BAKER ENCYCLOPEDIA OF
BIBLE PLANTS

BAKER ENCYCLOPEDIA OF

BIBLE PLANTS

FLOWERS AND TREES • FRUITS AND VEGETABLES • ECOLOGY

F. Nigel Hepper

First published in the UK
by Inter Varsity Press
38 De Montfort Street, Leicester
LE1 7GP, England

ISBN 0-85110-643-9

First published in the USA
by Baker Book House
Grand Rapids
Michigan 49516
USA

ISBN 0-8010-4361-1

Designed and created by
Three's Company
12 Flitcroft Street
London WC2H 8DJ

Worldwide co-edition organised
and produced by
Angus Hudson Ltd
Concorde House
Grenville Place
London NW7 3SA

Printed in the United Kingdom

Contents

Index of Plant Names

The English names are followed by the accepted scientific name; synonyms are indicated in the text. The Latin scientific plant names are followed by the authority and the plant family to which they belong. Illustrations in *bold italics*. Some insects and other organisms are also included. See also the General Index, p. 190.

Foreword

I am delighted to introduce Nigel Hepper's most recent book on Bible plants because I share many mutual interests with the author: a love of plants, a concern for the environment and a Christian faith. These attributes, as well as a long experience of fieldwork in Bible lands and much scholarly research in the libraries and herbaria of the world, give the author the unique qualifications that have produced this interesting and informative book. While it is the result of considerable scholarship from a long-serving botanist of the Royal Botanic Gardens, Kew, this book is beautifully presented in a format that is easy for the layman to understand. Kew has had an association with biblical plants dating back at least to the 1878 book by the Curator, J. Smith, *Bible Plants: their history*, which was published because of the help given to Smith by our second Director, Sir Joseph Hooker. I am particularly pleased to continue this tradition by providing a foreword for our current biblical expert who has already produced two books, *Bible Plants at Kew* and *Planting a Bible Garden,* that are very popular with many of our visitors.

In these days when much attention is being given to the importance of conserving the biodiversity of tropical rainforests and other species-diverse habitats, not much consideration is given to the plant species of the Middle East. The natural vegetation of that region has suffered more than many others because of its long period of human occupation. In the Bible, we read about the plundering of the cedar trees to build Solomon's temple and about animals, such as the hippopotamus (Job 40:15), which have long since become extinct in the region. Yet the plants of the Bible lands are of greater importance to mankind than those of most other parts of the world. The life-sustaining crops of wheat, barley, vines, olives, onions and pulses all originated within the geographical region covered by this book. The wild ancestors of these crops and such important trees as cedars, which now only occur in tiny remnants of natural vegetation, represent a vital resource for future crop breeding.

The author has described some of the environmental destruction of the region. It is to be hoped that this will stimulate a greater realization of the importance of conserving the botanical riches of Bible lands. This aspect should particularly challenge the Christian reader into active conservation. The Bible makes quite plain our responsibility for the care of creation. Adam was put in the Garden of Eden with the command to till (Heb. *abad*: to serve) and to keep (Heb. *shamar*: to preserve) the land. Since the Fall, disobedient humanity has been a poor steward of creation. In the light of our reconciliation to God and to creation through Christ who is the 'first born of all creation', the Christian should be foremost in taking care of the species which God created for our use and enjoyment.

'And out of the ground the LORD God made to grow every tree that is pleasant to the sight and good for food' (Genesis 2:9, RSV). We often forget the aesthetic side of creation that we are commanded to preserve. Let us not leave this responsibility to a secular New Age movement that does not recognize the great work of our Creator. God has given us the rich flora that is described here and we are to be its stewards, not those who eradicate it from the face of the earth.

This book, which is a completely new approach to the study of Bible plants because it combines history and archaeology with the botany, ecology and economic botany of the region, will appeal to a broader audience. Whether you study at home or go to the eastern Mediterranean region as a tourist, a pilgrim, a biologist or a Bible student, you will find a wealth of information here that will make your visit more interesting.

Professor Ghillean T. Prance
Director,
Royal Botanic Gardens, Kew

Introduction

The enormous amount of scientific and archaeological research that has been carried out in Bible lands in recent years is having a radical impact on biblical studies. New and exciting facts have been discovered, and many of the standard works have become outdated. Much of the information is published in scientific journals and in reports of excavations not readily available to the general reader. The present book brings together this information as it relates to plants and plant products mentioned in the Bible.

This is clearly a vast subject and I have tried to present the reader with information both old and new. During the preparation of this book I have had the privilege of field experience in the Eastern Mediterranean region as well as access to the immense collections of plants in the Herbarium of the Royal Botanic Gardens, Kew, and use of its world-renowned library. In this way I have been able to check, as far as possible from first principles, the species involved. This has been an absolute necessity, as otherwise previous errors of identification and names are perpetuated. Bare facts about foreign plants can make dry reading if they are not clothed in narrative and related to something familiar or interesting. To this end I have set the economic plants in a historical context by including notes on archaeological findings. In order to give an ecological setting to the wild plants, which should be of particular use to tourists with an interest in the flora, I have devoted chapters to the different types of vegetation and habitats of today.

My interest in ancient plants developed originally from an interest in Egyptology. My field trips to this region include a memorable visit to Egypt in 1963, with a journey up the Nile to Abu Simbel; in 1984 and 1985, I was attached to Cairo University for a few weeks; and I made other visits in 1990 and 1992. My tour of Jordan and Israel in March 1967 was notable for visits to Petra, Jerash and the Negeb, and was followed by another in 1969 to Mount Hermon and the hills of Upper Galilee. In 1977, and again in 1987, I went to Samaria, Mount Sinai and the Arabah. Numerous visits between 1985 and 1992, mainly in connection with the biblical garden at St George's Cathedral, Jerusalem, enabled further field study in Israel and Cyprus. Throughout the 1970s and 1980s, as botanical lecturer on Swan Hellenic Cruises, I visited historic sites in Italy, Greece and Turkey. Kew botanical expeditions to the Yemen and throughout tropical Africa have also proved useful in often unexpected ways.

For the sake of the non-scientific reader I have tried to keep the use of technical terms in the text to a minimum. However, certain particularly important words have been retained, and these have been defined when mentioned for the first time. A glossary is also included (p. 187).

English readers today are favoured with numerous translations and renderings of the Bible, which, when compared, often bring out fuller meanings of the original text. I have chosen the Revised Standard Version (RSV) for most quotations, supplemented by the Authorised (King James') Version (KJV), New English Bible (NEB), New International Version (NIV), and others, but have avoided detailed discussion of the respective merits of these versions. Many such comparisons were made by Moldenke in his *Plants of the Bible* (1952), to which reference may be made, although I do not always agree with his conclusions. Much more recent, and the result of a lifetime's fieldwork, is Michael Zohary's *Plants of the Bible* (1982), in which conclusions are often based on current Arabic plant names. I have used a simplified Anglicization for the Hebrew names and words. Young's *Exhaustive Concordance* has been very useful, but I have adopted a simpler spelling.

Sometimes I have taken up a figure of speech used in the Bible with a view to discussing its botanical basis. However, people today do not always appreciate the sentimental allusions popular in former years, and the shelves of second-hand bookshops are stocked with dusty works about flowers in flowery language. I have also shunned the mythology and legend that became associated with biblical, or supposedly biblical, plants. But the Bible is not a textbook on botany, and references to plants are often figurative or symbolic. In the Old Testament the vine symbolizes Israel; in the New Testament, Christ called himself the true vine, and communion wine symbolizes the blood of Christ shared by the Church. Metaphor and simile, too, are frequent. 'All flesh is grass', says Isaiah, 'and all its beauty is like the flower of the field. The grass withers, the flower fades ... but the word of our God will stand for ever' (Isaiah 40:6–8). One cannot expect a botanist to comment on 'All the trees of the fields shall clap their hands' (Isaiah 55:12 NIV), for this is poetry and we accept the language without question. But illustrations such as the parables of the sower, and of the fig tree, were used with great effect by Jesus during his ministry, and we can understand them better by knowing more about the plants and their ecology.

I have included many of my own colour photographs of the habit of trees and of plants in their habitats, as well as close-ups of flowers, fruits and leaves. As far as possible I have used living plants for my supplementary drawings, though a few have been made from material in Kew Herbarium or from other illustrations. Some of the drawings were done in the Holy Land itself. In order to make this book a bridge between botany and history I have also included a number of illustrations of archaeological interest taken from objects kept in the Manchester Museum, the Petrie Collection at University College, London, and the Palestine (Rockefeller) and Israel Archaeological Museums in Jerusalem. There are also some reproductions of Egyptian motifs from Wilkinson's *Manners and Customs of the Ancient Egyptians.*

The Illustrated Bible Dictionary (IVP, 1980), J. A. Thompson's *The Bible and Archaeology* (Paternoster, 1965), J. R. Harris' revision of A. Lucas' *Ancient Egyptian Materials and Industries* and many journals dealing with biblical history and archaeology have served as valuable sources of archaeological information. I have hardly drawn on the wealth of extra-biblical material on plants and agriculture contained in the Talmud, the book of Jewish Law. Much of it is outside the scope of this book, though in many respects it is a remarkable source of information. Other valuable sources include I. Löw's *Die Flora der Juden* in five volumes, Dalman's seven-volume work *Arbeit und Sitte in Palästina,* and, more recently published, a series of splendidly illustrated books by Nogah Hareuveni of Neot Kedumim.

References to publications cited and to others of particular interest are given in the Bibliography (pp. 188-9); those most frequently used are listed by author, and other publications are entered under the relevant chapter. Readers are advised to use the detailed indexes (pp. 6-11 and 190-1) in order to find all the references to plants and their products, since they are likely to be represented in several chapters.

The naming of plants

Some plants have well-known and accurate common English names, but many more have not. In a book of this kind one frequently mentions obscure plants that may or may not be known by their products. Plants of economic importance such as flax, which yields linen and linseed oil, are unambiguous. However, the fig presents a problem in so far as there are two kinds of figs in the Middle East, as well as many in other parts of the world. Instead of speaking simply of the fig, therefore, it is necessary to qualify it, differentiating the *common* fig from the *sycomore* fig.

Numerous species of wild plants of no particular economic importance have no English name. Although local people may know them by their vernacular names in Hebrew or Arabic, these give little guidance to English-speaking readers. For this reason it is much more satisfactory to use the botanical name, which is (or should be) both unambiguous and internationally understood. Some people are discouraged by these Latin names and make no attempt to master them; yet familiarity with a name dispels this fear, and accordingly it may be helpful to examine the constituent elements of a scientific plant name.

The full name has two parts: *genus* and *epithet*. For example, the well-known anemone of florists and gardens is scientifically called *Anemone coronaria*. It so happens that the English name and the scientific name for the plant are the same, i.e. *Anemone* (although some people call it wind-flower), but this is not usually the case. The category genus is used for a broad range of similar plants or species. Just as in English one qualifies anemone in order to be precise, e.g. wood anemone and Japanese anemone, so also in Latin there are *Anemone nemorosa*, and *Anemone japonica* (abbreviated *A. nemorosa*, etc.) where the descriptive adjective, or epithet, follows the noun.

One further category needs to be mentioned. The anemone is a member of the buttercup *family* or *Ranunculaceae* (after *Ranunculus*, the buttercup). The family is a larger assemblage of more or less similar or related plants, and it is often convenient to be able to place an unfamiliar plant in its family. Once the family of an unfamiliar plant is known, it is possible to recognize family characteristics, and perhaps to compare with greater ease and accuracy those that differ. Some more examples may help to explain the terms: the sycomore fig, *Ficus sycomorus*, belongs to the mulberry family, *Moraceae*; barley, *Hordeum vulgare*, is in the grass family *Gramineae* (or *Poaceae*); and the Cedar of Lebanon, *Cedrus libani*, is in the pine family, *Pinaceae.*

Strictly speaking, the name of the botanist who coined the plant's Latin name should be added, usually in abbreviated form. The name of the eighteenth-century Swedish botanist Linnaeus frequently appears simply as L., as in *Anemone coronaria* L. When a species was described in one genus and later transferred to another, the name of the original author is transferred with the epithet. Thus Linnaeus named a species of thistle as *Carduus syriacus,* which was later transferred by Cassini to the genus *Notobasis*; the full citation is therefore *Notobasis syriaca* (L.) Cass. For the sake of clarity, I have limited the citation of authorities of botanical names to the index.

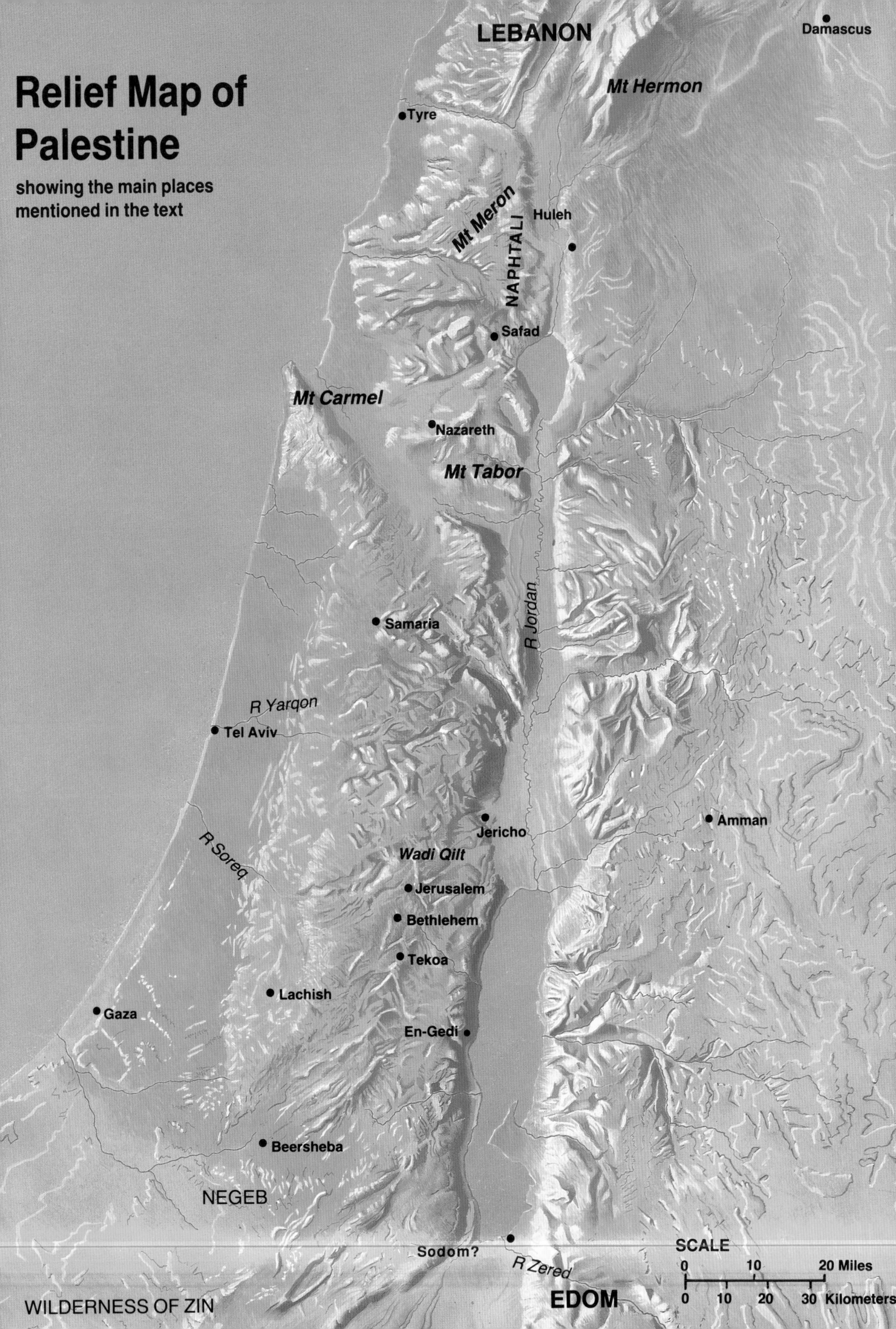

Relief Map of Palestine
showing the main places mentioned in the text
LEBANON
Damascus
Mt Hermon
Tyre
Mt Meron
NAPHTALI
Huleh
Safad
Mt Carmel
Nazareth
Mt Tabor
R Jordan
Samaria
R Yarqon
Tel Aviv
R Soreq
Jericho
Amman
Wadi Qilt
Jerusalem
Bethlehem
Tekoa
Lachish
Gaza
En-Gedi
Beersheba
NEGEB
Sodom?
R Zered
EDOM
WILDERNESS OF ZIN
SCALE
0
10
20 Miles
0
10
20
30
Kilometers

Acknowledgements

I am indebted to so many friends and colleagues that the task of acknowledging their assistance is a formidable one. Although I mention them by name, responsibility for the text, with any blemishes there may be, is entirely mine.

I must acknowledge those in Israel who unstintingly set about showing me their country and its plants. At the University of Tel Aviv, Professor and Mrs Jacov Galil were especially helpful in making arrangements for three of my visits and for reading my chapter on figs. I am also grateful to my guides Dr Jacob Friedman and Dr Daniel Eisikowitch. Similarly, in Jerusalem, the Department of Botany at the Hebrew University was placed at my disposal by Professor Naomi Feinbrun-Dothan, the late Professor Michael Zohary, Professor Clara Heyne and their staff: Drs Avinoam Danin, Uzi Plitman, Avi Shmida and Michael Avishai of the Botanical Garden. At Bar Ilan University, Dr Mordecai Kislev guided me through the desert – as a botanical archaeologist, he has a fund of information about Hebrew plant names in the Talmud and the Bible. I also found discussions with Professor Daniel Zohary about ancient crops very stimulating, especially when hunting wild cereals in the Negeb or in the cosmopolitan atmosphere of a café in Beersheba, as well as many times in my office at Kew. At Beersheba I benefited from the hospitality of Dr James Aaronson and Dr Allan Witztum, who included me on university field excursions. The splendid Field Study Centres of the Society for the Protection of Nature in Israel enabled me to stay in remote places to study the flora in reserves and archaeological sites of the Nature Reserves and the National Parks Authorities. Nogah Hareuveni and Helen Frenkley have often spared me time at their biblical landscape reserve, Neot Kedumim. Dr A. Weinstein kindly commented on the ecology chapters. The staff of St George's Cathedral, especially the Dean of the College, Dr John Peterson, have been a constant source of inspiration during my visits to Jerusalem.

Anyone who went round the Egyptian Museum in Cairo with the late Professor Vivi Tackholm, as I did in 1963, will agree that this was a memorable experience. Her successor, Professor Nabil El-Hadidi, was a great help in arranging my attachment to Cairo University for some weeks in 1984 and 1985, as well as other visits to Egypt. Fieldwork ranged from Aswan to Kharga oasis, Faiyum and the Mediterranean coast. I am grateful to Dr Hassan Ragab for his collaboration over papyrus and for guided tours of his Pharaonic Village at Giza.

In Britain my contacts have been numerous. I wish to thank the following for their assistance: Dr David Dixon in the Department of Egyptology, University College London; Terence Mitchell, formerly of the Department of Western Asiatics at the British Museum; Alan R. Millard and Professor Kenneth A. Kitchen of the University of Liverpool; Professor Donald J. Wiseman, formerly at London University; Nigel St-J. Groom, who kindly read the chapter on incense and Rev. Robert Amess of Richmond, who read my notes on symbolisms. My fellow members of the committee of the Palestine Exploration Fund have been supportive while I used the library to scan the archaeological journals for relevant information.

Professor William T. Stearn, formerly of the Natural History Museum, London, has made many useful comments, in spite of the constant demands on his time from others throughout the world who also value his scholarship. My colleagues at the Kew Herbarium have always been ready to make available their special knowledge of the Mediterranean flora; and the Director, Professor Ghillean T. Prance, kindly contributed the Foreword. Especial thanks go to my wife, Helen, who held the fort during my travels, endured long evenings while I wrote in my study and even had the patience to type my manuscript.

PART ONE:

WILD PLANTS

IN THEIR HABITATS

1. The Ecology of Bible Lands

'And God said, "Let the earth put forth vegetation, plants yielding seed, and fruit trees bearing fruit in which is their seed, each according to its kind, upon the earth." And it was so ... And God saw that it was good.'
(Genesis 1: 11–12.)

The lands covered by the biblical narrative extend at least from Italy to Iran, and from Greece to Egypt, although those on the periphery of this vast area are by no means as important as the Holy Land at the centre. Most of the momentous historical events recorded in the Bible occurred within that small portion of the earth's surface which came to be known as Palestine, between the Mediterranean Sea and the wastes of the Arabian Desert. Over the years the name Palestine has stood for several different areas – originally it was the ancient Philistia – nevertheless it is a useful geographical term for the region from Mount Hermon, south along both sides of the River Jordan, to the Sinai Desert. It is in this sense that we shall use it, without any political overtones. For the Hebrews of the Old Testament, this was the Promised Land: 'for the Lord your God is bringing you into a good land' (Deuteronomy 8:7).

Most of our material will of course deal with the flora and ecology of Palestine. In addition, Arabian spices and African timbers, Egyptian vegetables and Indian perfume, all call for attention.

PREVIOUS STUDIES

The modern urge for travel, and the relative ease and cheapness with which it can be fulfilled, has brought to the Middle East a large number of visitors of all types and interests. Even the average tourist to Palestine can be fascinated by its flowers and trees in springtime and want to know more about them, while Bible students often find that their botanical enquiries go unanswered for lack of available literature.

The natural history of the Bible has attracted considerable attention and many works have been produced, but these mostly take the form of factual encyclopedias or try to give spiritual lessons. When the ancient biblical manuscripts were translated into other languages scholars were faced, as they still are, with the problem of identifying the plants and animals mentioned. Cruden, in his great *Concordance* of 1737, declared somewhat despairingly 'that there is hardly anything less certain than the Hebrew names' of the plants and trees mentioned in the Scriptures! Even today we must admit that we sometimes do not know what species was intended. Frequently the line of least resistance was taken by translators, and the names of plants and animals likely to be known to readers were inserted. For example, in the KJV, in the parable of the sower, tares, a noxious weed of seventeenth-century English wheat fields, replaced the Mediterranean darnel grass of the Greek text.

Other scholars have been more scientific in their approach. In 1773, for instance, the King of Sweden appointed the renowned botanist Carl Linnaeus to the Swedish Bible Revision Committee. His fellow Swede, Professor O. Celsius, had already published his great two-volume work on biblical plants in 1745 and 1747, and then, in 1749, another Swedish naturalist

Below: Cross-section of Palestine.

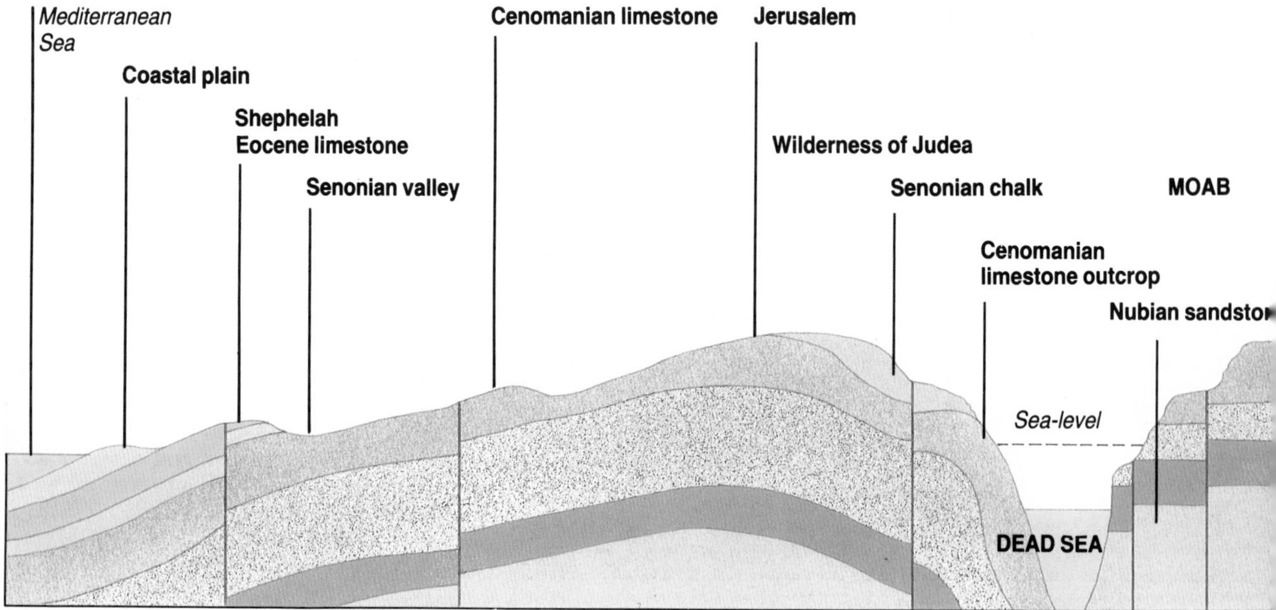

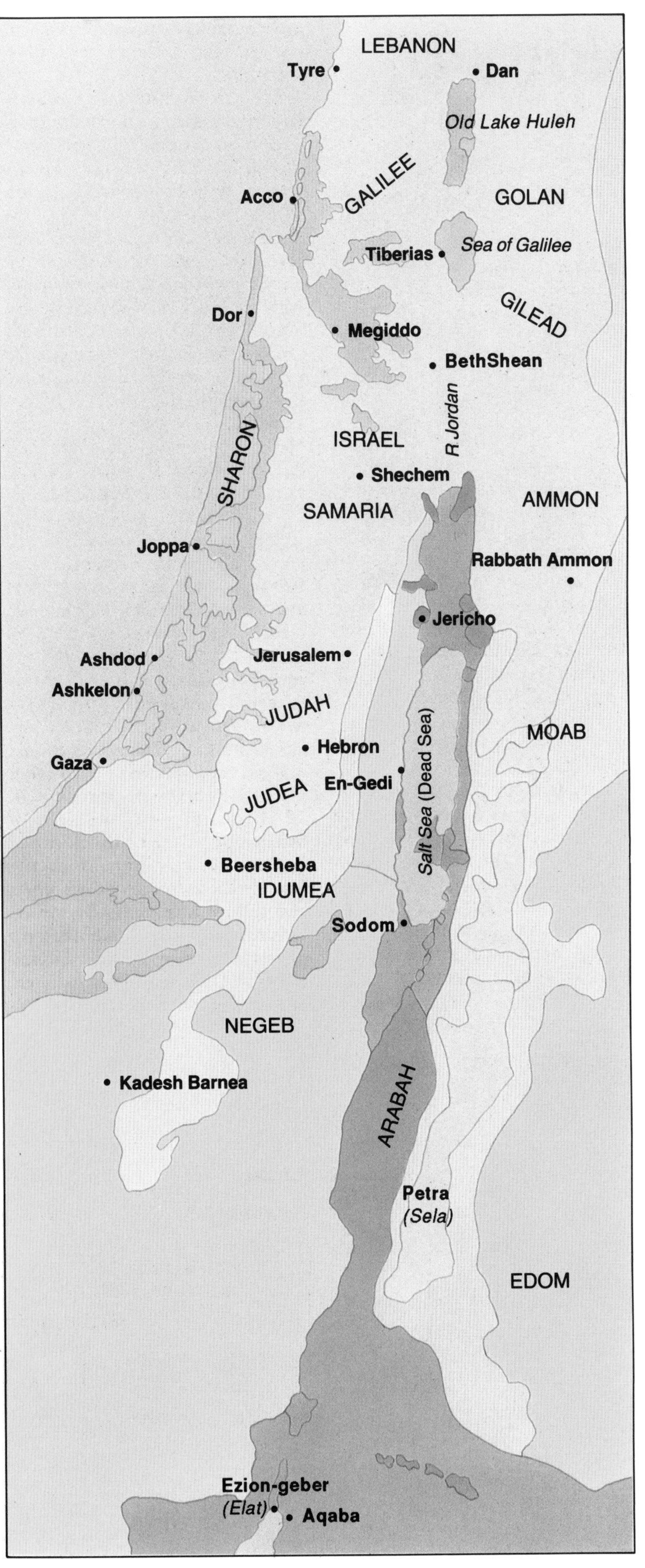

Forest and *maquis*

Coastal plain

Plains and valleys under cultivation

Semi-arid dwarf shrub vegetation

Deserts

Salt desert

Tropical vegetation

Sandy deserts

Left: Map of the Holy Land (Palestine in the terms of this book) showing what the vegetation may have been during biblical times. After M. Zohary (1982).

'Mediterranean' forest zone with Tabor and kermes oaks, styrax, carob, mastic shrubs and Aleppo pines. Herbaceous semi-steppe vegetation.

The coastal plain consists of sandy soil grassland or shrubs, occasionally mixed with Tabor oak, carob forests and mastic shrubs.

The deserts are plantless or vegetated in wadis only, mostly with dwarf shrubs. ('Irano-Turanian' and 'Saharo-Arabian'.)

The tropical vegetation ('Sudanian') includes wild and cultivated oases with acacia.

The sandy deserts are vegetated by white broom and saxaul.

F. Hasselquist went to Palestine to investigate the country. Hasselquist died there, but Linnaeus used his materials and notes to prepare a natural history of the country, which was published in 1757. Linnaeus submitted to the Bible committee a list of identifications of animals and plants in Genesis, the manuscript of which is carefully preserved with his collections in the rooms of the Linnean Society of London, where I have examined them. Linnaeus' revolutionary and practical system of nomenclature and classification made field investigations worthwhile, since the newly gathered material could be incorporated immediately into the new system. Young men, stimulated by Linnaeus' lectures, explored distant lands to investigate and collect plants and animals; in his later years, however, Linnaeus felt some remorse that he had been responsible for the loss of so many young lives in the cause of biological science.

Another noteworthy botanist was Pehr Forsskål, who died in the Yemen in 1763. He had joined an expedition financed by Frederick V of Denmark to investigate the plants and animals of the Bible for a new Danish translation. Even in the eighteenth century, Palestine was thought to have lost many biblical

Right: The Mediterranean coast at Caesarea. The coastal dunes are now much built-over and the inland plain, formerly marshland, is now agricultural.

characteristics that the Yemen would still retain. Although Forsskål discovered materials of great interest to the naturalist, much remained obscure. It was not until 1863 that the Palestine Exploration Fund of London sent Canon H. B. Tristram to make a detailed field study, which was published in 1867 as his *Natural History of the Bible*, and, in 1884, his monumental *Survey of Western Palestine: Fauna and Flora of Palestine*.

Many other works on botanical aspects of the region have been published, including *Bible Plants: their history* (1878) by John Smith, former Curator of the Royal Botanic Gardens, Kew, who, although he did not visit the Holy Land, had a deep knowledge of the Bible and a lifetime's experience of plants. Being blind, he never saw his book, and had dictated the text to his sister. John Smith was helped by the then Director of Kew, Sir Joseph Dalton Hooker, who travelled in Palestine during 1860 and also contributed the botanical sections of William Smith's *A Dictionary of the Bible* (1863). A century later, I feel honoured to follow in the steps of these illustrious predecessors at Kew, with entries in *The Illustrated Bible Dictionary*, and my books *Bible Plants at Kew*, *Planting a Bible Garden*, *Pharaoh's Flowers*, and now this volume.

Since the time of Tristram, the Smiths, and Hooker, many others have entered the field. The twentieth century has seen the intensive scientific study of the natural history of Palestine by resident scientists, and an understanding of the distribution and ecology of organisms which was quite unknown to former generations. The reader is referred to Michael Zohary's *Plant Life of Palestine* (1962) for a detailed analysis of the flora and vegetation, which I have found a most useful work. Many other Israeli publications are available in English or Hebrew. For cultivated plants an up-to-date account is that by Daniel Zohary and Maria Hopf, *Domestication of Plants in the Old World* (1988).

Right: Terraced hillsides west of Jerusalem, near Sataf, with re-growth bushes and trees in Mediterranean type *maquis* vegetation.

Left: The view eastwards from Mount Scopus in springtime, with the annual vegetation rapidly petering out down the Judean Desert towards the Dead Sea in the distance (March 1987).

PLANT GEOGRAPHY

Knowledge of geology, topography and climate is essential for an understanding of plant distribution and of the various types of vegetation. Such information is given in any good Bible atlas and in Y. Aharoni's *The Land of the Bible* (1979) and Denis Baly's *The Geography of the Bible* (1957). George Adam Smith's *The Historical Geography of the Holy Land* (1894, rev. 1931) although dated, is a beautifully written work, full of interest.

The study of plant geography has placed the flora of Palestine within a much wider context. Visitors who travel from the coast at Tel Aviv to the Dead Sea via Jerusalem traverse most of the plant geography territories and geological formations. Eastward, beyond the coastal sand dunes, the agricultural alluvial plains that formerly supported swamp or deciduous oak woodland can be seen. Rising to the bare Shephelah hills of Eocene limestone and crossing a narrow band of chalk, the road winds through steep limestone hills once covered by evergreen oak and *maquis* thickets. This is typical vegetation of the Mediterranean region, with its cool, moist winters and hot, dry summers. The visitor will encounter planted pine forests before reaching Jerusalem.

Just east of Jerusalem the rainfall decreases rapidly, agriculture ceases and this chalky, arid zone contains dwarf shrubs and annuals of the type that are distributed far to the east across the Syrian Desert to Iran – the 'Irano-Turanian region'. Adjoining the Dead Sea (the biblical Salt Sea some 400 m (1312 ft) below sea-level) and stretching far to the south is the true desert, where rainfall is erratic or almost non-existent. The plants in this area link up with those in the Sahara and across the Arabian Desert to the Sind, the area known as the 'Saharo-Arabian' or 'Saharo-Sindian region'. Finally, there are the small oases by the Dead Sea, where fresh-water springs support an assemblage of plants and animals that normally belong to tropical Africa: these are the 'Sudanian' enclaves; in fact African plants occur all along the hot Arabah valley.

Of course, there is no clear demarcation, and one type of plant may be found in more than one area. This is especially true of contemporary Palestine, where the effects of human intervention on the natural vegetation have radically altered the environment. Invasive desert species have colonized deforested areas; pine-tree plantations have replaced the oaks on the hills; swamps have been drained and goats have grazed everything within reach!

The visitor who gazes across the Sea of Galilee to the trees lining its opposite shore may not realize that these are Australian eucalyptus (*E. camaldulensis*). The highways are shaded by more eucalyptuses, and road embankments often stabilized by Australian acacias. Crops of American origin, such as maize and pumpkins, as well as Chinese oranges, dominate the agricultural landscape. Also often introduced from other lands are weeds of cultivation, such as the yellow Cape sorrel (*Oxalis pes-caprae*) from South Africa, conspicuous in vineyards in springtime.

Similarly, most of the ornamental plants in towns are of recent or ancient introduction, and sometimes, to the confusion of the amateur botanist, they seed into adjacent waste places. Thus the visitor struggling up the rough path on the Mount of Olives will see the shrubby South American tobacco *Nicotiana glauca* sprouting from

Above: Prickly-pear cactus (*Opuntia ficus-indica*) from the New World, now often grown in Palestine as a hedge and for its edible fruits. An olive tree is also shown here.

Above right: A shrubby tobacco (*Nicotiana glauca*) from South America, now naturalized in old walls and rough places in the Mediterranean region.

Right: Cape sorrel (*Oxalis pes-caprae*) introduced from South Africa and now abundant in vineyards and olive groves.

the base of stout stone walls – and be doubly confused by local guides who insist that this is the mustard-seed of the New Testament! The common cactus *Opuntia ficus-indica*, planted by Arabs as field boundaries, was also introduced from the New World, yet it is sometimes included in nativity scenes!

Modern handbooks

Handbooks naming and describing the plants of a region or country are usually called 'floras'. Such works are produced at several levels, according to intended readership. In modern Israel there is now literature at all levels from popular tourist booklets with numerous colour pictures to academic books, usually with monochrome illustrations and a Hebrew text. The standard work in English is *Flora Palaestina*, by Michael Zohary and Naomi Feinbrun-Dothan, in four volumes, with four additional volumes of drawings. Other works are listed on pp. 188-9, where titles on the flora of neighbouring countries are also given. There is also a vast literature on the flora of the Near East published in botanical journals. I have given an account of many of these papers, where relevant, in order to bring together the latest scientific information.

The remarkably diverse habitats in the small area of Palestine account for the high number of plant species known to occur there. Some 2780 species have been recorded (Feinbrun-Dothan & Danin, 1991), and additions are documented by the Plant Monitoring Center at Ha-Gilo, near Bethlehem. The mountains of Lebanon would add hundreds more to this total.

The conservation of nature

Ecology is the study of organisms in relation to their habitat or environment. Since plants are the ultimate source of food for all animals, the richness of the fauna in any given habitat usually depends upon the presence of suitable vegetation. Impoverish the plant life and the faunal diversity decreases, as the links in the food chains are broken. While some creatures are adaptable, others, such as butterflies, are totally dependent on certain species of plants and simply cannot exist if these are not available.

We must not so alter our environment that all natural habitats, with their delicate balances, are destroyed, and their diverse plant and animal species lost for ever. To this end nature conservation laws and practices are to be welcomed, and the national parks and nature reserves in Israel, Jordan and Lebanon mark a good beginning in providing varied habitats and refuges for threatened species. But such reserves occupy a minute total of the whole land area, and our concern must be with the best use of the complete environment, be it town or country. It is still not too late to conserve something of the natural flora and fauna, and I believe that nature conservation is obligatory if the heritage entrusted to us is to be passed on.

Bibliography

Aharoni, Y., *The Land of the Bible*, 2nd rev. ed. (London, Burns and Oates, 1979).

Baly, D., *The Geography of the Bible* (London, Lutterworth Press, 1957; rev. ed., New York, Harper and Row, 1974).

Celsius, O., *Hierobotanicon* (Uppsala, 1745, 1747), 2 vols.

Hasselquist, F., in C. Linnaeus (ed.), *Iter palaestinum* (Uppsala, 1757).

Smith, G. A. *The Historical Geography of the Holy Land* (London, Hodder and Stoughton, 1894).

Smith, J., *Bible Plants: their History* (London, Hardewicke and Bogue, 1878).

Smith, W., *A Dictionary of the Bible* (London, J. Murray, 1861–3): 3 vols; plants by J. D. Hooker.

2. Forest and Thicket

Then shall all the trees of the wood sing for joy before the Lord, for he comes.
(Psalm 96:12–13.)

The hot, dry summers and cool, moist winters of the Mediterranean region produce a characteristic evergreen thicket-woodland usually known as *maquis* – a word which has come to us through French from the Corsican dialect. The thick dark green leaves resist the drought of summer and provide a lovely fragrance that pervades the air, and mingles with the perfumes of the bright flowers and resins of the pines. This type of Mediterranean vegetation reaches its limit in Palestine, where it peters out into the semi-desert and desert of the Negeb.

DEFORESTATION

In favoured places the *maquis* supports some well-grown trees such as oaks forming an open woodland. But forests of oak originally covered more than half the area of lowland Sharon – a name actually translated as 'oak forest' in the Septuagint, the early Jewish Greek version of the Old Testament. The pioneer Israeli botanist Alexander Eig thought that the deciduous Tabor oak, which existed there until recently, formed the original oak forest; but now Nili Liphschitz and colleagues (1987) have shown that Tabor oaks replaced a woodland of evergreen Kermes oaks that used to grow there in biblical times. It seems that the Kermes oaks were cut down for timber during the Arab period (AD 800–1400) and, because the soil was too poor for agriculture, faster growing Tabor oaks replaced them. Extensive Tabor oak forests with widely spaced trees were present in Crusader times and down to the Napoleonic and late Islamic periods and although charcoal- and lime-burning have accounted for much destruction throughout Palestine, it was only during the nineteenth century, when the wood was required for Egyptian ships, that these Tabor oak forests were severely depleted. They were finally eliminated during the First World War, when the Turks used vast quantities of wood as fuel for their railways.

As the lowland forests were cleared, the land was rapidly colonized by halfa grass (*Desmostachya bipinnata*), only itself to be largely destroyed by modern agriculture using fertilisers, leaving just a few isolated trees.

Beyond the coastal plain the low foothills known as the Shephelah stretch from near Beersheba in the south to the Carmel range in the north. These foothills are composed of soft limestone and chalk which erodes into smooth slopes and valleys, contrasting with the rugged scenery of the hard limestone in Samaria and Judea.

The southern Shephelah borders the Negeb Desert and would always have been too dry to support forest; but from the latitude of Hebron northwards there is sufficient rainfall for the Mediterranean type of vegetation on the greyish soils (*rendzinas*). The original vegetation in the valleys can now only be guessed at, as alluvial soils rich in humus have accumulated there, and have been cultivated by farmers since biblical times. It is probable, however, that the Shephelah hills

Left: Eroded limestone plateau near Ramallah, with dwarf *batha* vegetation maintained by grazing goats; this was woodland in biblical times.

Right: Well-developed *maquis* near Gilo in the hill country of Judea. Evergreen Kermes oak (*Quercus calliprinos*) in the rear; storax (*Styrax officinalis*) in the middle ground, with yellow spiny broom (*Calycotome villosa*), and in the foreground spiny burnet (*Sarcopoterium spinosum*). April 1991.

were covered with an evergreen *maquis* composed of lentisk bushes and carob trees along the western side, while on the eastern side of the Shephelah there would have been Kermes oak and Palestine terebinth thickets, with some tall Aleppo pines and Kermes oaks. Today the uncultivated areas of the Mediterranean zone carry a lower evergreen vegetation about 1 m (3 ft) high called *garigue*, of shrubs such as rock-roses (*Cistus salvifolius, C. creticus*) and the sage *Salvia fruticosa*, or even the dwarf shrub community up to 50 cm (18 ins) high, termed *batha*, dominated by spiny burnet. So for forest to develop the succession would be *batha* to *garigue*, *garigue* to *maquis*, and *maquis* to *forest* – with each stage taking years longer than the previous one.

According to John Currid (1984), who has studied the history of the vegetation of the Shephelah, the changes have been caused by human activities such as wars in biblical times. For example, Nebuchadnezzar used local timber when he destroyed Lachish by fire. However, forests were also steadily cleared for building-timber, charcoal and tanning. Flocks of sheep and goats prevented the regeneration of trees, and an ever-increasing population led to overgrazing by herds and erosion. Wherever the land was suitable for agriculture, small plots were cultivated for cereals, and olives and vines were planted.

The same pattern of settlement and deforestation occurred in the hill country from Hebron to Gilboa. Here the soil is red (*terra rossa*) from the weathered limestone. As the demand for arable land increased, the steep hillsides were terraced (see chapter 7), decreasing the natural vegetation still more. Today the bare hillsides show little or no sign of the original *maquis* of evergreen oak and terebinth that once covered the slopes, except at the occasional nature reserve, such as that in the valley of Soreq or higher up at Gilo.

The old terraces around Gilo, near the monastery of Cremona, are still used as vineyards for the well-known wines bottled by the monks. The nature reserve of Ha Gilo spreads down the hillside, merging with the planted Aleppo pine forest. Kermes oaks and terebinths mingle with storax bushes (*Styrax officinalis*) (Hosea 4:13; Heb. *livneh*, poplar RSV) and yellow spiny broom (*Calycotome villosa*), while anemones and orchids flourish in the absence of grazing. Here one sees a tiny sample of what the hill country was like when Joshua declared to his people 'the hill country shall be yours, for though it is forest, you shall clear it and possess it to its farthest borders' (Joshua 17:18). However, even after this clearance, there were still enough trees on Mount Zalmon for Abimelech's people to cut boughs to burn the stronghold of Shechem (Judges 9:49).

Let us now look at several areas in some detail.

The majesty of Carmel[1]

Mount Carmel has always been associated with flowers and trees, and it was a rich source of timber in biblical times. Even today there are fine trees in the large national park and nature reserve, which is helping to conserve what was left of the natural vegetation after a disastrous fire in 1989.

The broad limestone ridge of Carmel stretches out to the Mediterranean, where it ends abruptly at Haifa. It was from this summit that Elijah's servant looked toward the sea and saw the cloud bringing rain which ended the severe drought (1 Kings 18:44). Steep slopes or cliffs run for many miles along each side of the ridge. Inland, the undulating downland near Megiddo is cut by the twisting road to the north. Occasional streams occur, with willows and blackberry thickets, and there are rock outcrops and woods. In early spring the scene is extraordinarily green and colourful as the masses of annual plants and bulbs break into flower, as described in chapter 4. In the *maquis*, the new red leaves of the terebinth (*Pistacia palaestina*), pink flowers of Judas trees (*Cercis siliquastrum*), pink and white rock-roses (*Cistus*) and the bright yellow

Above left: Rock-roses (*Cistus creticus*) are conspicuous in the *maquis*.

Above: An unusual parasite (*Cytinus hypocistis*) on the roots of rock-roses on Carmel.

spiny broom contrast with the dark leaves of the evergreen Kermes oak. In some places the deciduous Tabor oak and the evergreen oak grow together, but the latter is more common at higher levels. In at least one place a fine wood of large trees has survived due to prolonged protection by the Druse.[2] Nearby, the Aleppo pines become more numerous, a belt of them following the lighter rocks across the hillside; but they are subject to sweeping fires (Psalms 83:14). Rocky places and crags provide refuges for annuals and tough perennial plants, whose roots penetrate the crevices. From the higher points one can see that the sea is not far away, and the great cultivated plain stretches eastwards from industrial Haifa to Jezreel. North of the Vale of Jezreel the city of Nazareth lies in Lower Galilee, whose hillsides still carry oak and storax bushes, and beyond, the mountains of Upper Galilee, or Naphtali.

In the hill country of Naphtali[3]

As one climbs from the hot Upper Jordan valley north of Capernaum, snow-capped Mount Hermon lies to the north-east and the hills of Upper Galilee to the west. As the road turns westward into these lovely hills of Naphtali, it climbs steeply towards Safed, with the Sea of Galilee lying far below, and the Golan Heights beyond. The relative coolness of Safed and the fresh grassy hills around are welcome to many a visitor. Further west the plateau is broken by streams and tree-covered hills, orchards and occasional kibbutzim.

The highest point in Upper Galilee is Mount Meron, 1208 m (3900 ft), where a large nature reserve has been designated. This is a remarkable achievement, with rich Mediterranean vegetation, and an important diversity of habitats and species, preserved in spite of centuries of farming in the area.

In ancient times most of this hill country was densely populated and, according to the Jewish historian Josephus, the olives of Upper Galilee were famous. Even the lower slopes of Mount Meron, now within the reserve, were cultivated, and a few decrepit olives remain. The upper slopes were too bleak for anything but grazing and a good deal of woody growth has survived. With the designation of the reserve and the cessation of most grazing, the trees are now able to develop naturally. In the vicinity of the village of Meron there is already a fine forest of large evergreen oaks, long protected by the Arabs, who regarded the site as sacred. As on Mount Carmel, the evergreen oak is the principal tree, but, unlike Carmel, Mount Meron does not carry Aleppo pine. There is also another deciduous oak (*Quercus boissieri*), which, being confined to this region, is not likely to be mentioned in the Bible. The high altitude, with its cooler and moister climate, has enabled other trees, such as the Syrian pear (*Pyrus syriaca*) and wild cherry (*Prunus ursina*) – which here find their most southerly location – to become important constituents of the woodland.

The typical Mediterranean species are here, too, as impenetrable thickets which cover much of the reserve. Wild boar root for bulbs in the grassy patches occurring here and there. The numerous low limestone cliffs also provide open spaces of a different kind for small plants favouring stony ground. In early spring the air is filled with the fragrance of the spiny yellow broom (*Calycotome*), later supplanted by the taller Spanish broom (*Spartium junceum*). A sickly fragrance, however, is given out by the white flowers of the widespread Eastern hawthorn tree (*Crataegus azarolus*). Numerous strawberry trees (*Arbutus andrachne*), with their clusters of greenish-white flowers, are very striking, owing to the naked appearance of their smooth red-brown trunks. During March and April, the pure white and the crinkled pink flowers of shrubby rock-roses (*Cistus salviifolius* and *C. creticus* respectively) are to be seen everywhere. Ladanum (or laudanum) resin is yielded by some species of rock-rose (p. 147), and on a hot summer's day the resinous fragrance is typical of the dry evergreen vegetation so widespread in the Mediterranean region.

In some places the well-known myrtle (*Myrtus communis*) is to be found. This evergreen shrub or small tree has fragrant leaves, owing to the presence of numerous small glands which appear as pellucid dots if the leaf is held up to the light. Also fragrant are the white flowers which appear in profusion in the summer. Myrtle is such a delightful shrub that in Isaiah (41:19; 55:13) it is envisaged as replacing the thorny scrub of the wilderness. As the twigs of myrtle

(Heb. *hadas*) are amongst those used during the Feast of Tabernacles (Nehemiah 8:15), some people, with an eye to a quick cash profit, encourage the development of fresh green shoots by partially burning the bushes. Unfortunately this practice has been known to get out of hand and devastate large areas of carefully preserved natural vegetation and forest.

On the eastern side of Mount Meron the reserve joins with another around Wadi Ammud, known in biblical times as 'the waters of Merom', where the Canaanite kings encamped to fight with the Israelites (Joshua 11:5). As I descended the steep valley to the small gorge, the welcome sound of rushing water could be heard from the stream, which flows throughout the year. Rooted firmly between the boulders in the stream bed are oriental plane trees (*Platanus orientalis*, p. 73) of various ages, their flower-heads dangling among the leaves. This area is drier and milder than Meron itself, and the oak trees give way to extensive *maquis* of small shrubs. Rock-roses are the typical ones, though many members of the mint family also occur. Some are shrubby, such as the yellow Jerusalem sage (*Phlomis viscosa*) and the mauve three-lobed sage (*Salvia fruticosa*, formerly *S. triloba*); others are dwarf shrubs growing in rock crevices, such as wild thyme (*Coridothymus capitatus*) and hyssop (*Origanum syriacum*). The latter is usually regarded as the hyssop of the Hebrew purification rites (see p. 140). It grows as tufts of stems about 45 cm (18 in) high, and the small rounded minty leaves are covered with hairs of almost the same pale grey colour as the rock out of which it grows. The white flowers are insignificant, in small heads at the top of each stem. The wild rue (*Ruta chalepensis*) also occurs in this habitat. Like the culinary rue (*R. graveolens*), it forms a little bush 60 cm (2 ft) high. Its divided leaves are covered with pellucid glands full of the strongly smelling oil which is so characteristic of the plant. Rue was mentioned by Jesus (Luke 11:42, see p. 133).

In April, when spring has reached its climax, the hillsides of Upper Galilee are resplendent with new leaves and flowers (considered in detail in chapter 4). The heat of summer soon dries up the annuals and melts the snow across the valley on Mount Hermon, although drifts are plainly seen on a clear day on the higher summits of Lebanon due north of Mount Meron.

Right: Cedar of Lebanon (*Cedrus libani*) planted in Kew Gardens.

The glory of Lebanon[4]

Because of ruthless exploitation of the cedars for thousands of years, only a few remnants of the forests of Lebanon are left. Professor E. V. Beals, formerly of Beirut University, has made an interesting study of these remnant cedar forests (Beals, 1965). He concludes that, at one time, cedars (*Cedrus libani*) may have covered the western and northern slopes between 1400 m and 1800 m (4600–6000 ft), whereas nowadays there are only five distinct localities where cedars are found. In some areas natural regeneration is being encouraged, but unfortunately a massive planting scheme by the United Nations Development Fund has been interrupted by years of civil war. Military activity and grazing by goats present a continual problem everywhere, allowing uncontrolled cutting of old trees and widespread overgrazing. At the famous site of Baharre, trampling by numerous visitors prevented the growth of natural cedar seedlings, even before war aggravated the situation.

The cedar forests occur in an area with quite a high precipitation, which falls as snow during the winter. I recall flying over the Lebanese mountains at dawn one March morning when the sun was tinting with pink the snow-covered crests far below. The cedars could not be seen beneath their blanket of snow, from which they would finally emerge only during May. From then on, during the hot, dry summer months the cedars have to be satisfied with moisture already in the ground and with condensation from passing clouds.

Between the trees, providing there is sufficient light, an interesting ground flora develops. Many of these herbs and shrubs are species similar to those found in the Mediterranean zone, but others are more typical of Turkey and southern Europe. Accompanying the cedars in the northern localities are several important timber trees which should be mentioned. There is the Cilician fir (*Abies cilicica*), the Grecian juniper (*Juniperus excelsa*), cypress (*Cupressus sempervirens*), and at the lower levels the Calabrian pine (*Pinus brutia*). All of them are tall conifers bearing distinctive cones, except the juniper which has a berry. Although Lebanon is famous for its cedars – 'his appearance is like Lebanon, choice as the cedars' (Song of Solomon 5:15) – it is certain that the other trees were also felled for their timber.

The great cedars and other trees of Lebanon were felled by an army of men sent and provisioned by King Solomon. Hiram, king of Tyre, entered into a treaty with Solomon, and the timber was transported as rafts to a suitable point on the coast of Palestine (1 Kings 5:9). Rafts of this type had long been used to float logs from Lebanon across the sea to Egypt and thence up the Nile. In fact, Egyptian politics and territorial aspirations were for centuries directed towards Lebanon, to gain her timber supplies by treaty or by war. Other empires also wanted Lebanese timber. An Assyrian bas-relief now at the Louvre depicts galleys being used to haul cedars before ultimate transport to Assyria by land, presumably from a suitable place further north than Phoenicia (Lebanon). The scene dates from the time of Sargon II, about 720 BC, but there is little doubt that the trees for Solomon's temple three hundred years earlier were assembled in a similar manner. The relief has been described in the following way by Pottier (quoted by Offord, 1918):

'All the lower part of the relief depicts the sea at the entrance to a harbour dominated by two fortresses, one of these posted upon the foothills or rocks of the shore, on the right: the other resting upon a masonry foundation apparently based upon submerged rocks or a small islet, is at the extreme left of the design. Upon the sloping hillside, with two men standing nearby, are the trunks of trees waiting to be slid down to the water's edge. In the water itself are three galleys, two of these, having what seems to be horses' heads carved as prow ornaments, being rowed away from the shore, towing behind them the trunks of large trees, in one case apparently forming a sort of raft, but in the other they are corded to the ship and float separately. The third galley is being propelled towards the shore, with so far no towage, as it is coming in for the timber depicted as waiting to be removed. These are not war vessels as represented in Egyptian and other reliefs, but merchant ships, and were not intended for long journeys as they have no sails. Neither are they of any Mesopotamian type of galley. They are certainly Phoenician craft, employed in this case for Assyrian service.'

Calabrian pines (*Pinus brutia*) on the Troodos mountains in Cyprus (November 1991).

Timber from Lebanon was used by the Assyrians for their special buildings. For instance an inscription tells of a temple of Balawat having cedar doors bound with copper, and being roofed with cedar, just as Solomon roofed his temple. Soon afterwards Nebuchadnezzar of Babylon also imported cedars, and he records how:

'I cleft high mountains, I cut blocks of stone from the mountains, I opened paths, prepared roads for the transport of the cedars. On the canal Avakhtu, as though they were reeds of the river, I floated large cedars, tall and strong, of great beauty, of imposing aspect, rich product of Lebanon' (Moscati, 1968).

As the supply of Lebanon timber decreased, Sargon II turned to the Amanus hills and later to the Zagros mountains (Linder, 1986). Fresh supplies of Lebanon cedar were needed for the rebuilding of the temple at Jerusalem in 536 BC and, as in Solomon's time, floated down the coast to Joppa (Ezra 3:7). In the face of such exploitation, it is remarkable that any cedar forests remain.

Ancient forests of Cyprus, Turkey and westwards

The geographical position of Cyprus made it an attractive island for those who needed timber for ship-building and construction purposes. The Egyptians especially used it when the timber resources of Lebanon were unavailable owing to foreign occupation. Coastal pines and Troodos Mountain cedars were both obtained for ships (Ezekiel 27:3–9, see p. 163). We also know that Cyprus was thoroughly forested in ancient times, since Eratosthenes, quoted by Strabo, indicated that even the plains, where nowadays no tree is to be seen, were covered with woods (probably of oaks, pines and terebinths). With the discovery of copper on the island, before the Bronze Age, the demand for fuel and pit-props was such that it has been estimated that Cyprus must have needed the equivalent of sixteen times the timber that could have been grown on the island. As well as mining, agriculture was making its own demands on the lowland woods. However, there are still pine forests (*P. nigra, P. brutia*) in the Troodos mountains, as well as some cedars (*Cedrus libani* subsp. *brevifolia*) thanks to their

Spanish broom (*Spartium junceum*).

Jerusalem sage (*Phlomis viscosa*).

Etruscan honeysuckle (*Lonicera etrusca).*

Young foliage of the Palestine terebinth (*Pistacia palaestina*).

Wild Syrian pear tree (*Pyrus syriaca*) in full flower.

French lavender (*Lavandula stoechas*).

Right: These ancient Kermes oaks on Mount Carmel are protected. (June 1977.)

Far right: Open woodland and thicket on Mount Meron. The open soil is due to the activity of wild boar.

Ancient Kermes oak trees (*Quercus calliprinos*).

Aleppo pine, Kermes oaks, spiny broom and rock-roses.

Thyme (*Satureja thymbra*).

Myrtle bush (*Myrtus communis*).

Fruits of the eastern hawthorn (*Crataegus azarolus*).

Sage-leaved rock-rose (*Cistus salviifolius*).

Eastern strawberry tree (*Arbutus andrachne*).

Flower-head of the Eastern strawberry tree.

Tabor oak (*Quercus ithaburensis*) and yellow spiny broom.

Cistus creticus, C. salviifolius and *Salvia fruticosa*.

Left: Bushy *garigue*, with pink and white rock-roses and tri-lobed sage, east of Wadi Ammud (April 1969).

Far left: Woodland glade on the Carmel range in spring. The Tabor oak is sprouting new leaves; the yellow spiny broom is growing on old terraces.

Above: A forested valley on the Greek island of Lesbos, where Paul landed at the town of Mitylene.

conservation since the British occupation in 1878.

Cedar and fir forests also exist along the Taurus range of mountains in southern Turkey. These can still be seen from ships coming into port at Antalya. It was from here that cedar timber was exported for ship-building in ancient times. The north coast of Turkey from the Black Sea to Istanbul still has remnants of the deciduous forest of oaks, beech and maple which impressed Xenophon (c. 430–354 BC) in Persian times.

The western side of Asia Minor appears to have been more sparsely forested with Turkey oaks (*Quercus cerris*) and other deciduous trees. But visitors to Ephesus and Miletus today find these ports where Paul landed (Acts 14:1; 20:15) now several miles from the sea. There is no doubt that centuries of human settlement and activity deforested the neighbouring hills and river valleys far inland. Sediment washed down the eroded slopes was swept by the rivers into the broad valley, allowing the meandering waters to deposit their silt. Indeed, one of the rivers watering this flat agricultural vale is the River Meander! Although triremes were built at Ephesus by Lysander for the Spartan navy in 407 BC it seems that, even by this time, timber was being imported for them, and by late New Testament times timber importing was well established at Ephesus (Meiggs, 1982). It is probably over 2000 years since trees grew on the now grassy hills overlooking Ephesus, where reafforestation is belatedly taking place.

Most of the numerous islands in the Aegean Sea are unlikely to have been afforested. Samos and Rhodes were exceptions, with pine and cypress in abundance. Crete was also well endowed with forest, and is known for its exports of cypress and fir (*Abies cephalonica*); and Macedonia, much further north where the climate favours tree growth, was always self-sufficient in timber. In other parts of Greece, this was only the case in the higher mountains, where some fine fir forests still exist.

The Etruscans and Romans, on the other hand, had timber supplies close by in the Apennines. Here, Strabo tells us, they had pine and fir, as well as beech at lower altitude. Excavations at Acquarossa, near Viterbo in Italy, yielded carbonized timbers dating from about 500 BC of oaks, beech, elm, lime, maple and manna-ash (Meiggs, 1982). However, fine wood for special furniture and inlaid work timbers such as ebony (*Dalbergia melanoxylon*) and citron wood or thyine wood (*Tetraclinis articulata*), referred to in Revelation 18:12, needed to be imported from Africa (p. 160).

Cult worship

Groves of trees were associated with a Phoenician cult, and are frequently condemned in the Old Testament. It is not always clear, however, from the biblical account whether a grove of living trees is being referred to, or whether it was the column of wood with fertility significance known as the *asherah*. Typically the Phoenicians had a temple precinct set on a hill with a sacrificial altar and conical stone, or wooden *asherah*, in the middle, as well as a sacred grove and other features. In Deuteronomy such practices are condemned: 'You shall not plant any tree as an Asherah beside the altar of the Lord your God which you shall make' (Deuteronomy 16:21).

Immoral practices and incense-burning associated with the worship of Baal crop up repeatedly throughout the Bible, from the earliest times in the land of Canaan, and God laid down statutes for the destruction of the high places and the associated trees (Deuteronomy 12:1–3). The downfall of the people was often due to their turning back to such practices (2 Kings 16:4; 17:10–11; 2 Chronicles 33:2–3). The first sign of spiritual revival was the implementation of the Law, not legalistically but willingly, by the removal of such symbols and practices (2 Chronicles 23:17; 31:1; 34:4–7). Israel also turned to idols, which were forbidden by the Law (Exodus 20:4; Deuteronomy 4:23, 28), though these were recognized as foreign accretions and only useless pieces of wood (Deuteronomy 29:17; Isaiah 44:13–17; Jeremiah 10:3–5; Habakkuk 2:18–19).

Such practices are well known from extra-biblical sources, such as ancient art and architecture. In Assyria, a black basalt standing stone, or stele, of the period of

Right: Greek fir tree (*Abies cephalonica*).

Esarhaddon, the son of Sennacherib (680–609 BC), shows a sacred tree (p. 184). A common motif in ancient Sumer of the third millennium BC was of a sacred tree flanked by two rearing goats. Sacred date palms were often depicted in artwork of Mesopotamia.

FOREST TREES MENTIONED IN THE BIBLE

(see also Desert Trees, p. 63):

The cedar of Lebanon *(Cedrus libani)*

Individual old cedars (Heb. *erez*) develop massive trunks with spreading horizontal branches, while young trees are almost conical in shape. Along its branchlets the short sharp needle leaves are arranged in small tufts. The large female cones shatter on falling and release their winged seeds. Cedar timber was highly prized and used for Solomon's Temple (p. 157).

Carob *(Ceratonia siliqua), see p. 123.*

Judas tree *(Cercis siliquastrum)*

Hardly qualifying as a forest tree, the Judas tree, or tree of Judea, is frequent in the *maquis*. Although it is usually seen as a bush, with several stems and branches sweeping down to the ground, it can develop a trunk, especially when grown in a garden or park where it can attain a height of 7 m (over 20 ft). A member of the pea family (*Leguminosae – Caesalpinioideae*) it develops a mass of papery pods from the numerous pink flowers in clusters directly sprouting from its branches and twigs, usually before the leaves appear. Its name derives from the tradition that it was the tree from which Judas hanged himself (Matthew 27:5); possibly because the flowers look like drops of blood on the stem.

Cypress *(Cupressus sempervirens)*

The cypress (Heb. *teassur*; Isaiah 41:19; 60:13) is best known from the tall columnar form (var. *pyramidalis*) which is planted in gardens and around Arab graveyards, where it often forms a characteristic feature of the landscape. The true wild tree is more spreading, with scale leaves, but it still has a dense habit and yields very durable timber. Its small hard cones are almost spherical and contain winged seeds. The cypress occurs only in scattered sites in the Eastern Mediterranean region, although it is thought that it was more common in the past. During the Turkish occupation, up to 1917, cypress timber was even used to fuel railway locomotives, and a branch line was constructed to the forest near Petra.

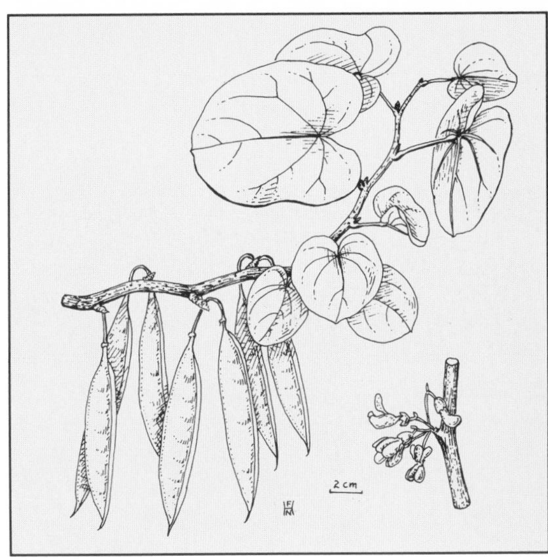

Above: Judas tree leaves, flowers and pods.

Pine trees *(Pinus species)*

Surprisingly, the Jerusalem or Aleppo pine (*Pinus halepensis*), though planted by the million on the hills of modern Israel, was never a common tree, owing to its stringent ecological requirements. It occurs naturally on soft chalky soils, where it matures into a fine tree with a large trunk attaining some 17 m (50 ft) in height. The long needle leaves are dark green and arise in pairs.

Pines are, of course, conifers,

Left: A Judas tree (*Cercis siliquastrum*) grown in a garden in Israel, where it is also part of the wild *maquis* vegetation.

Right: Stone pines (*Pinus pinea*) at Pergamon. These trees are umbrella-shaped and have edible seeds in their cones.

bearing cones containing seeds, which are usually winged, and which germinate easily given the right conditions. The Aleppo pine rapidly colonizes the ground from seed, but it appears to be restricted to certain soils, as the seedling cannot become established in soils which dry out too much in the summer heat. However, artificial planting of the saplings ensures that the roots are inserted at a deeper and moister level, and soil type ceases to be important. Hence the success of the plantations in areas where the pine was unlikely ever to have grown naturally. Lately, however, an epidemic of the scale-insect *Matsucoccus josephi* has been held responsible for the dying back of a considerable number of established trees; also processionary caterpillars (*Thaumatopoea wilkinsoni*) make their conspicuous cocoon-like nests in the upper branches.

Once the pine is established, the trees can withstand the severe conditions of the Palestinian hills, with their cool moist winters and extremely hot dry summers. However, they create very thick stands which cause the beautiful native flora to be shaded out of existence, and are very susceptible to fire, making them unsuitable for mass planting in Israel.

The modern Hebrew name of the Aleppo pine is *oren,* which occurs only once in the Bible: Isaiah wrote about the carpenter who 'plants *oren* [ash KJV; cedar RSV, NEB] and the rain nourishes it' and when it is grown it is used as fuel or is made into idols (Isaiah 44:14). However, Michael Zohary considered *oren* here to be the bay laurel (*Laurus nobilis*), and held that the Aleppo pine is *etz shamen* (Nehemiah 8:15; Isaiah 41:19), usually rendered as oil tree or wild olive.

Although the Aleppo pine is the only pine native to Palestine, in other parts of the Eastern Mediterranean region there are other species, such as the similar Calabrian pine (*P. brutia*) and the stone or umbrella pine (*P. pinea*), with its widely spreading crown and edible seeds possibly referred to by Hosea (14:8).

Terebinth or pistachio trees
(Pistacia species)

Although the RSV sources given here translate the Hebrew *ela* (or *alla*) as 'oak', as do other English versions of the Bible, it is in fact the word for the Atlantic terebinth (also

Right: Low *maquis* and *garigue* in Naphtali. The young red leaves of the Palestine terebinth (*Pistacia palaestina*) show up against the evergreen oaks; yellow spiny broom is in the foreground.

called pistachio or teil tree, *Pistacia atlantica*). Jacob hid foreign idols and rings under one near Shechem (Genesis 35:4); while later Joshua set up a stone under a terebinth, also near Shechem (Josiah 24:26). David's son Absalom met his end in a terebinth, as he was riding on his mule which 'went under the thick branches of a great oak [*ela*], and his head caught fast in the oak [*ela*] and he was left hanging between heaven and earth ... and [Joab] took three darts in his hand, and thrust them into the heart of Absalom while he was still alive in the oak [*ela*]' (2 Samuel 18:9, 14).

This tree gave its Hebrew name to the Valley of Elah, in which David fought Goliath (1 Samuel 17:19). Today this peaceful place, where I once saw a group of Palestine gazelles, is rocky and devoid of trees, but Professor Michael Zohary told me that there is no reason why the terebinth should not have grown there in biblical times. It is true that this deciduous tree does look like an oak, but it has pinnate leaves. It occurs from Dan to the central Negeb, inhabiting the drier mountains rather than the Mediterranean type of vegetation. It may have been more common in the past, even as far east as Northern Iraq, since it was referred to in Old Babylonian inscriptions (Stol, 1979). Many trees survive for hundreds of years as sacred trees because of local preservation; in Cyprus, for example, venerable trees are preserved beside ancient Greek Orthodox churches. But natural propagation from seed is difficult, as seedlings need minimal competition from other vegetation and suffer from the grazing of animals.

There is another much smaller terebinth, *Pistacia palaestina* (or *P. terebinthus* subsp. *palaestina*), which is a shrub or small tree common in the wooded hill country up to the highest parts. The brilliant red-brown colour of its new foliage in spring contrasts markedly with the dark green evergreen oaks usually growing nearby. Both these terebinths yield edible fruit that is still sold in Arab markets, but these are tiny balls unlike the modern pistachio nut (see p. 122). Another member of this genus, the mastic or lentisk (*P. lentiscus*), is an even smaller shrub, and is an important constituent of the Mediterranean shrub vegetation. The mastic usually grows about 1 m (3 ft) high, although it may reach three times this height, with numerous short branches in a dense evergreen growth. The compound (pinnate) leaves have several pairs of narrow leathery leaflets, while the tips of the shoots bear the small aggregated flowers. The cut stems of a variety of this shrub found on the Greek island of Chios exude a translucent gum which is the mastic used in medicine (p. 147).

Left: Mastic or lentisk bush (*Pistacia lentiscus*) in fruit. An evergreen shrub frequent in Mediterranean type *garigue* and *maquis*.

Plane tree *(Platanus orientalis), see p. 73.*

Oak trees *(Quercus species)*
The oak tree of the mountains is the Palestinian form of the evergreen Kermes oak (*Quercus coccifera*), which is known by Israeli botanists as the calliprinos oak (*Quercus calliprinos* or *Q. coccifera* subsp. *calliprinos*). Botanical classification of oaks is very difficult and few taxonomists agree on how it should be done or which names should be

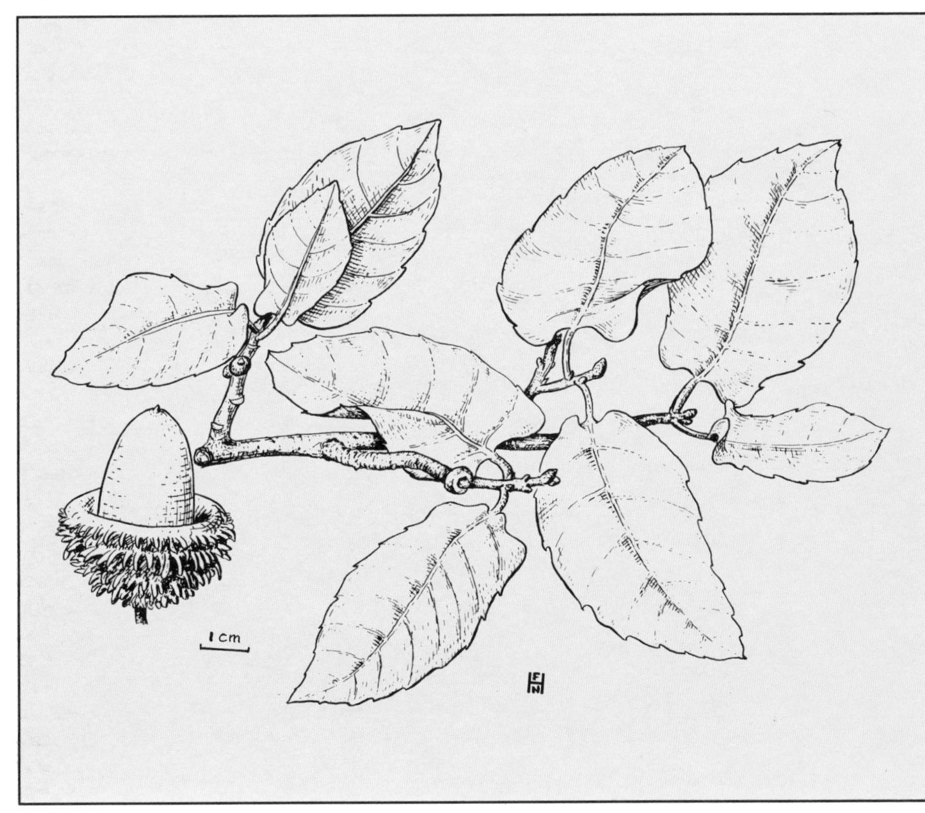

Below: A shoot of the deciduous Tabor oak (*Quercus ithaburensis*).

used. The trees vary a great deal and some botanists consider that a name should be given to each variation. For our purposes I am taking a broad view, using the comprehensive name *Q. coccifera*. The Palestinian form of it is often grazed down, but when protected it may grow into a large tree, apparently unlike the species elsewhere in the Mediterranean region where it is always seen as a shrub.

It has leathery leaves about 4 cm (1.5 ins) long with rather prickly margins, and its acorns, which mature in the second year and germinate only while fresh, are held in a cup covered with recurved and more or less prickly scales. As indicated earlier, Kermes oak must have covered considerable areas of the hill country from Carmel to Samaria and Hebron, and even today there are fine forests on the hills of Upper Galilee and Gilead. In Judea it now occurs as individual trees preserved as markers of tombs or as sacred groves, which reminds one of the frequent mention in Scripture of the evils practised 'under every green tree' (p. 30).

Perhaps the largest and most famous tree of this species is 'Abraham's oak' at Mamre. After separating from Lot 'Abram moved his tent, and came and dwelt by the oaks [RSV; plain KJV; terebinth NEB, NKJV; great trees NIV] of Mamre, which are at Hebron; and there he built an altar to the Lord' (Genesis 13:18). This tree is carefully protected by ugly ironwork, and a healthy youngish tree conveniently beside it is the obvious successor to the aged remnant (Hepper and Gibson, 1992). No doubt the old one visible today is itself the successor to a series of others on or near the same traditional site, which is held in reverence by Christian, Muslim and Jew, and an interesting botanical point about the site is that it is near the southernmost limit of the kind of vegetation in which this species of oak can exist. It may indicate that evergreen oak woodland used to occur in the Hebron region.

The deciduous Tabor or Valonea oak is widespread in the Eastern Mediterranean region, where it is known as *Quercus macrolepis* by some botanists, or as *Q. aegilops* by others. To Israeli botanists it is *Q. ithaburensis*, the Tabor oak.

It has a well-developed trunk up to 5.5 m (17 ft) before branching, giving trees up to 10 m (31 ft) in height. Usually, however, it is smaller, with wide spreading branches forming a rounded crown. The leaves are very variable in shape and size with coarse teeth on the margins and woolly hairs on the under surface. Towards the end of the year the leaves fall off, except in the warmer parts of the country such as the Upper Jordan valley, where they may persist throughout the winter. The yellow-green flower catkins appear in early spring and the pale new leaves impart a fresh appearance to the countryside; but soon the leaves darken and the trees appear to hang heavily on the hills of Lower Galilee, Carmel and to the east of the River Jordan, where they still occur as large scattered trees. The huge acorns, held in cups bearing large spreading or reflexed scales, mature before the end of the year and will not germinate if they are dried.

The practice of marking graves with oak and terebinth trees is still continued to this day and several fine evergreen oaks may be seen, for example, beside the road from Jerusalem to the coast. In the Bible both the oaks are known by the Hebrew words *allon* or *elon*, which refer usually to marker trees, such as the one on the boundary of Naphtali at Zaananim (Joshua 19:33). Sometimes a place name has been derived from the oak tree, for example the biblical Allon-bacuth – the oak of weeping – under which Deborah, Rebekah's nurse, was buried (Genesis 35:8).

---

[1] Isaiah 35:2.

[2] The Druse being a Muslim sect living in the region.

[3] Josiah 20:7

[4] Isaiah 35:2

[5] Teassur is one of the trees that Isaiah prophesied would grow in the desert (Isaiah 41:19, box tree KJV; box NEB). Since the evergreen box (*Buxus sempervirens*) only reaches the northern slopes of Lebanon and does not occur in Palestine proper, it is less likely to have been known to Isaiah than the common cypress tree (RSV).

Bibliography

Beals, E. W., 'The Remnant Cedar Forests of Lebanon', *Journal of Ecology* (Oxford, 1965), 53:679–94 .

Currid, J. D., 'The Deforestation of the Foothills of Palestine', *Palestine Exploration Quarterly* (London, 1984), pp. 1–11.

Danin, A., 'The Atlantic Pistachio: largest of Israel's trees', *Israel Land and Nature* (Jerusalem, SPNI, 1980), pp. 114–16.

Eig, A., 'A Historical and Phytosociological Essay on Palestinian Forests of *Quercus aegilops* ssp. *ithaburensis* in past and present', *Beihefte zum Botanischen Centralblatt* (1933), 51:233ff., Abt. II.

Hepper, F. N., and Gibson, S., 'Abraham's Oak', *Palestine Exploration Quarterly* (London, 1992).

Linder, E., 'The Khorsabad Wall Relief: a Mediterranean seascape or river transport of timbers?', *Journal American Oriental Society* (Ann Arbor, 1986), 106:273.

Liphschitz, N., and Biger, G., 'Cedar of Lebanon (*Cedrus libani*) in Israel during antiquity', *Israel Exploration Journal* (Jerusalem, 1991), 41:167–75.

Liphschitz, N., Lev-Yadun, S., and Gophna, R., 'The dominance of *Quercus calliprinos* (Kermes oak) in the central coastal plain in antiquity', *Israel Exploration Journal* (Jerusalem, 1987), 37:43–50.

Meiggs, R., *Timber in the Ancient World* (Oxford University Press, 1982).

Moscati, S., *The World of the Phoenicians* (London, Weidenfeld and Nicolson, 1968), p. 83.

Offord, J., 'How Cedars were Transported', *Palestine Exploration Quarterly* (London, 1918), pp. 181–3.

Paz, U., 'The Forests of Israel at the end of the Islamic Period', *Israel Land and Nature* (Jerusalem, 1981), 7(1):28–31.

Shamida, A., 'Kermes Oaks in the Land of Israel', *Israel Land and Nature* (Jerusalem, 1980), 6(1):9–16.

Stol, M., *On Trees, Mountains and Millstones in the Ancient Near East* (Leiden, Ex Oriente Lux, 1979).

See also General References: Feinbrun-Dothan and Danin (1991); Mouterde (1966–83); Plitmann, Heyn, Danin and Shmida (1983); Zohary (1962); Zohary and Feinbrun-Dothan (1966–86).

3. Thorns and Thistles, Fire and Fuel

'Cursed is the ground because of you ... thorns and thistles it shall bring forth to you.'
(Genesis 3:17, 18.)

Left: The white-veined leaves of Mary's milk-thistle (*Silybum marianum*) are similar to those of several other common thistles, such as *Notobasis, Scolymus* and *Carduus*.

Left: The Syrian thistle (*Notobasis syriaca*).

Even in these days of mechanization, thorns and thistles are a curse to farmers the world over. They are much worse for the peasant wresting a living with his hands at the fringe of the Near Eastern deserts, where prickly plants abound. The Bible frequently refers to thorns and thistles, sometimes in a metaphorical context, in which they are destroyed by fire in the same way that people are destroyed by wickedness (Isaiah 9:18–19). In this chapter it is convenient, therefore, to deal with thorns, thistles and other prickly and stinging plants, as well as the effect of fire on vegetation and the use of plants for fuel. We shall also consider the significant ecological and conservation issues arising from the use of fire.

It is often difficult to be sure to which plant the biblical text refers, since some twenty different words are used for thorns and prickly plants. Many of these appear to be general terms in common usage by Bible writers who were non-botanists. Commentators have made numerous suggestions for identification, the most recent by Professor Michael Zohary (1982) who based his conclusions on current Arabic names. Here I describe a selection of such plants to be seen in the Palestine region and relate them, as far as possible, to a scriptural context.

THISTLES AND OTHER PRICKLY WEEDS

Many prickly plants occur as weeds in cultivated and disturbed ground. Perhaps the most conspicuous, forming dense banks along the roads, is the milk-thistle, or Mary's thistle (*Silybum marianum*), with large prickly leaves characteristically white veined. In April it grows rapidly to over 1 m (3 ft) high, with the stout thistle-heads bearing pink (or white) florets. Perhaps Jesus was thinking of these shady stands when, in the parable of the sower, he spoke of the seed sown among thorns (Gk. *akantha*): 'this is he who hears the word, but the cares of the world and the delight in riches choke the word' (Matthew 13:22). Jeremiah (4:3) warned men not to sow 'among the thorns', but in broken fallow ground. The Syrian thistle (*Notobasis syriaca*) is difficult to distinguish from it unless in flower, as both have milky-veined leaves, but *Notobasis* does not usually grow quite so thickly. Its flower-heads are surrounded by long, unequal prickly leaves (bracts), while the milk thistle has shorter, equal ones.

Many other members of the aster family (*Compositae*) are conspicuously prickly. The spotted golden thistle (*Scolymus maculatus*) has yellow flowers surmounting an incredibly well-armoured stem, and

Below: The flower heads of Mary's milk-thistle (*Silybum marianum*) are usually pink, but in recent years white ones, var. *albiflorum*, have become more frequent in Palestine. Large stands of milk-thistle grow along waysides and at the edge of cultivation, where they would overshadow growing cereals.

Right: Roman nettle (*Urtica pilulifera*).

Far right: Fruiting heads of the slender safflower (*Carthamus tenuis*), a common thistle.

the white-veined and prickly-margined leaves present a formidable defence against browsing animals. It flowers in the summer and its knee-high grey stems persist throughout the winter in fallow fields. M. Zohary equates it with the thistles of Isaiah 34:13 (Heb. *hoah*, bramble KJV). Much more slender is the silvery thistle (*Carduus argentatus*) with spots of silver on its leaves and purplish flowers. In red soil the star thistle (*Centaurea iberica*) radiates its long spines from its yellow flower-heads. This is said to be the cursed thistle of Genesis 3:18 (Heb. *dardar*). Yet another thistle is the slender safflower (*Carthamus tenuis*), allied to the safflower used as a dye (see p. 171). It infests fields in the hill country after harvest, and produces small pink flower-heads the following year. Another bad weed of cultivation, the Crete eryngo (*Eryngium creticum*) in the parsley family, is recognized by its mauve-tinged wiry stems and sharp, narrow leaves. Its broader basal leaves are edible and used as bitter herbs at Passover (Numbers 9:11) (p. 130).

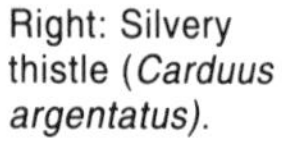

Right: Silvery thistle (*Carduus argentatus*).

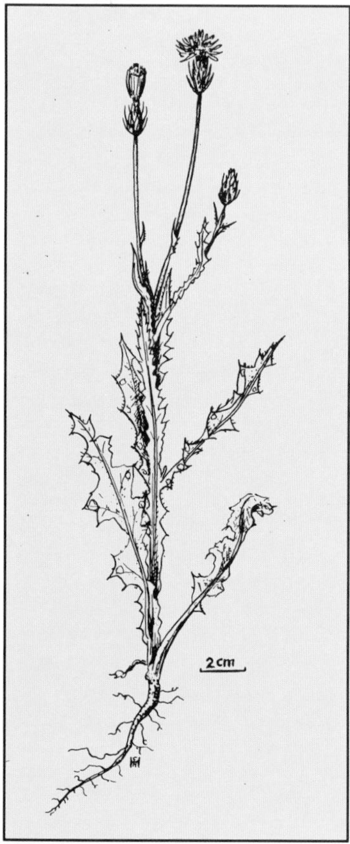

Two members of the pea family, *Leguminosae*, are also worthy of note as prickly plants. One of the worst weeds of barley fields is the upright rest-harrow (*Ononis antiquorum*), which has sharply pointed axillary spines along its erect 25 cm (9 ins) high stems, and pink flowers. The other is a small dull undershrub about 30 cm (12 ins) high – the field prosopis (*Prosopis farcta*), which infests fields and roadsides in the plains and valleys. It is one of the plants occurring naturally in open communities of the semi-desert region which has spread to suitable inhabited regions far outside its former range. One should beware of walking through this uncomfortably spiny plant, which can often be recognized by the large old insect-galled pods remaining among its maze of grey branchlets.

Thorny plants were an important source of fuel in biblical times, especially the spiny burnet (*Sarcopoterium spinosum*) that is characteristic of the low-growing *batha* type of vegetation. The peasant farmer was glad to be rid of such prolific and unproductive plants. However, in an almost treeless country where fuel is hard to come by, many of the thorny shrubs provide more heat than annual plants. They burn readily with a bright, noisy flame: 'as the crackling of thorns [Heb. *cirah*] under a pot, so is the laughter of the fools' (Ecclesiastes 7:6). Even fresh thorns will burn, as indicated by the psalmist speaking of the wicked: 'sooner than your pots can feel the heat of thorns [Heb. *atad*], whether green or ablaze, may he [God] sweep them away!' (Psalm 58:9). M. Zohary equates the Hebrew *atad* with the Christ thorns *Ziziphus spina-christi* and *Z. lotus*. The metaphor of wickedness as thorns burnt up in judgement occurs several times in the Bible. 'Godless men are all like thorns [Heb. *qots*] that are thrown away ... and they are utterly consumed with fire' (2 Samuel 23:6–7). 'For wickedness burns like a fire, it consumes briers [Heb. *shamiyr*] and thorns [Heb. *shayith*]' (Isaiah 9:18). Also there is the promise that 'the light of Israel will become a fire, and his Holy One a flame, and it will burn and devour his thorns [Heb. *shayith*] and briers [Heb. *shamiyr*] in one day' (Isaiah 10:17).

Nettles

Before we come to the thorn-bushes we should deal with the herbaceous stinging nettles. In most English versions of the Bible two Hebrew words are translated

Left: Spiny burnet (*Sarcopoterium spinosum*, formerly *Poterium spinosum*), a principal species of the *batha* type of vegetation.

Far left: Syrian acanthus (*Acanthus syriacus*). Acanthus leaves provided an art motif for Greek architecture.

as nettles: one is *harul* (Job 30:7; Proverbs 24:31; Zephaniah 2:9) and the other is *qimmos* (Isaiah 34:13; Hosea 9:6). Moldenke (1952) summarizes the view expressed by various authors who suggest other species such as charlock (*Sinapis arvensis*) and the Syrian acanthus (*Acanthus syriacus*); but I am satisfied that true nettles (*Urtica* species) were intended. M. Zohary (1982) considered the 'brier' of Isaiah 55:13 (Heb. *sirpad*) and Ezekiel 2:6 (Heb. *seravim*) could also be rendered 'nettles'. As we have seen in chapter 3, these weeds occur in abundance in unattended cultivation, such as 'the field of the sluggard' (Proverbs 24:30–31).

There are three annual stinging nettles in Palestine, and a rare perennial in the Huleh swamps (*U. hulensis*). Like nettles elsewhere, they follow cultivation and quickly invade waste places, especially the damper spots with a high nitrogen content in the soil. One frequently comes across the Roman nettle (*U. pilulifera*), and another annual *U. membranacea*, amongst ruins (Isaiah 34:13; Hosea 9:6; 10:7), while the small nettle (*U. urens*) is a weed of more open habitats such as fields.

Stinging nettles do not simply prick the skin, as in the case of a thistle, but they actually inject a fluid into the victim. This acetic acid is the irritant causing the well-known inflammation which mercifully disappears as soon as the acid has been dispersed within the body. Withered nettles therefore have no further ability to sting.

HEDGES AND THORNY SHRUBS

Isaiah described a vineyard which was hedged (Isaiah 5:5, Heb. *mesukah*), and so did Jesus: 'there was a householder who planted a vineyard, and set a hedge [Gk. *phrygmos*] around it' (Matthew 21:33). Living hedges were probably not grown in biblical times, their place being taken by low stone walls topped by branches cut from any convenient thorny shrub, such as spiny burnet and both Christ thorns (*Ziziphus lotus, Z. spina-christi*): 'therefore I will hedge up her way with thorns; and I will build a wall against her, so that she cannot find her paths' (Hosea 2:6). This kind of hedge is still frequently to be seen in biblical lands. It is also likely that temporary barriers were made around plots by simply piling up cut thorns to keep out animals and thieves, as I have often seen in tropical Africa.

A common hedge seen nowadays around Arab gardens is the huge prickly pear, *Opuntia ficus-indica,* which is a comparatively recent introduction from the New World. The best hedges in the hill country are those of alaternus (*Rhamnus alaternus*), which has rather large leathery leaves but no thorns. Closely related to it is the Palestine buckthorn (*R. palaestinus*), although it looks very different, having small, spoon-shaped leaves and short, stout thorns sticking out in all directions. It is a common shrub of the *maquis,* and its natural distribution extends much further south than the alaternus. If given the chance, and not chopped or grazed as so frequently happens in the wild, it will form a rounded, well-armed bush. One I saw in a naturally-protected rocky corner at Petra was 2 m (6 ft) high and as much across, with numerous clusters of small greenish-yellow flowers very sweetly scented.

On the red soils of the hill country the common Mediterranean spiny broom (*Calycotome villosa*), which is smothered with yellow flowers in spring, is a fiercely armed bush about 1 m (3 ft) high. Often growing with it are the eastern hawthorns (*Crataegus azarolus* and *C. aronia*) which make small trees. They have decorative white flowers with a sickly smell and stem thorns in the axils of the divided leaves. As many fruit-stones of hawthorn were found during excavations of ancient Lachish, it is thought that the inhabitants gathered the red or yellow fruits and ate the flesh around the stones, just as Arabs still do. These little fruits are called haws, while the fruits of the rose are hips. Only the Phoenician and the dog-rose occur in Palestine. The Phoenician rose (*Rosa phoenicia*) favours damp places where its charming white flowers contrast with its fiercely armed stems. The dog-rose (*R. canina*) prefers shady Palestinian oak woods and its well-known pink flowers are often seen in British hedges.

Desert thorns

Beside the thorny acacia trees (mentioned in chapter 5), there are many prickly desert shrubs, especially the spiny zilla (*Zilla spinosa*), after which Zillah, wife of Lamech, was named (Genesis 4:23), according to M. Zohary. Its bluish cruciform

Right: A spiny shoot of boxthorn (*Lycium shawii*) photographed in the northern Egyptian desert.

flowers are held behind the fierce thorns. The small camel thorn (*Alhagi maurorum*) is common in Egypt and in the Arabah as a troublesome weed in salty places and where the water is not far beneath the surface. The plant has small white pea-flowers.

Widespread in the desert and the drier parts of Palestine are prickly boxthorns (*Lycium europaeum, L. shawii*, and others in puzzling variety). Their long branches with greyish leaves form impenetrable thicket clumps. Small mauve flowers reveal that they belong to the nightshade family (*Solanaceae*). In most English versions of the Bible the words translated bramble or brier probably refer to the boxthorn. For instance, when Jotham told his parable of the trees to those who had made Abimelech king, he spoke of the trees which 'said to the bramble [Heb. *atad*] "Come you, and reign over us" ' (Judges 9:14), although M. Zohary thought *atad* to be Christ thorn. The prickly boxthorn is also probably the brier which Gideon threatened to use as flails, together 'with the thorns of the wilderness' (Judges 8:7), the latter being either Christ thorn (*Ziziphus spina-christi*) or Egyptian balsam (*Balanites aegyptiaca*).

Some authors consider the brier of Micah 7:4 to be the hoary nightshade or Jericho potato (*Solanum incanum*), owing to the similarity of its Hebrew name *chedeq* to its Arabic one. However, since it is a tropical plant limited to the Jordan valley and oases by the Dead Sea, it is unlikely to have been well known elsewhere (see p. 55). True brambles do also occur in Palestine and these may be intended in certain passages, such as 'thorns and snares are in the way of the perverse' (Proverbs 22:5, Heb. *tsen*). Only the holy bramble, or blackberry (*Rubus sanguineus*, formerly *R. sanctus*), is at all common, growing beside streams in the hilly areas and forming dense tangles. In ancient times, when the country was less densely populated, it was probably more frequent. Its pale pink flowers produce red to black fruits among the prickly stems and compound leaves. A plant of this bramble is considered to be the 'burning bush' of Mount Sinai (p. 62).

Figurative allusion of thorns

It is interesting to note the way in which the concept of the curse of thorns and thistles is continued throughout the Bible. The fact that thorns are useless and fit only to be burnt lends itself to figurative allusion: 'godless men are all like thorns [Heb. *qots*] that are thrown away ... and they are utterly consumed with fire ' (2 Samuel 23:6, 7). Prickly plants are often contrasted with the pleasant and the fruitful:

'*In that day every place where there used to be a thousand vines, worth a thousand shekels of silver, will become briers and thorns. With bow and arrows men will come there, for all the land will be briers* [Heb. *shamiyr*]; *and thorns* [Heb. *shayith*], *and as for all the hills which used to be hoed with a hoe, you will not come there for fear of briers and thorns; but they will become a place where cattle are let loose and where sheep tread*' (Isaiah 7:23–25).

'*For no good tree bears bad fruit ... for figs are not gathered from thorns* [Gk. *akantha*], *nor are grapes picked from a bramble bush* [*Gk. batos*]' (Luke 6:43, 44). It is reasonable to equate *batos* with the true bramble *Rubus sanguineus*. Paul wrote about his thorn in the flesh as 'a messenger of Satan' (2 Corinthians 12:7; Gk. *skolops*).

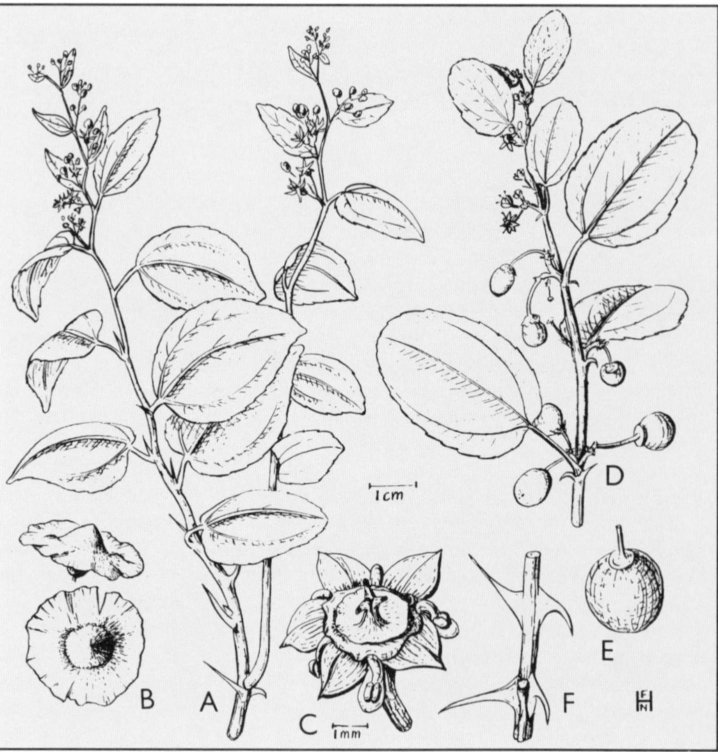

Right: The two Christ thorns: A–C the Syrian Christ thorn (*Ziziphus spina-christi*); D–F *Paliurus spina-christi*.

Above left: A tree of the Syrian Christ thorn (*Ziziphus spina-christi*) at Neot Kedumim in early spring before its leaves developed. The very spiny twigs could have been used to make Jesus' crown of thorns.

Above: Thickets of the holy bramble (*Rubus sanguineus*) growing along a stream on the Carmel range of hills, with dead stems of the golden thistle (*Scolymus maculatus*) in the field; willow trees (*Salix acmophylla*) can be seen in the distance.

Crown of thorns

When Jesus was mocked before Pilate, the soldiers :

'*stripped him and put a scarlet*[1] *robe upon him, and plaiting a crown of thorns*[2] *they put it on his head, and put a reed in his right hand. And kneeling before him they mocked him saying, "Hail, King of the Jews!" And they spat upon him, and took the reed and struck him on the head*' (Matthew 27:28–30). The striking upon the head would have driven the thorns into Jesus' brow. Here, too, was the curse of the ground around his head (Genesis 3:17–18).

On the spur of the moment the soldiers took a thorny plant growing close at hand to make the crown. What grew within easy reach? Even now on the rocky hillsides of Jerusalem the spiny burnet (*Sarcopoterium spinosum*) grows in profusion. Perhaps this was used; present-day Hebrew botanists believe so. Older botanists, such as Linnaeus in the eighteenth century, thought that the common spiny shrub or tree popularly known as the Syrian Christ thorn (*Ziziphus spina-christi*) was the plant, hence Linnaeus gave it an appropriate epithet. About the same time Miller considered that the crown of thorns was made from the so-called European Christ thorn and named it accordingly *Paliurus spina-christi*. Others have suggested the boxthorn (*Lycium* species) and the lotus Christ thorn (*Ziziphus lotus*); the former is unsuitable, and the latter a subtropical shrub occurring in the Jordan valley and thus not immediately available in Jerusalem. The *Paliurus* Christ thorn, on the other hand, has a southern European distribution, at present extending only to Syria and Mount Tabor. However, in New Testament times oak *maquis* was probably still found along the Judean hills, and it is possible that this shrub was found further south than nowadays. An interesting confirmation of the presence of *Paliurus* in the vicinity, at least during very ancient times, is the identification of wood fragments by Dr A. C. Western (1961) from the Jericho pre-pottery period. On present evidence, however, the plant most likely to have been used for the crown of thorns is *Ziziphus spina-christi*.

Another suggestion was by Hart (1952), that the crown of thorns was composed of the spines at the base of date-palm leaves. This interesting, but less plausible, idea is based on the radiate crown frequently depicted on Greek and Roman coins and which would have been well known to the Roman soldiers. The crowned head indicated a divine ruler, and such a crown, viewed from the front, appears to have radiating spikes, incidentally like that on the Statue of Liberty. Hart maintains that the palms at Jerusalem, such as those used on the first Palm Sunday, would have been readily available. The lower leaflets of the date palm are reduced to thorns (and in fact all the leaflets are sharply pointed) and they could have been plaited or tied to a band around Jesus' head. If he was adorned with a mock-radiate crown, the soldiers were mocking his divinity as well as his kingship, although it would not have been an instrument of torture in the same way as the other type of crown mentioned above.

FIRE IN FIELD AND FOREST

'*Fire has devoured the pastures*' (Joel 1:19). Here Joel graphically describes the spreading of fire in natural vegetation and its resulting destruction (see also Psalm 83:14; Isaiah 10:17–19; Jeremiah 21:14; James 3:5). So what is the ecological effect of burning a field or a forest? This depends on several factors, such as the type of vegetation burnt and the frequency of burning. Thus grassland can recover rapidly, probably within a season, with no lasting damage, unless the fires are so frequent that they prevent seed formation. Even thickets recover a few years after a fire, but a thicket is often a stage in the development of woodland, so burning may set back the vegetation to its previous stage. Since trees take longer to develop than herbs or shrubs, fires at intervals of as long as a decade may effectively prevent the development of forest in a locality otherwise suitable for the growth of trees. Intense grazing and agriculture must also be taken into consideration when discussing the effects of fire on the vegetation in the past. For instance, fire raging through pine forest or *maquis* may kill so many trees that grazing, agriculture or soil erosion prevent fresh development of forest, even without further fires.

It is unlikely that thick oak forests would have easily caught fire, but dry thickets (the *garigue*) accompanying the open hill woodland (the *maquis*) of ancient

Right: An Arab preparing a fire for cooking. Wood is used when available, whilst animal dung is an alternative fuel widely used in treeless areas.

Palestine would have beeen very susceptible to burning, which would in turn scorch the oaks. Coniferous woodlands, on the other hand, are easily burnt, owing to the resinous nature of the timber and leaves. James pointedly comments: 'how great a forest is set ablaze by a small fire!' (James 3:5–6). Cedars, being conifers, must have suffered from fires down the years as Zechariah graphically described: 'open your doors, O Lebanon, that the fire may destroy your cedars!' (Zechariah 11:1). Likewise the fir and cypress trees of Lebanon would suffer, and the Aleppo pines in Palestine, too.

In countries such as Palestine where there is a prolonged dry season, the natural vegetation becomes scorched and tinder-dry. When a fire is started, whether deliberately or by accident, there is the possibility that it will sweep rapidly through cornfields and grassland, as Isaiah indicated: 'as the tongue of fire devours the stubble, and as dry grass sinks down in the flame, so their root will be as rottenness and their blossom go up like dust' (5:24). Trees may be affected, too, as Joel vividly expresses: 'for fire has devoured the pastures of the wilderness, and flame has burned all the trees of the field' (Joel 1:19). Fire in grassland sweeps uphill even more rapidly than on level ground, especially when driven by the wind, and it may eventually reach the forest itself: 'as fire consumes the forest, as the flame sets the mountains ablaze, so do thou pursue them [God's enemies] with thy tempest' (Psalms 83:14, 15).

Fuel

Since the discovery of fire as a useful and valuable provider of warmth and for cooking purposes, fuel has been needed. Until recently, when coal, gas, oil and other modern fuels became available, plants had to be used in their raw state to supply fuel requirements. Even animal dung and charcoal, which have been used in the Middle East since time immemorial, are plant products. In biblical times the ordinary peasant, such as the widow of Zarephath who looked after Elijah (1 Kings 17:10), gathered sticks for cooking purposes, and nobody expected to pay for fuel, except in times of distress (Lamentations 5:4). Bundles of sticks were also obtained from orchards and vineyards after the annual pruning. The local Arab

Right: Arab fuel-gatherers cut and collect large quantities of spiny burnet (*Sarcopoterium spinosum*) on the *batha* hills near Tekoa. (March 1985.)

Left: Charcoal burners in Palestine. Vast quantities of charcoal were required for iron and other metal smelting.

Below: Charcoal burning on the West Bank. (Photograph: Three's Company.)

women in the rich vineyard country around Hebron still collect the prunings and load huge bundles on to diminutive donkeys. As I watched them doing this, I wondered whether Isaiah had in mind such a scene: 'when its boughs are dry they are broken; women come and make a fire of them' (Isaiah 27:11). Jesus also referred to the practice: 'the branches are gathered, thrown into the fire and burned' (John 15:6).

The nomadic Bedouin still cut many of the tougher desert plants for fuel. In the Negeb I have seen heaps of wormwood (*Artemisia monosperma*) awaiting collection with the help of camels, but in areas where the loose sand is bound together by the wormwood, excessive and frequent cutting may have an erosive effect by making the sand more liable to be blown about by the wind. Similarly in parts of the hill country where undershrubs such as the spiny burnet (*Sarcopoterium spinosum*) are extensively used for fuel, as already mentioned, the hillsides become so badly eroded that the thin layer of soil is washed away, trees cannot establish themselves and the areas become artificially made deserts. However, the use of such plants for fuel is very ancient. As long as the population's fuel requirements do not exceed the regrowth rate of the plants little damage is done; but with the increase of population, heavy grazing and thoughtless cutting, the results are catastrophic and sometimes irreversible.

Jesus mentioned the use of wild plants for fuel when he spoke of 'the grass of the field, which today is alive and tomorrow is thrown into the oven' (Matthew 6:30). Frequent biblical references to the burning of chaff (Heb. *mots*) and stubble (Heb. *qash*) are again used metaphorically for the wicked. They 'are like stubble, the fire consumes them; they cannot deliver themselves from the power of the flame' (Isaiah 47:14). And Christ's 'winnowing fork is in his hand, to clear his threshing floor, and to gather the wheat into his granary, but the chaff [Gk. *achuron*] he will burn with unquenchable fire' (Luke 3:17). The fine, light chaff resulting from winnowing corn was probably used to produce evanescent heat when needed. Generally all chaff, stubble and thorns were worthless and fit only for burning. However, if the fire did get out of hand and consume the stacked and standing grain, restitution had to be made (Exodus 22:6).

When Joshua and Caleb spied out the land of Canaan, one of their objects was to find out whether there was wood, presumably for fuel and timber (Numbers 13:20). Later Isaiah (44:15) wrote of a planted tree that 'becomes fuel for man; he takes a part of it and warms himself, he kindles a fire and bakes bread'. But the felling of trees with the simple hand-axes available presented a formidable task not likely to be undertaken by the ordinary person. Dead forest trees and fallen branches would mainly have been used, as well as poor quality fruit trees, and both John the Baptist and Jesus used as a warning the burning of poor or diseased fruit trees: 'every tree that does not bear good fruit is cut down and thrown into the fire' (Matthew 7:19; also Luke 3:9).

Biblical references to timber as fuel usually relate to sacrificial fires (e.g. Leviticus 1:8). The Mishnah[3] even states that 'all wood is ritually

Right: Copper dross covering hills near Hazeva in the Arabah valley. Charcoal prepared from the acacias growing in the wadis was used for copper smelting. Charcoal-burning was responsible for the clearance of many trees in all parts of Palestine.

pure for the altar fire, saving olive wood', though 'old olive may be sold for [domestic] firewood'. We also learn from the same source that dried olive leaves and olive cake – the pulp remaining after the oil has been extracted from the seed – were used for fuel, together with 'grape seeds and grape skins of the seventh year'. Olive wood burns with a characteristically pleasant aroma and gives out great heat, as it is highly resinous, even when fresh. The roots are especially favoured as fuel, probably because the trunks of old felled trees are of more value as timber than fuel. However, they present a great problem to anyone preparing them for fuel, since the wood is hard and the grain is extremely twisted. I once watched a man and a boy in a back-yard in Jerusalem energetically wielding a sledge-hammer and cold-chisel on an enormous olive root-stump. It gave real meaning to Ecclesiastes 10:9: 'he who splits logs is endangered by them'.

Charcoal

The use of charcoal as a fuel is very ancient indeed and its production has until recent times constituted an important minor industry in many Mediterranean countries. Charcoal is formed by heating wood in a kiln with regular, but limited, amounts of air. This retarded combustion drives off the volatile components of the wood and leaves behind the carbon, good quality charcoal having a fixed carbon content of about 80 per cent. Primitive kilns, such as were used in biblical times, were constructed with sods surrounding a stack of wood and each charge took many days to burn through before the charcoal was ready.

The role of charcoal in the progress of civilization has been enormous, for without it any advance in metallurgy beyond the most primitive methods would have been difficult, if not impossible. This is because very high temperatures are required for the smelting of ores, and charcoal was until comparatively recent times the only fuel known that would produce sufficient heat.[4] The use of charcoal by metal workers is referred to by Isaiah: 'the ironsmith fashions it [the idol] and works it over the coals ... and forges it with his strong arm' (44:12), and 'I have created the smith who blows the fire of coals, and produces a weapon for its purpose' (54:16). Ezekiel, in allegorical context, refers to its use in the purification of a copper cooking pot (Ezekiel 24:11). Charcoal, the first smokeless fuel, was expensive and so was not normally used for baking purposes (but see Isaiah 44:19). Jesus, however, cooked fish on it (John 21:9). Charcoal fires or braziers were used for heating where smoke was not wanted, such as in the royal palace (Jeremiah 36:22) and in the High Priest's courtyard (John 18:18), and small quantities were used in censers (Leviticus 16:12) by the priests.

Readers of the Scriptures in biblical times would therefore have been very familiar with charcoal and it was natural for writers to allude to it metaphorically (Psalms 18:8; 140:10; Ezekiel 1:13; Romans 12:20). Charcoal is ignited by embers and glows when burning, unlike raw wood which bursts into flame – a characteristic well known to Solomon who wrote 'as charcoal to hot embers and wood to fire, so is a quarrelsome man for kindling strife' (Proverbs 26:21; see also Romans 12:20).

Burning charcoal was probably used in sieges to shower upon the attackers, and incendiary arrows were also used on suitable occasions: 'a warrior's sharp arrows, with glowing coals of the broom tree' (Psalm 120:4; Heb. *rothem*; juniper KJV). Writers now agree that this refers to the white broom (*Retama raetam*), which is said to produce excellent charcoal and at one time was extensively used for that purpose. As this broom is a shrub rather than a tree (see p. 60), only the roots and trunk would be of sufficient size for charcoal-making.

-----

[1] The colour of the robe was scarlet according to Matthew, and purple according to Mark and John, but there is no contradiction here since the context clearly shows that a garment of the royal colour was used (see dyes, p. 170).

[2] The Greek word *akantha* simply means thorns, without identifying the species. The idea that it refers to the Acanthus plant is ridiculous!

[3] The Mishnah is a collection of precepts forming the basis of the Talmud, and embodying Jewish oral law. R. J. Forbes (1958) gives further references to statements within the Jewish writings concerning fuel and fire, and also deals with the history of heating, refrigeration and lighting in the ancient world.

[4] Charcoal has a high calorific value, 12–14,000 British Thermal Units per pound, which compares favourably with the best bituminous coal.

Bibliography

Forbes, R. J., *Studies in Ancient Technology* (Leiden, Brill, 1958), vol. 4.

Hart, H. St. J., 'The Crown of Thorns in John 19:2–5', *Journal of Theological Studies* (Oxford, 1952), pp. 66–75; plates 1, 2.

Western, A. C., 'The Identity of some Trees mentioned in the Bible', *Palestine Exploration Quarterly* (London, 1961), pp. 89–100.

See also General References: Feinbrun-Dothan and Danin (1991); Plitmann, Heyn, Danin and Shmida (1983); Zohary, M. (1962); Zohary and Feinbrun-Dothan (1966–86).

4. Flowers of Fields and Hills

'All flesh is grass, and all its beauty is like the flower of the field.'
(Isaiah 40:6.)

No colour photograph can do justice to the glory of a Palestinian spring. Happy is the visitor who arrives at the height of the flowering season and gazes across an open hillside where cultivation and grazing are not too intense and the wild plants have been allowed to develop in full profusion. One is struck by the richness of colour and the diversity of species. In this chapter we deal with some of the herbaceous plants that grow in grassy and rocky places, around archaeological sites or as weeds of cultivation.

As spring is short in the Mediterranean region, flowering is concentrated into a few weeks between February and April before the summer drought sets in. Plant growth begins, however, after the first rains in November, during the moist, cool season of the year. When the warmth of the sun encourages the development of flowers they appear in rapid succession, quickly fading and setting seed. Their transient appearance has not escaped the notice of poet or prophet, for the 'flower of the field' and 'flower of the grass' is frequently referred to in the Scriptures as symbolic of the brief span of human life (Psalm 90:5; Isaiah 40:6; James 1:10; 1 Peter: 24–25). During April the 'latter rains' cease first in the plains, where the herbaceous vegetation soon dries up, to be followed by that on the hills. Throughout the hot summer the plants and seeds remain dormant until the rains return in November.

FLOWERS ON THE ROCKY HILLSIDES

We have already seen how the Mediterranean woodland offers numerous places where herbaceous plants may grow. With the development of primitive agriculture open places were greatly extended. Where forest once covered the hills, thicket (*maquis* and *garigue*) replaced it; where thickets were cleared, low shrubs and perennial herbs (*batha*) took over, while in open ground annuals and other herbaceous plants flourished. This process is reversible to a certain extent in the moister regions, providing there are sufficient remnants of the original vegetation to re-colonize the land and there is enough time for each stage to develop. We have seen that the natural regeneration of an oak woodland, for example, would take many decades. Open places on the rocky limestone hillsides provide ecological niches for a variety of interesting perennial plants, as well as annual weeds, which also colonize cultivated ground.

Bulbous plants are an important element in these habitats. The development of a food store which can persist during dry summer conditions often takes the form of a bulb or tuber, according to the species. Familiar bulbs such as tulip, narcissus, star-of-Bethlehem, and wild onion, occur in Palestine, as well as the tuberous asphodel and orchids; the corms of anemone, crocus and cyclamen; and rhizomes of iris. Many of them flower at a time when their leaves are not present. An example of this is the sea squill (*Urginea maritima*), the very tall flowering of which is so conspicuous in the Mediterranean region in late summer, although it develops its broad leaves during the winter in dense greyish-green tufts. The star-of-Bethlehem (*Ornithogalum narbonense* subsp. *brachystachys*) often occurs on gravelly hillsides in such profusion that its white flowers have the

Below left: A blaze of springtime colour with poppies, mallows, chamomile and other annuals on an archaeological site near Eshtemoa, south of Hebron (late March 1987).

Below: Annuals flowering on the slopes of Tel Lachish include yellow crown daisy, scarlet corn poppies and the mauve stock *Erucaria hispanica*.

Chamomile (*Anthemis palestina*).

Corn marigold (*Chrysanthemum segetum*) at Hazor.

Corn poppy (*Papaver subpiriforme*).

Reversed clover (*Trifolium resupinatum*).

Dove's dung (*Ornithogalum narbonense* subsp. *brachystachys*).

Crocus biflorus, similar to the Palestinian *C. hyemalis*.

Mallow-leaved bindweed (*Convolvulus althaeoides*).

The rare oncocylus iris (*Iris lortetii*).

Shield clover (*Trifolium clypeatum*).

Wild cyclamen (*Cyclamen persicum*).

Squirting cucumber (*Ecballium elaterium*).

Natural rock garden, with buttercup, onion and orchid.

Antirrhinum siculum on a Jerusalem wall.

Holy hawk's-beard (*Crepis sancta*).

Wild anemone (*Anemone coronaria*).

Wild carrot (*Daucus carota* subsp. *maximus*).

Right: Asian or turban buttercup (*Ranunculus asiaticus*).

Far right: Yellow scabious (*Scabiosa prolifera*), red pheasant's eye (*Adonis aleppica*) and pink hairy flax (*Linum pubescens*) growing near Hazor (April 1991).

appearance of bird droppings, hence its biblical name of dove's dung (Heb. *chiryonim*). Its bulbs were sold for food during the siege of Samaria: 'the fourth part of a kab [cab] of dove's dung for five shekels of silver' (2 Kings 6:25). This works out at 300 ml (10 fluid ounces) for 57 gm (2 ounces) of silver – a very expensive foodstuff in spite of its low quality. In fact another European species, the umbelled star-of-Bethlehem (*O. umbellatum*), is poisonous, and Professor Tackholm (1954) points out that this species could not have been eaten as stated by Moldenke and others. *O. narbonense* subsp. *brachystachys*, on the other hand, appears to be edible. It has a short flowering up to about 10 cm (4 ins) high with green-striped white flowers appearing at the same time as the narrow grass-like leaves.

The rose of Sharon and lily of the field

We will now consider some of the more important and spectacular flowers, as it is of little value to detail what numerous authors have suggested for the identity of the biblical rose and lily (Song of Solomon 2:1; 4:5; 6:2; Isaiah 35:1).[1] It is interesting to note that the Hebrew word *shushan*, usually rendered 'lily', may be derived from a root meaning six, which fits well with the petal number of the Madonna lily (*Lilium candidum*). This well-known garden bulb with fragrant white flowers occurs very rarely in the Mediterranean type of vegetation of Carmel and Galilee. It is doubtful whether it was ever very common in Palestine, although in Crete it was the most frequent floral motif of Minoan art, where it is depicted in the murals at the palace of Knossos. It symbolized purity and grace for the Greeks and Romans from early days, and perhaps for the same reason it was grown and applauded by the Hebrews.

Other wild monocotyledons (with flower parts in sixes) are the blue hyacinth (*Hyacinthus orientalis*), the ancestor of the cultivated bulb, and the equally popular polyanthus narcissus (*Narcissus tazetta*). The latter is common in the hills and moister parts of the Sharon Plain and could be the 'rose of Sharon'. Flowering during the winter months, its white petals contrast with the short orange cup (corona) in each of the clustered flowers. Garlands of these flowers have been found in Egyptian tombs of the Graeco-Roman period. Various species of *Crocus* also flower during the winter in Palestine, even with the onset of rain, yet the sand lily (*Pancratium maritimum*) produces its fragrant white flowers in the heat of summer. The latter is also known as the sea daffodil, as it occurs in coastal sand dunes where its twisted leaves can be seen long after flowering time.

Turning to the New Testament, the well-known reference to lilies of the field is no clearer than those in the Old Testament:

'And why are you anxious about clothing? Consider the lilies [Gk. *crina*] *of the field, how they grow; they neither toil nor spin; yet I tell you, even Solomon in all his glory was not arrayed like one of these. But if God so clothes the grass of the field, which today is alive and tomorrow is thrown into the oven, will he not much more clothe you, O men of little faith?'* (Matthew 6: 28–30)[2].

Why should not any decorative and well-known plant be this lily of the field? The wonderful succession of scarlet produced by anemones, tulips, Asiatic ranunculi and poppies, in that order, spans the whole of spring, and M. Zohary considers these to be the spring flowers (Heb. *nitzanim*) of Song of Solomon 2:12. So similar are they in form and colour that from a distance they may easily be confused.

The anemone (*A. coronaria*) is traditionally identified as the 'lily of the field'. It is widespread in the Mediterranean region and its flowers can be found in several colours. Recent research in Israel has shown that there is a genetic basis for this variation which accounts for the dominance of a certain colour in a particular region. Around Jerusalem, for instance, the scarlet form is more frequent than the blue, while on the basalt slopes near Capernaum one sees the hillside flecked with the blue and white flowers. I have been impressed by some of the wild plants having a particularly brilliant scarlet colour which does not appear in cultivated ones. The Asiatic ranunculus, or buttercup (*Ranunculus asiaticus*), is also scarlet-flowered, but is distinguishable from the anemone by the presence of reflexed sepals.

Quite different from either of these, but also with a scarlet flower, is the mountain tulip (*Tulipa agenensis*, also called *T. montana* and *T. sharonensis*). When I saw one

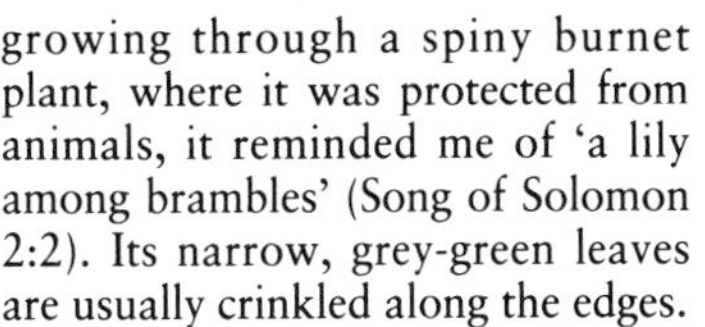

growing through a spiny burnet plant, where it was protected from animals, it reminded me of 'a lily among brambles' (Song of Solomon 2:2). Its narrow, grey-green leaves are usually crinkled along the edges.

Corn poppies (*Papaver rhoeas, P. subpiriforme* etc.) are annuals inhabiting disturbed ground and their seeds are in capsules, unlike the anemone and ranunculus, which are perennials and have their seeds in separate nutlets. Pheasant's eye (*Adonis cupaniana, A. aleppica*) are also annuals with scarlet flowers, but with nutlets like the anemone.

It is quite impossible to deal adequately with the enormous number of different species of flowering plants to be found on the hillsides, so this text is supplemented by colour photographs and explanatory captions. As already mentioned, some 2780 species of plants have been recorded from Palestine alone – which is a large number for such a small region – and most of them are herbaceous. The greater proportion occur in the Mediterranean zone, where the diversity of habitats provides many ecological niches. Of these spectacular flowers I am most impressed by the combination of the showy pink hairy flax (*Linum pubescens*), the pale yellow scabious (*Scabiosa prolifera*) and the deep blue pimpernel (*Anagallis caerulea*) trailing about their roots. In grassy places and in abandoned fields several species of the daisy family form conspicuous blocks of yellow or white according to the season. The crown daisy (*Chrysanthemum coronarium*) and the corn marigold (*C. segetum*) have bright yellow flowers which appear in early spring, while the various species of white chamomile (*Anthemis*) take over later.

Many members of the wallflower family (*Cruciferae*) are conspicuous, too, growing in masses as weeds of cultivation. The white wall rocket (*Diplotaxis erucoides*) is a noxious weed of alluvial soil, flowering early in the year and similar to the garden rocket (*Eruca sativa*), one of the cultivated and gathered herbs (2 Kings 4:39; Heb. *oroth*). They are followed by the yellow flowers of charlock (*Sinapis arvensis*) and white mustard (*S. alba*). The black-mustard (*Brassica nigra*) occurs along roadsides and in fields, especially in Galilee, yet many writers have been puzzled as to why this plant, if it is really the mustard (Gk. *sinapi*) of Matthew 13:31–32, should have been selected by Jesus as a tree in which birds perch, for it grows as a tall herb. (This is discussed further on p. 133.) The hoary mustard (*Hirschfeldia incana*) also makes yellow large areas of waste ground.

Members of the pea family (*Leguminosae*) are so abundant that they deserve special mention. At all altitudes one finds the clovers, especially the carmine-red reversed clover (*Trifolium resupinatum*) and the pinkish-white clover (*T. clypeatum*). Birds-foot trefoils (*Lotus*) and milk vetches (*Astragalus*) are as common in the Mediterranean region as they are in the desert.

Roadsides and margins of fields often provide a sanctuary for a varied collection of decorative plants. Mallows (*Malva nicaeensis, Malva sylvestris, Alcea setosa*) and members of the parsley family, such as the wild carrot (*Daucus carota*), are typical of this habitat. Often there are prickly plants (see chapter 3), such as the spotted golden thistle (*Scolymus maculatus*) and the field prosopis (*Prosopis farcta*), and especially huge stands of milk thistle (*Silybum marianum*) and Syrian thistle (*Notobasis syriacum*), which are also a feature of rubbish heaps where there is a high nitrogen content. Excavations and tips of soil often have their own plants, especially various species of orache (*Atriplex*) and goosefoot (*Chenopodium*). A typical and amusing plant of waste places around the Mediterranean is the squirting cucumber (*Ecballium elaterium*) which jet-propels its seeds with considerable force when the fruits reach maturity.

Many of the grasses (Genesis 1:11; Heb. *deshe*; 1 Peter 1:2; Gk. *chortos*) are short-lived annuals such as the wild oat (*Avena sterilis*) and brome grass (*Bromus scoparius*), but there are some perennials like the three-awned grass (*Aristida coerulescens*) and cocksfoot (*Dactylis glomerata*). Grass mown for hay as fodder during summer is referred to in Psalm 72:6 and Proverbs 27:25. The ancient practice of putting grass sods on house roofs, which is still to be seen in such diverse places as Syria, Iceland and Sweden, is mentioned by Isaiah (37:27), and in Psalms (129:6), and reference made to the lack of moisture in such situations preventing the grass from growing. The most conspicuous grass occurring as a weed of cultivation is the bulbous barley (*Hordeum bulbosum*), which has

Above far left: Polyanthus narcissus (*Narcissus tazetta*), possibly the 'rose of Sharon'.

Above right: Poppy anemone (*Anemone coronaria*).

Above: The Madonna lily (*Lilium candidum*) is now restricted to one or two localities in Mount Carmel and Upper Galilee.

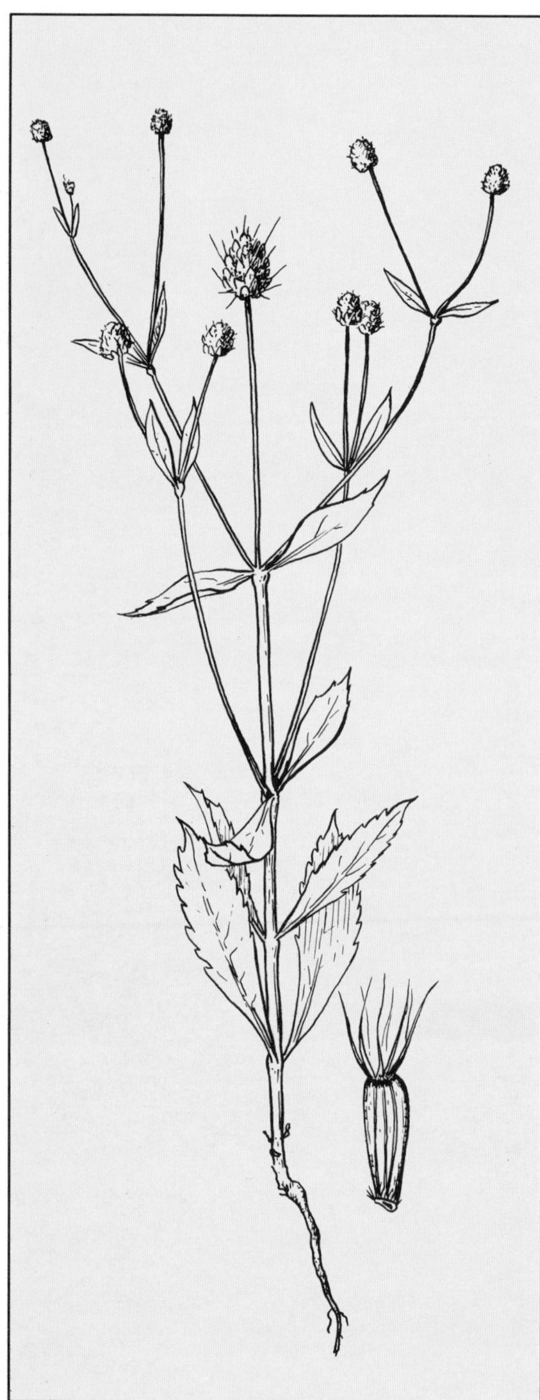

Above right: Egyptian campion (*Silene aegyptiaca*), which often inhabits the ground in vineyards and orchards.

Above: Syrian scabious (*Cephalaria syriaca*).

long-bearded ears carried at least 1 m (3 ft) high. Near Mount Hermon this barley is particularly abundant, and it was there that wild wheat was first found by botanists, but that story is told in chapter 8.

WEEDS OF CULTIVATION

Primitive agricultural methods have been used until very recently in Palestine, and in many parts of the Near East methods are little changed from those used in biblical times. A typical weed flora is found in cultivated ground, with many perennial plants as well as annuals. One may wonder how these perennials manage to survive the repeated ploughing, until one realizes that their roots or bulbs are usually deep in the soil and below the level reached by the primitive plough. Anybody who has tried to dig up a tulip from a field will have been surprised at the depth of the bulb – if they ever reached it. Some plants, such as the lion's leaf (*Leontice leptopetalum*), are actually encouraged by the action of the shallow plough which merely cuts the large corm, giving rise to numerous cormlets each capable of developing into a new plant. In this way a field can soon become infested with this weed. When a modern deep plough is used, however, the bulbs are raised to the surface, where they are exposed to the sun and perish. Bulbs rot rapidly when the fields are irrigated during the summer months, their natural resting period.

Irrigation is increasingly practised as piped water becomes more widely available, and even Arab fields are losing perennial weeds which used to survive traditional agricultural methods. Similarly chemical sprays are having a devastating effect upon annual weeds of cultivation throughout the world. This, no doubt, is in the interests of increased food production but it is nevertheless changing the flora.

The prophet Hosea wrote that the judgement of those who reject the Lord 'springs up like poisonous weeds in the furrows of the field' (Hosea 10:4). The Hebrew word *rosh* in this verse is rendered 'hemlock' in some English versions, but hemlock (*Conium maculatum*) is not a weed of cultivated ground, although it may be found in shady waste places in Palestine. An alternative is the veined henbane (*Hyoscyamus reticulatus*) which occurs in ploughed fields at the edge of the desert; I have seen it near Beersheba and at Damascus. It stands about 60 cm (2 ft) high with viscid, hairy foliage and yellowish pink-veined flowers. In most of the other regions of Palestine the most eligible plant is probably the Syrian scabious (*Cephalaria syriaca*) with poisonous seeds. Another plant is mentioned by Job, while defending his integrity: he said 'let thorns grow instead of wheat, and foul weeds [Heb. *bosa*] instead of barley' (Job 31:40). Syrian scabious or henbane may have been the ones he had in mind, or perhaps the prickly upright rest-harrow (*Ononis antiquorum*) as suggested by some botanists, but not the corn cockle (*Agrostemma githago*) (as KJV), which was never a common plant in Palestine.

Certain weeds possess adaptations which enable them to survive in the special conditions imposed by cultivation. For example, some annuals grow with cereals and are often harvested with them, such as the darnel grass (*Lolium temulentum*) and the common Syrian scabious (*Cephalaria syriaca*), both of which have been identified with the biblical tare (p. 88). Their fruits are similar to grains of corn and are sown with them the following year.

Mimicry of lentil seeds likewise occurs in the corn bedstraw

Purple-top sage (*Salvia horminum*).

Everlasting *(Helichrysum sanguineum).*

Golden henbane (Hyoscyamus aureus).

Jagged sage *(Eremostachys laciniata).*

Anatolian orchid (*O. anatolica*).

Viper's bugloss (*Echium angustifolium*)

Heron's bill *(Erodium gruinum).*

White mignonette (*Reseda alba*).

Rough alkanet (*Anchusa strigosa*).

Right: Caper (*Capparis spinosa*), said to be the 'hyssop that grows out of the wall'.

Opposite: White asphodel (*Asphodelus aestivus*, formerly *A. microcarpus*) often occurs around ancient ruins, as well as in dry, sandy places.

(*Galium tricornutum* (*G. tricorne*)) which has been found in Palestinian deposits of the Early Bronze Age (Feinbrun, 1938). Helbaek also found it during excavation of seventh-century BC Nimrud, where fifty-eight species of weeds were systematically recorded, as well as sixteen kinds of cultivated or gathered plants.

PLANTS OF TERRACED HILLSIDES

Although most of the conspicuous terraces of the hill country of central Palestine may have been constructed after biblical times (see p. 78), Isaiah implies that terraces were known to him (5:1–2). Today, many of these terraces are abandoned or semi-derelict, or have been overplanted with Aleppo pines. Other terraces, near Arab villages, continue to be maintained as olive groves, vineyards and mixed almond and fig orchards, with cereals, coriander and fodder crops in between the trees.

The weed flora depends on the management of the terraces. In a vineyard that is regularly harrowed, for instance, there may be a pink carpet of Egyptian campion (*Silene aegyptiaca*) with Syrian speedwell (*Veronica syriaca*) in early spring. An olive grove with less attention often has a meadow of the daisy family, including hawk's-beards (*Crepis sancta, C. palaestina*) and chamomile (*Anthemis* species), as well as numerous clovers and other pea family already mentioned. The diversity is astonishing and its beauty is breathtaking.

In some ways terraces combine the characteristics of cultivated fields and rocky hillsides, since the stone walls offer ecological niches to both types of plant. Crevices between the limestones give sanctuary to wild cyclamen (*Cyclamen persicum*), orchids (*Orchis* species), wild onions (*Allium* species), and numerous mints (e.g. *Coridothymus capitatus, Origanum syriacum, Teucrium polium*).

The hyssop that grows out of the wall

Finally, a note about plants which find refuge between the stones of old buildings. Such plants are simply making use of artificial 'cliffs', cliffs being their natural environment. When Solomon spoke of the 'trees, from the cedar that is in Lebanon to the hyssop that grows out of the wall' (1 Kings 4:33) he may have been referring to the caper (*Capparis spinosa* and its varieties). This shrub has long spindly branches which sprout out between rocks in the desert or hang down the walls of buildings. At the base of the grey-green leaves are two sharp reflexed spines. The decorative white flowers are about 6 cm (2·5 ins) across with a large number of spreading stamens rising from the centre. The fruit is carried on a long stalk which, strictly speaking, is part of the ovary and is characteristic of the mainly tropical caper family. The flower buds are pickled and used as an appetizer – Ecclesiastes 12:5 laments the time when they lose their zest (NEB).

Perhaps the most conspicuous and decorative wall-inhabiting plant is the golden henbane (*Hyoscyamus aureus*) which sprouts out of the Wailing Wall in Jerusalem, as well as from those of old castles and ruins elsewhere in Palestine. It is a herbaceous plant with large golden flowers bearing distinct black blotches near the centre. Another attractive plant on Jerusalem's walls is the white-flowered snapdragon (*Antirrhinum siculum*), a modern introduction from Europe. It is similar to the well-known garden snapdragon (*A. majus*) with pink flowers that still grows wild on cliffs in Upper Galilee. Less conspicuous with its green flowers, but even more frequent than the foregoing, is the pellitory-of-the-wall (*Parietaria diffusa*), which usually grows at the foot of walls.

---

1 Translators of the biblical texts have great difficulty in deciding on the identity of these plants, as is shown by these references in the several English versions: Song of Solomon 2:1; rose KJV, NKJV, RSV, NIV; asphodel, lily NEB, REB; wild flower, lily GNB. Isaiah 35:1; rose KJV, NKJV; crocus RSV, NIV; asphodel NEB; flowers GNB.

2 See also Luke 12: 27–28; NEB uses asphodel and balsam, for some of the words rendered lily in other versions.

Bibliography

See General References: Alon (1969); Feinbrun (1938); Feinbrun and Koppel (1960); Feinbrun-Dothan and Danin (1991); Plitmann, Heyn, Danin and Shmida (1983); Zohary, M. (1962); Zohary and Feinbrun-Dothan (1966–86).

5. The Wilderness and its Plants

'The Lord your God led you forty years in the wilderness.'
(Deuteronomy 8:2.)

Few people can have known the desert better than Moses after spending eighty years in Sinai: forty as a shepherd and forty as leader of the wandering Israelites (Acts 7: 30–36). He may even have noticed some of the characteristics that enable plants to survive the hard climatic conditions of the desert. Nowadays we can analyse these characteristics scientifically and see how well some plants are adapted to a rigorous environment.

In most deserts there is rain at some time or other, but if there is no water available the desert remains lifeless. The amounts may be small and may occur irregularly. However, thunderstorms produce flash floods, with an enormous quantity of water eroding the ground as it pours down the dry wadis. Temporary pools also form in the desert. Topography is very important: even slight depressions can collect surprising amounts of run-off which will support vegetation, as the Nabataeans knew well and used to their advantage. Whereas bare rocks and encrusted loess throw off the water, rainfall sinks into sand. Away from the depressions, the plants are scattered and widely separated from one another as their roots compete for available moisture.

ADAPTATIONS TO THE DESERT ENVIRONMENT

With the coming of the winter rains, seeds of desert annuals lying in the sand absorb the moisture, swell and quickly sprout into growth. Many dry seeds of desert plants develop a covering of jelly on contact with water. This has been found to act as a kind of safety-valve, which guards against the seed germinating when the amount of rain is insufficient to ensure the growth of the seedling into a mature plant. Should the amount of moisture be too small, then the jelly will dry up and the irreversible mechanism of germination will not have been initiated. Only when the jelly is saturated, and there is still surplus moisture to enter the seed coat, will the interior of the seed be activated into growth.

Once the seeds have germinated, the growth of short-lived desert plants is extremely rapid, and flowering takes place quite soon after the rain has fallen. After a few weeks the life cycle is complete and, with the ripening of the fruit and the dispersal of the seed, the parent plant withers away, leaving the desert seemingly devoid of life once more. These are known as annual plants, or, more strictly, ephemerals, which have a brief period of existence and could, since their life

Right: The rainless Egyptian desert, looking from Saqqara northwards to the great pyramids at Giza.

Left: Jointed anabasis (*Anabasis articulata*), a leafless shrub with succulent stems occurring in the salty desert.

cycle is so short, have more than one generation in a single year if there were sufficient moisture to support them.

Woody plants, such as the white broom and acacia trees, survive for many years if their long roots can tap moisture deep below the surface. Perennial herbs also live for two or more years, but their aerial shoots die down each year. There are two principal types of such herbaceous plants. One group manages to survive in the desert owing to its swollen or succulent leaves, which reduce the proportion of surface area of the leaf to its volume, and so ensure a minimum of evaporation. The second type includes the bulbous plants, such as wild tulips and narcissi, common in the Mediterranean region, as well as corms like the crocus. Having flowered and seeded, the plant 'retreats' into its bulb, where sufficient food and moisture are stored to see it through to the next growing season. Bulbous plants are found in localities where there is an adverse season, such as drought in summer or cold in winter, so they are by no means restricted solely to desert conditions.

Desert plants have certain protective devices to prevent loss of water. These include a thick waxy skin (cuticle) or a protective covering of dense hairs, as in the wormwood (*Artemisia herba-alba*), which reduces the air movement past the leaf surface and cuts down moisture loss. Plants of dry habitats frequently possess reduced leaf surfaces. For example, the leaves may be very small and insignificant, or appear only for a time on the young shoots, their function of food manufacture (photosynthesis) being performed by the green stems. Some of these species, such as the white broom (*Retama raetam*) and saxaul (*Haloxylon persicum*), are known from their appearance as switch plants. Others (e.g. a sea-blight, *Suaeda asphaltica*) drop their leaves altogether during the heat of summer, while some plants (e.g. spiny burnet, *Sarcopoterium spinosum*) have smaller summer leaves.

Surprisingly, there is sometimes abundant water in the desert, but at a depth not normally available to the ordinary plant. Deep root systems enable certain desert species to tap these reservoirs. The problem, however, is for the plant to reach such depths despite insufficient moisture in the intervening soil. This is normally achieved by rapid growth of the roots during a period when moisture is available in the upper layers, and once the roots have reached the permanent water-table the aerial parts can remain green and lush. The colocynth (*Citrullus colocynthis*) has an elongated root system which maintains large green leaves on its stems trailing over the dry sand during the summer, as its enormously long roots reach the water-table (p. 126). The roots of a tamarisk tree (*Tamarix aphylla*) measured in Iraq were found to extend some 11 m (36 ft) below the surface of the desert (p. 64).

Very important in salty deserts and sea-shores are those species with a high sap pressure. Ordinary plants absorb water from the soil through the roots by osmosis. The soil-water is normally a very dilute solution of mineral salts (most of which can be utilized by the plant), but the cell sap in the roots is a much stronger, or denser, sugar solution, which tends to draw the soil-water into them. Now, should the soil be very salty and therefore denser than usual, this tendency will be more or less neutralized until a stage is reached when the soil-water solution *outside* is stronger, or denser, than that inside the plant-cells, and water is then withdrawn from the roots by the reverse process of ex-osmosis. This is, in fact, what happens when salt is spread on a path to kill the weeds. But if the concentration of sap in the roots is much greater than even a strong salty solution, then water will continue to be absorbed by such plants, which are called halophytes, or salt-loving plants. The leaves of these plants are usually thick and fleshy (e.g. *Nitraria retusa*, *Zygophyllum dumosum*) or leathery (e.g. *Atriplex halimus*).

Let us now look at the desert vegetation in certain well-known Palestinian sites.

Below: White wormwood (*Artemisia herba-alba*).

Right: The Dead Sea beyond the ruins of Qumran, where biblical scrolls were found in the caves. The Rift Valley, well below sea-level, lies in a rain-shadow and is hot desert country.

The Wilderness of Judea

The famous desert road to Jericho winds down through the hills from Jerusalem. It descends 1100 m (3575 ft) in 24 km (15 miles), measured as the crow flies. Looking east from Mount Scopus to the Dead Sea it can be readily appreciated that this wilderness lies in the rain shadow of the Judean hills to the west. The glaring white chalk is virtually devoid of vegetation, except for annuals after winter rain. It was after an exceptionally rainy winter in 1967 that I had the opportunity to examine the flora near the Inn of the Good Samaritan (Luke 10:25–37), a well-authenticated site and now detached from the new road. The even wetter spring of 1992 yielded a torrent down Wadi Qilt and a profusion of vegetation right down to Jericho.

The haze of green on the slopes beside the upper stretches of the road rapidly decreased further downhill, where the rain had been lighter. It was noticeable even in March that the northern slopes were greener than the southern ones which catch the full force of the sun. Almost all the plants were very short-lived annuals of a few centimetres high, often with brightly coloured flowers. The pea and wallflower families were particularly frequent. Not only individuals of the same species, but different genera of the same family were represented within a small area. Such a diverse flora is typical of the desert. As well as annuals, some bulbs flourished in the short spring, but there were no trees or shrubs. However, nearby, showing as black dots all over the white hillsides, occurred the rounded shrubs, *Chenolea arabica* and *Suaeda asphaltica*, that can withstand severe drought.

Somewhere in this region lived John the Baptist during his ministry. He wore a garment of camel's hair and a leather girdle around his waist, and his food was locusts and wild honey (Matthew 3:4). Clearly John lived frugally, and the locust insects (Gk. *acrides*) on which he fed used to be common in Palestine. These are unlikely to have been the locust beans which come from the

Below: The Judean Desert east of Tekoa, towards En-Gedi (April 1987).

carob tree growing in the Mediterranean vegetation zone (see p. 123), despite being called St John's bread in many different languages. It was also in this wilderness that Jesus himself suffered hunger and temptation for forty days (Luke 4:1–2).

The Judean Desert stretches southwards opposite the lower Jordan, past Qumran and Masada, along the whole length of the Dead Sea some 388 m (1275 ft) below sea-level, until it links up with the Arabah and the Negeb. It rises from the Dead Sea as a spectacular naked white wilderness, stretching westwards to Tekoa and Hebron, high on the hill country.

The ruins of the Qumran community, near the caves where the Dead Sea scrolls were first found in 1947, lie well above the sea, but below the main crags of the Judean Desert. This area is totally arid and devoid of vegetation, save for a few annuals in the early part of the year and occasional low shrubs along the wadis and north-facing hillsides.

Much further south lies the great stronghold of Masada. This spectacular flat-topped hill, detached from the main range, was the scene of the great siege of AD 70–73. While 960 Jews took refuge in Herod's fortified palace, 10,000–15,000 Romans raised a massive causeway nearly to the summit upon the western side. Dried fruit had been stored for food, and rainwater trapped in the rock-cut cisterns, and according to Josephus cultivation would have been possible in the 'fat soil' put there by Herod for vegetables, but the refugees still had a good supply of food when they committed mass suicide. Yadin actually saw massed crown daisies after rain and he planted pomegranates with some success.

Oases in the Rift Valley

Jericho, 'the city of palm trees' (Deuteronomy 34: 3), owes its long history to the spring of fresh water that irrigates much agricultural land nearby, which contrasts with the salt desert around it. Another spring occurs at En-Gedi, where David took refuge from Saul (1 Samuel 23:29). It lies midway along the western shore of the Dead Sea, and supports a tropical African (or Sudanian) kind of vegetation which is not found elsewhere in Palestine. M. Zohary (1962) considered that when there was a warmer climate all over the country such tropical plants were much more widespread, but as the climate cooled they were restricted to the warmer rift valley. Previously botanists had assumed that African species spread up the Arabah taking advantage of the tropical conditions.

The history of human occupation of these oases is extremely long, and by Solomon's time the 'henna blossoms in the vineyards of En-Gedi' (Song of Solomon 1:14) were famous. Nowadays the little plain between the Dead Sea and the dry escarpment is even more intensively irrigated, early fruits and flowers constituting an important industry. All this has had a disastrous effect upon the natural vegetation, which is now restricted to the less accessible screes and cliffs near the trickles of life-giving water from the springs. Fortunately a sizeable area constitutes a strict nature reserve designed to preserve the remaining plants and the tropical birds associated with them.

Some of the plants at En-Gedi and other tropical oases are mentioned in the Bible. There are several candidates for the vine of Sodom (Deuteronomy 32:32), one of them the hoary nightshade (*Solanum incanum*), sometimes called the Jericho potato. It has a wide distribution in tropical Africa, where I have also seen it forming prickly thickets in overgrazed grassland. In Palestine it occurs in the hot Jordan valley and in the oases by the Dead Sea, and it may be the 'brier' (Heb. *chedeq*) mentioned in Micah 7:4. Growing about 1 m (3 ft) high, its rather large leaves with wavy margins are covered with pale stellate hairs. Stout curved prickles occur here and there on the leaves and abundantly on the stems. The rather large mauve flowers give way to yellow tomato-like fruit which, however, dry up internally and become powdery. Early writers evidently confused them with the light fruits of the Sodom (or Dead Sea) apple (*Calotropis procera*). Although the size of a large apple, the latter are softly inflated and filled with plumed seeds. One meets with this striking plant in drier parts of tropical Africa, as well as in the Nile valley and the Dead Sea region. It stands over 2 m (6 ft) high, and its pale grey, corky branches become quite woody. The large leathery grey-green leaves yield a poisonous white juice. However the vine of Sodom is most likely to be the colocynth (*Citrullus colocynthis*) (p. 53)

Above: The Sodom apple (*Calotropis procera*) in flower.

Two trees characteristic of En-Gedi oasis are the Egyptian balsam (*Balanites aegyptiaca*) and the horse-radish tree (*Moringa peregrina*), which yield balanos oil and ben oil respectively and so are described in chapter 15 (p. 150). These are wild species, still growing there, but the balsam reputed to have been cultivated by Solomon is no longer present. That was the opobalsamum or balm of Gilead (*Commiphora gileadensis*) described later (p. 148).

Saltworts by the Dead Sea

The intense heat and stillness combine with the lunar aspect of the landscape to make the area due south of the Dead Sea a most unusual place. In certain places near the southern shores of the Dead Sea undisturbed natural vegetation of a very special type can still be seen. I was fascinated by the association of plants growing in parched conditions with a high concentration of salt in the soil.

The salt-loving plants (or halophytes, see p. 53) grow where they are best adapted. In places with a constant supply of salty water or where a freshwater spring joins the sea, beds of the common reed and the Arabian rush occur; but where the ground is only flooded now and again in winter quite a bushy vegetation of tamarisk develops.

The most characteristic family of salty places is the goose-foot family, *Chenopodiaceae*. The well-known glassworts (*Salicornia*) of salt marshes, saltworts (*Salsola*), oraches (*Atriplex*) and seablites (*Suaeda*) all belong to this family. The pea family is represented by the camel thorn (*Alhagi maurorum*) and field prosopis (*Prosopis farcta*), both prickly dwarf shrubs.

The shrubby orache, *Atriplex halimus*, which occurs in many salty places around the Dead Sea and in the Arabah, is a grey-leaved bush about 1.5 m (4 ft 6 ins) high. It is usually regarded as the 'mallow' or saltbush picked for food by the disreputable young men who teased Job (30:4). The Hebrew word *malluah*, often rendered mallows in English, implies saltiness – which applies to both the habitat and the leaves of *Atriplex* and many other species of its family.

Most of the shores of the Dead Sea are sterile wilderness. The southern area is now greatly changed by vast salt pans and associated industrial works, but it can never have had any vegetation to speak of.

Huge cliffs of solid rock-salt stand beside the western shore road, indicating times past when the level of the Dead Sea was much higher. One can almost see the pillar of Lot's wife amongst the many columns of eroded rock-salt in this area! Plants are seldom to be seen here, unless they scrape a root-hold here and there in the less exacting conditions along the roads. Beside the sea itself the rocky beach is lifeless and it is not until one is well above the spray line that some plants appear. Succulent shrublets of *Anabasis articulata* and *Salsola tetrandra* are accompanied by annual herbs of the desert only after the infrequent rain, for this is true desert as well as a salt one.

To the north of the Dead Sea and west of the Jordan is an expanse of grey, water-scoured, saline mud, which in summer turns to fine dust, with scattered shrublets of the Palestine seablite, *Suaeda palaestina*, and sparse annuals in the winter. Perhaps it was of this area that the psalmist was thinking when he wrote of God turning 'rivers into a desert, springs of water into thirsty ground, a fruitful land into a salty waste, because of the wickedness of its inhabitants' (Psalm 107:33–34).

Right: A branch of the shrubby orache (*Atriplex halimus*).

Acacias in the Arabah

The Arabah extends south of the Dead Sea and is part of the Great Rift Valley system stretching down the Red Sea and along the African lakes. Moses and the Israelites apparently trekked through the Arabah during their wanderings in the wilderness, but their precise route is not clear, except that they ascended to the eastern plateau by the valley of the River Zered (Numbers 21; Deuteronomy 2).

Away from the Dead Sea the desolate gravel and sand of the valley floor is not usually salty. The winter rains wash fresh water down from

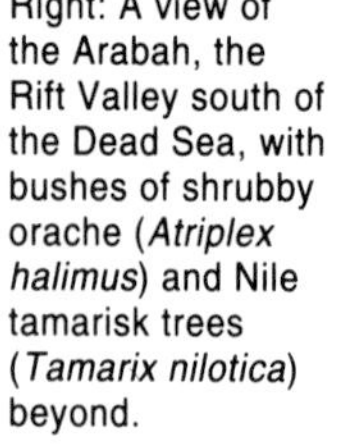

Right: A view of the Arabah, the Rift Valley south of the Dead Sea, with bushes of shrubby orache (*Atriplex halimus*) and Nile tamarisk trees (*Tamarix nilotica*) beyond.

Above left: The parasitic acacia mistletoe (*Loranthus acaciae*) has been considered, with little justification, to be Moses' burning bush.

Above: Tumbleweeds - the biblical 'rolling thing' - occur in deserts where dried up plants are swept away by the wind. Here a large plant of *Salsola kali* is stopped by a fence in the Negeb.

the eastern hills of Edom and, on the other side, from the Negeb (Psalms 126:4). Great banks of shingle thrown up in the dry water courses (wadis) harbour many different plants, while deeper rooted trees and shrubs concentrate along these runnels. The most conspicuous are the flat-topped acacia trees (*Acacia tortilis, A. raddiana*, p. 63) called *shittim* in Hebrew, a name retained in some English versions of the Bible.

Acacias are referred to in the Bible as occurring north of the Dead Sea, in an area opposite Jericho, and to the east of the Jordan, where the Israelites encamped at Abel-Shittim, literally the 'field of acacias' (Numbers 33:49). Another place-name mentioned is Beth-Shittah, or 'the house of the acacia' (Judges 7:22). We also find that in the Day of the Lord 'a fountain shall come forth from the house of the Lord and water the valley of Shittim' (Joel 3:18) – perhaps the Arabah was intended, although other places have been suggested that are unlikely ever to have supported acacias.

A scarlet-flowered mistletoe (*Loranthus acaciae*) often grows on acacias, as its scientific name implies. This parasitic shrub, like other mistletoes, has special attachment pads (haustoria) which grow into the host and tap its sap in order to obtain sufficient nourishment to supplement that made in its green leaves. Some authors consider it to be the burning bush seen by Moses (see p. 62)

A characteristic shrub or small tree of the Arabah and Arabian desert is the white saxaul (*Haloxylon persicum*, Heb. *ada*), which M. Zohary (1982) considered gave its name to Adah, wife of Lamech (Genesis 4:23). It has the appearance of a tamarisk or broom with leafless twigs, but it is another member of the goose-foot family. Arabs know it as the *ghada* tree and value it as a camel fodder and good fuel in the desert.

The Arabah dries up very quickly due to the intense heat, and the annual plants have to complete their life cycle while the moisture lasts. Spindly shrubs of the switch-like *Ochradenus baccatus*, a relative of mignonette, occur in the wadis, as well as dense banks of the extremely spiny zilla (*Zilla spinosa*), with mauve flowers like those of stocks. Other plants of African affinity occur here, as well as many species of desert annuals, but nowhere are individual plants thick on the ground.

Some of the herbaceous plants (e.g. *Gundelia tournefortii*) or small shrubs (e.g. *Salsola kali*) form loose balls when they dry up in the summer. A strong dry wind can send numerous balls tumbling like wheels along the open stony desert, effectively scattering their seeds as they go. Such plants are descriptively called 'tumbleweeds', and the psalmist may have had them in mind when he wrote 'O my God make [thy enemies] like whirling dust [marginal reading: a tumbleweed; a wheel KJV; thistledown NEB] – like chaff before the wind' (Psalms 83:13). Isaiah says the nations 'will flee far away, chased like chaff ... before the wind and whirling dust [rolling thing KJV; thistledown NEB] before the storm' (Isaiah 17:13).

Another plant, not a tumbleweed but one that may be considered as a 'rolling thing', is a colocynth, whose ripe fruits are like small yellow melons. It is, however, extremely light and when caught by the wind is swept along at speed until smashed against a rock, freeing the seeds within. The colocynth (*Citrullus colocynthis*), is a member of the gourd or marrow family (*Cucurbitaceae*) which grows in the deserts of the Middle East. As already mentioned (p. 53), its long roots enable it to tap supplies of water hidden beneath the dry surroundings to maintain its trailing branches and large leaves, even in the heat of the day. Its bitter fruits lie on the hot sand like a cluster of outsize yellow eggs waiting to be blown away.

A little desert annual that has often been taken for a tumbleweed is now known not to be distributed in that way, in spite of it curling up into a ball. This is the famous resurrection plant or rose of Jericho (*Anastatica hierochuntica*), which belongs to the cabbage family (*Cruciferae*). In winter it forms a leafy rosette a few inches across, with clusters of small white flowers. When flowering is over, the branches curl upwards and meet overhead, forming a ball-like framework which is, however, still firmly attached to the ground by its dead root. It stays like this until the rain comes, when the branches uncurl in an unexpected manner. One that I found near the Dead Sea took less than half an hour to open out, hence its popular name, as well as its scientific name, derived from the Greek *anastasis*, resurrection. In the

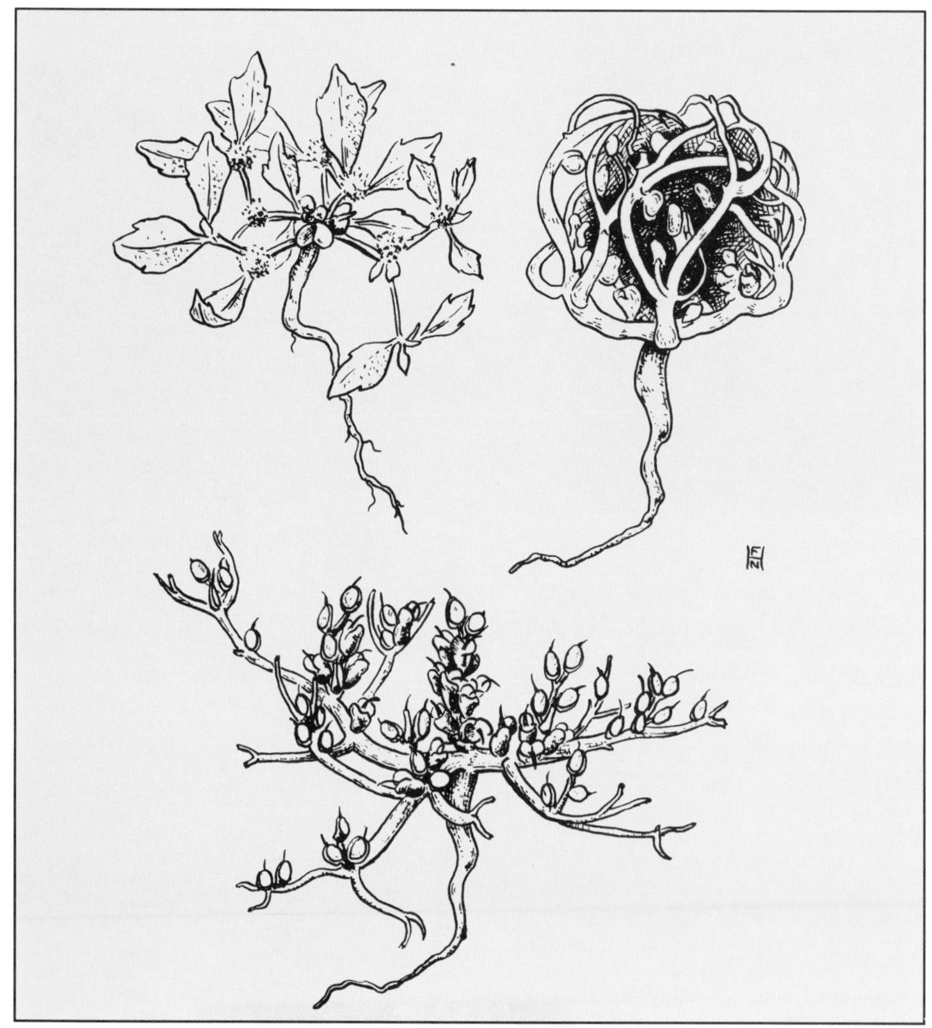

Above: The so-called rose of Jericho (*Anastatica hierochuntica*) curls up when dry and opens out after rain.

desert, where it may have to wait years for rain, research has now found that the seeds of this plant are released by the physical impact of heavy raindrops.

The Arabah stretches southwards with increasing aridity. From either side it is joined by wadis which are in some places huge canyons cutting back into the hills of Edom in the east and into the Negeb in the west. They are reminders of the massive erosion caused by the torrential rain during the wet, or pluvial, period some thousands of years ago. The most famous canyon on the Edom side is Petra, which we shall consider next.

Petra: the cleft rock

Petra lies deep in very arid country, with the Arabian Desert to the east and the Arabah and Sinai to the west. Only to the north is there a finger of moister land, along the heights of Moab and Edom, parallel to the Dead Sea. Westerly winds drop their rain on the Judean hills and leave the Arabah in a rain shadow, only to encounter more mountains on the Jordanian side, which benefit from further rain. Petra receives less moisture than Moab, but more than the region immediately to its south, where absolute desert continues to the Red Sea. So it is that traces of the Mediterranean type of vegetation may still be found at Petra, and the country around it is cultivated during the spring.

I followed the usual tourist route to Petra, approaching from the east by the direct desert road between Amman and Aqaba, parallel to the King's Highway that Moses tried to use (Numbers 20:17). The flat, stony 'hammada' along the desert route is nearly devoid of vegetation, but after turning westwards near Ma'an, a change is noticeable. The undulating nature of the ground and higher rainfall allow some plant life, at least along the depressions. A little farther west the limestone hillsides are dotted with tufted plants of the white wormwood (*Artemisia herba-alba*), and patches of intense cultivation around the occasional springs. Towards the Arabah I could see in the distance the crests of the pink sandstone hills above Petra heralding a striking change in the landscape. Widespread cereal cultivation takes place on the terraced hillsides as the road descends Wadi Musa, with its fine spring of cool sweet water. However, there is no evidence that the Israelites entered Petra, in spite of traditional associations with both Moses and Aaron; the latter appears to have died before they reached that area (Numbers 20:28).

The white limestone is cut through by Wadi Musa to expose the pink Nubian sandstone beneath it. The dry crags of Petra are entirely composed of this wind- and water-eroded sandstone. Deep gorges have been gouged out of the rock, and it was here that the early inhabitants chose to make their dwellings. A city was established within a natural fortress, with a defile as the only entrance, in reality the dry bed of Wadi Musa. This ravine, called the Siq, is over 30 m (100 ft) deep and 2 km (1·2 miles) long. As I went along the rock-strewn track it became narrower and darker until it was only a few feet across. Then it opened abruptly to reveal a great classical façade that might have been cut yesterday from the living rock, so clearly defined were its features. The cliffs towered all round, and I looked up the hemmed-in valley towards what used to be the centre of the metropolis, with its amphitheatre and rock-cut tombs and temples and fantastically sculptured weather-worn rock.

Pink-flowered wild oleander bushes (*Nerium oleander*) have long since taken over the valley floor where once the highroad lay. Although the monuments one sees at Petra date from Hellenistic and New Testament times, evidence of a much earlier Edomite settlement has been found. This accords well with the biblical narrative (Jeremiah 49). For many centuries Petra served as a centre for the plundering of the spice caravans. About 300 BC, however, the Nabataeans began to establish there a city with tolls levied on the merchants heading for

Gaza, and although the New Testament says little about Idumaea, at that time it was at the peak of its wealth and power. The Greek Empire, and later the Roman, demanded huge quantities of spices and other exotic products, and the impregnable fortress of Petra flourished for several hundred years. After about AD 100 it slowly decreased, after the diversion of southern trade routes across the Red Sea to Egypt and the northern ones to Palmyra. Never was Edom to rise again, as was prophesied by both Isaiah and Jeremiah: 'they shall name it No Kingdom There, and all its princes shall be nothing. Thorns shall grow over its strongholds, nettles and thistles in its fortresses ... There shall the owl nest' (Isaiah 34: 12–13, 15). As I wandered through the abandoned remains, one of the first plants I saw was a Roman nettle, and thorn-bushes abounded amongst the vanished glories. Later that day as the shadows deepened an owl hooted from high up amongst the weird weather-worn rocks – there shall the owl nest, indeed!

Unlike most of the popular tourist localities in the Palestine region, Petra remained inaccessible until recent years and its plants are still imperfectly known. Most of the small plants are short-lived annuals or bulbs, which appear for a few weeks in the spring and wither away after setting seed. For the rest of the year, the ground is dry and sandy with only the odd dwarf shrubs, looking like prickly pin-cushions.

After rain in springtime the sandy ground develops a fairly rich herbaceous flora. In some years, however, the rain is light and the plants develop poorly, with the small stunted annuals producing flowers and seeds at the earliest opportunity. Nearly all the plants have to compete with the ubiquitous herds of black goats. Only certain unpalatable or thorny species, such as shaggy sparrow-wort (*Thymelaea hirsuta*) (p. 177) and Palestine buckthorn (*Rhamnus palaestinus*) (p. 37), tend to lushness, for even in springtime when the vegetation is at its height, other plants are grazed back into rounded cushions.

While the area is essentially desert, with scorching sun and very high temperatures for much of the year, the broken nature of the ground, with its patches of deep shade and moisture between the rocks, does provide a diversity of habitats for plants. The twisting staircase up to the High Place leads past sandy ledges with straggly narrow-leaved daphne (*Daphne linearifolia*), a shrub characteristic of Petra. Phoenician junipers (*Juniperus phoenicea*) also occur all over the cliffs as solitary gnarled bushes or small trees having the appearance of cypresses, and add spots of deep green to the pink and sandy scene.

For some 1700 years the only commercial crop at Petra has been corn, grown in small patches here and there among the ruins, where black-garbed Bedouin women keep off marauding goats. There still remain, however, reminders of the vanished spice trade. I spotted a clump of *Aloe vera* growing at the base of the stairs leading to El-Deir Temple, the so-called Monastery. The stiff sword-like leaves of this succulent plant yielded the bitter aloes of the ancients (see p. 152). Perhaps this very clump of a slow-growing plant is a living survivor of that long-past age.

The Negeb

In ancient times a great trade route to Gaza followed the Arabah, entering Wadi Ramon or mounting up the Ascent of Scorpions (Akrabbim) to the high land of the Negeb. Wadi Ramon is also known as Makhtesh Ramon, *makhtesh* being the Hebrew for mortar or mixing-bowl. This huge valley enclosed by sheer cliffs cuts back westwards into the heart of the rugged mountainous part of the Negeb. The banks of

Above: The central area of Petra is reached by a single narrow gorge. Wild oleander bushes (*Nerium oleander*) grow on the valley floor; Phoenician juniper (*Juniperus phoenicea*) and narrow-leaved daphne (*Daphne linearifolia*) inhabit the cliffs (March 1967).

Left: White broom (*Retama raetam*) growing in sandy places among the rocks at Petra. Black goats roam everywhere, nibbling most plants within reach (March 1967).

Above far right: A rare desert iris (*Iris atropurpurea*).

Above right: This uncommon parasite, the red cynomorium (*Cynomorium coccineum*) grows on the roots of desert shrubs.

Above: Another striking parasite plant found in the desert is the giant broomrape (*Cistanche tubulosa*).

shingle and loess along the broad valley bottom provide refuge for numerous annuals when the briefly flowing torrents have subsided, early in the year.

To the south-west of Wadi Ramon lies the desolation of the Wilderness of Paran and the main part of the Sinai Peninsula, which was never cultivatable. West of the Wadi is Kadesh-Barnea, where the wandering Israelites settled for a time (Numbers 32:8). It lies to the south of an area that may with skill be cultivatable in places, by conserving such moisture as there is. The Nabataeans, much later, became successful agriculturalists by using the rainwater from huge catchment areas to irrigate small plots of cultivation. Remnants of their earthworks may be seen to this day (p. 79).

Between Kadesh-Barnea and Beersheba, which marks the northern limit of the Negeb, lies a vast area of undulating desert, and cultivation becomes increasingly possible as Gaza and the coast are approached. The northern Negeb is by no means uniform in its natural vegetation. In depressions where moisture temporarily collects there is often a good growth of shrubs such as the white broom, *Retama raetam*. This leguminous bush is covered by myriads of small white flowers in early spring. It is usually 1.5 m (5 ft) high but it may be as much as 3 m (10 ft) and is very widespread in the drier parts of Palestine, offering the only available shade for miles around. When Elijah fled from Queen Jezebel and came to Beersheba he 'went a day's journey into the wilderness, and came and sat down under a broom tree ... and he lay down and slept under a broom tree; and behold, an angel touched him' (1 Kings 19:4–5; Heb. *rothem*: juniper KJV)

Occasionally the roots of white broom and other desert and salt-loving shrubs are parasitized by a grotesque plant, the crimson cynomorium (*Cynomorium coccineum*). Some authors hold that it was this succulent parasite that was used for food by destitute people in the desert, not the poisonous white broom roots themselves (Job 30:4: juniper roots KJV). The evidence for this interpretation is slender and in my opinion hardly acceptable. The RSV neatly avoids the problem by rendering this verse: 'they pick mallow and the leaves of bushes, and to warm themselves the roots of the broom'.

Whether the cynomorium is really mentioned in Scripture or not, it deserves further comment from a botanical point of view. As a total parasite the whole plant is devoid of chlorophyll and the leaves are reduced to mere scales. However, it is a flowering plant, not a fungus – as suggested in the NEB footnote to this verse. The 20 cm (8 ins) high, club-shaped aerial portion of the plant carries numerous small flowers, which are either female or male with one stamen, or occasionally bisexual. Although it is reputed to be scarlet, the plants I have seen are really crimson and are pollinated, I suspect, by flies attracted to their meaty appearance.

The bare hills of the northern Negeb, where the wind has blown away the sand, are peppered with little clumps of the white wormwood (*Artemisia herba-alba*), which is used medicinally. It is a tough little perennial daisy, capable of enduring immense changes in temperature and extreme drought conditions. The aromatic, divided

Right: A desert tulip (*Tulipa systola*).

Left: The Negeb desert in springtime after rain supports scattered plants and small bushes, especially along the wadis where moisture collects.

leaves of the white wormwood are covered with silvery hairs, which help to reduce water loss.

In flatter areas of the central Negeb, as well as vast areas of trans-Jordan, a stone desert (known as hammada) is sparsely vegetated with succulent-leaved little bushes of bean caper, *Zygophyllum dumosum*, as well as other small specialized perennials, and, of course, with annuals after rain.

Soil conditions markedly affect the plant growth. Thus the fine loess, which covers large areas of the Negeb, throws off the rain from its crust into the depressions. However, when, as often happens, the loess is covered by a thin layer of sand, the rain is trapped by the sand and sinks into the loess. In such areas a surprisingly rich flora is found, including the rare oncocyclus iris (e.g. *I. atropurpurea*), which is now closely protected by nature conservation laws. The common white asphodel (*Asphodelus aestivus*) is another species with tuberous roots, and it stands like a sentinel, with white flowers and tufts of narrow leaves. It has a wide tolerance, ranging from the moist Carmel and Jerash hills to the desert conditions of the Negeb, often growing in trampled ground by ancient ruins. Bulbous plants such as tulips (*Tulipa systola*), the yellow star-of-Bethlehem (*Gagea*) and also the white star-of-Bethlehem (*Ornithogalum*) grow here too.

Numerous annuals almost cover the ground in a rainy year, and I had the good fortune to visit the Negeb at such a time. I shall always recall the all-pervading fragrance of the mauve carpet of night-scented stock (principally *Matthiola livida*) stretching on either side of the road for many miles between Beersheba and Arad. During the day it was hardly noticeable, but at dusk the flowers opened and became strongly fragrant. In a dry year the plants are small and stunted, each bearing only one or two flowers.

Deep sand-dunes are limited to the north-western portion of the Negeb, and there is evidence that they are very old and well anchored. The principal anchoring plant is a panic grass, *Panicum turgidum*, which has the ability to bind together more or less mobile sand. Panic grass usually occurs with a wormwood, *Artemisia monosperma*, which is gathered by the Bedouin for fuel (see p. 41). The shrub shaggy sparrow-wort (*Thymelaea hirsuta*) is also frequent in such sandy places. It grows about 1 m (3 ft) high and its profuse branches bear numerous small, succulent leaves of a bright green colour. The flowers are pale yellow, heavily scented, and the male and female flowers occur on separate plants. The twigs are extremely tough and are used as rope by the Arabs (Danin, 1983). It is possible that these were the new ropes with which Delilah bound Samson (Judges 16: 7–9; green withs KJV). Although Moldenke and others consider that willow twigs were used, willows are not found in Gaza, where the Samson incident took place.

Beersheba is the commercial centre of the Negeb Desert, although it lies at the northern edge. Large areas around it are semi-desert, and in wetter years good corn crops are obtained. However, drought and the prospect of famine are always very real, even to the semi-nomadic Bedouin, whose migration northwards in drier years causes considerable social and economic problems.

This ancient pattern proves that overall, the climate, as reflected by the rainfall, has changed little in historic times. The changes in vegetation that have taken place in Palestine may, therefore, be attributed to human intervention, which results in desiccation, soil erosion, and the development of quite different plant communities from those originally present. For example, conspicuous shallow excavations (Heb. *liman*) to trap rainwater in the Negeb, are planted with eucalyptus trees (*E. occidentalis*). The spread of native desert plants into areas formerly unsuited to them is a notable change. Once the ground is opened up, light-requiring desert species can spread into areas in which competition is reduced or non-existent. The coastal dunes, which penetrate well into the Mediterranean vegetation zone, are colonized by many desert plants.

The burning bush at Mount Sinai

The historic monastery of St Catherine at the foot of Mount Sinai (Horeb) is no longer isolated and remote. A new highway from Cairo to the Gulf of Elat brings coachloads of tourists to the pink-walled settlement surrounded by towering mountains, traditionally where Moses received the Ten Commandments (Exodus 19: 3–25). The monastery itself commemorates the burning bush: 'the angel of the Lord appeared to [Moses] in a flame of fire out of the midst of a bush [Heb. *sneh*]; and he looked, and lo, the bush was burning, yet it was not consumed' (Exodus 3:2; see also Acts 7:30). Today the monks at the monastery carefully tend a bush of the holy bramble (*Rubus sanguineus*), which grows behind railings enclosing a chapel, evidently under the impression that it was Moses' burning bush. Actually, its natural distribution is in the moister Mediterranean zone where it is common, and the only remarkable fact about it, in my opinion, is that it can grow in Sinai.

Moldenke (1952), and others before him, have considered that a plant can actually be assigned to this vision; for example, the scarlet-flowered mistletoe (*Loranthus acaciae*) (p. 57), that spectacularly parasitizes acacia trees in the Arabah. Another suggestion is the *Dictamnus albus*, variously known as fraxinella, dittany and gas-plant, which inhabits woods in Lebanon far from Sinai; it is covered with glands which, during calm hot weather, release oily vapour that can ignite. Even the Sinai hawthorn (*Crataegus sinaica*) has been suggested, and M. Zohary (1982) mentions two other desert plants – the senna bush (*Cassia senna*) and the bladder senna (*Colutea istria*), both having yellow pea-flowers, with an Arabic name *sneh*, similar to the Hebrew.

However, I personally doubt whether the occasion of the burning bush has a scientific or botanical explanation. Moses would have been familiar with such plants after spending many years in the desert. Perhaps this manifestation was similar to 'the glory of the Lord [that] filled the temple' (2 Chronicles 7:1) and other incidents when radiant light signified the presence of God.

If this was where the Israelites assembled, the extensive plain between the mountains and within sight of the monastery would have provided a suitable camping ground, particularly because of the smooth-faced red granite from which the mountains are built which, during the winter months, channels the rain into grooves and soft rock dykes, whence it flows as clear water springs (Danin, 1983). When I explored the neighbouring valleys with a Bedouin guide, I was amazed to see running streams supporting poplars, cypress and groups of olive trees; and some Bedouin, tending small patches of good soil, were actually raising crops of several fruits and vegetables in this barren region.

Pilgrims ascending Moses' mountain (Jebal Musa) are likely to notice little more than a scattering of wormwood (*Artemisia herba-alba*) in the stony soil. The spectacular views from the summit provide a lunar landscape devoid of vegetation. However, the flora of Sinai is generally very diverse, with a total of 812 species recorded, while the Israeli deserts as a whole yield 1130 species (Danin, 1983). Much of the Sinai Peninsula is mountainous with a varied rock formation; red granites, black volcanic and pink sandstone compose the highland areas of the centre and south, while vast sandy areas occur in north and west Sinai and Negeb.

Sweet water and manna

Scholars still dispute over the route taken by the Israelites during the exodus from Egypt (Exodus 13: 17–18). However, I think there is

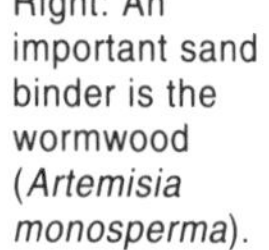

Right: An important sand binder is the wormwood (*Artemisia monosperma*).

Left: At St Catherine's Monastery in Sinai a protected bush of holy bramble (*Rubus sanguineus*) is considered to be Moses' burning bush (March 1987).

no doubt that they crossed the Sea of Reeds (Heb. *Yam-suph*), the marshy area now traversed by the Suez Canal, and not the Red Sea of modern terminology (see p. 71).

When the Israelites reached Marah they found the waters bitter, that is, salty and undrinkable. After the people complained, Moses was shown a tree, a branch of which he cast into the waters, which became sweet and drinkable (Exodus 15: 22–25). Speculation as to which tree was responsible for this miracle has yielded no satisfactory answer.

The next place reached by the Israelites was Elim where there were twelve springs and seventy palm trees (Exodus 15:27). These would be date palms, characteristic of oases in the desert of Sinai, which indicate that water is close to the surface. The Arabian rush (*Juncus arabicus*) and Nile tamarisk (*Tamarix nilotica*) are associated with the palms.

This tamarisk is often attacked by a scale insect which excretes sugary honey-dew. Bodenheimer (1947) considered that this could have been the manna. However, it is difficult to collect and there are other species of desert plants, such as *Hammada salicornica*, which also yield small amounts of sugary liquid. Large quantities of manna were collected daily by the wandering Israelites, who did not know what it was – *manna* being the Hebrew for 'what is it?' (Exodus 16:15). 'It was like coriander seed, white, and the taste of it was like wafers, made with honey' (Exodus 16:31). It would not keep overnight, yet Moses kept an omer in a jar for future generations to see (Exodus 16:33; Hebrews 9:4). Unfortunately this exhibit is no longer available!

Further speculation about the identity of manna has been made by many authors (Moldenke, 1952, and others). They considered it could have been a mixture of a blue-green alga *Nostoc*, and various lichens *Lecanora*, which blow about and 'fall from heaven'. This is such an uncommon phenomenon we can rule it out. I think we should recall once more that Moses was familiar with desert lore, yet he did not give a name to this heavenly bread. Although there is a natural explanation for the quails (Exodus 16:13), I doubt whether the same can be said for the manna. Moses knew as well as Abraham that Yahweh *yireh* (Jehovah *jireh*) – the Lord provides.

DESERT TREES MENTIONED IN THE BIBLE

(see also Forest Trees, p. 31)

There are only a few species of trees in the desert and most of these are referred to in the Bible. We have already mentioned them in their habitat and here they are described in more detail.

Acacia trees *(Acacia species)*

In the Arabah there are two common species of acacia (*A. raddiana* or *A. tortilis* subsp. *raddiana*, and *A. tortilis*) as well as several rarer ones (Heb. *shittah* singular, *shittim* plural). *A. raddiana* has more of a distinct trunk than *A. tortilis* which tends to shoot from the base. They are about 3 m (10 ft) high and branched in the upper part to give the typical spreading crown. The branchlets are very spiny and bear numerous small leaves which are finely divided into tiny leaflets. As a member of the mimosa family, acacias have characteristic tiny, pale yellow flowers clustered into small heads which festoon the trees during the winter and spring. The slender bean-like pods twist and loop before ripening. Acacias were the only trees available for timber by the Israelites during their wanderings in Sinai, so they were used for the construction of the Tabernacle and other wooden objects (see p. 156).

A. tortilis grows almost entirely in the hot Arabah valley, while *A. raddiana* can tolerate cooler conditions far and wide in Sinai. The white acacia (*A. albida* or *Faidherbia albida*) has a scattered

Right: Acacia tree (*Acacia albida*) near Jezreel, where a group occurs as a remnant of a wider distribution during a warm period.

distribution as a relict in lowland Israel, including the Sharon plain and Lower Galilee. It has creamy flowers and thick orange pods.

Egyptian balsam *(Balanites aegyptiaca)*, see p. 150.

Juniper *(Juniperus phoenicea)*
The Phoenician juniper, also known as the Phoenician cedar, is a small tree looking more like a cypress than a juniper. It has a wide distribution round the Mediterranean, and extending into the higher parts of Sinai and Arabia where it usually occurs at an altitude of about 760 m (2500 ft). The trees in the latter localities are the only remains of a far larger number in former times. Even the small size of the trees nowadays indicates that the larger specimens have been felled for timber or for charcoal production. Some of the leaves are needle-like and spreading, while other leaves on the same tree are like scales, and overlap.

The Phoenician juniper was the 'cedar wood' used by the Levites during the sacrifices, in association with hyssop and scarlet (Leviticus 14: 4–6; 49–52; Numbers 19:6) (p. 140). Although this juniper is near the limit of its natural range in southern Palestine, it was certainly available to the Israelites. The resinous twigs and timber would have been pleasantly fragrant, and the hyssop, too, must have added its own scent to the pyre. There may also be a connexion between the Levitical use of the juniper wood and the significance attached to 'cedar' by the Egyptians, whom the Israelites had so recently left. It is worth noting that the word 'cedar' has been, and still is, used for various species of *Juniperus*, as well as for the true cedar (*Cedrus*). The Egyptians used cedar and juniper wood for coffins and shrines, and the 'cedar' oil from juniper wood (as well as juniper berries), employed for anointing the dead bodies of royal and prominent persons, must have been of particular significance to them.

This is the 'desert shrub' of Jeremiah 17:6 and 48:6 (Heb. *ar-ar*; heath, KJV; juniper, NEB, bush, NIV), and not the brown-berried juniper (*Juniperus oxycedrus*) indicated by Moldenke (1952), which has a Mediterranean type of distribution.

Ben oil or horseradish tree *(Moringa peregrina)*, see p. 150.

Date palm *(Phoenix dactylifera)*, see p. 116.

Atlantic terebinth *(Pistacia atlantica)*, see p. 122.

White broom *(Retama raetam)*, see p. 60.

Tamarisk *(Tamarix species)*
Several species of tamarisk occur in the desert zone, but only one of them is really a tree, the leafless tamarisk (*T. aphylla*). It is slender, with weeping leafless branches, the trunk becoming gnarled in old age, up to 10 m (91 ft) high. In late summer and autumn the decorative white flowers occur in numerous narrow heads. The trees grow as odd individuals on the plains and in wadis, and it was at Beersheba that 'Abraham planted a tamarisk tree [Heb. *eshel*; grove KJV; strip of ground NEB] ... and called there on the name of the Lord, the Everlasting God' (Genesis 21:33).

The shrubby tamarisks grow in wadis where the soil is often salty. The Nile tamarisk (*T. nilotica*) is summer flowering; the flowers are white, and the twigs are often white, too, being caked in salt. The Jordan tamarisk (*T. jordanis*), is a tree limited to the Jordan valley, also with white flowers.

Bibliography

Bodenheimer, F. S., 'The Manna of Sinai', *Biblical Archaeologist* (Baltimore, 1947), 10(1):2–6.

Cloudsley-Thompson, J. L., and Chadwick, M. J., *Life in Deserts* (London, Foulis, 1964).

Danin, A., *The Desert Vegetation of Israel and Sinai* (Jerusalem, Cana Publishing House, 1983), with extensive bibliography.

Donkin, R. A., *Manna: an Historical Geography* (The Hague, Dr W. Junk, 1980).

Evanari, M., Shanan, L., and Tadmor, N., *The Negev* (Cambridge, Mass., Harvard University Press, 1971).

Harlan, J. R., 'The Early Bronze Age Environment of the Southern Ghor and the Moab Plateau', *Studies in the History and Archaeology of Jordan* (Amman Antiquities, 1985), 2:125–40.

Kirkbride, D., 'The environment of the Petra region during the pre-Pottery Neolithic', *Studies in the History and Archaeology of Jordan* (Amman Antiquities, 1985), 2:117–24.

Zohary, M., and Orshan, G., 'Ecological Studies in the Vegetation of the Near East Deserts: II Wadi Araba', *Vegetatio* (Den Haag, 1956), 7:15–37.

See also General References: Feinbrun-Dothan and Danin (1991); Plitmann, Heyn, Danin and Shmida (1983); Zohary, M. (1962); Zohary and Feinbrun-Dothan (1966–86).

6. *Reeds and Willows*

'Can papyrus grow where there is no marsh? Can reeds flourish where there is no water?'
(Job 8:11.)

In the eastern Mediterranean region rainfall is restricted to the winter season, so many of the streams dry up during the summer, and do not support typical water-loving plants. Indeed, in the drier areas the seasonal streams, called wadis, may run for only a few days in the year – and then sometimes as dangerous torrents (Psalm 124:4) – and the plants growing along them are almost entirely desert species, taking advantage of the residual moisture. Nevertheless, there are some rivers and streams, as well as marshes and pools, with interesting aquatic plants. On the eastern side of the country the snows of Lebanon and Mount Hermon ensure a continuous supply of water for the River Jordan, which passes through the Huleh valley and the Sea of Galilee before reaching the barren Dead Sea. The coastal plain on the western side of the hills used to support extensive marshlands, now drained.

In this chapter we look at the water-loving plants of the Jordan Valley and of the coastal plain.

The Huleh swamp

A hundred years ago Canon Tristram, during his survey for the Palestine Exploration Fund, described the Huleh swamp of the northern Jordan valley as inaccessible, because of the luxuriant growth of papyrus sedge (*Cyperus papyrus*) and malarial mosquitoes. Huleh remained so until the 1950s. At that time the natural basalt dam, which had impeded drainage at the southern end of the swamp, was blown up and the water-level fell dramatically, enabling the cultivation of large areas. However, water was retained in a swampy lake, embanked by keen naturalists and designated the 'Hula Nature Reserve'. It has great scientific value, especially as a staging-post for birds migrating between Europe and Africa and as the only Israeli habitat for various animals and aquatic plants, other species of which were exterminated during drainage (Paz, 1979).

Papyrus and common reed grow so thickly in the reserve that few other plants are able to compete with them. There is a distinct zoning of species including the knotweed (*Polygonum acuminatum*), which grows round the base of the papyrus and spreads into

Left: A portion of Huleh swamp now forms the 'Hula Nature Reserve'. In the foreground is the yellow flag (*Iris pseudacorus*), and beyond lies the Jordan tamarisk (*Tamarix jordanis*), in flower, with willow trees. The major part of the reserve is covered by papyrus and common reed, conserving important biodiversity.

Above: The white water-lily (*Nymphaea alba*) is now on the verge of extinction, as are several other aquatic plants and animals in Palestine.

open water. Sometimes blue- or white-flowered water-lilies (*Nymphaea caerulea, N. alba*) star the water surface. The pink-flowering rush (*Butomus umbellatus*) occurs in the shallows with tufts of the yellow flag (*Iris pseudacorus*). This is the southernmost locality for the iris. Visitors to these papyrus swamps can imagine what it was like in the Nile Delta of ancient Egyptian times. Murals in some of the Egyptian tombs depict a pharaoh or a nobleman in similar swamps, standing on a skiff made of bundles of papyrus, ready to spear fish or fell a duck with a throw-stick.

Sea of Galilee (Lake Tiberias)

This is Israel's only freshwater lake and a vital resource for the water which is piped all over the country. Although this is not the place to discuss the sensitive issues relating to water and its profligate use, the effect of excessive demand on the lake level and the ground water resources has been dramatic. Intense development, coupled with unusually low rainfall in the 1980s, has aggravated the situation. From a botanical aspect, little aquatic flora can develop around the lake because of its variable shoreline.

River Jordan

The upper Jordan valley, north of the Sea of Galilee, is very different from the lower Jordan, between Tiberias and the Dead Sea. The crystal clear fresh water gushing from the caves and springs at Baniyas, or passing along the rocky river bed in the nature reserve at Dan, sustains water-loving plants, such as willow (*Salix acmophylla*), plane tree (*Platanus orientalis*), and oleander (*Nerium oleander*), and a wealth of marsh species well known in Europe. Regrettably, part of this is now being destroyed for the sake of hydro-electric power, transforming the river near the lake into a canal.

Many side-streams feed water into the Jordan and the Sea of Galilee. They come from the Golan Heights to the east and the

Right: The River Jordan near Dan supports a rich waterside vegetation (April 1969).

Opposite: This waterfall from the Golan Heights provides spray for the plant-life around it and water for the River Jordan north of the Dead Sea.

Right: The papyrus plant is a tall sedge, *Cyperus papyrus*, with a large mop-like head.

Galilean hills to the west, and many of them flow perennially, supporting plane trees, oleanders and many others. However, the numerous fish-ponds in the valley are usually kept clear of weeds and do not develop an aquatic flora.

The lower River Jordan is markedly salty, owing to the saline springs around the Sea of Galilee. There are still extensive remnants of the forest that formerly lined both banks of the Jordan. These consist principally of stands of Jordan tamarisk (*Tamarix jordanis*) at the water's edge and taller Euphrates poplar (*Populus euphratica*) on the bank. In biblical times it was 'the jungle of the Jordan' (Jeremiah 12:5) which was the habitat of wild animals, including lions (Jeremiah 49:19; 50:44; Zechariah 11:3). This riverine forest occurred on the narrow overflow bank (the *zor*), which the Israelites encountered when they crossed the Jordan (Joshua 3:15). The salt flats towards the Dead Sea are mentioned in chapter 5 (p. 56).

The coastal plain

Much of the rainwater running off the western side of the Judean hills sinks into the soil or is used by agriculture or evaporates, which leaves little to reach the sea. Inland from the coastal sand-dunes there is a line of very low hills composed of calcified sand called *kurkar*. In ancient times these formed such an effective barrier that extensive swamps developed on the coastal plain, with oak trees in the drier areas. At Evan Yehuda Nature Reserve I was interested to see these kurkar hills through which, as long ago as the Roman period, an east–west channel was cut in order to drain the swamps behind. By now, all these marshes have been drained and the rich soil used for agriculture or building developments, leaving few habitats for the native water-loving plants. Patches of reeds in ditches, both north and south of Carmel, provide a habitat for other aquatic plants. Unfortunately the only permanent

Below: Papyrus plants illustrated on an ancient Egyptian sheet of papyrus (British Museum).

river, the Yarqon, is now heavily polluted, as are some of the streams nearer to Jerusalem, especially the Soreq.

Marsh-plants in the Bible

There are many biblical references to marshes and water-plants but it is not always certain to which species they refer, since the designation, as in most languages, is not precise. However, the Hebrew *agmon* and *gome* are usually translated by rush or papyrus; *suph* by bulrush or flag, and *qane*, and the Greek equivalent *kalamos*, by reed. It is therefore convenient to consider together the water-loving plants occurring in the region.

Papyrus

We have already seen that this tall sedge is the dominant plant in the Huleh swamp. Its stout green stalks are triangular in section, 4 m (13 ft) or more high. The terminal head of leafy bracts and brown scaly flowers forms a mop-like ball. Although these heads are present throughout the year, during the winter months no flowers form and the head is made up entirely of narrow green bracts. Wind can easily cause the heavy head to bend over on the slender upper part of the stalk, and it was possibly this characteristic, broken appearance that Isaiah had in mind when he criticized the kind of fasting that made a man 'bow down his head like a rush' (Isaiah 58:5; Heb. *gome*; bulrush KJV; rush RSV). Other authors consider this reference is to the plume-like flower-head of the common reed (*Phragmites*), but it cannot be to the rush *Juncus*, which has no heavy flower-head.

At the base of the papyrus stalk is the true stem, which is a very thick, prostrate rhizome, with shallow roots spreading into the mud. The rhizomes become matted and the stalks rise close together to form a dense thicket. In ancient Egypt the rhizomes were baked, boiled or eaten raw, as they are full of starch.

The conditions for papyrus to flourish are found in swamps where the water is shallow and nearly constant in level. Job knew these conditions when he asked:

'Can papyrus grow where there is no marsh?

Can reeds flourish where there is no water?

While yet in flower and not cut down, they wither before any other plant.

Such are the paths of all who forget God; the hope of the godless man shall perish' (Job 8:11–13).

The Huleh marshes are at the extreme northern limit of the natural range of papyrus, and some authors even consider it was brought there from Egypt. Papyrus is widely distributed in tropical Africa, where it forms the sudd in the Sudanese portion of the Nile, and the papyrus islands in Lake Chad. Yet it does not now grow as a wild plant in the Egyptian Nile, except for one recently discovered clump of doubtful antiquity. There is no doubt, however, that papyrus was naturally wild in Egypt, the most convincing argument being given in the wall paintings of hunting scenes; and another being the proliferation of papyrus products in Egypt from earliest times. Papyrus was later cultivated, by which time immense changes had taken place in the Nile Delta, due to silting, diversion of tributaries and direct human interference. As a shallow-rooted plant with stringent ecological requirements, papyrus is vulnerable to these changes, which it found wholly adverse. Indeed, Isaiah foresaw a disastrous circumstance when

'the waters of the Nile will be dried up, and the river will be parched and dry; and its canals will become foul, and the branches of Egypt's Nile will diminish and dry up, reeds and rushes will rot away' (Isaiah 19:5–6).

As canals were constructed further up the Nile, the flow of the river was diminished to such an extent that sea-water began to pass upstream along the Nile and its tributaries. Since papyrus cannot withstand very saline conditions and soon succumbs, the remaining wild population was doomed to extinction. Moreover the plant was in great demand for paper and other products, so by Roman times, conservation and cultivation became essential. When the demand for papyrus ceased, due to the use of other materials for paper, the cultivation of the plant quickly stopped and Egypt was left with neither a wild population nor a cultivated one.

Papyrus is, of course, famous for the writing material of the same name which is described in chapter 19. The plant was also used for baskets (p. 174), cords (p. 176) and in symbolic ornamentation (p. 182).

We should not close this section without mentioning the use of papyrus for skiffs (Job 9:26; skiffs of reed RSV). Isaiah refers to 'vessels of papyrus upon the waters' of the Nile (Isaiah 18:2) and gives an accurate description of these boats, common in Egypt, which were made of bundles of papyrus stalks tied together at their ends. Small papyrus boats were very thick in the middle and pointed at each end. The larger ocean-going ships, however, had a high curving prow and stern. Thor Heyerdahl, the Norwegian explorer, believes that

Above: A papyrus boat under construction at Dr Ragab's Pharaonic village near Cairo.

Right: The common reed (*Phragmites australis*). Reed stems had many uses, such as for arrows and wickerwork.

wooden ships were modelled in the shape of earlier papyrus ones and in 1970 he actually built and sailed a large vessel of papyrus across the Atlantic Ocean with seven men aboard. The type of vessel rendered 'galley' in Isaiah 33:2[1] would probably have taken several people.

As mentioned above, Egyptian paintings frequently represent kings and nobles using papyrus rafts for hunting and fishing in the Nile-side marshes, and the tomb of Tutankhamun contained golden figures of the young king standing on model papyrus boats. Because the internal pith of the papyrus stalk contains a network of large intercellular air spaces, the stalks are light and buoyant, so that, although the rafts could support someone standing, they were very light when dry and could be carried on the shoulders. Today papyrus boats are still being made in the Sudan and by the people who live on islands in Lake Chad. During a visit to Chad in 1969 I poled along one of these craft in a standing position. It was about 5 m (16 ft) long and surprisingly heavy, since much water is soaked up by the stalks after prolonged immersion.

Reeds

We now come to the aquatic grasses collectively known as reeds (Heb. *qane*), of which two concern us. One is the common reed and the other is the giant reed.

The common reed is a tall grass, now called *Phragmites australis*, though better known as *P. communis*, which occurs in shallow lakes and slow streams throughout the world. It has a slender creeping stem (rhizome) which travels for immense distances through marshes, at intervals throwing up erect leafy stems. In summer these stems, similar to slender bamboo canes, bear the familiar plume-like flower-heads which are over 2 m (6 ft) high. Reed beds grow very dense where they are given plenty of moisture throughout the year, in areas such as swamps and riverbeds. Some varieties will survive surprisingly dry conditions, however, enabling them to grow in sandy localities, provided these are sometimes flooded. Some reeds can also withstand salty conditions, which enables them to grow in wet places near the Dead Sea, together with the sugar reed, *Saccharum spontaneum* var. *aegyptiacum*, which can rather easily be confused with the giant reed.

The giant reed, *Arundo donax*, is a very tall grass, which grows in large clumps on river banks just above the water level, unlike the common reed which usually roots in the water itself. The large plume-like flower heads are borne late in the year on stems up to 5 m (16 ft) high. The stout bamboo-like stems are hollow except at the leaf nodes. Thus a small section of stem, cut just below a node and again a few inches above it, provides a convenient box, such as the one in which Judas Iscariot stored the disciples' money: 'he was a thief, and as he had the money box [Gk. *glossokomon*; not bag, as KJV] he used to take what was put into it' (John 12:6; see also 13:29).

Reeds were used for many purposes, such as baskets, roofing material, mats, strainers, pens and arrows (see chapters 18 and 19). Wind instruments, such as the pipe or flute of biblical times, were also probably made from the giant reed. Thus we read in the Old Testament that 'all the people said, "Long live King Solomon!" And all the people went up after him, playing on pipes' (1 Kings 1:39–40). In the New Testament we find 'flute players' mourning the death of the ruler's daughter (Matthew 9:23).

Reeds are often mentioned in the Bible, although it is not always clear which species is intended. The servant mentioned by Isaiah (Isaiah 42:1–3), whom Matthew identified with Jesus, was not one to

'wrangle or cry aloud, nor will any one hear his voice in the streets; he will not break a bruised reed or quench a smouldering wick, till he brings justice to victory; and in his name will the Gentiles hope' (Matthew 12:19–21).

Reeds are brittle, and a bruised or damaged reed is easily shattered and broken. For this reason one cannot use a damaged reed as a staff because the sharp pieces will pierce one's hand (2 Kings 18:21).

The characteristic shaking of the tall reeds in the wind was used by Ahijah to illustrate how 'the Lord will smite Israel, as a reed is shaken in the water' (1 Kings 14:15). Likewise, Jesus asked the people who flocked to see John the Baptist: 'what did you go out into the wilderness to behold? A reed shaken by the wind?' (Matthew 11:7; Luke 7:24). In other words, did they expect the unusual sight of a marsh plant growing in the desert? A man in fine clothes; or a prophet?

When Jesus was crucified, one of the bystanders 'ran and took a sponge, filled it with vinegar, and put it on a reed [Gk. *calamos*], and gave it to him to drink' (Matthew 27:48; see also Mark 15:36). The account in John's Gospel (19:29) refers, in most translations, to the sponge being put on hyssop (Gk. *hyssopos*). There has been much ensuing speculation about the identity of this stick used to offer the drugged sponge (see also p. 152).

Any straight stick would, of course, have been suitable, especially one of the true reeds, *Arundo* and *Phragmites*, though I doubt whether the reed-mace (*Typha*), another suggestion, would have been readily available or sufficiently strong. Moldenke (1952) and others reject the possibility of marjoram

Left: The lotus water-lily (*Nymphaea lotus*)

Far left: The sharp rush (*Juncus acutus*). Rush stalks were used as writing pens and for mats.

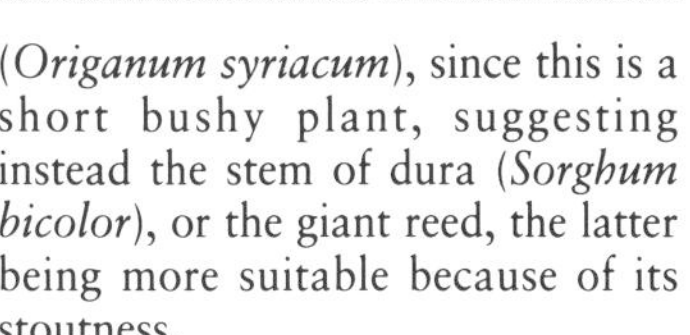

(*Origanum syriacum*), since this is a short bushy plant, suggesting instead the stem of dura (*Sorghum bicolor*), or the giant reed, the latter being more suitable because of its stoutness.

However the popular idea of a tall cross is unfounded. In fact the feet of the person crucified would only just have cleared the ground, and Jesus' mouth could have been reached with the aid of quite a short reed, or even with a bunch of twigs. On the other hand, John's observations are generally detailed and accurate, and some scholars have plausibly suggested that this *hyssopos* should read *hyssos*, Greek for a javelin shaft. Like other issues, this much debated crux remains an open question.

A 'reed' was a standard measure of six cubits which, at 445 mm (17.5 ins) per cubit, was 2.67 m (8 ft 9 ins) in length, the thickness and height of the wall around the temple area as recorded by Ezekiel (40:5). Other parts of the temple were also measured with a reed (Ezekiel 42:15–20). The golden rod used to measure the holy city in Revelation 21:15 may likewise be regarded as a standard measuring-reed in length.

Rushes, bulrushes and cat-tails

The seven fat cows of Pharaoh's dream fed upon the vegetation on the banks of the Nile (Genesis 41:2; 18; meadow KJV; reed grass RSV; reeds NIV). Some grasses occur in this type of marshy vegetation as well as sedges and rushes (*Juncus* species). They may also be intended in Isaiah 9:14, 19:15 (Heb. *agmon*; rush KJV; reed RSV, NIV). Several species of *Juncus* are recorded for Palestine and Egypt. The toad rush (*J. bufonius*) is small, while the maritime rush (*J. maritimus*), the Arabian rush (*J. arabicus*) and the sharp rush (*J. acutus*) are the largest ones, growing in salty, sandy places by the sea or inland. The tufts have numerous erect stems like green porcupine quills 60–90 cm (2–3 ft) high. The stems are cylindrical with very sharp points, and the cluster of small, chaffy flowers arises at one side, somewhat below the tip. These species have for long been very important for mat-making, as pens in Pharaonic times and as tapers when stripped and soaked in olive oil (p. 108).

The English plant name bulrush has been a source of confusion in several ways. In Exodus 2:3 the KJV and RSV translated the Hebrew *gome* as 'bulrush' instead of papyrus, which was the plant used for Moses' basket. In popular English usage there is a misapplication of the name bulrush for the cat-tail or reed-mace (*Typha* species), when it properly applies to the tall, slender aquatic sedge, *Scirpus lacustris*, that occurs in ponds throughout Europe and the Near East.

There are two similar species of reed-mace or cat-tail in the Near East: *Typha domingensis* (formerly called *T. angustata*) and *T. latifolium*. It was among stands of reed-mace that Moses' floating papyrus basket was found, though English versions translate the Hebrew *suph* as flags (KJV) or reeds (RSV, NIV). Reed-mace develops large stands, often in competition with the common reed. It also grows in the saline swamps at the north end of the Red Sea, which in Hebrew is *Yam-suph*, literally 'sea of reeds' or 'reed-sea', through which the Israelites passed (Exodus 14:18 mgn) (However, Batto, 1984, has challenged this meaning in favour of the Red Sea.) Reed-mace has tall cylindrical inflorescences about 2 m (6 ft) high, which are composed of a multitude of minute brown flowers which persist long after maturity.

Water-lilies

Occasionally on the open water of the Hula Reserve one can see beautiful water-lily flowers – the white *Nymphaea alba* and the blue *N. caerulea*. A yellow water-lily (*Nuphar lutea*) grows in shallow stagnant water in other parts of the country. Water-lilies used to occur abundantly in the lakes of the Nile Delta and in pools beside the Upper Nile. Conditions have changed, however, and, like the papyrus, which has disappeared from Egypt, water-lilies are now very rare. But in ancient times the white lotus, *Nymphaea lotus*, and the blue one, *N. caerulea*, were so well known that the lotus[2] became symbolic of Upper Egypt, just as the papyrus was symbolic of Lower Egypt. For the use of the lotus in ornamentation in Egypt and the lily-work (Heb. *shushan*) on the capitals of Solomon's temple (1 Kings 7:19 ff) see chapter 20.

Willows and poplars

There are several trees and shrubs associated with wet places of the Near East. Willows (*Salix* species) are typical streamside trees, to which several allusions are made in the Bible. Isaiah, for instance, tells that the Lord will 'pour [his] Spirit'

Above: Leaves of the white poplar (*Populus alba*).

Right: A Euphrates poplar tree (*Populus euphratica*), with an eastern plane tree (*Platanus orientalis*) to the right and reed-mace (*Typha domingensis*) in the pool. (Tel Aviv Botanical Garden.)

upon the descendants of Jacob who 'shall spring up like grass amid waters, like willows [Heb. *arabim*] by flowing streams' (Isaiah 44:4). They are mainly small trees, with trunks growing from the bank or the stream and their roots in the water. Frequently a fallen tree may be found lying across the water or in mud, yet still leafy and full of vigour. The ability to form roots from almost any living woody portion is very characteristic of willows. Small leafy twigs soon take root with the result that a willow thicket may arise in a short time. However, Ezekiel was apparently referring to the easy rooting of the poplar, which roots like the willow, in his allegory of the vine: the eagle 'placed it beside abundant waters. He set it like a willow twig, and it sprouted' (Ezekiel 17:5; willow KJV, RSV; poplar NEB).

In Palestine and other Near Eastern Bible lands the distribution of willows today is severely restricted by the diminishing number of pools and permanent watercourses. The two native species of willow most frequently encountered are *Salix acmophylla* and *S. alba*, while a third species, *S. triandra*, is much rarer; a fourth one, *S. pseudo-safsaf*, occurs in the hot Jordan valley, and a fifth, *S. subserrata*, grows in Egypt.

The willow *Salix acmophylla* is the species most usually found in the northern half of Palestine, on river banks or even on the beds of shallow streams. It is a small tree, which may develop several trunks, each about 30 cm (12 ins) thick. In winter the brittle twigs appear red and glossy, and in early spring the flowers are borne on typical, short, willow catkins, soon to be followed by the long narrow leaves. In spite of their lack of petals and dull colouration, the flowers do contain nectar which attracts pollinating insects.

It should be mentioned that the weeping willow (*S. babylonica*) nowadays occurs as a cultivated tree in Palestine as well as in the vicinity of ancient Babylon, but its native home is probably China. Hence it could not have been the real 'willow' of Babylon, after which Linnaeus named it. The trees on which the exiled Hebrews hung their harps (Psalm 137:1–2, KJV) were doubtless the Euphrates poplar.

Poplars are closely related to willows. The Euphrates poplar (*Populus euphratica*) and the white poplar (*P. alba*) occur naturally in the Near East, though others are planted, such as the white-trunked black poplar (*P. nigra* var. *afghanica*) at Mount Sinai. It was also the Euphrates poplar rather than the willow that was referred to by Isaiah (44:4). The reason for the confusion is easily explained when one sees the young leaves of the Euphrates poplar and compares them with those on older stems. The young leaves are long and narrow, like those of willows, while older ones are rounded or angular in outline.

The white poplar would have been used by Jacob when he 'took fresh rods of poplar and almond and plane, and peeled white streaks in them, exposing the white of the

Left: A basal shoot of the Euphrates poplar, showing the narrow young leaves. The mature leaves are much broader.

rods' (Genesis 30:37) which he set before Laban's flocks. It is a tall tree with white bark and leaves. The bark is said to be a popular medicine and the soft timber is used for certain kinds of carpentry.

Oleander

Some writers consider the oleander to be the plant intended where most versions have 'willows' (e.g. Leviticus 23:40). More certain references to the oleander are found in the Apocrypha: 'as a rose plant in Jericho' (Ecclesiasticus 24:14 KJV) and 'as a rose growing by the brook' (Ecclesiasticus 39:13 KJV); and M. Zohary (1982) includes the reference to 'the field which is called Ardath' (2 Esdras 9:26) on linguistic grounds. The oleander (*Nerium oleander*) occurs along rocky seasonal watercourses on the Carmel range and in the drier mountain areas, especially to the east of the Jordan, where it forms thickets 2 m (6 ft) or more high, often in association with the chaste-tree, *Vitex agnus-castus*.

The willow-like leaves of the oleander are retained throughout the year. They occur opposite one another, in twos and threes, and are leathery with back-rolled margins. In summer the large pink flowers appear in masses and transform the valleys into ribbons of colour. As the long, woody, V-shaped fruits, so characteristic of the periwinkle family *Apocynaceae*, develop they ripen and dry, splitting lengthwise and the two woody valves curl back, liberating enormous quantities of plumed seeds. Every part of the oleander is poisonous and its white sap is dangerous.

Tamarisk

As already mentioned, the banks of the River Jordan, meandering between the Sea of Galilee and the Dead Sea, are still today thickly clothed with poplars and skirted with Jordan tamarisk (*Tamarix jordanis*) (p. 68).

Plane tree

Certain other streamside trees are apparently much rarer now than they used to be. We have seen that the oriental plane (*Platanus orientalis*) is typical of the Upper Jordan and its tributaries, where the tree grows among the rocks in the stream bed. It is more widespread in

Below: Oleander bushes (*Nerium oleander*) in flower along the bed of a stream on the Carmel range.

the eastern Mediterranean, and in the hills of Iraq. This species is one of the parents of the well-known hybrid London plane, the other parent being the western plane (*P. occidentalis*) from North America. The large size and huge branches of the oriental plane were used by Ezekiel to illustrate his prophecy against Egypt (Ezekiel 31:8; chestnut tree KJV; also Genesis 30:37; Heb. *armon*). The characteristic flaking bark of the plane tree makes pale-coloured patches all over its trunk. The flowers are borne in four or five spherical pendulous heads, which break up on maturity, liberating the plumed seeds, which are blown away by the wind. The large, lobed, digitate leaves occur alternately on the branchlets, and the base of the leaf-stalk completely encloses the axillary bud until the leaf falls in autumn. The RSV names the plane as one of the trees that shall be set in the desert (Isaiah 41:19; Heb. *tidhar*), but M. Zohary considers this to be laurustinus (*Viburnum tinus*), a rare shrub of Carmel, now often cultivated.

Elm

Even a few elm trees (*Ulmus canescens*) occur on the banks of streams in the mountains of Ephraim, but as Palestine is the southern limit of the elm genus, it is doubtful whether it was ever common. In the KJV the rendering of Hosea 4:13 as 'elms' (for *elah*) should properly refer to terebinth. However, M. Zohary (1982) concludes, on linguistic grounds, that elms were intended in another verse usually rendered as 'he plants a cedar and the rain nourishes it' (Isaiah 44:14).

Ash

More widespread is the Syrian ash (*Fraxinus syriaca*). This still grows by one stream on the Sharon Plain and near Beth Shean, as well as near Dan where it grows luxuriantly beside the rushing torrent of the Jordan headwaters. Although it is not a large tree, its characteristic winged fruits, familiarly known as ash keys, enabled me to pick it out even in a leafless state among other species in the riverside forest.

There is a reference to the 'ash' in Isaiah 44:14 (KJV) for the Hebrew *oren*. This is one of the trees said to have been planted and used for the carving of idols, but since this is the only occurrence of that Hebrew word in the Bible, there has been considerable discussion as to its meaning. Some authors believe it refers to the Aleppo pine, cedar (as RSV) or one of the other coniferous trees, and not to the ash tree, in spite of the latter's availability and the suitability of its wood. Löw (1926) and M. Zohary (1982), however, treat *oren* as the bay tree (*Laurus nobilis*; see p. 32).

---

[1] *si*-boat: Professor Wiseman indicates that this word in the Hebrew text has been borrowed from Egyptian.

[2] The Eastern sacred lotus, *Nelumbo nucifera* (= *Nelumbium speciosum*) is often confused with the ancient Egyptian lotus (see Darby *et al.*, 1977). *Nelumbo* was not introduced into Egypt until the Greek Ptolemaic period. Although it is also in the water-lily family, both the leaves and flowers are held well above the water-level. The fruit is like a pepper-pot and its seeds were eaten as bread.

Bibliography

Heyerdahl, T., *The Ra Expeditions* (London, George Allen and Unwin, 1971).

Paz, U., 'The Hula Reserve – Pioneer of Nature Conservation in Israel', *Israel Land and Nature* (Jerusalem, 1979), 5(1):24–27.

Van Zeist, W., 'Past and Present Environments of the Jordan Valley', *Studies in the History and Archaeology of Jordan* (Amman Antiquities, 1985), 2:199–204.

See also General References: Feinbrun-Dothan and Danin (1991); Plitmann, Heyn, Danin and Shmida (1983); Zohary, M. (1962); Zohary and Feinbrun-Dothan (1966–86).

PART TWO:
CULTIVATED
AND USEFUL PLANTS

7. Tillers of the Ground

'Now Abel was a keeper of sheep, and Cain was a tiller of the ground.'
(Genesis 4:2.)

In Genesis we read of Abel becoming a pastoralist and Cain an agriculturalist. This took place somewhere in the Middle East where the wide valleys of the Fertile Crescent have a long history of human settlement and agriculture. But it is to the mountains of that region, in present-day Iraq and Turkey, that we must look for the origins of agriculture.

Origins of agriculture

Early people were wanderers, hunting animals and gathering wild plants. They were dependent on their skills as hunters, on the abundance of quarry and on the presence of suitable plants. Eventually they learned to domesticate animals and to cultivate food plants which obliged them to settle, at least temporarily, before they moved on to fresh grazing.

Amidst the prehistoric forests that covered the hills of north-eastern Iraq in about 7000 BC, a group of people settled in a village we now know as Jarmo. Excavations have shown that they kept goats and pigs as domestic animals, and that they cultivated two kinds of wheat, barley and several pulses. We also know that, at about the same time, much further to the west, at Jericho, a town was established and the inhabitants had domestic animals and probably cultivated cereals. Grains and legumes have been found there, but not from the earliest levels.

A thousand years earlier, however, a New Stone Age city, Catal Hüyük, now known to have the earliest evidence of farming, was developing high up on the Turkish Plateau. Victor Pearce and James Mellaat, who excavated the site, see it as thorough vindication of the Bible statement that Cain built a city (Genesis 4:17). Not, of course, that Cain built Catal Hüyük, but that a city is now known to have been built in the Neolithic period, with the agricultural provisions to support it that this implies. Indeed, carbonized grains have been found there in great quantity, with wheat (identified by Helbaek as einkorn and emmer), as well as barley, occurring at the lowest levels. The grain was stored in bins provided in every house, which also had mortars for de-husking and querns for grinding. At a later level, even bread wheat (*Triticum aestivum*) was discovered. (The origin of the various cereals is discussed in detail in the next chapter.) These grains were associated with seeds of peas and vetches, as well as the nuts of almonds, Atlantic pistachio (*Pistacia atlantica*) and acorns.

Back in Palestine, the study and identification of ancient pollen grains deposited in layers of silt at the bottom of the Sea of Galilee have shown the succession of vegetation in the surrounding area as cultivation increasingly affected the environment. Uri Baruch, of the Hebrew University, has found that there was only a limited impact until about 2000 BC, when large-scale forest clearance began. For the next 2000 years olives were increasingly cultivated, but forest regeneration occurred from about AD 500 when further clearance again reduced the wild vegetation to a more weedy flora.

The spread of agriculture meant that food sources became fairly reliable, which enabled commerce to develop and expand to regions not previously occupied. The way was open for the great civilizations of Mesopotamia and Egypt, and for their impact on world history. Agriculture did not originate in their luxuriant valleys, as used to be thought, since there would have been too much competition from the natural vegetation. It originated in the wooded rocky hills where competition was less intense and where the ancestors of modern crops were already growing in the open spaces between the trees.

C. O. Sauer (1952) propounded

Below: A water-wheel driven by an ox in Egypt (February 1963).

Left: Cultivation of melons along the banks of the River Nile as the water level decreases. Seen here in February 1963 before the Aswan High Dam controlled the water flow.

interesting ideas about the development of crops from the wild species. He, and the Russian botanist, N. I. Vavilov, before him, considered that the region in which large numbers of natural species are located should be regarded as the origin of the crops derived from them by the early farmers. This implies a diversified terrain such as one finds in hilly districts, where even different climates occur within quite a local area. One side of a single mountain, for instance, may be hot and dry, while the other is cold and moist, and such conditions allowed the selection and development of strains of plants that could be cultivated. Sauer also considers the date palm, the olive and the fig, which are all important biblical plants, as some of the oldest cultivated flora of the Mediterranean region. He notes that they are all reproduced by cuttings, which he regards as an ancient practice. More recently, D. Zohary and M. Hopf have drawn together much information on this subject in their *Domestication of Plants in the Old World* (1988).

Climate and seasons

Peasant farming is still the basic industry in most of the biblical lands. In an agricultural community the whole year is governed by the seasons and the requirements of the crops: 'For everything there is a season ... a time to plant, and a time to pluck up what is planted' (Ecclesiastes 3:1–2). Pastoral societies, in which animal husbandry is the main occupation, also depend on the seasons. During the excavation of Gezer on the Shephelah hills a tablet dating from 925 BC was unearthed inscribed with a verse in biblical Hebrew which seems to be a mnemonic ditty for children. Here is Albright's translation (in Pritchard, 1950):

'His two months are [olive] harvest
His two months are planting [grain],
His two months are late planting;
His month is hoeing [pulling] up of flax
His month is the barley harvest
His month is harvest and feasting;
His two months are vine-tending,
His month is summer fruit.'

Successful agriculture needs regular supplies of water. Life-giving rain is so important that good crops depend on its falling in sufficient quantity at the right time of year, or famine ensues. The 'early rain' (Heb. *yowreh*) signals the end of summer in November, the germination of seeds and the greening of the land. The 'later rain' (Heb. *malqowsh*; latter KJV) during April, often mentioned in the Bible (Deuteronomy 11:14; Job 29:23), is especially important to ensure a good crop since it falls when the grain is coming into ear. Precipitation in the form of hail, however, can be catastrophic, especially if it occurs during the summer, when it beats down the crops, fruiting vines and sycomores (Exodus 9:25; Psalm 78:47).

Snow falls in Jerusalem occasionally, as it did in Old Testament times (2 Samuel 23:20; 1 Chronicles 11:22), and can be disastrous, since the weight of it breaks boughs and freezes the crops and wildlife. It is preceded by unusually cold weather, as I recall during visits in March in both 1967 and 1992, when I was unprepared for such low temperatures. On the higher hills and mountains snow lies for many weeks each year, and as I flew from Damascus to Amman, I could see the snowy hills of Bashan, as well as those of Hermon and Lebanon (Jeremiah 18:14).

In Palestine the rainless summer lasts for six months, while in the Nile Valley little or no rain falls even in winter, and the people are entirely dependent on river-water for irrigation. At several places along the Nile one can see the ancient stone-cut nilometers, which measured the height of the flood in ancient times in order to calculate the taxes that were to be levied. The higher the water level the better the crops and the greater the payment – an estimated income-tax! Floods brought silt to fertilize the soil, and, when the water receded, irrigation channels of varying sizes were filled with water by means of buckets, or later by water wheels.

The ancient *shaduf*, with a bucket on the end of a balanced pole operated by one man, is fast disappearing from the Nile in Egypt in favour of power pumps. In Deuteronomy there is a description of the flat fields of Egypt, where the farmer used his bare feet to stop the irrigation channel with mud and in this way diverted the water to another channel:

'For the land which you are entering to take possession of it is not like the land of Egypt, from which you have come, where you sowed your seed and watered it with your feet, like a garden of vegetables' (Deuteronomy 11:10).

Later, the prophet Isaiah, using the same thought, pictured the Lord having 'dried up with the sole of [his] foot all the streams of Egypt' (2 Kings 19:24).

Right: Egyptian field irrigation, where water trickles along muddy channels. The water can be diverted by using the foot to block the flow with mud; Kharga Oasis (February 1985).

Terraces

In contrast to the rainless Egyptian climate, the Promised Land would be 'a land of hills and valleys, which drinks water by the rain from heaven'. Different farming techniques were required. While plains such as the Vale of Jezreel and the Jordan valley could be cleared and ploughed to provide food for the cities of Beth Shean and Jericho, the rocky mountains around Jerusalem had to be terraced to catch the rainfall and retain the soil.

Below: A traditional *shaduf* reconstructed at the Ragab Pharaonic Village, with papyrus swamps beyond.

From at least the late Iron Age period farm units were developed with high stone-walled alleyways for animals, such as that used by Balaam and his ass (Numbers 22:24), to protect the crops growing on either side. The abundant stones were cleared from the ground to create walls to retain the soil as terraces, often utilizing the natural outcrops of the horizontal strata. The retaining walls were backed by gravel and sand for drainage, and extra soil brought from unused areas was enriched with household waste and manure. No wonder that Isaiah wrote about 'a very fertile

Left: Parched soil cracking into polygons. Mosaic laws laid down sound agricultural, social and ecological guidelines which, if disobeyed, would lead to disastrous crop yields.

Left: An ancient walled road between fields in Samaria, such as Balaam might have ridden along in Moab.

hill' on which the vineyard was dug and cleared of stones and planted with choice vines (Isaiah 5:1–2).

An increasing number of archaeological studies are being made of ancient Holy Land landscapes and the communities populating them, to find out how they lived and what they grew.[1]

Run-off agriculture

In the desert, clearance of loose stones greatly helped the efficient run-off of rainwater and the collected stones were piled into little heaps which in many places are still visible. Stone-collecting was a common practice elsewhere in Palestine, as ploughs unearthed many from the shallow soil. Perhaps the prophet had this in mind when he wrote: 'I will make Samaria as an heap of the field, and as plantings of a vineyard: and I will pour down the stones thereof into the valley' (Micah 1:6, KJV). The prophet Hosea also wrote 'if in Gilgal they sacrifice bulls, their altars also shall be like stone heaps on the furrows of the field' (Hosea 12:11).

In some parts of the desert local cultivation is possible when rainwater running off the dry ground is collected and channelled to the fields. During Old Testament times the Negeb and Judean deserts were populated by both herdsmen and cultivators. A run-off cultivation was developed along the wadis by the Israelites and later, during the inter-testamental period, by the Nabataeans. In the Negeb one can still see these low terraces constructed to ensure the best use of every drop of water. Aerial photographs reveal large channels for diverting flash-floods to the cultivated areas which served the associated townships, such as Avdat, built on commanding sites nearby. Even light rain was utilized for irrigation, by collecting water from a large area of stony hillside into an intricate system of channels directed towards the relatively deep valley soils. The water brought fertilizing silt, while at the same time leaching away any accumulation of harmful salts.

The Nabataeans were so successful at their desert run-off agriculture that it continued until the Arab conquest after AD 630. At Shivta and Avdat, successful reconstructions of some of their fields and water systems in recent years have become well known (Michael Evenari *et al.*, 1971). I shall always recall my amazement on seeing patches of bright green wheat in a wilderness of sand, and even more surprising was an orchard of apricot trees in full flower! It must be stressed, however, that these fields represent a minute proportion of the desert, as it is impossible to cultivate the barren hillsides.

This type of agriculture should not be confused with the extensive area of cultivation near Beersheba, which lies in a region normally receiving sufficient rain to allow some sort of crop each year. (However, to ensure a constant economic return, it is now irrigated by water piped from the Sea of Galilee.) There is general agreement that the climate has not changed in historical times, although minor fluctuations do occur. The seasons in the Mediterranean are very unpredictable, for one winter may be wet, only to be followed by a series of dry ones.

Dew

Dew is also important in supplying moisture in dry-country conditions. The rapid cooling encountered in the desert at night induces condensation of atmospheric moisture as dew, expecially near the coast, and arguments as to whether plants benefit from dew have now been settled in the affirmative by scientific experiments carried out in the Negeb. Melons and other crops on which dew forms have more leaves and yield more fruit than those deprived of the moisture (Duvdevani, 1964). Several biblical references to dew imply its beneficial effects, which are now scientifically vindicated (Genesis 27:28; Deuteronomy 33:28; Haggai 1:10, etc.).

We have seen that most of the rain being brought by the north wind (Proverbs 25:23) falls during the winter. The vegetation slowly develops during the cooler months, and with the warmth of spring in

Right: Boundaries between neighbouring properties were sometimes indicated by sea-squill bulbs (*Urginea maritima*); such landmarks could not easily be removed.

March and April the whole country is colourful and fragrant. In good years even parts of the desert are green. But then the burning, dry, easterly and southerly wind known as the *sirocco* (Arab. *hamsin*; Heb. *sharav*) suddenly begins to blow. The air is full of dust, and almost overnight the plants are shrivelled up, just as Jesus said: 'And when you see the south wind blowing you say, "There will be scorching heat"' (Luke 12:55). The result was well known to the prophets, who likened the transience of man's life to that of vegetation, 'All flesh is grass, and all its beauty is like the flower of the field. The grass withers, the flower fades when the breath of the Lord blows upon it' (Isaiah 40:6; 1 Peter 1:24). Crops suffer as much as the wild plants, and people find the conditions distressing, as I know from experience in the Negeb, Egypt and tropical Africa.

Preparation of the land

Peasant agriculture on the hills of Palestine involved the clearance of forest and scrub in order to make small terraced fields from which the stones were removed, as mentioned above. The plains were more easily prepared, unless they were too dry or too wet for agriculture. The fields were marked out with stones, or even lines of trees or growing bulbs, and it was a serious offence to remove these landmarks (Deuteronomy 19:14; Job 24:2; Proverbs 22:28; 23:10).

The land in Israel was privately owned, as it was in neighbouring countries other than Egypt, where it was nationalized under the Pharaohs. Land was passed on from father to son and was not lightly disposed of; hence Naboth refused King Ahab his vineyard (1 Kings 21). There were many peasant farmers and large land-owners, the king having his own estates and temple property.

According to Mosaic Law the people were to leave the land fallow every seventh year (Exodus 23:11; Leviticus 25:3–7). The practice of fallowing fields helped to restore fertility from the weathering of the soil, and to conserve humus from ploughed-in weeds. This practice was continued until quite recent times, even in England, when the need for crop rotation was acknowledged and fertilizers became available to the farmer. In Egypt, however, the annual flood brought abundant nutrient- and humus-rich silt which enabled several crops to be grown every year. Hence I am apprehensive about the present situation in the Nile valley, following the construction of the Aswan High Dam, since this maintains a steady flow of water down the River Nile and deprives the surrounding land of silt. Unless the value of the silt is made good by the addition of expensive fertilizers, the Egyptian farmer will be cultivating a wasting asset.

Basic crops were the first essential for the peasant farmer, with barley and wheat being the most important in Palestine. Olives for oil and vines for grapes and wine were the other mainstays of the peasant economy (Deuteronomy 7:13). Of course, other crops were grown, the diet also being supplemented with animal products and wild herbs, as we shall see elsewhere in this book. Ploughing was accomplished with a primitive animal-drawn wooden plough, which was later equipped with an iron-tipped ploughshare, such as the one dating from the twelfth century BC, found in excavations at Gibeah. It is interesting to recall that this was the very place where Saul slaughtered the yoke of oxen (1 Samuel 11:7).

Albright (1949) points out that when the Hittite Empire was destroyed in about 1200 BC their monopoly of iron was broken and iron tools displaced copper. Their techniques passed to the Philistines, and by the time of the divided kingdom of Israel in the tenth century BC, iron was the principal metal for plough-tips and sickles, as well as for weapons. The famous passage in Isaiah recalls how the Lord 'shall judge between the nations ... and they shall beat their swords into ploughshares, and their spears into pruning hooks' (Isaiah 2:4).

The area that a pair of yoked oxen could plough in a day was used as a measure of land. The unit in Hebrew is *semed*, rendered as acre in English (1 Samuel 14:14; Isaiah 5:10). After ploughing, the clods were broken with oxen-drawn disc-harrows or nail-studded boards. The ordinary hand implement was the hoe, originally made from a simple forked branch. Later it was improved to form a wooden blade inserted into a wooden handle. A cord tied back the blade to the handle to take up the strain of working. These agricultural operations were picturesquely and figuratively expressed by Hosea:

'*Judah must plough,*
Jacob must harrow for himself.
Sow for yourselves righteousness,
reap the fruit of steadfast love;
break up your fallow ground,
for it is the time to seek the Lord,
that he may come and rain salvation upon you' (Hosea 10:11–12).

Pests and diseases

Ancient agriculture was not immune from pests, which the people usually regarded as God's punishment. The greatest pest was the locust in its various stages of development, referred to in the KJV as 'caterpillar' and 'cankerworm'. Locusts descended in plagues every few years and literally devoured the crops (Psalm 105:34–35) The farm-

Left: A Druze farmer ploughing with oxen in northern Israel; April 1969. Here, unlike the irrigated Egyptian fields, the farmer is dependent on rainfall.

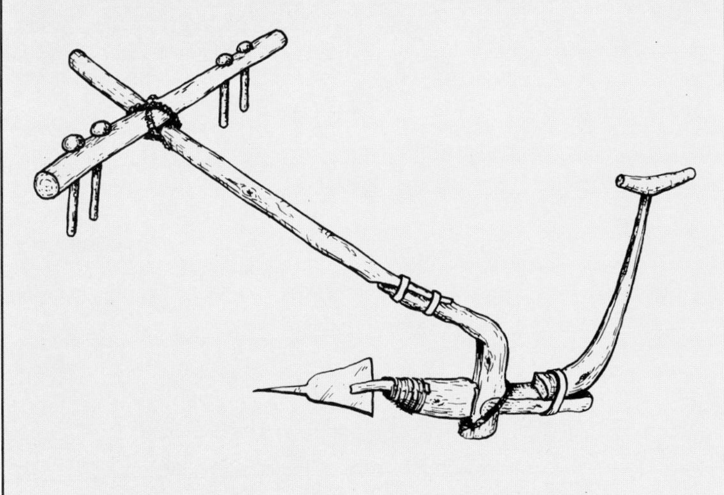

Left: A traditional wooden plough with iron share.

ers were helpless against locusts, but in Assyria caterpillars and other insects affecting trees were fumigated by burning bitumen. It is surprising to learn that the Assyrians also used bitumen to seal tree-wounds, and on sticky bands to keep away ants, in a similar manner to modern practice (Forbes, 1921; 1928).

A toll of the crops was taken by fungal diseases, referred to in the Bible as wasting, blight and mildew (Deuteronomy 28:22; Amos 4:9; Haggai 2:17; Heb. *shiddaphown, yeraqown*). Grasses, including the grain crops, are subject to rust disease, which manifests itself as rust-like streaks on the leaves. The commonest rust-fungus is *Puccinia graminis*. The grain itself is often diseased with a fungus called smut (*Ustilago nuda*), which gives the ears a sooty appearance. Another is the ergot (*Claviceps purpurea*), which replaces each grain by a hard black nodule. This is the fungus' reproductive body which can poison humans who may eat it in flour. Many other fungal diseases affect plants, usually with a specific fungus infecting a certain species.

Propagation

It appears that grafting is an ancient practice (Romans 11:24). Choice varieties of fruit trees have long been grafted on to the stock of poor fruiting trees which, however, possess a good root system. Olive and carob trees are typical examples, as well as the hawthorn, to which apples are now grafted. In this way good crops can be obtained quickly, especially by using wild stocks naturally scattered over the hillsides. Many of the Mediterranean tree crops are obtained by using cuttings rather than seed; this is because the seeds, being unimproved by artificial selection, do not yield fruitful progeny.

Agricultural festivals

Agricultural communities, such as those formed by the Israelites, often derived their festivals from the seasonal calendar. In Exodus (23:16) they were told to

'keep the feast of harvest [or the Feast of Weeks], of the first-fruits of your labour, of what you sow in the field. You shall keep the feast of ingathering [or Succoth, the Feast of Tabernacles] at the end of the [Hebrew] year, when you gather in from the field the fruit of your labour.'

The first-fruits were to be offered to the Lord (Exodus 34:26), but rich harvests would only be forthcoming if the Law were observed (Leviticus 26:3 ff). The Feast of Weeks coincided with the wheat harvest, which ripens later than barley (see Exodus 9:32). The Feast of Ingathering occurs during the grape harvest, when the people lived in the vineyards in temporary shelters – tabernacles or booths – made of branches to keep off the sun, rather than the rain, since grapes ripen at a dry time of year. Little shelters and watchtowers among crops, such as 'the lodge in a cucumber field' (Isaiah 1:8),[2] are frequently found in many parts of the world to protect them from animals, birds and thieves. At harvest time labour became even more important, since the grapes were picked and pressed on the spot and the whole family took to the vineyards for a time of work and celebration. These feasts developed into formal rites and thanksgiving for the town-dweller too:

'On the fifteenth day of the seventh month, when you have gathered in the produce of the land, you shall keep the feast of the Lord seven days; on the first day shall be a solemn rest, and on the eighth day shall be a solemn rest. And you shall take on the first day the fruit of goodly trees, branches of the palm trees, and boughs of leafy trees and willows of the brook; and you shall rejoice before the Lord your God seven days' (Leviticus 23:39–40; see also Nehemiah 8:14–18).[3]

Some Bible gardens

Most scholars now believe that the word Eden in Genesis (2:8 ff; 3:24), where God planted a garden, has come to us from a Sumerian or Akkadian word meaning 'plain'. In

Above: An ancient Egyptian mural showing a gardener drawing up water between papyrus and water-lilies; cornflowers are in flower and mandrakes in fruit; a pomegranate bush is over the gardener's head.

other words, the garden was situated on a plain, and Eden is not a proper name at all. Subsequently it became known as Paradise, which is an anglicized form of the Persian word for a walled garden. (For a fuller account, see *The Illustrated Bible Dictionary*, pp. 332–4, 934–5.) A walled garden was owned by the wealthy, and in dry regions it needed a ready supply of water for irrigation. Indeed, Isaiah likens the righteous to a watered garden (Isaiah 58:11).

We have a precise plan of an Egyptian garden drawn on the tomb of its owner, a general in the army of Pharaoh Amenophis III in about 1400 BC. The garden was walled and the geometrical layout allowed the numerous criss-crossing irrigation channels to reach the vines trained over pergolas, as well as the lines of date palms and other trees such as pomegranates. The rectangular ponds would have been bright with water-lilies, especially the blue water-lily which was favoured for its scent. Clearly, the Egyptians were keen on their gardens, which possessed symbolic meaning (Wilkinson, 1990).

In biblical times gardens were essentially for fruit trees and vegetables, rather than for floral display, although fragrant herbs and ornamental pools were often included. For example, Solomon boasted:

'I made great works; I built houses and planted vineyards for myself; I made myself gardens and parks, and planted in them all kinds of fruit trees. I made myself pools from which to water the forest of growing trees' (Ecclesiastes 2:4–6).

Some indication of the plants grown by Solomon is given in Song of Solomon 4:12–14, although these verses are poetic and include imported spices. In Assyria, soon after Solomon's time, Ashurbanipal is known to have had trained gardeners to maintain his botanical and zoological gardens and a park; and the hanging gardens of Babylon were one of the seven wonders of the ancient world (Wiseman, 1983).

Fragrant herbs were highly prized in ancient times, and vegetables and culinary herbs were also surprisingly diverse. Ahab, king of Israel, wanted to convert Naboth's vineyard into a vegetable garden (RSV), or a 'garden full of herbs' (KJV), because it was near his palace in Jezreel, and it was procured for him by Queen Jezebel at the cost of Naboth's life (1 Kings 21).

The trees planted in gardens were usually fruit trees, such as olives, figs, and pomegranates. These little orchards were shady retreats, like the garden of Gethsemane, on the Mount of Olives, where it was Jesus' custom to go (Luke 22:39). The rock-hewn sepulchre in which Jesus' body was laid must have been set in a garden since after his resurrection, when he revealed himself to Mary, she supposed him to be the gardener (John 20:15).

Much is also known about gardens in Greece, while in Italy there have been excavations in a garden at Pompeii where the positions of the trees have been revealed by the study of the layout of their decayed roots. Attempts are being made to reconstruct ancient gardens, and there are many biblical gardens containing assemblies of plants mentioned in the Bible. The largest is at Neot Kedumim near Lod,

Right: A riverside vegetable garden such as the Israelites would have had for growing leeks, onions and garlic when they lived in Goshen.

Left: A Bible garden incorporating plants mentioned in the scriptures, planned and planted by the author at Redcliffe College, London 1984.

where the Director, Nogah Hareuveni, demonstrates plants of Jewish interest. I have recently established one at St George's College, Jerusalem, and there is another at Tantur Ecumenical Center near Gilo. The Hai-Bar Biblical Zoo north of Elat includes animals of ancient times. Many other biblical gardens exist in the USA, England, Australia and New Zealand, and are listed in my *Planting a Bible Garden* (1987). A pharaonic garden surrounds the Agricultural Museum at Giza in Egypt.

This chapter has set the background for those that follow. We shall now deal with the crops in detail, starting with the staff of life – the cereals – and then moving on to the fruit trees, vegetables and spices, before considering plants used for purposes other than food.

---

[1] Palestinian excavations and detailed laboratory studies of the plant finds have been undertaken by such scholars as Helbaek, Van Zeist, Liphschitz, Kislev, Gibson, and La Bianca. Sites in Turkey and Syria have been studied by Hillman and colleagues in London; Egyptian botanical material is being examined by Rowley-Conway, El-Hadidi and colleagues; and Mesopotamian by Van Zeist, to name only a few.

[2] M. Zohary points out that, although the Hebrew *miqshah* is usually translated 'cucumber field', the word means melon field, where shelters were put up by the owner to foil thieves.

[3] Nogah Hareuveni (1979) has much to say about these agricultural festivals from a Jewish point of view, with detailed plantings and reconstructions at his 700-acre biblical landscape reserve, Neot Kedumim, east of Lod. For example, the four tree species of the Feast of Tabernacles, in Hebrew *succoth* (Leviticus 23:40), that Jews take home for the festival, are shown by the construction of a large booth of palm leaves supported on palm and sycomore trunks, with live trees planted nearby. The palm represents the desert wanderings of the Israelites. A stand of Euphrates poplar (*Populus euphratica*) represents the 'willows' of the Jordan bank where they encamped prior to crossing the river. The third species (the 'leafy trees') is represented by the myrtle bushes of the hillside thickets; and the fourth is the citron (*Citrus medica*; Heb. *etrog*), now traditional at Succoth as the 'fruits of goodly trees', although to me the grapevine more accurately represents the fruit of the Promised Land after settlement.

Bibliography

Duvdevani, S., 'Dew in Israel and its Effects on Plants', *Soil Science* (New Brunswick, 1964), 98:14–21.

Edelstein, G., and Gibson, S., 'Ancient Jerusalem's Rural Food Basket', *Biblical Archaeology Review* (Washington, 1982), 8(4):46–55.

Evenari, M., Shanan, L., and Tadmore, N. H., *The Negev: the Challenge of a Desert* (Harvard University Press, 1971).

Hawkes, J. G., 'The Origins of Agriculture', *Economic Botany* (New York, 1970), 24:131–3.

—. *The Diversity of Crop Plants* (Cambridge, Mass., Harvard University Press, 1983).

Helbaek, H., 'First Impressions of the Catal Hüyük Plant Husbandry', *Anatolian Studies* (Ankara and London, 1964), 24:121.

McKay, A. I., *Farming and Gardening in the Bible* (Emmaus, Penn., Rodale Press, 1950).

Mellaart, J., 'A Neolithic City in Turkey', *Scientific American* (New York, 1964).

Moens, M.-F., *Ancient Egyptian Gardens of the New Kingdom* (Leuvain, 1982).

Pearce, E. K. V., *Who was Adam?* (Exeter, Paternoster Press, 1970).

Petrie, W. M. F., *Tools and Weapons* (London, Egypt Exploration Fund, 1917).

Pritchard, J. B., *Ancient Near Eastern Texts*, 2nd ed. (Princeton University Press, 1950), p. 320.

Raikes, R. L., 'The Climate and Hydrological Background to the Post Glacial Farming in the Middle East', *Studies in History and Archaeology of Jordan* (Amman Antiquities, 1985), 2:267–72.

Rohde, E. S., *Garden-craft in the Bible* (London, Herbert Jenkins Ltd, 1927).

Sauer, C. O., *Agricultural Origins and Dispersals* (New York, American Geographical Society, 1952).

Stager, L. E., 'Farming in the Judean Desert during the Iron Age', *Bulletin of the American Schools of Oriental Research* (Washington, 1976), 221:145–58.

Van Zeist, W., 'On Macroscopic Traces of Food Plants in Southwestern Asia', *Philosophic Transactions* (Royal Society of London, 1976), B.275:27–41.

Wilkinson, A., 'Gardens in Ancient Egypt: their location and symbolism', *Journal of Garden History* (London, 1990), 10:199–208.

Wiseman, D. J., 'Mesopotamian Gardens', *Anatolian Studies* (London, 1983).

8. Wheat and Barley

'God is bringing you into a good land ... a land of wheat and barley.' (Deuteronomy 8:7–8.)

There were two cereals in biblical Palestine, wheat and barley, both originating in the eastern Mediterranean region and both self-pollinating, unlike most grasses which cross-pollinate. Their classical names, *Triticum* and *Hordeum* respectively, have been taken over as their scientific names. Of the cereals we know nowadays, rice (*Oryza*), millet (*Panicum*) and dura (*Sorghum*) seem not to have reached the Mediterranean area from East Asia and Africa before Christian times. Oats (*Avena*) and rye (*Secale*) were late-comers into cultivation, although developed from species wild in the Mediterranean region. Wild oats and rye were always present as weeds in cereal fields, but they only developed as crops in their own right wherever wheat could not be relied upon to yield good crops, such as in the northern latitudes. Indian corn, or maize (*Zea*), has been grown around the world only after the opening up of America. All of these belong, of course, to the grass family *Gramineae.*

The riddle of the origin of cultivated wheat and barley has been only recently unravelled. It is a classic example of how archaeology and botany can work together to mutual advantage. First it was necessary to find out which cereals were cultivated in ancient times and then to seach for their wild progenitors. Careful identification of grains from excavations of known age was followed by the collection and examination of numerous wild and cultivated cereals; the relationship of these was then established through studying their ecology, genetic composition and breeding behaviour, as summarized by D. Zohary and M. Hopf (1988). Perhaps the story is still not complete, for further discoveries could still be made.

Right: Ploughing and harvesting wheat, depicted on the end wall of the tomb of Nakht at Thebes, Egypt, *c.* 1400 BC.

WHEAT AS FOOD

Grains of wheat[1] are found abundantly in most excavations carried out in the Middle East. Various sites in Mesopotamia have yielded wheat, as well as barley, dating from the beginnings of farming in about 6500 BC (Helbaek, 1966; Hopf, 1969). Ancient primitive wheats were bearded like present-day barley, with long bristles called awns. This cultivated wheat, known as emmer, is very similar to a wild wheat growing naturally in northern Palestine and southern Syria. Even the grains of the wild and cultivated emmer wheat are similar in size, the cultivated one being only slightly the larger. The very important difference between them is that whereas the ear of the wild plant shatters and breaks up immediately it is ripe, leaving only the standing straw, the ear of cultivated wheats remains intact. One can imagine how difficult it would be to cut and carry a field of wild emmer as most of it would break up and fall away before it reached the barn! A crop of standing wheat, on the other hand, will not disintegrate when cut, and subsequently it can be carted away and stacked.

Artificial threshing is necessary to separate the grains, and winnowing clears away the chaff. In the primitive cultivated wheats, like their wild ancestors, the kernel of the grains was tightly invested by some of the chaffy parts (glumes) of the individual flowers, which could only be separated by pounding in a mortar.[2] It is only the comparatively modern wheats that lose their glumes on threshing and expose the naked kernel, about which more will be said later.

No doubt in ancient times in the Syrian region wild grasses were collected for food long before they were cultivated. In a good year and in the right place, ample supplies for a small family could be gathered. According to Professor Jack Harlan (1967) of Oklahoma University, who, in an experiment, harvested wild cereals at the rate of about 2 kg (4 lb 8 oz) per hour, it was very hard work pulling off the ears with his hands. By cutting them with a reconstructed flint sickle blade he increased his productivity to nearly 2.45 kg (5 lb 8 oz) per hour, but some of the ripest fell off during cutting.

In the last chapter we saw that

once nomadic peoples had stored a quantity of food, they would have been immobilized until it was more or less consumed. This meant a sedentary life for at least part of the year, during which time, perhaps, they learnt to domesticate wild animals and cultivate some wild plants. Among the latter must have been wild wheat, and when varieties were found which did not shatter they could be harvested more successfully. By keeping some grain for sowing each year, these early farmers became largely independent of wild plant resources which were always liable to be uncertain. Agriculture was thus established.

Botanically there were three distinct kinds of cultivated wheat: *einkorn wheat*, *emmer wheat* and *bread* (or *common*) *wheat*. Each of these three kinds of wheat have different chromosome numbers.[3] Wild einkorn and emmer were important constituents of the ground flora of open deciduous oak woodland in the northern part of the Fertile Crescent. The trees in this type of woodland are well spaced, and wild cereals grew in massive profusion in the absence of the domesticated animals which nowadays graze them. As both of these wheats were gathered in the wild state, so both came into cultivation, together with barley.

An interesting fact is that cultivated cereals, because they do not shatter on ripening, are entirely dependent on the farmer for their perpetuation as they have lost their dispersal mechanism. The grains have to be threshed and sown, while the wild cereals thresh and sow themselves, as it were, by breaking up the ears, thus ensuring their survival. The long whiskers or awns on wild grasses twist according to atmospheric moisture, and once the grains are on the ground they rapidly screw themselves into the soil, which affords both protection from birds and good conditions for germination. Cultivated cereals do not need awns, and farmers tend to select those varieties that do not possess them. Replacement of the enclosed (or hulled) grain types, such as einkorn and emmer, by the naked grain macaroni (or hard) wheat (*Triticum durum*) took place shortly before the Roman period. This is the wheat that has been characteristic of the Mediterranean region and gave it the typical *pitta* or flat bread, as well as the Italian macaroni and other pasta. It is true to say that *durum* wheat has retained its dominance until the present time, but it is being replaced by modern 'bread wheats' which have hitherto been more typical of the northern temperate zone.

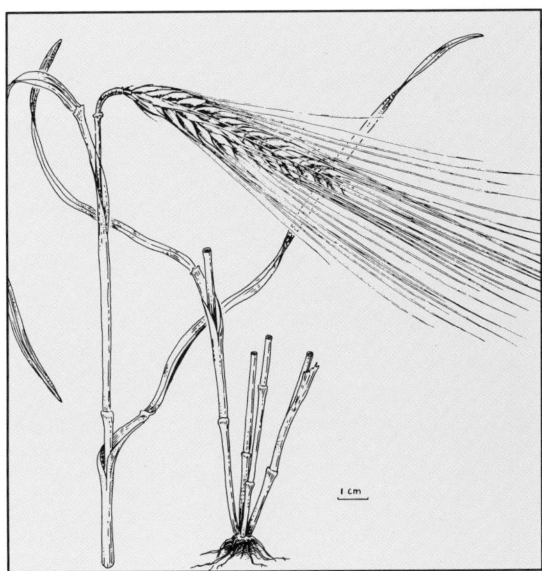

Above left: This bread wheat (*Triticum aestivum*) is bearded, whereas most modern varieties of it are without these awns.

Above: Barley (*Hordeum vulgare*).

Only recently has the origin of bread wheat (*T. aestivum*) been understood. It has the hybrid ancestry of a wild goat grass (*Aegilops squarrosa*), which has a wide natural distribution in northern Iran and adjacent Caucasus, crossed with cultivated *T. turgidum* (which includes the emmer *T. dicoccum*). The hybrid apparently arose one or two millennia after cultivation of emmer wheat started. The full story is very complicated. Briefly, it involved acquisition of certain chromosomes from each parent and the subsequent doubling of the chromosome complement.

Archaeological and botanical studies have jointly increased our understanding of ancient cereals. One of the earliest finds of cultivated wheat was from imprints of coarse grains, probably of emmer, in clay plaster from a burnt house in southern Jordan, at a place not far from Petra. They may have dated from about 7000 BC (Helbaek, 1966). Although some grains of einkorn and bread wheat, dating from a pre-pottery level and from the Early Bronze Age (about 2500 BC) respectively, are said to have been unearthed from the ruins of Jericho, by far the most important early wheat was emmer (Hopf, 1969). In fact emmer is the only wheat known in Egypt until later times. Einkorn is not recorded at all there, which is not surprising, as it is a wheat favouring a cooler climate. Egyptologists are now certain that bread wheat has not been found in any deposit earlier than Graeco-Roman times (Dixon, 1969). However, we now know from excavations that bread wheat was the principal variety in Palestine at the time of Sennacherib's attack on Lachish in 701 BC. It comprised 99 per cent of the samples examined by Helbaek.

In the dream that troubled Pharaoh he saw 'seven ears growing on one stalk, full and good', typifying the seven years of plenty. This apparently fantastic kind of wheat is known to this day in Egypt. According to Tackholm and Drar (1941), the Arabs call it the 'seven-headed wheat' from the branching habit of its ear. It is a variety of the rivet wheat (*T. turgidum*), which is very similar to hard wheat (*T. durum*) in the emmer group. No examples appear to have been specifically recorded from ancient Egypt, but this is hardly surprising considering the finds are usually as grains rather than as the whole ears by which this kind would be most readily recognized.

The RSV and other versions have substituted 'spelt' for the obviously incorrect 'rie' (rye) of the KJV in Exodus 9:32: 'the wheat and the spelt were not ruined [by thunder and hail], for they are late in coming up'. Although two cereals are

Right: Wild barley (*Hordeum spontaneum*) on the Shephelah hills.

distinguished here, there is no evidence for the presence in Egypt, at such an early date, of spelt wheat (*T. spelta*),[4] which is a primitive hard-grained bread wheat. Neither was rye (*Secale cereale*) ever grown there, since this is a central European crop which requires a cool climate. The cereal intended by the Hebrew word *Kussemeth* in that verse, as well as similar words in Isaiah 28:25 and Ezekiel 4:9, may indicate a kind of wheat known to the Egyptians as *swt*, possibly the hard wheat, which, as noted above, is related to emmer (Tackholm and Drar, 1941; see also, Darby *et al.*, 1977).

As to the yield of ancient and modern wheat, the following comparison is of interest. A good modern variety grown in Britain yields an average of 4 tonnes/tons per hectare, which would be equivalent to a volume of 3000 litres (600 imp. gallons). *The Illustrated Bible Dictionary* (1:516) provides evidence from the Babylonian city of Mari which indicates that 1 iku (= 3600 square metres) produced 1 ugar (= 1200 litres) of grain. This converts to 3330 litres per hectare, which is nearly 10 per cent more than modern yields!

'Barley also and straw for the horses'[5]

In biblical times barley (Heb. *seoreh*; Gk. *krithe*) was staple food for horses and humans alike (2 Kings 4:42; John 6:9), and it still forms an important part of the diet in some Near Eastern countries. Barley (*Hordeum vulgare*, including *H. distichum* and *H. hexastichum*), was the principal cereal in early times, largely giving way to wheat by the Iron Age (second millennium BC). The primitive cultivated barley excavated in earlier archaeological deposits has the grains in two rows, one on each side of the ear. It was very similar to wild barley except that, like cultivated wheat, the ears did not break up on ripening but remained intact during harvesting. This 'two-rowed barley' (*Hordeum distichum*) must have been selected directly from the wild barley (*H. spontaneum*) naturally growing in the park-like oak woodlands of the hills in the Fertile Crescent and right up to the fringe of the desert.

The origin of barley with six rows of grains – three on each side – which appears in later archaeological deposits is more speculative. This 'six-rowed barley' (*H. hexastichum*), which is our common malting and cattle fodder cereal, was thought until recently to have arisen from a wild barley grass (*H. agriocrithon*) with the grains in six rows. But the latter has now been shown not to be a truly wild species, since it is a hybrid resulting from chance crossing of cultivated and wild barleys. In the absence of any other progenitor, we are now thrown back to assuming that the cultivated six-rowed barley arose by mutation from the two-rowed, which in turn was derived from the wild *H. spontaneum*. Both the wild barley and the cultivated barley have the same chromosome number (2n = 14).

Other cereals

We have already seen that wheat and barley were the ancient cereals of the Near East. However, some authors consider that dura and millet are mentioned by the prophet Ezekiel.[6]

Dura (*Sorghum bicolor*, also called *S. vulgare*) is a tall reed-like grass with large round grains. It is of tropical African origin and it was not a crop plant in the ancient Middle East. It was cultivated in Palestine during the New Testament period and rapidly became a very important crop in the warmer low-lying areas. The thick old stems of the previous year's crop could therefore have been available at Jerusalem to the Roman soldiers, who used a 'reed' (Gk. *calamus*) to strike Jesus' thorn-crowned head (Matthew 27:29–30; Mark 15:19) (See also p. 70).

A sower went out to sow

The parable of the sower, recorded in Matthew 13, Mark 4 and Luke 8, relates a typical life-history of seeds sown in the rough fields of Palestine. Jesus' accurate observations bear careful examination from a botanical point of view, as well as study of the spiritual aspects of the parable which we cannot deal with here. The account tells us much about seed germination and the subsequent growth of the seedling to fruition. In ancient farming the seed was broadcast[7] by hand from a seed basket as the sower walked along, scattering the seed on the roughly prepared ground, where it was likely to meet with a variety of conditions.

Ideal conditions for germination comprise a supply of moisture, atmospheric oxygen and warmth. A great deal of interesting research has been carried out at Kew and elsewhere on the requirements of different species, and their remarkable adaptations according to their usual habitat. Seeds of temperate lands often need to be chilled before they will germinate properly, yet this would kill tropical seeds. Others need light, but most have to be in the dark, a requirement met by covering the seed with soil which also protects them from birds and other seed-eating creatures: 'some [seed] fell along the path ... and the birds of the air devoured it' (Luke 8:5). Cereals and grasses with bearded (or awned) grains rapidly burrow into the soil and the whole grain is screwed into the ground by the daily variation in atmospheric moisture, as mentioned above. But if the soil is compacted like that on

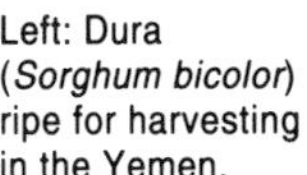

Left: Dura (*Sorghum bicolor*) ripe for harvesting in the Yemen.

a path the grain will neither be covered nor will it be able to bury itself in the soil.

Once below ground, moisture diffuses into the seed, and when sufficient is absorbed, the stored starch is turned into sugars.[8] A point is soon reached when the process is irreversible and the food reserves become increasingly available to the live embryo, the so-called 'germ', enabling it to grow. First the young root (radicle) bursts the seed coat and extends downwards into the soil where it absorbs moisture; then the young cereal shoot (plumule) with its single seed-leaf (cotyledon) pushes upwards. At this stage the seedling needs sufficient moisture to maintain deep growth of the roots, but shallow soil over rocks would soon dry up in the heat of the sun and the seedling would be scorched (Matthew 13:5–6). Even when there is sufficient depth of soil and moisture, a seedling must have light to make its own food, since the period immediately after germination is critical. As the young plant has used its reserves stored in the seed, it must quickly make more by developing green chlorophyll, which turns water and carbon dioxide into sugars and other substances. If weeds grow up and overshadow the young corn it is deprived of light, and the competition is altogether too much for its survival: 'Other seeds fell upon thorns, and the thorns grew up and choked them' (Matthew 13:7).

Finally, the parable of the sower relates how the seed which fell on good soil 'brought forth grain, some a hundredfold, some sixty, some thirty' (Matthew 13:8). This may be contrasted with Haggai's picture of those who have 'sown much, and harvested little' (Haggai 1:6). It is quite true that ears of corn yield different amounts of grain according to the nourishment of the plant or its hereditary constitution.Of course the stage of fruition cannot be reached at all if the seed remains unsown and ungrown. Jesus, speaking of his own self-sacrifice, said that 'unless a grain of wheat [Gk. *kokkos*] falls into the earth and dies, it remains alone; but if it dies, it bears much fruit' (John 12:24), thus implying that the grain 'dies' in order to give rise to new life.

Returning to the sower and his seed, we conclude that during the great famine at the time of Joseph the Egyptians must have consumed

Left: Ploughed stony ground in the hill country of Palestine, ready for the sowing of cereals.

Above: Sacks of grain on sale in a market in northern Yemen, 1975.

Above right: Darnel grass (*Lolium temulentum*), the weed mentioned in the Parable of the Tares.

their sowing seed, for they said 'there is nothing left ... give us seed, that we may live ... so Joseph bought all the land of Egypt for Pharaoh' (Genesis 47:18–20). The people became servants and Joseph said 'Now here is the seed for you, and you shall sow the land. And at the harvests you shall give a fifth to Pharaoh, and four-fifths shall be your own, as seed for the field and as food' (Genesis 47:23–24). Joseph wisely stressed the retention of a proportion as sowing seed.

Professor William T. Stearn (1965) has drawn attention to the startling fact that:

'if for some six years men failed to sow their wheat, maize, millet, rye and rice, these basic crops would vanish from the world and with them most of humanity, and the human survivors would lack the means of creating them anew. Cultivated plants are mankind's most vital and precious living heritage from remote antiquity. Behind the bread wheat lie 9,000 years of cultivation, in every one of which men somewhere tilled the soil, sowed the seed, gathered the harvest and put aside part of it for the next season's sowing. Without foresight in thus saving seed the cultivation of the wild grasses ancestral to our cereals could never have started' (p. 282).

In our day, it is increasingly important that environmental campaigners stress the need to conserve the diversity of wild organisms, not least because they represent a genetic resource with practical applications.

The Mosaic laws dealt with cleanliness in sowing seed in the following way:

'And if any part of their [unclean animals'] *carcass falls upon any seed for sowing that is to be sown, it is clean; but if water is put on the seed and any part of their carcass falls on it, it is unclean to you'* (Leviticus 11:37–38).

Another law to maintain purity of stock and avoid hybridization is found in Leviticus 19:19: 'You shall not sow your field with two kinds of seed'. The intention is clear when it is linked with the preceding law: 'you shall not let your cattle breed with a different kind'. Although cereals are self-pollinated, most other crops are cross-pollinated.

Darnel or tares[9]

There are numerous biblical references to reapers (e.g. 1 Samuel 6:13) and the harvest is frequently referred to both allegorically and symbolically of the last days. Thus in the parable of the weeds or tares (Gk. *zizania*; Matthew 13:24), the men say they sowed good wheat seed, that is, not mixed with weed seeds, yet weeds have come up amongst the corn. The weed intended here was the darnel grass (*Lolium temulentum*). The farmer was not to pull up these grass plants, as they looked very similar to the young wheat plant. Only when they were in ear, ready for harvesting could the two be distinguished: then 'I will tell the reapers, "Gather the weeds first and bind them in bundles to be burnt, but gather the wheat into my barn".'

Darnel is an annual grass about 30–60 cm (1–2 ft) high and widespread in the Mediterranean region, although decreasing nowadays due to the availability of cleaner sowing seed. The toxic properties of flour containing a proportion of darnel seed are attributable to the poisonous alkaloid temuline ($C_7H_{12}N_20$) produced by a fungus very often present in the grain. It causes dizziness and other unpleasant effects, even death on occasions. Darnel has evidently been a serious pest of cornfields since the earliest times. It has been found mixed with samples of barley and emmer wheat preserved in ancient Egyptian tombs, and was also well known in Palestine where it has been found in grain samples excavated in Lachish. However, in Assyria its poisonous properties were put to medicinal use.

HARVEST TIME

Harvest has always been a time of great labour, celebrated with much rejoicing at its successful conclusion. As the ears of corn reach maturity the grains dry off, the plant itself shrivels and changes colour: 'the fields are already white for harvest' (John 4:35).[10]

In early Old Testament times the reapers used hand sickles, of flints set into wood or bone with a wooden handle; but long before the coming of Christ, iron sickles were being used. The standing corn stalks were grasped below the ears and cut off in the middle; the handfuls of cut corn were bundled into sheaves

Left: Threshing in the traditional Arab manner, near Nazareth; Mount Tabor can be seen in the distance. (June 1977.)

and tied up with some of the straws. The sheaves were placed in stooks (shocks) to dry out or to await collection by pack animals or in a cart (Amos 2:13) for stacking before threshing.

Barley ripens before wheat. In Palestine it is ready for harvesting after the 'latter' or 'spring rains' have swelled the grain, in late April and May according to latitude and altitude. The wheat harvest is several weeks later, hence several times in the Bible we find a precise indication of the time of year reckoned by the barley or wheat harvest (Exodus 9:32; Ruth 1:22).

The law laid down certain rules for the reapers. Of course, one could not reap a neighbour's field with a sickle, but it was permissible to 'pluck the ears with your hand' (Deuteronomy 23:25) – a practice regarded as work by the Pharisees, who criticized the disciples for doing this on the Sabbath (Matthew 12:1–2; Mark 2:23–24; Luke 6:1–2). Gleaning was widely practised by the destitute, such as Ruth, who followed the reapers (Ruth 2). The Law stated that 'When you reap the harvest of your land, you shall not reap your field to its very border, neither shall you gather the gleanings after your harvest' (Leviticus 19:9; 23:22). Likewise for the sake of the poor, the harvester who has 'forgotten a sheaf in the field ... shall not go back to get it' (Deuteronomy 24:19).

Very detailed instructions were given regarding the offerings to be

Below: Harvesting, threshing and checking the stored grain in ancient Egypt. (From Wilkinson, *Manners and Customs*.)

Right: An Arab harvester gathers threshed wheat for winnowing near Nazareth.

made at the time of harvest (Leviticus 23:9–21). This was followed by the great Feast of Tabernacles or more literally the 'festival of booths,' set out in Leviticus 23 and Deuteronomy 16. This festival was an extension of the 'feast of ingathering' laid down in Exodus 23:14, which was of redemptive significance rather than simply a harvest festival.

Threshing the grain

Separating the grain from the ears was carried out on the threshing floor, a circular plot of stamped down soil which often acted as a focal point of village life.[11] The sheaves were undone and thrown on to the floor, where the straws were trodden on by animals or had a threshing sledge pulled over them (Deuteronomy 25:4; Hosea 10:11). Beneath the wooden boards of a threshing sledge metal studs protruded, which knocked out the grains and chopped up the straw. One I saw being used in 1977 in Arabic Nazareth had sharp stones inserted into holes bored into the timber. Such an instrument is referred to by Isaiah (41:15) as: 'new, sharp, and having teeth'. But Amos (1:3) mentions 'threshing sledges of iron', and 1 Chronicles 21:20–23 tells how Ornan and his four sons were threshing wheat in Jerusalem with oxen pulling wooden threshing sledges, when King David bought their threshing floor for an altar. It was here that King Solomon raised his temple after his father David's death. Cattle used for threshing were not to be muzzled, according to the Law of Moses (Deuteronomy 25:4; 1 Corinthians 9:9).

Because the threshing floors were often sited in exposed places they were also conspicuous, and in times of famine or occupation of the country it was inadvisable to use them. Thus we find Gideon 'beating out wheat in the wine press, to hide it from the Midianites' (Judges 6:11). The wine-press was so confined that, instead of employing cattle to pull a sledge, Gideon had to beat out the grain with sticks, a method usually kept for the more delicate seeds such as those of fitches (*Nigella sativa*) and cumin, or cummin (*Cuminum cyminum*):

'*For the fitches are not threshed with a threshing instrument, neither is a cart wheel turned about upon the cummin; but the fitches are beaten out with a staff, and the cummin with a rod*' (Isaiah 28:27–28 KJV).

The chopped straw (stubble of KJV) and chaff – botanically glumes – had to be separated from the grain by winnowing. Sir Flinders Petrie often found wooden winnowing fans – really shovels – in his Egyptian excavations. They are so shaped that the rounded backs could be held one in each hand. Petrie (1917) explained that 'the

Right: A threshing board used near Nazareth (June 1977).

trodden out grain and chaff was scraped up from the threshing floor, upon the boards, and lifted up till it could be tossed on high for the wind to blow away the chaff'. George Adam Smith in the last century observed peasants in Palestine, as I have more recently seen in the Yemen and Africa, utilizing the welcome daily winds occurring during the heat of summer for their winnowing in the ancient manner. Isaiah (30:24) wrote of winnowing 'with shovel and fork', while John the Baptist pictured Christ with 'his winnowing fork ... in his hand, and he will clear his threshing floor and gather his [good] wheat into the granary, but the [evil] chaff he will burn with unquenchable fire' (Matthew 3:11–12). Elsewhere we find that 'the wicked ... are like chaff which the wind drives away' (Psalm 1:4). The frequency of such references shows that winnowing was a common sight in biblical times, familiar to everybody.

The winnowed wheat was sieved and re-sieved to retain the stones and other impurities while the grain fell through. Sieves were wooden with leather or wickerwork crosspieces. The method of using sieves is depicted by Amos when he tells how the Lord will shake Israel 'as one shakes with a sieve, but no pebble shall fall upon the earth' (Amos 9:9). Jesus promised the apostle Peter that Satan would sieve him like wheat – as indeed he did (see Luke 22:31–34).

Storage

Once the grain was clean it had to be stored in a dry, pest-proof place. Storage jars of earthenware, dating for instance from the eleventh century BC, were found abundantly at Ai, and were probably sufficient for small quantities. Larger amounts were stored in dry subterranean cisterns or in 'barns'. The latter (Gk. *apotheke*), were probably of lath and plaster construction suitable for the storage of fruit and vegetables and sometimes of grain.

Since grain was exacted by the authorities as tax, large silos were necessary in the residences of the district governors. Massive sunken granaries have been found at Megiddo, Hazor and elsewhere. Store-cities are several times mentioned in the Bible; they were essential in times of war and as a precaution against possible siege. Thus 2 Chronicles 17:12–13 records how 'Jehoshaphat ... built in Judah fortresses and store-cities, and he had great stores in the cities of Judah'. Later, Herod the Great stored food in his refuge of Masada, which was still in good condition nearly a century later when the Jews were besieged there (p. 55).

Grain was such a familiar article of commerce that dry measures of capacity were frequently derived from receptacles commonly used for it. Thus a 'donkey load' of cereal became the measure of one *homer* or *cor*, equivalent to about 220 litres (about 48 imp. gals). There were ten *ephahs* to the homer, and each ephah therefore had a capacity of 22 litres (about 5 imp. gals). An ephah was subdivided into tenths (*omers*). A person could hide in an ephah receptacle, while an omer bowl was used to collect manna. In the New Testament the bushel (under which one does not hide a light: Matthew 5:15; Mark 4:21; Luke 11:33), was a container for measuring a bushel of cereals, equal to 8.75 litres (about 2 imp. gals).[12]

Although the straw and chaff are waste products of threshing and winnowing, straw has its own uses as bedding. Even as early as Genesis we read of Laban providing 'straw and provender for the camels' (Genesis 24:32); it was also used as bedding for asses (Judges 19:19) and for horses (1 Kings 4:28).

The most famous use for straw is, of course, for bricks. Oppressed by their Egyptian taskmasters, the Hebrew slaves had to produce the same number of mud-bricks when no straw was provided as they had done before (Exodus 5). Chopped straw or stubble helps to bind the mud together, but it should be mentioned that there are numerous instances of Egyptian sun-dried bricks which never contained straw, and one should not assume that all such bricks were necessarily made by the Hebrews! Straw is only really necessary in brick-making when the proportion of fine grain clay to sand is rather low. Surprisingly, the binding action is principally a chemical one, since the straw decays and releases acid which increases plasticity. The use of straw for similar reasons in pottery is very ancient, too, for ware containing it has been found in Jericho (stratum IX), dating from as early as the Neolithic period, during the fifth millennium BC.

Corn in Egypt

Many claims have been made for the germination of 3000-year-old wheat grains from Egyptian tombs. Popular opinion is still inclined to believe these stories, although there is no scientific evidence that 'mummy wheat' has ever sprouted. In fact, most of the seeds of numerous kinds found in the tombs were in a poor state of preservation and extremely dry or even carbonized. There can be little doubt that any grains which have produced healthy plants were cunningly introduced into the tombs or somehow switched with the ancient grains.

Many species of plants have been scientifically tested for the longevity of their seeds and several long-term experiments have been carried out. Some plant seeds are known to lose completely their ability to grow (that is, their viability) after a few

Left: Mud bricks with binding straw; Yemen 1975.

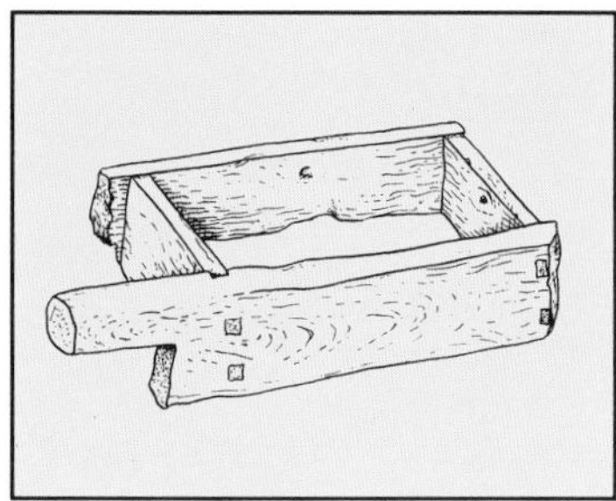

Right: A wooden mould for brick-making in Egypt; Kahun, 17th dynasty. (Manchester Museum.)

Far right: A modern demonstration of grinding grain on a saddle quern into flour; Ragab Pharaonic Village.

weeks. Yet seeds of other species, such as beans, remain viable for years, while seeds of weeds infesting cultivated ground may germinate erratically over many years, much to the grief of the farmer.[13]

Although the dry atmosphere of the Egyptian tombs has preserved in a remarkably complete state most of the objects hidden in them, living seeds rapidly become too dry to germinate. Inside a seed the 'germ', which is the living embryo, is dormant, with the life processes continuing at a greatly reduced rate. But a very small amount of moisture is essential to this life. In any event, protoplasm (the living contents of cells) ages in a way we cannot fully explain and there comes a time when life ceases altogether and it is incapable of reproducing itself.

OUR DAILY BREAD

Perhaps the simplest way of preparing cereals for eating is by roasting the grains on a hot stove or on a flat piece of iron. The fresh, not fully dried, seed is preferable. This parched grain (Heb. *galah*, meaning 'roasted') is referred to several times in the Bible. Boaz offered some parched barley to Ruth in the harvest-field itself (Ruth 2:14). David took an ephah of parched grain to his brothers when the men of Israel confronted Goliath and the Philistine army in the valley of Elah (1 Samuel 17:17). Later, parched corn was amongst the provisions given to David and his men when they fled from Absalom (2 Samuel 17:28). Clearly, it was a very common food in the Near East, and is known from ancient Egyptian and Assyrian records, too.

Before true bread can be made, flour has to be prepared. In Old Testament times the grains were rubbed out on a saddle quern or pounded with a pestle in a mortar:[14] 'Crush a fool in a mortar with a pestle along with crushed grain' says Proverbs 27:22, 'yet his folly will not depart from him.' The rotating quern appears to have been introduced later, and it was certainly widely used by the Greek period. Coarse, stone-ground flour of ancient times usually included a considerable quantity of grit. Preserved examples of Egyptian bread even glisten from the reflected particles, hence it is no wonder that molar teeth were often severely worn down!

Several kinds of bread were baked in every home as the 'daily bread' (Matthew 6:11; Heb. *qemach*), which was flour mixed with water, salt and leaven. Leaven, or yeast, was not added for unleavened bread, which often took the form of wafers (Heb. *raqiq*), probably like the delicious flat bread, *pitta*, still commonly served in Mediterranean countries.[15] They were cooked on hot flat stones or metal sheets. The dough was kneaded in special shallow troughs of wood or pottery such as those referred to in Exodus 12:34 (see also Jeremiah 7:18). If thick loaves were required they were baked on the walls of brick ovens. Such loaves were of wheat, as in the Tabernacle (Exodus 25:30) or barley, such as the five small loaves carried by the lad at the feeding of the five thousand (John 6:9).

Before baking took place it was necessary to allow time for the leaven to make the dough rise (Hosea 7:4). Leaven (Heb. *chametz*, *seor*, Gk. *zyme*) is yeast, a simple, single-celled fungus (*Saccharomyces cerevisae*). It was obtained from a portion of unsalted dough left from a previous mixing, which was then thoroughly kneaded with the new dough. The purpose of leaven is to aerate the dough by fermentation to make a less stodgy loaf. Carbon dioxide gas given off during fermentation leaves numerous small holes which greatly improve the texture of the baked loaf. A small amount of alcohol is also produced which is rapidly dispersed during baking. The process of fermentation breaks down sugar by the action of bacteria on the yeast. In new dough, however, there is no free sugar in the starchy flour. It is only when the starch in old dough has been converted by other decaying organisms into sugar that fermentation can proceed. (Nowadays sugar is mixed with yeast to hasten the action.)

This association of decay and fermentation with leaven, like corruption and sin, may explain the prohibition of its use in certain Hebrew offerings, and is dealt with elsewhere (p. 93). The symbolic evil of leaven was taken up by Jesus when he warned the disciples to beware of the 'leaven' of the Pharisees and Sadducees (Matthew 16:6). However, on another occasion he likened the action of yeast in dough to the development of the Kingdom of God (Matthew 13:33). During the Passover Festival, the Feast of Unleavened Bread lasted seven days, commemorating the hasty departure of the Hebrews from bondage in the land of Egypt (Deuteronomy 16:3). This feast is still kept, and it is frequently referred to in both the Old Testament (Numbers 9:11; Ezra 6:22, etc.), and the New Testament (Luke 22:1; Acts 12:3).

Left: An Arab-style bread oven constructed at the Ragab Pharaonic Village.

The importance of the grain (corn) crop in ancient times may be judged from the fact that famine usually resulted from the failure of the corn, due to drought in the uncertain Mediterranean climate. Even Egypt, which was not directly dependent on rain, had its famines when the Nile flood failed (Genesis 47). Of the trio grain, wine and oil, frequently associated with one another in the Scriptures, grain was the most important. It was so much the staple food that in Ezekiel we read of the Lord threatening to stretch out his hand against a sinful land 'and break its staff of bread and send famine upon it' (Ezekiel 14:13; see also Haggai 1:10–11).

Famine was caused all too frequently by the ravages of war and siege when the bread supply failed. On such occasions the price of grain – the raw material for home-baked bread – gives a good indication of prevailing conditions. For example, at the lifting of the siege of Samaria 'a measure of fine meal was sold for a shekel, and two measures of barley for a shekel' – still a high price, but no doubt lower than during the siege, if any had been available. It is interesting to note here the price differential between fine meal of wheat (presumably) and barley – a differential also recognized in famine conditions in Revelation 6:6, 'a quart [Gk. *choinix*; measure KJV] of wheat for a denarius, and three quarts of barley for a denarius'.

Beer

Cereals, especially barley, were used for brewing beer – the strong drink of the Bible (Heb. *sekar*). Albright (1949) points out that the frequency of beer jugs as well as wine craters in excavations of Philistine habitation in Palestine gives a useful confirmation of the biblical impression that the Philistines were 'mighty carousers'. The jugs were fitted with strainers similar to the holes pierced in modern tea-pots, to prevent the beer drinker from swallowing barley husks. When beer is produced, yeast is used to ferment the barley which has been partly germinated. Germination converts the starch into sugars, as described above, which are themselves converted into alcohol and carbon dioxide.

The cereal offering

Fine quality flour (Heb. *solet*) was required for the Israelite meal[16] offering and precise details are given in the Old Testament. For instance: 'When any one brings a cereal offering as an offering to the Lord, his offering shall be of fine flour; he shall pour oil upon it, and put frankincense on it' (Leviticus 2:1). But 'for a sin offering; he shall put no oil upon it, and shall put no frankincense on it' (Leviticus 5:11). Likewise there were commandments concerning the use of leaven in the offerings:

'And this is the law of the sacrifice of peace offerings which one may offer to the Lord. If he offers it for a thanksgiving, then he shall offer with the thank offering unleavened cakes mixed with oil, unleavened wafers spread with oil, and cakes of fine flour well mixed with oil. With the sacrifice of his peace offerings for thanksgiving he shall bring his offering with cakes of leavened bread' (Leviticus 7:11–13).

Leviticus 2 laid down the law that leaven and honey shall not be in the cereal offering intended for burning. The meal offering should always be salted, and those of first-fruits were to be of crushed new grain with oil and frankincense to be burnt as an offering to the Lord. The manner of making the offerings is described in Leviticus 6 and 7. Fine flour was also used in combination with animal sacrifices as specified in, for example, Exodus 29:40, Numbers 28:12; 29:3, 4. Occasionally the corn for the meal is specified, such as barley in cereal offering for jealousy (Numbers 5:15) and fine wheat flour for the wave offering (Exodus 29: 2, 23).

Above: Bread on sale in the Old City of Jerusalem.

This is not the place, however, to deal exhaustively with these Hebrew offerings of the Old Covenant, even though they touch on botanical aspects. They were part of the solemn ritual and service to God and the reader who is interested in following the details of Hebrew sacrifices and offerings is referred to the admirable article in *The Illustrated Bible Dictionary.*[17]

Bread of the Presence, Bread of the Passover and the Bread of Life

Akin to the cereal offering were the loaves continually displayed in the tabernacle. These twelve loaves – presumably one for each of the tribes – were known as the showbread or the bread of the presence of God (Exodus 25:30). They were set in two rows, with frankincense, on a special table. Each loaf was surprisingly large, being made from two-tenths of an ephah of fine flour, which works out at over four litres (almost 1 imp. gal.) of flour. No wonder David and his men were satisfied with the showbread obtained from the priest, in their flight from Saul (1 Samuel 21:1–6)! According to the Law, however, the bread was only allowed to be eaten by the priests in the Holy Place when they changed the loaves each sabbath day (Leviticus 24:5–9).

Bread was of central significance in the Jewish religion. We have already referred to the unleavened bread eaten at the Passover, reminding the Jews of the flight from Egypt, and above, to the ever-present Showbread. Jesus himself took up this imagery, proclaiming 'I am the bread of life: he who comes to me shall not hunger, and he who believes in me shall never thirst' (John 6:35); and in the upper room inaugurating the Lord's Supper by breaking the Passover bread with the words 'Take, eat; this is my body' (Matthew 26:26).

---

[1] Heb. *chittah*, Gk. *sitos*; also *dagan* and *bar* in the sense of corn or grain.

[2] Botanically the chaff segments of grass flowers are called glumes. The unit of harvesting was therefore the whole spikelet of several flowers. Such invested grains are usually called *hulled*.

[3] For readers unfamiliar with chromosomes a word of explanation may be necessary. Each living plant and animal cell has a certain number of pairs of minute sausage-shaped bodies called chromosomes (from Gk. *chroma*; stain or colour, as they stain heavily in prepared microscope slides) which carry in them the genetic characters of its own species. In the male and female reproductive cells (i.e. in the pollen grain and ovule respectively in plants) the process of meiosis halves the number of chromosomes, and the original number is restored when the sex cells unite on fertilization. Each of the ordinary cells of einkorn contains fourteen chromosomes (i.e. seven pairs), except the reproductive cells in the flowers, each of which has seven single ones, and it is termed a *diploid* wheat. Emmer wheat, however, has twenty-eight chromosomes and as this is four times the basic number of seven it is called a *tetraploid*. Bread wheat, with forty-two chromosomes, is a *hexaploid*. (The reproductive cells of einkorn, emmer and bread wheats have seven, fourteen and twenty-one chromosomes respectively.) Scientific understanding of inheritance via chromosomes sheds light on Genesis 1:11: 'let the earth put forth vegetation, plants yielding seed, and fruit trees bearing fruit in which is their seed, each according to its kind'. Each species has continuity of its hereditary composition and widely separate species cannot turn into something else, as Jesus (Luke 6:44) and James (3:12) both knew.

[4] Unfortunately einkorn wheat (*T. monococcum*) is sometimes called *small spelt*, a practice not recommended owing to its possible confusion with true spelt.

[5] 1 Kings 4:28.

[6] Heb. *dochan* (Ezekiel 4:9) – *pannag* (Ezekiel 27:17) respectively, but on linguistic grounds *pannag* actually refers to unripe figs, rather than the common millet (*Panicum miliaceum*), a small annual grass with tiny grain used for bread and porridge. Stol (1979) considers *pannag* not to be a cereal but the resin galbanum from *Ferula* species (p. 142).

[7] Not only cereals were sown broadcast, as Isaiah says: 'Does he who ploughs for sowing plough continually? does he continually open and harrow his ground? When he has levelled its surface, does he not scatter dill [fitches KJV], sow cummin, and put wheat in rows and barley in its proper place, and spelt as the border?' (Isaiah 28: 24–26). The RSV reference to wheat in 'rows' should not, I think, be taken in the modern sense of single drills but rather as patches between other crops. However, recent experiments with ancient farming techniques at Butser Archaeological Farm in southern England show that harrowing to cover the seed after sowing tends to set the grains in rows! The vaguer rendering of the KJV seems better.

[8] This is similar to the action of saliva in our mouth which breaks down by enzymes carbohydrates, such as starch, into simple sugars, such as glucose.

[9] The translators of the KJV used the word 'tares' which in seventeenth-century England were wild vetches (*Vicia*) of cornfields. In Palestine the Syrian scabious (*Cephalaria syriaca*) is closely associated with grain crops so it has been suggested as the weed of this parable. Many other plants have been mentioned as possibilities, and a very interesting study on the subject is being pursued by Dr W. van der Zweep of Holland, who has found that *zizania* is rendered in different languages as one of the worst local weeds (van der Zweep, 1984).

[10] R. A. Cole (*The Illustrated Bible Dictionary* 1:307) notes that 'white' in this verse literally means 'gleaming'; the Greek language is rich in words contrasting light and shade rather than actual colours.

[11] The stamping of the soil prior to threshing is referred to allegorically in Jeremiah 51:33: 'the daughter of Babylon is like a threshing floor at the time when it is trodden; yet a little while and the time of her harvest will come'. More recent sites are paved.

[12] Latin *modius*; the British bushel has about twice the capacity.

[13] Quite exceptional were the weed seeds which germinated after being buried for about 1700 years, associated with datable remains unearthed in 1965 during Danish archaeological excavations. Prior to that find the record was held by 300-year-old seeds of Indian Lotus (*Nelumbo nucifera*) seeds which were germinated after being found at the bottom of a lake in Manchuria. Russian scientists claim that they have been able to raise vines to maturity from grape seeds which had lain underground in sealed amphoras for many hundreds of years. They were planted in Georgia in about 1960 when the vessels were excavated by archaeologists on the Black Sea coast of the Caucasus. A claim has been made for the germination of arctic lupin seeds estimated to be 10,000–15,000 years old, found in 1954 in frozen Alaskan deposits! Although the information given by A. E. Porsild, C. R. Harrington and G. A. Mulligan (in *Science* 158: 113, 1967) is convincing, it has been challenged by Prof. H. Godwin of Cambridge in *Nature* 220: 708–9, 1968) and the matter must remain open for the present.

[14] Both these methods are still widely practised in remoter parts of Africa, such as Northern Nigeria, where I have seen the women simply rub their guinea corn with a rock on a boulder – a tedious, back-breaking occupation – and pound grain with a large pestle and mortar. Crushed corn for eating is *seber* in Old Testament Hebrew.

[15] This thin type of bread probably arose because of a common use of flour from the emmer and hard wheats, which lack the adhesive property of gluten and do not enable proper dough to be made.

[16] 'meal' or 'cereal' of later translations of the Bible, was unfortunately rendered 'meat' in the KJV, an archaic and now a misleading use of the word.

[17] *The Illustrated Bible Dictionary 3*: 1358–68.

Bibliography

Barton, L. V., *Seed Preservation and Longevity* (London, Leonard Hill, 1961), pp. 4–6.

Bor, N. L., *Flora of Iraq* (Baghdad, Ministry of Agriculture, 1968): vol. 9: wheat, pp. 194–208; barley, pp. 244–57.

Dixon, D. M. 'A Note on the Cereals in Egypt', in P. J. Ucko and G. W. Dimbleby (eds), *The Domestication and Exploitation of Plants and Animals* (London, Duckworth, 1969), pp. 131–42.

Godwin, H., 'Evidence for the longevity of seeds', *Nature* (London, 1968) 220:708-9.

Harlan, J. R., and Zohary, D., 'Distribution of Wild Wheats and Barley', *Science* (Washington, 1966), 153:1074–80.

Helbaek, H., 'Commentary on the Phylogenesis of *Triticum* and *Hordeum*', *Economic Botany* (New York, 1966), 20: 350–60.

Hillman, G. C., 'Traditional Husbandry and Processing of Archaic Cereals in Recent Times', *Bulletin on Sumerian Agriculture* (Cambridge, 1984, 1985): 1:114–52, 2:2:1–31.

Hopf, M., 'Plant Remains and Early Farming in Jericho', in P. J. Ucko and G. W. Dimbleby (eds), *The Domestication and Exploitation of Plants and Animals* (London, Duckworth, 1969), pp. 355–9.

Porsild, A. E. , Harrington, C. R., and Mulligan, G. A., *Science* (Washington, 1967) 158:113.

Staudt, 'The Origin of Cultivated Barleys: a discussion', *Economic Botany* (New York, 1961), 15:205–12.

Stearn, W. T, 'The Origin and Late Development of Cultivated Plants', *Journal Royal Horticultural Society* (London, 1965), 90:279–91, 322–40.

Stol, M., *On Trees, Mountains and Millstones in the Ancient Near East* (Leiden, Ex Oriente Lux, 1979), pannag, pp. 68–71.

Storke, J., and Teague, W. D., *A History of Milling: Flour for Man's Bread* (Minneapolis, 1979).

Youngman, B. J., 'Germination of Old Seeds', *Kew Bulletin* (London, 1952), 6:423–6.

Zeuner, F. E. , 'Cultivation of Plants', in C. Singer, E. J. Holmyard, and A. R. Hall (eds), *A History of Technology* (Oxford University Press, 1954), pp. 353–75.

Zohary, D., 'The Progenitors of Wheat and Barley in Relation to Domestication and Agricultural Dispersals in the Old World', in P. J. Ucko and G. W. Dimbleby (eds), *The Domestication and Exploitation of Plants and Animals* (London, Duckworth, 1969), pp. 47–66.

—. 'Origins of South-West Asiatic Cereals: wheat, barley', in P. H. Davis, P. C. Harper, and I. C. Hedge (eds), *Plant Life of South-West Asia* (Edinburgh Botanical Society, 1971), pp. 235–47.

—. 'The Origin of Cultivated Cereals and Pulses in the Near East, *Chromosomes Today* (New York, John Wiley, 1973), 4:307–20.

Zweep, W., van der, 'Linguistic, artistic and folklore aspects of tares in the biblical parable', in R. Vickery (ed.), *Plant Lore Studies* (London, Folklore Society, 1984).

9. Grapes and Wine

'I am the true vine, and my Father is the vinedresser.' (John 15:1.)

Perhaps no biblical plant so typifies the land and its people as does the vine. Vineyards, vines and wines are mentioned throughout the Bible. The first vineyard encountered is that planted by Noah after the flood (Genesis 9:20), presumably in the Mount Ararat region. Remarkably, it is in this very area, near the southern end of the Caspian Sea, that many botanists regard the cultivated grape as having arisen from its wild ancestors. Later we find vines (Heb. *gephen*) and vineyards (Heb. *kerem*) frequently mentioned in the Scriptures; the Promised Land was to yield the famous trio of grain, wine and oil (Deuteronomy 7:13). Solomon established many vineyards, especially at En-Gedi (Song of Solomon 1:14). The prophet Isaiah must have known vines and vineyards very well since he often referred to them figuratively, as we shall see. To Zechariah a fruiting vine was a symbol of peace (8:12) and a place under which to sit peacefully (3:10).

Extra-biblical evidence of the vine in Palestine comes from Egyptian sources. For instance, the soldiers of Pharaoh Pepi I felled vines, as well as fig trees, during the campaign in 2375 BC. In more tranquil times Palestinian wines were imported into Egypt, usually as tribute from a subservient people. For example, during the Egyptian Eighteenth Dynasty, in about 1360 BC, while the Hebrews were still in captivity, records relate how wine was obtained as tribute from the Isle of Ruad (then known as Arvad) off the Phoenician coast, as well as from 'Djahi' and from 'Retenu', the Egyptian names for Palestine and Syria. In the same period, Tutankhamun's tomb was furnished with wine from the royal vineyards in the Nile Delta (Hepper, 1990).

In the palace at Nineveh, beautiful stone reliefs of the seventh century BC depict grapevines in Ashurbanipal's garden. These reliefs, now in the British Museum, show the vines twined round a tree, said to be the earliest example of this method of training vines that was in common use by Roman times (Albenda, 1974). Any modern visitor to excavated Pompeii in Italy will see wine shops at many a street corner, with marble counters into which great flagons were let; and a large vineyard has been excavated near the town (Jashemski, 1973).

Below: A vineyard at the foot of Tel Lachish, with the grape vines (*Vitis vinifera*) supported on metal poles for clean table grapes (March 1987).

VINEYARDS

Jesus described in a parable a vineyard in Palestine during New Testament times (Matthew 21:33): 'There was a householder who planted a vineyard, and set a hedge around it, and dug a wine press in it, and built a tower'. It differed little from that described by Isaiah in the Old Testament. In both cases a protective hedge or wall, a convenient wine-press and a watchtower were necessary: 'My beloved had a vineyard on a very fertile hill. He digged it and cleared it of stones, and planted it with choice vines; he built a watchtower in the midst of it, and hewed out a wine vat in it' (Isaiah 5:1–2).

In Samaria today old, and now disused, terraces have been studied by Professor Shimon Applebaum (1978). During a visit with him he showed me that the stones cleared from the ground had been used to build the terrace walls thicker than necessary in order to use up the surplus stones. Yet more stones were piled on rock outcrops, and some had been used for the towers that had long since collapsed. But in Judea, I was able to enter beehive-towers on terraces still maintained as orchards and vineyards.

Although these towers date from well after Isaiah's time, their function remains the same. The vinedresser or manager would take his family there shortly before the grape harvest, in order to protect the fruit from animal and human thieves. There would probably also be temporary booths or leafy shelters (Isaiah 1:8), but in the heat of

Left: An old watchtower in Judea used to protect vines, olives and other crops at fruiting times (June 1977).

the day the thick stone walls of the single-roomed tower, where the watchers lived, kept the interior remarkably cool. According to measurements taken by Dr Zwi Ron the inside air temperature keeps 5°C (11°F) lower than that outside – and differences of up to 13°C (28°F) have been recorded.

Nearby was a great cistern hewn out of the ground and lined with stone and plaster. It was filled by run-off rainwater from the hillside that was first diverted to a simple sedimentation tank from which the cleaner water overflowed into the pit. Shallow wine-presses are often seen on the terraces where the fresh fruit could quickly be trodden by bare feet. The expressed juice drained from the pulp into the vat for fermentation (see p. 101).

Constant attention to the maintenance of the vineyard is necessary, since failure to prune and hoe makes the vines yield sour or 'wild grapes', and the vineyard (in Isaiah 5:7, symbolic of ancient Israel), deserved no further tending. Hoeing between the rows in a vineyard is essential to keep the weeds down, or 'briers and thorns shall grow up' (Isaiah 5:6) which would compete with the vines for moisture and hinder their growth.

Much of the maintenance, as well as the planting in Old Testament times, would have been in the hands of women (Proverbs 31:16; Song of Solomon 1:6). In Jeremiah's day, when Nebuchadnezzar sacked Jerusalem and took the wealthier people captive to Babylon, only the poorest were left to tend the vineyards (Jeremiah 52:16). From Jesus' parables we learn that landlords had to hire labourers to work in their vineyards (Matthew 20:1–16), or they were let out to tenants (Matthew 21:33–41; Luke 20:9–16). Fathers also expected their sons to help with the work (Matthew 21:28–31). The Law laid down that it was permitted to eat grapes from one's neighbour's vines, but not to gather them into a container (Deuteronomy 23:24). Moreover grape-gatherers must not glean afterwards, in order to leave some for the poor and needy (Deuteronomy 24:21).

Irrigation

Isaiah shows his knowledge of the importance of water to the vine and viticulture when he writes: 'A pleasant vineyard, sing of it! I, the Lord, am its keeper; every moment I water it' (Isaiah 27:2–3). Ezekiel also refers to the need of water by the vine in his allegory (Ezekiel 17, and 19:10).

Grapevines need abundant water during the winter so that the soil is thoroughly wet when the leaves appear and the shoots elongate in spring. Should available soil water be exhausted before growth is completed, serious damage can result. Prolonged wilting may be irreversible and, if it is allowed to go too far, the growing portions shrivel up and growth ceases. Insufficient ground-water causes a change in the colour of the vine plant and results in the dropping of the lower leaves. Hence the hills are terraced to prevent rainwater run-off, as well as to stop soil erosion. If drought conditions continue, the vines either produce smaller grapes, or some of the unripe grapes may drop, a condition that is more noticeable during the period after flowering and setting. Irrigation of vines needs to be done before any of these drought symptoms appear, in order to ensure a good crop. However, they should not be watered late in the season after a drought, or new growth will be stimulated which would exhaust food reserves in the plant, without the new leaves being able to restore them before the onset of winter.

The roots through which the water is absorbed and transported are extensive and often penetrate to

Right: A grapevine in winter after severe pruning. The new growth in spring will trail over the rock and onto the ground (Gilo, March 1985).

depths of 2–4 m (6–13 ft) in light soils, although most of them will be found in the upper 0.6–2 m (2–6 ft) of soil. Some roots are said to have been traced to a depth of 12 m (40 ft) (Winkler, 1962)! In shallow, stony ground, such as is encountered in the hill country of Judea, root growth is either greatly limited or else the roots must penetrate fissures in the rock in order to obtain moisture. Roots must maintain active growth if they are to develop the minute root hairs just behind the tip. As the root grows in length, the root hairs furthest away from the tip shrivel up as corky tissue covers the root; and they are replaced by new hairs developing from the younger cells nearer the tip. It is through these root hairs that moisture is absorbed; if the roots are damaged so that the young tips are lost, the plant cannot obtain sufficient water to replace that lost through the leaves, and wilting results.

Pruning

Pruning of the vines takes place during winter dormancy, and, except for side shoots, not at the height of development (Isaiah 18:5). The previous season's growth is cut back and the long leafless twigs are used for fuel (John 15:6). Pruning helps to ensure that the fruit is of good quality, for otherwise during the following season there would be too many clusters of fruit to be nourished by the roots, resulting in only poor grapes. Jesus was familiar with these principles when, after likening himself to a vine, he said: 'Every branch of mine that bears no fruit, he takes away, and every branch that does bear fruit he prunes, that it may bear more fruit' (John 15:2). There is a very close parallel between these sayings and the following excerpt on pruning vines from a modern manual:

'If the vine seems weak it should be pruned more severely than the year before – that is, leave fewer fruit buds – in order to strengthen it by diverting more of its energy from crop production to growth and to replenishing the store of reserve food materials. [In subsequent years] the grapes will be of good quality and the vine will be invigorated' (Winkler, 1962).

In Palestine vines are commonly severely pruned each year to produce short erect trunks, so-called 'head-pruned' vines, for wine production. The spurs left on the trunk after pruning produce the cane and flower clusters during the summer. Peasant farmers who cannot afford supports for the vines simply prop up the trunks on a pile of stones and let the branches trail on the ground, as they did in biblical times. Even in commercial vineyards wine grapes are often unsupported, although supports are provided in varying degrees of complexity to ensure clean fruit for the table. Different methods of pruning are also adopted to encourage the formation of better fruit. One system, cordon-pruning, develops an upright vine trunk about a metre (3 ft) high, with usually two horizontal branches forming a letter T. Sometimes several tiers of lateral branches are developed on either side of the trunk, with spurs annually sprouting the slender canes bearing flowers.

Propagation

The use of seeds to propagate vines is inadvisable, since they usually produce seedlings that are inferior to the parent plant, and there is no means of knowing the fruiting quality of the new plant until it has reached maturity. Propagation of grapevines is usually by means of cuttings and, to a lesser extent, by layers or grafts.

Cuttings are taken in winter from shoots formed the previous summer on good, well-grown vines. They are about 30 cm (1 ft) long with four or five buds, and with the lower end cut just below one of the buds. When the cuttings have been inserted in moist ground for some weeks, a layer of new tissue (the callus) will form over the cut end and this produces young roots. Once the roots have started to grow, in the early spring, the sap will flow and stimulate development of the aerial buds and unfolding of the leaves.

In biblical times too, cuttings would have been the normal method of propagation. We see from Isaiah 5:1, 2 that careful selection of the best varieties of vine was made: 'My beloved had a vineyard ... and planted it with *choice* vines' (Heb. *soreq*).

Little foxes and other pests[1]

The only pests of the vine mentioned in the Bible, apart from the neighbour's domestic cattle and sheep (Exodus 22: 5; Jeremiah 12:10), are wild animals: 'the little foxes that spoil the vineyards' (Song of Solomon 2:15) or: 'The boar from the forest ravages it, and all that move in the field feed on it' (Psalm 80:13). Foxes are fond of fruit, and by running along the rows of vines they would be liable to damage the trailing grapes. Wild boar, deer and other herbivores were even more likely to feed upon an unprotected vineyard. In Malachi 3:11 we find the promise to those who bring the full tithes, that the Lord 'will rebuke the devourer [margin: 'devouring locust'] for you, so that it will not destroy the fruits of your soil; and your vine in the field shall not fail to bear'. Perhaps the KJV throws more light on the last phrase: 'neither shall your vine cast her fruit before the time in the field'. Unripe grapes may be dropped if the vine is burnt or is too dry, or suffers from excessive heat or salinity.

Wild grapes

In Isaiah 5:2, 4 we find a reference to wild grapes, and Jeremiah similarly writes figuratively 'Yet I planted you [Israel] a choice vine, wholly of pure seed. How then have you turned degenerate and become a wild vine?' (Jeremiah 2:21). It is now thought that the 'wild grapes' and 'wild vine' (Heb. *beonshim*) in Isaiah 5:2, 4, would be better rendered as 'unripe', 'rotten' or even 'diseased' grapes. In that case, the Bible makes no mention of a really wild grape, which is hardly surprising since it is not truly wild in Palestine.

The wild plant (*Vitis sylvestris*) occurs from southern Europe to the Caspian and Himalayas. It has separate plants for male and female flowers, unlike the cultivated vines which have both sexes in the same flower. Wild vines have more seeds than cultivated ones, which may even be seedless.

BIOLOGY OF THE GRAPEVINE

Growth begins in the spring only when a mean daily temperature of 10°C (50°F) has been reached. As the weather becomes warmer, so the speed of growth accelerates until flowering time, after which the rate of growth decreases. Some six weeks after growth has started, flowering begins and fruit enlargement takes place rapidly. During July and August, the grapes are developing, but they are sour and set one's teeth on edge (Jeremiah 31:29; Ezekiel 18:2). They become ripe in the late summer, when harvesting takes place. As the grapes ripen the shoots stop growing, and by harvest time there is little or no new growth. The bark changes from green to a darker colour and the leaves are retained until after they too have changed colour (Winkler, 1962).

The long trailing branches of the vine carry numerous divided five-lobed leaves which develop on alternate sides of the shoot. Each flower cluster, like the tendrils, is opposite a leaf. In fact it is fairly clear that the tendrils are modified flowerless inflorescences, as there are many gradations between a complete inflorescence and a true tendril.

There are two kinds of buds on vines – the leaf buds and the fruit buds – as in many other woody plants. The leaf buds produce only elongated shoots bearing leaves and no flowers, while the fruit bud expands to produce two or three flower clusters opposite the fourth, fifth, or sixth leaf. The flowers and leaves are developed within the bud during its formation the previous autumn. Nearly all the flowers are bisexual and set fruit. The few flowers with male parts alone (staminate flowers) cannot, of course, produce fruit. At flowering time the green petals (the corolla) are shed in one piece as a little cap (the calyptra),

Above: Flowers of the grapevine (*Vitis vinifera*) and one inflorescence with a partial tendril.

Left: Growing grapevines with unsupported branches; the grapes will be used for wine rather than for the table.

Right: Mature grapes ready for picking.

while the five petal segments remain united at the top. The flowers open when the temperature rises to 16°C (61°F) or more, and after the calyptra has fallen the stamens spread out, shedding the pollen. It seems that the pollen of a flower is simply shed on to its own pistil to effect pollination. Sometimes insects transfer the pollen, but the flowers are inconspicuous and there is little nectar to attract them. The fragrance of vine flowers is very noticeable at certain times, and Solomon knew of it when he wrote that winter is past and 'the vines are in blossom; they give forth fragrance' (Song of Solomon 2:13). The grapes – black and green – ripen between July and October, depending on the site and variety.

Grapes and raisins

Vines were so abundant in ancient Palestine that grape seeds have been found in most, if not all, of the excavated sites. At Lachish, for instance, which was occupied for very many centuries, grapes were found in all the samples of seeds in both the Early Bronze Age and the Iron Age deposits (third and first millennia BC). Hans Helbaek, who investigated the plant remains there, concluded that the vine was commonly grown at Lachish, and that grapes were consumed with the daily meals (Helbaek, 1958). Grapes were eaten fresh at the time of harvest (Isaiah 65:21), and dried – as raisins – for eating at all times of the year.

Nowadays raisins are usually prepared from seedless grapes, which were probably unknown in biblical times, although two varieties (Sultania and Kishmish) are certainly ancient and may go as far back as those days. What we know as the yellow 'sultana' is the dried grape of a seedless variety which, prior to drying in the sun, is dipped into a boiling solution of potassium carbonate or caustic soda (lye) with an emulsion of olive oil. It is quite possible that a similar process, using a solution of wood ash, was current in biblical days, a process which, according to Crowfoot and Baldensperger (1932), is still used by Arabs.

Little black raisins were a speciality of Corinth, hence our name 'currants' for them. Undoubtedly most of the raisins of ancient times were simply sun-dried surplus grapes, including the seeds, producing a larger muscat type of raisin. Grapes spread in the sun take two or three weeks to dry. If they are caught in an autumn shower at this stage, the raisins are spoilt, so a cover is available for spreading over the drying frames should rain threaten. Analysis of raisins shows that they have a rich supply of sugar, amounting to as much as 70 per cent of their weight. Such a high sugar content would rapidly revive a famished person such as the Egyptian fed on raisins by David's men (1 Samuel 30:12), and compressed cakes of raisins (Isaiah 16:7) are very sustaining (Song of Solomon 2:5).

Place-names

It is no wonder that many Palestinian place-names derive from local crops. When Joshua and Caleb spied out the land they brought back a huge bunch of grapes from the valley of Eshcol, which is the Hebrew for a cluster (Numbers 13:23). Their word for grape is *anab* (or *enab*) and a place of that name (Joshua 11:21) occurs near Hebron, where vines are still extensively grown on the terraced hillsides. Not far away is the valley of Soreq in which Delilah lived (Judges 16:4), *soreq* referring to the choice vine or the tendril of the vine. Mount Carmel has the meaning 'the hill of the vineyard of the Lord', and is well known for its wines (Goor, 1966 and 1968), although experts consider the ground too alkaline. Conversely, places sometimes gave their names to wines. The fragrant 'wine of Lebanon' was famous (Hosea 14:7) and the wine from Helbon near Damascus was sold in the market of Tyre (Ezekiel 27:18).

Symbolism of the vine

In the Old Testament the symbolism of the vine as the people of Israel is clearly shown in Psalm 80, where the writer reminds God that:

'Thou didst bring a vine out of Egypt;
thou didst drive out the nations and plant it.
Thou didst clear the ground for it;
it took deep root and filled the land.
The mountains were covered with its shade,
the mighty cedars with its branches;
it sent out its branches to the sea,
and its shoots to the River'
(Psalm 80:8–11).

Yet the psalmist questions the Lord for the violence that has apparently overtaken the nation which he still likens to a vine in a vineyard:

'Why then hast thou broken down its walls,
so that all who pass along the way pluck its fruit?
The boar from the forest ravages it,
and all that move in the field feed on it' (Psalm 80: 12–13).

Finally the psalmist implores God to tend his vine:

'Turn again, O God of hosts!
Look down from heaven, and see;
have regard for this vine,
the stock which thy right hand planted.
They have burned it with fire,

they have cut it down;
may they perish at the rebuke of thy countenance!'
(Psalm 80:14–16).

Jeremiah (6:9) saw the enemy, like grape-gatherers, gleaning Israel of everything. The prophet Hosea also likens Israel to a vine '... a luxuriant vine that yields its fruit'. Unfortunately, 'The more his fruit increased the more [pagan] altars he built' (Hosea 10:1).

Jesus' parable of the man who established a vineyard, and, at the grape harvest sent his servants and finally his son (typifying the prophets and the Messiah) to collect the fruit (Matthew 21:33–41), may be compared with the passage in Isaiah 5:7 where Israel is described as 'the vineyard of the Lord of hosts'. No doubt Jesus used the vineyard advisedly for his parable, since the vine is so frequently symbolic of Israel; a golden vine was placed over the entrance to Herod's temple in Jerusalem. Jesus' familiarity with it is shown when, speaking of the church, he said: 'I am the true vine and my Father is the vinedresser ... I am the vine, you are the branches' (John 15:1 ff.).

Wine

In wine-growing districts the grape harvest is a busy time, with baskets of juicy fruit contrasting with the dry, end-of-summer ground. In the less advanced areas loaded donkeys still carry the grapes to the vats as they have done for centuries past. Crushing the fruit with bare feet ensures that the bitter seeds are not broken. In a village in Portugal I recall seeing treaders at work up to their knees in blood-red juice crushing the grapes as more are loaded into the vats (Nehemiah 13:15; Isaiah 63:2; Revelation 14:20). In biblical Palestine vineyards typified the country and, as we have seen, small wine-presses were built alongside them to receive the fresh, ripe grapes. The angel in Revelation 14:17–19 is seen harvesting grapes with a sickle before throwing them into the great wine-press – here expressed in symbolic terms. As the juice ran from the crushed grapes it was collected in jars or stone-cut vats beside the press, which itself was often simply hewn out of the bed-rock.

Grape-juice, or must, ferments naturally, for it contains minute yeast organisms which break down the rich sugar content into alcohol and carbon dioxide.[2] Grapes maturing in hot climates have more sugar and less acid than those in cooler places. When there is a certain balance between the amount of sugar in the grapes and their acidity, then they are ready for wine-making. Should the fruit be injured during harvesting, however, this balance will be upset and decay organisms will spoil the wine.

After six weeks fermentation of the must, the new wine is left for another month while the sediment, or lees, collects at the bottom of the stone jars. The new wine (Heb. *tirosh*, Gk. *gleukos*) is decanted from the lees (Heb. *shemarim*). Jeremiah uses this for an illustration:

'Moab has been at ease from his youth and has settled on his lees; he has not been emptied from vessel to vessel, nor has he gone into exile; so his taste remains in him, and his scent is not changed' (Jeremiah 48:11).

The sediment consists not only of yeast but of pips, skins and stalks, to be thrown away. New wine in which the fermentation process may not be quite complete will continue to give off a certain amount of carbon dioxide gas. This explains why Jesus said: 'Neither is new wine put into old wineskins; if it is, the skins burst, and the wine is spilled, and the skins are destroyed; but new wine is put into fresh wineskins, and so both are preserved' (Matthew 9:17; also Luke 5:37). Hard old skins, unlike soft new ones, would not expand to make room for the carbon dioxide. The use of the word 'bottles' in KJV, instead of 'skins', makes this illustration more difficult to understand.

Long-term storage of wine, however, was in earthenware jars. Jars found in Egyptian tombs, such as Tutankhamun's, were carefully plugged with rushes or vine leaves, and a vent was sealed with a layer of mud after the last of the gas had escaped. Each jar was labelled, and often dated to record the year of vintage. Archaeologists find jar-handle stamps a valuable means of dating excavations and learning about contemporary trade routes.

Grapes were not the only fruit from which wine was prepared in Egypt and Palestine. The writer of the Song of Solomon wrote of 'spiced wine to drink, the juice of my pomegranates' (8:2). In ancient Egypt wines from palm sap, dates, figs and other fruits were also well known.

Noah succumbed to wine (Genesis 9:21); Jotham said 'it cheers gods and men' (Judges 9:13); the Nazirites (Numbers 6:3; Luke 1:15) and the Rechabites (Jeremiah. 35:5 ff.) abstained, and priests were forbidden wine when they officiated (Leviticus 10:9). Elsewhere in the Bible warnings against excess are given: 'be not among winebibbers' says Proverbs 23:20, and 'he who loves wine and oil will not be rich' (Proverbs 21:17). We are also told in the Old Testament that 'wine is treacherous' (Habakkuk 2:5), and that its effects are potentially disastrous (Proverbs 23:29-32; Jeremiah 13:12–14).

Yet wine was used as a disinfectant for wounds (Luke 10:34), and, mixed with water (Proverbs 9:2, 5), was the drink of the people in a hot and thirsty land. It was also a special drink at festival time: Nehemiah and Ezra told the people to drink 'sweet wine' to celebrate

Left: Harvesting grapes, treading them and bottling wine in ancient Egypt; a mural in the tomb of Nakht at Thebes, *c.* 1400 BC.

Right: The Seder meal at Passover in a Jewish family. During this meal wine is drunk.

their rediscovery of the Law (Nehemiah 8:10); and Jesus and his mother celebrated a wedding at Cana in Galilee where, when the wine ran out, he miraculously turned water into wine of better quality than that provided by the hosts (John 2:3–10).

In Old Testament times wine was used as a drink offering or libation to the Lord (Exodus 29:40; Numbers 28:14; 29:6) and similarly to the Egyptian 'queen of heaven' (Jeremiah 44:17). But in the New Testament we find the simple Jewish Passover meal transformed into the Lord's supper: 'Jesus took bread, and blessed, and broke it, and gave it to the disciples and said, "Take, eat, this is my body." And he took a cup, and when he had given thanks he gave it to them, saying, "Drink of it, all of you; for this is my blood of the covenant, which is poured out for many for the forgiveness of sins" ' (Matthew 26:26–28; see also 1 Corinthians 11:23 ff.).

Vinegar

Wine (Heb. *yayin*, or *sekar*; Gk. *oinos;* strong drink) can turn into vinegar (Heb. *chomets*, Gk. *oxos*) by the action of the bacterium *Acetobacter* in the presence of air. Acetic acid is produced and, providing it is not too strong, the result is a refreshing acidic drink, such as that taken by the harvesters and labourers in Ruth 2:14 (KJV). In New Testament times it was popular with the Roman army, who called it *posca.*

---

[1] Mention should be made of the greatest pest of vines, the insect *Phylloxera vastatrix,* and its repercussion on modern vineyards. This pest is an aphid, allied to the well-known greenfly, which lives on the roots of the vine. It is a native of North America and was, therefore, not known in the Old World until comparatively recently. In about 1860 it was introduced into France and rapidly eliminated some three-quarters of the French vines, reaching Palestine in 1890. As a result of these attacks, which have now spread to most areas of the world where the European vine is cultivated, vineyards are planted with vines grafted on to American species or are hybrids of vine with a natural immunity to phylloxera (Ordish, 1972).

[2] The yeast *Saccharomyces cerevisae* acts only on hexose sugars (glucose, fructose and mannose). Cane sugar with a larger molecule is first broken down by enzyme action to hexose before fermentation begins.

Bibliography

Albenda, P., 'Grapevines in Ashurbanipal's Garden', *Bulletin of the American Schools of Oriental Research* (Baltimore, 1974), 215:5–17, figs 1–15.

Applebaum, S., Dar, S., and Safari, Z., 'The Towers of Samaria', *Palestine Exploration Quarterly* (London, 1978), pp. 91–100.

Goor, A., 'History of the Grape-Vine in the Holy Land', *Economic Botany* (New York, 1966), 20:46.

Goor, A., and Nurock, M., *The Fruits of the Holy Land* (Jerusalem, Israel Universities Press, 1968): grape-vine, pp. 18–45.

Jashemski, W. F., 'The discovery of a large vineyard at Pompeii', *American Journal of Archaeology* (1973) 77:33-6.

Negruli, A. M., 'The Evolution of Cultivated Grapes', *Piroda* (1940), pp. 37–46. (Summary in *Plant Breeding Abstracts* [Cambridge, 1946], 16:220.)

Ordish, G., *The Great Wine Blight* (London, J. M. Dent and Sons, 1972).

Rainey, A. F., 'Wine from the Royal Vineyards', *Bulletin of the American Schools of Oriental Research* (Baltimore, 1982), 245:57–62.

Ron, Z., 'Agricultural Terraces in the Judean Mountains', *Israel Exploration Journal* (Jerusalem, 1961), 16:33–49; 111–12.

Vassilczenko, I. T., *Botanical Journal USSR* (Leningrad, 1964), 49:487–502.

Winkler, A. J., *General Viticulture* (University of Califo.nia Press, 1962).

10. The Olive Tree and its Oil

'His beauty shall be as the olive tree.'
(Hosea 14:6, KJV)

Clearly the olive tree was admired by the prophet Hosea. He must have been very familiar with the shady, grey-green trees that still abound in the Holy Land and elsewhere in the Mediterranean region. It has been said that the power of ancient Greece was made possible by the cultivation of the olive, which provided rich fruits from rocky countryside that could produce little else. Greek myths tell how a dove brought an olive twig from Phoenicia to Athens, where it was planted on the Acropolis to become their first olive tree. The Greeks dedicated the olive to their goddess Athena; it was symbolic of peace and prosperity; and olive leaves were used to crown Olympic champions. It seems, therefore, that the well-known association of the olive with the dove of peace owes as much to Greek mythology as to the biblical account of the dove returning to Noah's ark at the end of the flood (Genesis 8:11). Even so, the olive is one of the most important and symbolic plants mentioned in the Bible.

Here we trace the history of the olive tree, its cultivation and propagation, the harvesting of its fruit and the production of olive oil. Olive fruits provided the rich and poor alike with oil for cooking, lighting, cosmetics and medicine; while olives pickled in brine were an important food throughout the year. Also its hard, figured timber was used for special furniture, panelling and statues (1 Kings 6:23, 33), and its oil anointed prophets and kings (Judges 9:8–9). It was, with grain and wine, the third great product of the Promised Land (Deuteronomy 7:13).

THE OLIVE TREE

The olive (*Olea europaea*; Heb. *zayith*, Gk. *elaia*) is an evergreen tree usually about 5 m (16 ft) high, or much taller if unpruned. Young trees have a rather smooth silvery-grey bark, but with age the slender trunks become stout, fluted and knobbly. Many old trees actually develop holes in the sides of the trunks which themselves are hollow: the holes result from old side branches rotting away. The numerous branches form a dense, shady tree which is favoured by animals in the heat of the day.

An enormously spreading root system extends around each tree in order to absorb sufficient moisture in the dry conditions in which it normally grows. Hence the trees are well spaced out in the groves, being planted 11 m (36 ft) apart, although irrigated trees are much closer together. Wide spacing allows plenty of light to reach the crown for best fruit ripening.

Olive leaves are narrow and sharply pointed, grey-green on the upper surface and white on the underside owing to a complete covering of minute white scales, which help to keep down water loss from the tree. Flower buds develop among the leaves on the previous year's wood and they open in May. There are ten to forty flowers carried on each short inflorescence and the white flowers themselves are small with the parts in fours, but with only two stamens. Flowering begins when trees are at least five or

Left: An ancient olive tree in the Garden of Gethsemane.

Below: A small olive grove between Jerusalem and Bethlehem, with ploughed soil between the trees for cereal cultivation.

Above: Leafy olive shoots with flowers and fruits.

six years old and they are said to be at their best between forty and fifty years old, although many large ancient trees still bear regular crops.

A land of olive trees

The Israelites were promised many things for which they had not laboured, including vineyards and olive trees which they had not planted (Deuteronomy 6:11), thereby implying that olive cultivation was well established by the Canaanites at the time of the exodus in the thirteenth century BC. The Promised Land was to be 'a land of olive trees and honey' (Deuteronomy 8:8).

The hilly country of Samaria and the Shephelah is excellent for olives, but Judea around Hebron rises too high for successful cultivation. The olive tree thrives on hillsides, where drainage is better than in the valleys, and when the summer warmth ripens the fruit. However, for flower buds to form, a few degrees of frost or at least near-freezing temperatures are required during the winter. A hard frost will kill an olive tree, which requires an average annual temperature of 15°C (59°F), coupled with winter rainfall, to thrive. These conditions are met with in the Mediterranean region not far from the coast. Nowadays olives are grown successfully in Australia, California and other areas with this type of Mediterranean climate.

The olive groves of biblical times were usually quite small – we should call them orchards, rather than plantations – olives often dominating the gardens of those days.

Olive groves

The olive tree has been important in the Holy Land for so long that many place-names indicate the presence of olive groves, olive-presses or something to do with the oil. Sometimes the place-names are translated in the English Bible versions, as for example in Judges 15:5 which reads 'And when he had set the fire to the torches he let the [300] foxes [or jackals] go into the standing grain of the Philistines, and burned up the shocks and the standing grain, as well as the olive orchards'. According to Goor (1966), the last phrase should more properly remain as the Hebrew place-name Kerem Zayit, which means olive grove, and if he is correct, it is interesting that the animals apparently set fire to this village as well as to the corn. However, an olive grove could be burnt in the way described, as it was customary for cereals and other crops to be grown between the widely spaced trees.

The Mount of Olives

Undoubtedly the most famous locality embodying the name of the olive is the Mount of Olives, or Olivet. During my first visit to Jerusalem I stayed for a week in one of the hotels on its summit and had a fine view across the Kidron valley to the Old City. The hill is a flat-topped ridge with steep rocky sides, up which David and the people reluctantly trudged when Absalom tried to seize the throne (2 Samuel 15:30). Jesus frequently retreated there amongst its cool and shady trees, and even stayed there immediately before the Passover (Luke 21:37). After the Last Supper, 'he came out, and went, as was his custom, to the Mount of Olives' (Luke 22:39), 'and they went to a place which was called Gethsemane' (Mark 14:32) – which means oil-press. Today the traditional site of the garden of Gethsemane is full of ancient olive trees, and it is easy to imagine it as the place of the oil-press, to which the fruit was brought from the trees growing around about on the hillside.

The Mount of Olives is 830 m (2794 ft) high and is widely thought to have been the place of the ascension of Jesus. We read that the disciples returned to Jerusalem immediately after the ascension 'from the mount called Olivet' (Acts 1:12), although Luke (24:50) records that the disciples were led out by Jesus before the ascension as far as Bethany, which lies just beyond the Mount of Olives. In the Old Testament, Zechariah prophesied the coming day of the Lord.

'On that day his feet shall stand on the Mount of Olives which lies before Jerusalem on the east: and the Mount of Olives shall be split in two from east to west by a very wide valley; so that one half of the Mount shall withdraw northward, and the other half southward' (14: 3–4).

Much has been made of this passage through the years and Olivet is held in particular reverence, although largely for different reasons, by Jew and Christian alike.

Wild olives

The wild olive mentioned by Paul in Romans 11:17 is the oleaster (*Olea europaea* var. *sylvestris,* formerly *O. oleaster*).[1] This is a small tree or shrub common in the Mediterranean region, where it grows among oak *maquis* in rocky uncultivatable areas not far from the coast. Oleaster closely resembles the olive except that its fruit is smaller and the flesh is hardly oily. Turrill (1951) thought that the oleaster was a degenerate cultivated olive. Although there are relics of abandoned olive groves with degenerate cultivated olive trees, there are also real oleasters which D. Zohary and Spiegel-Roy (1975) consider to be truly wild and the ancestor of the olive. They remark on the early domestication of the olive, evident from the discoveries of seeds in ancient sites. One such excavation at Teleilat Ghassul, north of the Dead Sea, dates from the Chalcolithic period (3700–3500 BC), and the numerous olive stones found there were associated with cereals, dates and pulses, which were obviously cultivated in a region that could not support wild olive trees.

Another relative, and possible ancestor, of the cultivated olive, is *Olea europaea* subsp. *cuspidata* (formerly *O. africana*). I have seen these trees wild, high up on tropical east African mountains and in the Yemen, and it has a wide distribution across the Middle East to China. Another wild olive, *Olea europaea* subsp. *laperrinei,* occurs in the Sahara. This was the one favoured by Professor P. E. Newberry (1937) as the ancestor of the cultivated olive. He carried out an interesting archaeological investigation on the origin of the olive and its cultivation. He recalled how the ancient Egyptians hunted with throw-sticks made of olive wood. Their hieroglyph for an imported oil called *thnw* was a throw-stick sign together with one or three circular bowls like those traditionally used for the storage of olive oil. The country from which the oil came was called *Thnw*, oil-land. He went on to deduce from evidence of old grinders found in the Libyan Desert, and from another Egyptian hieroglyph meaning oil and representing such a grinder, that the region adjoining the Nile Delta on the west was the cradle of olive culture. Although olives are not grown there now, probably due to destruction of the trees by goats, and by military operations, and possibly to a change in climate, he regards that region as the original land of *Thnw* oil.

However, Lucas (1962) gives a salutary word of warning:

'References to olive trees, olives, and olive oil in translations of Egyptian texts are to be treated with caution and cannot be regarded as valid evidence for the early cultivation of the tree in Egypt, since in many cases it is the Egyptian words for the Moringa tree and its bean oil that have been incorrectly interpreted as olive. In fact the word for olive does not occur before the nineteenth dynasty, though a fragment of a mural painting of the eighteenth dynasty (fourteenth to sixteenth century BC*), shows part of a small olive tree with several olives growing on it.'*

Another picture of the same period shows a hand holding an olive twig which is bent under the weight of fruit. Cyril Aldred (1973) observes that the olive in this case substitutes the traditional bouquet usually offered to Akhenaten's sun disc god, Aten. So 'perhaps the olive, an exotic tree recently imported into Egypt, inspired the artist'. It is clear that the olive could never become widespread in Egypt itself, at least in the present climatic conditions, but this need not invalidate Newberry's thesis for the North African origin of olive culture.

Grafted olives

The grafting of cultivated olives upon wild ones has been practised in olive culture for a very long time. A traditional reason for grafting is the belief that the wild olive (or oleaster) is able to resist drought because of its taproot. However, there is no foundation for this theory. Numerous adult wild olive trees dug up in North Africa showed no trace of taproots. In fact it has been shown that the original roots of the olive tree, however it was propagated, are replaced by an entirely new system of roots which arise from the knobs which appear at the base of the trunk. These knobs (also called ovuli) are cut off and root easily to form new trees; leafy cuttings are also used. Grafting is, however, primarily a means of obtaining rapid propagation of a desirable cultivated variety of olive.

At first reading, the apostle Paul's argument in Romans (11: 17–24) about the wild and cultivated olive appears to be somewhat involved. He likens Israel, God's chosen people, to a cultivated olive tree, a symbol of spiritual richness, from which God has broken off some of the branches. In place of the Jews he has grafted in faithful Gentiles – here typified by the formerly useless wild olives (Gk. *agrielaios*) – to partake of the richness of the cultivated tree (Gk. *kallielaios*). Paul rightly regards this operation as 'contrary to nature', for one would expect the cultivated olive to be grafted upon the wild stock; by using this analogy he accentuates the richness of God's grace in the salvation of Gentiles.

Left: The Mount of Olives, Jerusalem. The Garden of Gethsemane lies to the left of the Church of All Nations (in the centre). Olive trees and date palms can be seen in the foreground; columnar cypress trees (*Cupressus sempervirens* var. *pyramidalis*) and Aleppo pines (*Pinus halepensis*) are planted on the opposite slope.

Above: Branches being lopped from an olive tree on the Mount of Olives.

Right: The same olive tree two years later, showing new growth.

Aged trees and new shoots

Olive trees are too valuable to be felled for fuel or timber like ordinary trees. Only when they are old and decrepit may they be felled, and then usually at ground level with the roots intact, for even an ancient tree will sprout fresh suckers from its base. Olive trees are often rejuvenated in this way by vigorous pruning, for lopping large branches encourages new growth that will bear fruit. It may have been the olive that Job had in mind when he observed:

'For there is hope for a tree, if it be cut down, that it will sprout again, and its shoots will not cease. Though its root grow old in the earth, and its stump die in the ground, yet at the scent of water it will bud and put forth branches like a young plant' (Job 14:7–9).

How long can an olive tree live? As they are invariably hollow, it is impossible to count the annual growth rings on aged trees. Present-day visitors to Gethsemane will see huge gnarled trees with trunks 2 m (6 ft) in diameter and be assured, as I was by enthusiastic guides, that they are 2700 years old! Were these trees seen by Jesus as he walked on the Mount of Olives and in the Garden of Gethsemane? They are certainly many centuries old, but we do not know for sure even whether the traditional site of the Garden is really the one that is now recognized as such. We do know, however, that Titus Vespasian destroyed all the trees in that area during the siege of Jerusalem in AD 70. To Jews, the felling of this kind of tree was against Mosaic Law, which laid down that even

'When you besiege a city for a long time, making war against it in order to take it, you shall not destroy its trees by wielding an axe against them; for you may eat of them, but you shall not cut them down. Are the trees in the field men that they should be besieged by you? Only the trees which you know are not trees for food you may destroy and cut down that you may build siege-works against the city that makes war with you, until it falls' (Deuteronomy 20:19, 20).

Nevertheless, regrowth by means of olive suckers could have taken place after the destruction, as well as at any time since. We could not expect the orderly grove in a garden with neat paths that we see today to have existed unchanged over the centuries. A neglected tree soon becomes surrounded by a host of upright shoots springing from the base, as the psalmist knew when he wrote 'your children will be like olive shoots around your table' (Psalm 128:3). At the base of old trees in Gethsemane there are such shoots which may one day take the place of the parent trees. The progeny, however, may be of inferior wild stock on to which the cultivated variety had been grafted, as explained above.

Olives as fruit

The fruit of the olive is the most

Left: A felled olive tree sprouting new shoots from its base.

important product of this valuable and useful tree. For the Hebrews it has for long been the principal fruit tree, thriving in conditions of soil and climate that would appear to be unfavourable for such a rich product. Curiously enough, mention of the eating of the fruit itself hardly appears in the Bible, yet it is known from the frequent occurrence of olive stones in archaeological excavations of the Holy Land that olives were eaten from the earliest times. At Lachish, for example, they have been found at all levels since the Early Bronze Age in the third millennium BC.

As olives were so widely cultivated the fruit was available to both rich and poor and constituted an important part of their diets. It was eaten in several ways, according to the variety of olive tree. Those that yielded the best oil were often not suitable for pickling or salting for the table. On the other hand dual-purpose varieties were developed which combined both characteristics, and should the fruit not be sold for pickling it could be returned to the press for oil.

Many writers mention that there are only four varieties of olives, but like most cultivated plants a much larger number has been recognized, each with its own characteristics and often its own local name. The purely oil-producing fruit trees were widely grown in biblical times and yielded heavier crops than the more valuable table kinds. Table olives were prepared in several ways according to variety. The fresh fruit was eaten, as it is today, in its natural state, usually with salt, or it could be pickled in vinegar, cooked or merely dipped in boiling brine, or dried. The bitterness could be reduced by treating with a hot alkaline solution before pickling.

The ripe fruit is about 2 cm (0.75 in) long, ellipsoid in shape and botanically known as a drupe, that is, having the same structure as a cherry. The three layers of the fruit are readily distinguishable, with a violet-blue skin (epicarp), oily flesh (mesocarp) and horny stone (endocarp), within which lies the solitary seed. The green unripe fruit is usually pickled. In ancient times the favourite olives for pickling grew in irrigated groves, while the vast majority thrived on the dry hillsides. Although the fruit is perfectly formed by the end of July it is still green, and the oil content of olives increases progressively until the skin turns black when it is really ripe. At maturity the pulp may contain at least 75 per cent oil.

Harvesting of oil olives takes place in the autumn: during October for green table olives and December for black ones. The fruit is either carefully handpicked, or simply beaten or shaken off the trees on to nets or cloths spread below them. Knocking with long poles is liable to damage the fruit badly, with the result that it tends to ferment quickly and spoil the quality of the oil. The prophet Isaiah was familiar with such methods of harvesting when he recalled the gleanings left in the tree with 'two or three berries in the top of the highest bough' (Isaiah 17:6; 24:13; shaking KJV; beating RSV). Mosaic Law stated that when the Israelite beat his olive tree he should not go over the boughs again as the gleanings must be left for 'the sojourner, the fatherless and the widow' (Deuteronomy 24:20).

How much fruit is obtained from each olive tree? Most of the varieties grown around the Mediterranean today are probably little different from those of biblical times, and it is reckoned that each tree yields 10–20 kilograms (22–44 lbs). Oil yields vary from about 1.3–2.6 kilograms (2 lbs 8 oz–5 lbs) per tree. After the tree has produced a good crop it will generally bear sparsely the next year. In Deuteronomy 28:40 there is reference to the olive casting its fruit to such an extent that there would not be sufficient oil for the people to anoint themselves, although there were abundant trees throughout the land. The regular dropping, or casting, of the flowers and young fruit is a well-established fact, with only a small proportion of the flowers actually reaching maturity in a normal season, as Eliphaz the Temanite knew (Job 15:33). Fruit production may be reduced even further by such factors as insufficient pollination of the flowers, lack of moisture or lack of plant food. Pests, such as the olive fruit fly (*Dacus oleae*), can also attack the fruit before maturity by laying eggs inside, and cause heavy dropping. It is estimated that the tree normally loses 80 per cent of its fruit between flowering and ripening. Not more than 5 per cent of the flowers set fruit in the first place, with only 20 per cent of these reaching maturity six or seven months after flowering. Thus less than 1 per cent of the flowers actually produce ripe fruits, according to Pansiot and Rebour (1961).

Below: Harvesting olives as depicted on a Greek vase *c.* 520 BC. The men are beating the branches with sticks to make the fruit fall, while a boy is up the tree and another gathers olives into a basket.

Right: An olive press reconstructed at Ha Gilo. The upright stones crush the fruit.

Olive oil

Olive-presses were usually located near the source of supply of the fruits to avoid carrying them long distances. The rock-hewn presses were large enough to take quantities of fruit for pulping by a heavy vertical stone wheel that could be rotated by one or two people, or by an animal pushing a horizontal bar. The camel or donkey turning the stone was blindfolded to prevent giddiness as it walked round and round. I was amazed at the size of the upright millstone which is still used at Bethany beside the traditional site of Mary and Martha's house. Similar oil-mills, with stone and press, have been set up as exhibits at Ha Gilo and Tantur near Bethlehem, the Israel Museum, Tirat-Yehuda and Neot Kedumim. In New Testament times, the Romans used a type of olive mill (*trapetum*) that could be worked either by water, or, more usually, by manpower.

When the fruit was crushed it was either trodden to press out the oil or, more usually, the pulp was placed in special rope baskets about 7 cm (3 ins) thick, piled on top of one another in a large press with a long wooden beam weighted by heavy stones. The oil and watery liquid squeezed out was separated in settling vats, for example the huge round pots found at Ekron, with two holes for draining off the surplus water.

Micah (6:15) warned that because the Lord's people had done the works of the house of Ahab they would 'tread olives, but not anoint [themselves] with oil', for they would be captives. Small quantities of oil were prepared by beating the olives in a mortar and pestle, or simply with a stone. This is indicated in Exodus (27:20) 'And you shall command the people of Israel that they bring to you pure beaten olive oil for the light, that a lamp may be set up to burn continually'. Oil prepared in this way is said to be particularly pure (Leviticus 24:1–3). It seems that the press found in a sacred precinct at Tel Dan in 1979 provided oil for the lamps, as well as for the anointing ceremonies, in the tenth to ninth centuries BC.

Small pottery lamps are commonly found in excavations of ancient sites in Palestine. The early lamps made around the time of the captivity of Israel in Egypt were open bowls with a rim, while the later ones of New Testament times had a central hole into which olive oil was poured, and a short spout with another hole for the wick. In contrast with these lamps, which were for interior illumination, torches were used outside. These consisted of old rags soaked in olive oil just before ignition. According to some authorities, these are wedding torches, which would make the reference to them particularly significant in the parable of the wise and foolish virgins, the latter having no oil for their unsoaked torches (Matthew 25:4 RV mgn).

Olive oil was used extensively in Old Testament times for cooking purposes. In fact it was an essential part of everybody's diet, as is shown by the repetition in the Bible of the trio oil (Heb. *yitshar*), wine and grain (e.g. Deuteronomy 7:13; 11:14; 12:17; 18:4 etc.). Olive oil was mixed with meal for cakes, for frying meat and for eating with bread and stews.

During the construction of the temple, Solomon sent to Hiram of Tyre in each year 20,000 cors (homers) of both wheat and barley, 20,000 baths of wine and the same of olive oil (2 Chronicles 2:10). To give some idea of the vast numbers of olive trees that must have been grown in the land at that period, 20,000 baths was equivalent (at 22 litres per bath) to 440,000 litres, which would work out at just over 12 ml (4 fluid ounces) daily for each of the 10,000 workers. At an average yield of 1840 ml per tree, I estimate that this would have been the annual output of 239,130 trees: a full orchard of olive trees properly spaced would be expected to have 48 trees per acre. Solomon must therefore have despatched the product of some 4981 acres or 2015 hectares of olive groves!

Recent excavations at Ekron revealed that the Philistines' main product was olive oil – at least 1000 tonnes/tons flowed from their presses after a good harvest. It was produced in rectangular buildings divided into three rooms for production and storage.

Symbolism and anointing

The anointing of people and objects with olive oil has a long history and a sacred significance. We first meet the practice in the Bible when Jacob, after he had seen the vision of a ladder from earth to heaven, poured oil (Heb. *shemen*) upon the rock that had been his pillow (Genesis 28:18). Later in the same place God spoke to him and Jacob again poured oil on a stone pillar (Genesis 35:14). By this symbolic act he set aside that place, which he called Bethel, as holy. Anointing was presumably a well-established practice even at that early date.

Later, we see Moses being commanded by God to prepare holy anointing oil with a fixed composition (see chapter 14) for the anointing of the tent of meeting, the Tabernacle, and all its contents. The furniture and utensils were thereby consecrated 'that they may be most holy; whatever touches them will become holy' (Exodus 30:29), and Aaron and his sons were also anointed 'that they may serve me as priests' (Exodus 30:30). In Leviticus (8:10–11) we find Moses putting

Above left: The pulp from crushed olives is pressed to extract the oil.

Above: Olive oil was used in pottery lamps. The hole in the centre allowed the oil to flow inside; a flax wick was pushed into the spout on the left.

this into practice, with the altar itself being anointed seven times. Furthermore, Moses had to warn the people of Israel of its holiness:

'It shall be for you most holy. And the incense which you shall make according to its composition, you shall not make for yourselves; it shall be for you holy to the Lord. Whoever makes any like it to use as perfume shall be cut off from his people' (Exodus 30:36–38).

Throughout the Old Testament, anointing signifies the holiness of the anointed objects or persons, their separation to God, and also divine authority.

From the anointing of the priest it was a simple step to the anointing of the king or of the king-designate 'They anointed David king over the house of Judah' (2 Samuel 2:4; see also Judges 9:8–9; 1 Kings 1:34); and prophets, such as Elisha (1 Kings 19:16). Jotham's story of the trees (Judges 9:8–15) stresses the role of the olive tree in this respect. Personal anointing (Psalm 104:15; Micah 6:15) on the other hand was not symbolic, for in the dry Mediterranean climate the cool, smooth olive oil is pleasantly soothing (Isaiah 1:6) for the skin and as a hair-dressing (Psalm 23:5).

All these anointings, apart from the personal one, were regarded as acts of God, and of sanctifying significance. For example, when the prophet Samuel poured oil on Saul's head he said: 'Has not the Lord anointed you to be prince over his people Israel?' (1 Samuel 10:1). Anointing with oil is associated with the outpouring of the Holy Spirit in both the Old Testament (e.g. 1 Samuel 16:13; Isaiah 61:1), and the New Testament (e.g. Acts 10:38; 1 John 2:20).

---

[1] The name oleaster has also been applied to *Elaeagnus angustifolia,* which is an unrelated small tree occurring sporadically in Western Asia along the coast. Some commentators (see Moldenke, 1952) have taken the Hebrew *ets shemen*, and its variants, meaning literally oil tree, to indicate this species. Although unrelated to the olive, its fruits yield an inferior oil and the better varieties are edible. I am doubtful about this being the biblical plant as the contexts usually clearly indicate the real olive stressing the oil it yields (1 Kings 6:23; 31–33; 1 Chronicles 27:28; Micah 6:7). In any case, M. Zohary (1962) points out that *Elaeagnus* is introduced into Palestine and was probably not there in biblical times. He thinks that the Aleppo pine is the species intended, which agrees with the KJV rendering of Nehemiah 8:15. Pine yields a resin which could be considered an oil in popular language.

Bibliography

Aldred, C., *Akhenaten and Nefertiti* (London, Thames and Hudson, 1973).

Gitin, S., 'Ekron of the Philistines: Part II: Olive-oil suppliers to the world', *Biblical Archaeology Review* (Washington, 1990), 16(2):33–42.

Goor, A., 'The Place of the Olive in the Holy Land and its History through the Ages', *Economic Botany* (New York, 1966), 20:223–43.

Goor, A., and Nurock, K., *Fruits of the Holy Land* (Jerusalem, Israel Universities Press, 1968): olive, pp. 89–120.

Newberry, P. E., 'On some African Species of the Genus *Olea* and the Original Home of the Cultivated Olive-Tree', *Proceedings of the Linnean Society* (London, 1937), Session 150:3–116.

Pansiot, F. P., and Rebour, H., *Improvement in Olive Cultivation* (Rome, FAO, 1961).

Peleg, Yehuda, 'How Ancient Olive Presses Worked', *Israel Land and Nature* (Jerusalem, 1981), 6:98–103.

Stager, L. E., and Wolff, S. R. , 'Production and Commerce in Temple Courtyards: an olive press in the sacred precinct at Tel Dan', *Bulletin of the American Schools of Oriental Research* (Baltimore, 1981), 243:95–101.

Turrill, W. B., 'Wild and Cultivated Olives', *Kew Bulletin* (London, 1951), 6:437–42.

Zohary, D., and Spiegel-Roy, P, 'Beginnings of Fruit Growing in the Old World', *Science* (1975), 187:319–27.

11. Figs and Sycomore Trees

'One basket had very good figs, like first-ripe figs, but the other basket had very bad figs, so bad that they could not be eaten.'
(Jeremiah 24:2.)

The fig tree is one of the most familiar in Mediterranean lands, where it is often seen in courtyards, hemmed in by white plastered walls and red pantiled houses. There are some eight hundred species in the genus *Ficus*, each having its own life cycle. Young fig trees are almost shrubby in growth with several grey-barked stems and thick twigs which exude a milky juice when cut. As they grow older one or two trunks thicken but the white wood is soft and of little use as timber. Leafless in winter, the fig tree bursts its buds in late spring and the coarse, lobed leaves are fully developed by the time the owner needs the shade during the heat of the summer months, like Nathaniel in New Testament times (John 1:48, 50). To this day a fig tree and a carefully trained vine are frequently found together beside a house and one is reminded of the scriptural references to the security of every man who sits under his vine and under his fig tree whom none shall make afraid (Micah 4:4).

Fig orchards

Orchards of the common fig (*Ficus carica*) are often seen in Palestine. On brilliant days in early spring I have seen orchards of leafless fig trees on the limestone hills, where the ground was smothered by pink Egyptian campion (*Silene aegyptiaca*), as well as the less conspicuous Syrian speedwell (*Veronica syriaca*) with rich blue flowers. The trees are spaced well apart as the roots not only penetrate the ground deeply, but spread out laterally for a great distance. When they are planted like this, fig trees have a rounded crown supported by a stout trunk. A young fig tree grows rapidly and may start to bear fruit when seven years old and continue for several decades, but fig trees usually become unprofitable after some fifty years. Mature side shoots need to be shortened in summer to encourage little fruits to develop on them which will mature the following year.

LIFE HISTORY OF THE FIG

Few people realize how specialized is the life history of the fig. The primitive common fig (*F. carica*) has two forms which correspond to male and female. The many-seeded fig fruit is the female, which is composed of numerous minute flowers lining the interior of a fleshy cavity, with only an obscure hole at the top through which the pollinating insect, the fig-wasp (*Blastophaga psenes*) creeps. The story of fig pol-

Right: Scattered common fig trees (*Ficus carica*) on the limestone plateau north of Jerusalem, before the leaves have developed (March 1985).

Above left: Baskets of fresh and dried figs.

Above: Half a fig fruit, showing the cavity lined with florets.

lination is a fascinating one, and demonstrates an extraordinary interdependence between the fig and this insect. Details of the pollinating process, and of the practice known as caprification, are given at the end of this chapter.[1]

Wild figs

The common fig, like the olive, grapevine and date palm, has been in cultivation from very early times, at least since the Early Bronze Age. It originated from the wild *F. carica* in the Mediterranean area, but is related to many wild species growing in the region towards Afghanistan. In Palestine today wild fig trees often grow in rocky places, especially where bats congregate. As the bats fly into their caves or cliff roosts they drop the seeds of figs on which they have been feeding and some of them develop into trees. Nowadays it is difficult to tell which ones are truly wild and which are naturalized through bat and bird dispersal. The trees one finds in the wild are of inferior quality as they have arisen from such seeds which, when they occur in good soil, are eradicated by the farmers and replaced by better varieties raised from cuttings.

The fig tree in the Bible

The first reference to the fig tree in the Old Testament, and probably the most famous, is that in Genesis; after eating fruit of the forbidden tree in the Garden of Eden, Adam and Eve 'knew that they were naked; and they sewed fig leaves together and made themselves aprons' (Genesis 3:7). Hence for centuries artists and sculptors have depicted nude figures wearing fig leaves! Metaphorical references to the fig abound in the Scriptures, such as Jotham's parable of the trees 'And the trees said to the fig tree, "come you, and reign over us." But the fig tree said to them, "Shall I leave my sweetness and my good fruit?" ' (Judges 9:10–11).

In the New Testament Jesus used the fig tree in a parable as a sign of the times – perhaps of when he would return: 'From the fig tree learn its lesson: as soon as its branch becomes tender and puts forth its leaves, you know that summer is near' (Matthew 24:32). By 'tender' he may have been referring to the abundance of milky latex present in the thick twigs during the spring. Jesus used the fig tree in another parable where the practice of manuring unfruitful trees is mentioned (Luke 13:6–9). The village of Bethphage, where Jesus cursed the fig tree (Matthew 21), actually means the 'house' or 'place of unripe figs', while Bethany is the 'house of figs'. There are other place-names derived from figs, such as Almon-diblathaim (Almon of dried figs) of Numbers 33:46, and Taanath-shiloh (the fig of Shiloh) of Joshua 16:6.

The curious incident of the cursing of a fig tree by Jesus, recorded in Matthew 21 and Mark 11, is an interesting case which has been explained in various ways. H. V. Morton, whose observations on the fig have often been quoted by other writers, thought that Jesus, seeing the small male figs that had come through the winter (called *tagsh* by the Arabs, probably *paga* in Hebrew), assumed the tree to be barren. But Asaph Goor (1968) thinks that the tree could have been a wild one, or a Greek variety which is known to need caprification. This does not explain, however, what a fig tree was doing in leaf at the time of Passover, which is too early to find a normal tree in leaf. Professor F. F. Bruce (1970) comments that for all the show of foliage, it was a fruitless and hopeless tree. He considers it to be an acted parable: the fig tree, green but barren, spoke of the city of Jerusalem where Jesus found much religious observance, but no response to his message from God. The withering of the tree was thus an omen of the disaster which, as he foresaw and foretold, would shortly fall upon the city.

Fig fruits in the Bible

From the various references to figs in the Bible and other historical literature,[2] there is no doubt that the fruit formed a very important part of the diet of ancient civilizations in the Near East. It was one of the seven fruits of the Promised Land (Deuteronomy 8:8). Figs may be eaten fresh or dried, but the first ripe fig was reckoned a very dainty morsel. Isaiah graphically pictures the first ripe fig: 'when a man sees it, he eats it up as soon as it is in his hand' (Isaiah 28:4). Both Hosea (9:10) and Nahum (3:12) use a similar analogy. Jeremiah contrasts the wholesome first ripe figs to overripe bad figs, which are only fit for destruction, and likens them respectively to Judah in captivity and that part of Judah remaining in Jerusalem (Jeremiah 24:1–10). The basket of 'summer fruit' (Heb. *qayits*) of Amos' vision (Amos 8:1 ff.) is usually understood to be a basket of overripe figs, and is probably a play on another Hebrew word, *qets*, meaning 'end', which fits the theme of the vision. Destruction of the fig trees and other fruits was a calamity: 'For a nation has come up against my land ... It has laid waste my vines, and splintered my fig trees; it has stripped off their bark and thrown it down; their branches are made white' (Joel 1:6, 7).

In the dried state, figs were an important food all the year round and valuable in wartime, especially during sieges. Supplies were stored in fortified cities and strongholds, such as Masada, where remnants have been found during excavations. The best figs were dried individually, the second best were strung together and dried, while ordinary figs were pressed into lumps (Heb. *debhela*). These caked figs were commonplace and ready at hand; hence Abigail could send David two hundred cakes of figs together with other offerings (1 Samuel 25:18), and later David's men gave a piece of one of these to the hungry Egyptian (1 Samuel 30:12). Isaiah apparently found the application of a cake of figs beneficial to Hezekiah's boil (2 Kings 20:7; Isaiah 38:21). In this respect it is interesting to note that in ancient Assyrian medicine the fig was used in plasters and there is evidence that it was efficacious.

Right: New leaves in springtime on young fig trees, with small fruits already developing.

The sycomore[3] of Jericho

The Scriptures also mention another kind of fig – the sycomore – which has a different life cycle. To many people the sycomore is known only from the reference to it in the New Testament when Zacchaeus climbed into one to see Jesus entering Jericho (Luke 19:4). Zacchaeus was a small man who could not see over the shoulders of other people, but he would have had little difficulty climbing up one of the massive sycomore trees as their knobbly trunks often branch near the ground. Presumably this tree was planted beside the road in Jericho, just as the sycomore is used as a street tree in modern Tel Aviv.

Although the sycomore is a kind of fig (*Ficus sycomorus*), in Egypt and Palestine during biblical times it was more important for its timber than for its fruits. Perhaps that explains Isaiah's statement (Isaiah 9:10) that the cut down sycomores would be replaced by cedars, which could be used for better timber. It has now declined in frequency in most parts of the Eastern Mediterranean as the fruits are inferior to the common fig.

Although the sycomore is known to have occurred in Egypt since predynastic times, before 3000 BC it is reckoned to be of tropical African origin. It thrives only in warmer areas such as the Nile valley, the Jordan valley and in western Palestine, where it was very common in Old Testament times (1 Kings 10:27; 2 Chronicles 1:15; 9:27). The psalmist recalls the disastrous effect of cold in Egypt: 'He destroyed their vines with hail, and their sycomore trees with frost' (Psalm 78:47 KJV). Trees were planted near the villages and towns, so that the fruit was readily available and advantage could be taken of its shade. The coarse heart-shaped leaves persist on the tree throughout the year, except in certain areas, where they may be lost in cold weather. For instance I have seen a tree in Thebes covered with leaves in February, yet the large trees in cooler windswept Tel Aviv were almost bare in March.

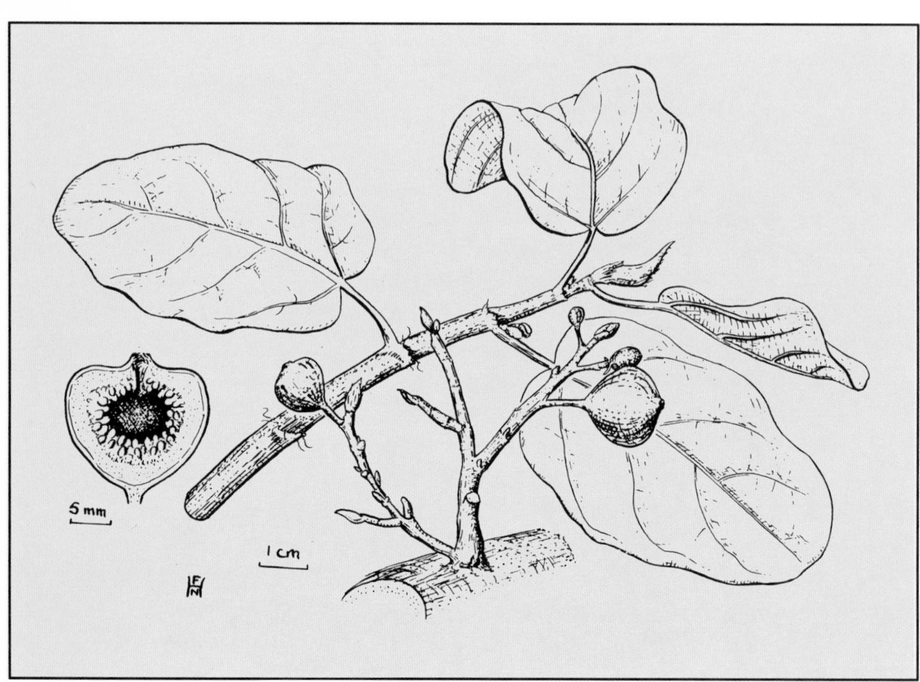

Below: Leaves and fruits of a sycomore fig.

LIFE HISTORY OF THE SYCOMORE FIG

The sycomore, like the common fig, also has a fascinating reproductive life cycle involving a remarkable association with certain wasps. This has only recently been worked out in detail, and I am indebted to my friend Professor Jacov Galil of Tel Aviv University for allowing me to report on his work in this area, and

Left: A sycomore fig tree (*Ficus sycomorus*) planted along a street in Tel Aviv in 1977, with Professor Jacov Galil, who has studied the biology of the sycomore and other figs.

to reproduce some of his illustrations. Again, full details are given at the end of this chapter.[4]

A dresser of sycomore trees

An ancient Egyptian relief of a sycomore clearly shows the figs bearing a characteristic cut, and many of the ancient figs, found in Egyptian tombs by Galil, bear deep scars on them, indicating that they were cut at an early stage of development. This is a very old practice which still continues in Egypt, Cyprus, and possibly elsewhere too. It is mentioned indirectly in the Bible where Amos describes himself as 'a herdsman, and a dresser of sycomore trees' (Amos 7:14). Part of the sycomore dresser's work was to climb the sycomore trees at the appropriate time and laboriously cut each small fig with a long-handled knife.

Only very recently has a scientific explanation of this practice been put forward by Galil. He has shown that the wounded fig liberates ethylene gas, which is now well known as a fruit ripener. Ethylene is used commercially for that purpose by introducing the gas into storage rooms of oranges, bananas and other fruits. The extraordinary feature of the sycomore is, however, that after the cutting operation the tiny immature fig suddenly begins to enlarge, and within three days it has increased its size ten times. In this case the ethylene apparently acts as a growth stimulator as well as a ripener. Clean, edible figs result, but not for the reason formerly propounded, that the cut was to release the insects.

There are hundreds of species of figs, especially in the tropics, evidently each with its own pollinating insects, beautifully adapted and interdependent. In this chapter we have dealt with only two of the species, and have revealed a wealth of botanical and biological interest. Perhaps it was a recognition of such extraordinary details in nature that led the psalmist to say 'O Lord, how manifold are thy works! In wisdom hast thou made them all; the earth is full of thy creatures ... living things both small and great' (Psalm 104:24–25)

----

[1] For the common fig, the pollinating insect, the winged female fig-wasp (*Blastophaga psenes*), hatches inside a 'male' fig (called 'caprifig') where the egg has been laid in one of the numerous short-styled flowers. Even before the female emerges, the grotesque little male insect mates with it and as the female pushes its way out of the apical hole of the fig it is dusted with pollen from the anthers situated around the hole. Once free, the winged female fig-wasp seeks out a young female fig and creeps inside where it walks over the florets, spreading pollen as it goes. Although it tries to lay eggs, the long styles of the florets in this type of fig prevents the insect from laying its eggs. Consequently no larvae develop in the florets, but, as pollination has been effected, the seeds do! Each seed develops from one of the tiny flowers lining the interior of the fruit.

Most cultivated varieties of fig produce fruits even without pollination by the fig-wasp, a process known as parthenocarpy, but other varieties (the Smyrna figs) will not develop ripe fruit in the absence of pollen brought by the pollinating insect. Caprification ensures a supply of the pollinating wasps by the farmer selecting and distributing caprifigs among the female fig trees so that when the insects emerge they will easily enter the young figs and pollinate them (Condit, 1947). The general scheme has long been known and the practice of 'caprification' is a very ancient practice, although it is only quite recently that its scientific complexities have been unravelled.

This outlines the story of fig pollination and explains the way in which the fig and insect depend upon one another. If one asks why there is a continual supply of fig-wasps during the warmer months, when each wasp lives for only a few days, the answer is that the caprifig trees bear three crops a year. Each caprifig may contain several hundred wasp eggs and some of the females fly off and enter young female figs, while others lay their eggs more profitably in the next crop of caprifigs, and so on for the following ones. The wasp eggs take about seventy days to hatch, or fewer in the hot season. The caprifigs appearing early in the year, at about the same time as the leaves, are called *profichi*; those produced during the summer are the *mammoni*; while the autumnal ones are known as *mamme*. The latter have to over-winter and may be frosted or blown off by strong winds, but sufficient survive for the insects to infect the *profichi* the following spring.

[2] Heb. *teenah*: fig, fig tree; Heb. *paga*: early green fig of Song of Solomon 2:13 only; Gk. *olynthos*: untimely fig of Revelation 6:13

Right: Immature sycomore fruits on a tree trunk, showing the cuts that were made earlier (Cyprus 1991).

Far right: Knives used by sycomore growers in Egypt to gash the young fruits. (After Galil.)

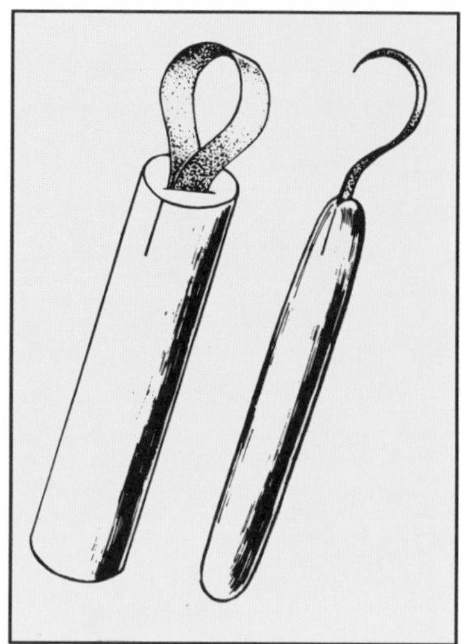

only; Gk. *syke:* fig tree; *sykon*: fig, whence the botanical term syconium for the fig fruit described above. Goor (1965) and Goor and Nurock (1968) deal extensively with references to the fig in the Talmud, as well as in the Bible.

[3] The spelling sycomore of KJV, NEB is preferable to sycamore of RSV, NIV since it is derived from the Greek *sykomoraia* and the Hebrew *shiqmah*. It also helps to distinguish the fig from the modern popular usage of sycamore for species of *Platanus* in USA and *Acer* in Britain. The sycomore fig is also known as the mulberry fig.

[4] I have already described the pollination and structure of the flower head ('syconium') of the common fig, from which the sycomore differs in several respects.There are two kinds of syconium in the common fig, but only one in the sycomore. The sycomore's male flowers are present in the upper portion of the same young fig as the female ones, of which there are stalked and unstalked florets. In its original home in tropical Africa the normal pollinating wasp (*Ceratosolen arabicus*) can lay its eggs only in the stalked flowers, as its ovipositor is not long enough to tackle the unstalked ones, which develop seeds in the normal way. The stalked flowers do not, therefore, produce seeds as they become galled and support the young wasps which, after four or five weeks, emerge into the cavity of the fig. Tiny wingless males develop first and mate with the females while still inside the galled flowers, and then a few of the males bore holes near the closed mouth of the fig enabling the females to escape. Before squeezing through the holes the winged females load special pockets on their legs with pollen before flying away to a different young fig. This it enters by the opening at the top, breaking off its wings on the way through. During egg-laying the female unloads the pollen from her pockets and thereby pollinates the florets which eventually set seed. All this has been filmed by Galil's team in a very clever piece of research. So the life cycle is completed, but that is not the full story, since in Africa five other wasps are involved in the following ways.

In the Mediterranean region the sycomore never sets seeds, a fact first noted by Theophrastus at about the time of Alexander the Great, and now we know why. Presumably when the sycomore was taken to Egypt from tropical Africa the pollinating wasp, *Ceratosolen*, did not go with it, or perhaps the winters there are too cold for this tropical insect to survive. However another wasp did follow the tree. It is *Sycophaga sycomori* which has a life cycle similar to that of *Ceratosolen* already described but with an important difference, namely that it lays eggs in *both* the stalked and unstalked flowers. Its ovipositor is long enough to achieve this and, besides, there are no special pockets on its legs to carry pollen. The formation of any seeds is therefore prevented.

A further point of interest is that another species of wasp, *Apocrypta*, parasitizes the larvae of *Sycophaga* by piercing through the outside of the developing fig with its long ovipositor until it reaches a galled flower in which it deposits its own egg at the expense of the first occupant. The mature female *Apocrypta* wasps escape from the fig through the holes bored by the *Sycophaga* males as the former conveniently emerges after the latter!

It is interesting to notice what remarkable synchronization of events takes place in this sequence. For instance there is a gap of four or five weeks between the full development of male and female florets of the fig, which coincides exactly with the time required for the wasp to complete its growth from egg to perfect insect. Likewise the parasitic wasp *Apocrypta* starts to pierce the fig only when galls have been formed inside it.

When the pollinating insects have completed their life cycle, the still undeveloped fig grows rapidly in size and eventually ripens. It is, however, unpalatable, since it contains numerous galls with dead male wasps and possibly some females which did not escape. Examination of ancient figs from Egyptian tombs by Galil has revealed the presence of both *Sycophaga* and its parasite *Apocrypta* wasps in them which showed that this is a long-standing sequence of events in the sycomores of the Mediterranean region.

Bibliography

Bruce, F. F., *The New Testament Documents* (London, IVP, 1970).

Condit, I. J., *The Fig* (Waltham, Chronica Botanica, 1947).

Galil, J., 'An Ancient Technique for Ripening Sycomore Fruit in East Mediterranean Countries', *Economic Botany* (New York, 1968), 22:178–90.

Galil, J., and Neeman, G., 'Pollen Transfer and Pollination in the Common Fig', *New Phytologist* (London, 1977), 79:163–71.

Galil, J., Stein, M., and Horowitz, A., 'On the Origin of the Sycomore Fig *(Ficus sycomorus L.)* in the Middle East', *Gardens Bulletin* (Singapore, 1976), 29:171–205.

Goor, A., 'History of the Fig in the Holy Land from Ancient Times to the Present Day', *Economic Botany* (New York, 1965), 19:124–35.

Goor, A., and Nurock, M., *The Fruits of the Holy Land* (Jerusalem, Israel Universities Press, 1968): fig, pp. 46–69.

Morton, H. V., *In The Steps of the Master* (London, Rich and Cowan, 1934) p. 388.

Wiebes, J. T., 'Co-evolution of figs and their insect pollinators', *Annual Review of Ecology and Systematics* (Palo Alto, 1979), 9:1–12.

12. Pomegranates, Dates and Other Fruits

'Pomegranate, palm, and apple, all the trees of the field are withered; and gladness fails from the sons of men.'
(Joel 1:12.)

We have already seen how important are the vine, olive and fig in the economy of the Mediterranean peoples. Several other fruits and nuts were frequently grown during biblical times. These feature prominently in contemporary records and their remains are often found during archaeological excavations in Palestine. However, we cannot begin to discuss fruit in the Bible without first mentioning the forbidden fruit – the so-called apple – given to Eve by the serpent in the best-known story of the Old Testament: 'You may freely eat of every tree of the garden; but of the tree of the knowledge of good and evil you shall not eat, for in the day that you eat of it you shall die' (Genesis 2:17). 'When the woman saw that the tree was good for food, and that it was a delight to the eyes, and that the tree was to be desired to make one wise, she took of its fruit and ate, and she also gave some to her husband, and he ate' (Genesis 3:6).

Later, the Mosaic Law had much to say about fruits: 'The first of the first fruits of your ground you shall bring into the house of the Lord your God' (Exodus 23:19). This was echoed in Proverbs: 'Honour the Lord with your substance and with the first fruits of all your produce; then your barns will be filled with plenty, and your vats will be bursting with wine' (Proverbs 3:9–10). God had promised them a fruitful 'land of wheat and barley, of vines and fig trees and pomegranates, a land of olive trees and honey' (Deuteronomy 8:8) – the famous 'seven varieties', seen by Jews, such as Nogah Hareuveni (1980) of Neot Kedumim, as being very significant.

Once the trees were planted it was not until five years later that the fruit could be eaten, since the fruit of the first three years was reckoned as unclean, and that of the fourth as dedicated to God (Leviticus 19:23–25).

Fruits also entered into ritual festivals, for example the sauce (Heb. *haroset*) eaten with unleavened bread at Passover (Heb. *pesah*) was prepared from dates, figs, raisins and vinegar. In the New Testament, when Jesus identified his betrayer during the Last Supper as 'one of the twelve, one who is dipping bread into the dish with me' (Mark 14:20; John 13:26), it would have

Left: Orchard terraces above Dan, in the shadow of snow-capped Mount Hermon (April 1969).

Right: Flowers of the pomegranate (*Punica granatum*).

been this sauce to which he was referring. Jesus had often illustrated his discourses with examples from nature and horticulture, and fruit trees were no exception to this (Matthew 7:16–19; 12:33; Luke 3:9; 6:43, 44).

POMEGRANATE

The flower of the pomegranate is so attractive that the shrub is almost worth growing just for the sake of these waxy red blossoms. But it is, of course, for its fruits that it has been cultivated for thousands of years. In the Mediterranean region their refreshing, watery juice is greatly appreciated in late summer.

The pomegranate (*Punica granatum*) originated from wild ancestors occurring near the southern Caspian Sea, where they still grow on the hills and along the rivers. They are rank and thorny in comparison with the cultivated plants, which in warm localities will grow into small trees, although they are usually seen as many-stemmed shrubs about 2 m (6 ft) tall. Being deciduous, they are leafless during the winter, with the rather narrow leathery leaves appearing in late spring. Cuttings are used for propagation, rather than seeds which yield inferior varieties.

Flowering takes place during the hot season, the flowers being self-pollinated. Fruits are ready for gathering at the end of the dry summer, before the cooling rains begin. The pomegranate fruit is round, tinged with pink, yellow and purple, and crowned by the persistent, enlarged calyx, and it hangs downwards on the branchlets. The rind is hard and tough; it contains tannins and red dye nowadays used in the manufacture of Morocco leather. When opened, a multitude of seeds is revealed, each enclosed in its own juice-filled sac. Small wonder that the inhabitants of the region esteemed the fruit and used it as a motif for ornamentation, as its shape is characteristic and easily recognized. They also saw the numerous seeds as being symbolic of fertility.

Ancient Egyptian inscriptions referred to pomegranates being brought back from Canaan during their campaigns, and I have seen them engraved on the stonework of Pharaoh Thutmoses III's temple at Karnak dating from about 1480 BC. Some interesting evidence of pomegranates in Canaan *c.* 1650 BC was found in the course of Kathleen Kenyon's excavations of Jericho. She found an attractive wooden bowl in the form of a pomegranate, having a lid of one half with minute dowels to hold it to the other half. Recognizable remains of real pomegranates were also found nearby (Kenyon, 1952). Fragments were also found in Bronze Age ruins of Gezer, while in caves near En-Gedi, overlooking the Dead Sea, other ancient pieces, as well as whole dried fruits, were excavated. A silver half shekel dating from the first Jewish revolt (AD 66–70) bears on the reverse side a stem with three pomegranates surrounded by the inscription 'Jerusalem the Holy'.

In Hebrew the pomegranate is known as *rimmon,* which is frequently mentioned in the Bible.[1] For instance, these fruits were brought back by the spies from the Promised Land, together with figs and grapes (Numbers 13:23). In fact the pomegranate was so common that it gave its name to many places, such as En-Rimmon, which means the spring of the pomegranate, mentioned in Nehemiah 11:29 and elsewhere. Solomon wrote of the pleasant fruits of the pomegranate (Song of Solomon 4:13; 6:11; 7:12), and 'the juice of my pomegranates' (8:2). Today the juice, known as grenadine, is still a popular cordial in Mediterranean countries.

Pomegranates are first mentioned as ornaments in Exodus 28:33–4 (and 39:24–6) where they were used along the hem of the robe of the ephod: 'pomegranates of blue and purple and scarlet stuff, around its skirts, with bells of gold between them, a golden bell and a pomegranate, a golden bell and a pomegranate, round about on the skirts of the robe'. The bells were in the form of the pomegranate flower, alternating with the fruits. The fruits in brass were similarly used ornamentally in Solomon's temple to decorate the capitals of the pillars: 'there were two hundred pomegranates, in two rows round about' (1 Kings 7:20; see also 2 Kings 25:17; 2 Chronicles 3:16; 4:13; Jeremiah 52:22–23). By tradition, Solomon's crown was modelled on the persistent calyx surmounting the fruit. Remarkably, the Israel Museum acquired in 1978 an ivory carved pomegranate the size of a thumb with a hole for a shaft handle at the base and inscribed in old Hebrew 'belonging to the Temple of the Lord'. Scholars assume that it was used by priests in Solomon's temple at Jerusalem (Avigad, 1990).

THE DATE PALM

The date palm (*Phoenix dactylifera*) is only known in cultivation in the drier subtropics, although its wild relatives are to be found from the Canary Islands eastwards to Bengal and Sikkim. The most likely suggestion for the origin of the date is that it was developed in the hot deserts of the Middle East (D. Zohary and Hopf, 1988). It seems to be one of those useful plants which in the remote past was selected from some wild stock, but which is now dependent on cultivation for its continuation. Fortunately, date palms can withstand considerable

Left: A basket of ripe pomegranates (*Punica granatum*). The pomegranate fruit hangs downwards when it is ripe. The interior contains numerous seeds enveloped in juicy sacs. Pomegranates adorned the priestly robes and temple columns of ancient Israel.

salinity and even irrigation with brackish water, often the only water available in deserts.

Although date seeds can produce new plants, the seedlings would have little chance of survival in the dry date groves since they need plenty of water, and without being irrigated at the right time most trees would quickly die. However, mature trees can withstand long periods of flooding, and I have seen them in the middle of the Nile waters above Aswan where the old dams impounded the water around their roots for most of the year. Such treatment causes poor growth and ultimate death, but for shorter periods of inundation no damage is normally done.

In the date palm the usual method of propagation is by suckers at the base of the parent tree which are induced to root by heaping soil around them. When sufficient roots have been formed, the off-shoots are transplanted to a nursery or to their permanent positions. After four or five years the tree begins to flower, but good crops are not usually expected before the tree has reached its eighth year.

The trunk grows about 30 cm (1 ft) a year for the first fifty years or so, after which the rate begins to decrease and few new leaves are developed. The large tuft of leaves at its crown may rise to as much as 21 m (75 ft) above the ground and such trees would be over a hundred years old. Each leaf is immense, reaching some 6 m (23 ft) in length, with a stout midrib and numerous lateral leaflets similar to an enormous feather. The palm family, incidentally, may be divided into those with leaves like the date and those with fan-shaped leaves, such as occur in the doum palm (*Hyphaene thebaica*), which, unlike most others, is easily recognized by its forked trunk. The doum is common along the Nile and extends to southern Arabia, with its last outpost near Elat, although it is not mentioned in the Bible.

In these countries, where timber has always been scarce, the stout straight and woody midribs of date palms have for long been valuable as poles for roofing and for simple furniture. In the Bible the leaves are referred to as branches, and to the lay person they are more like branches than leaves. They were used by Moses and the Israelites in the Sinai Desert to construct booths for the Feast of Tabernacles (Leviticus 23:40), and they are still used by Jews even on city balconies. It was palm 'branches' that the people of Jerusalem took to welcome Jesus as he rode a donkey into the city on the first Palm Sunday during his triumphal entry (John 12:13).

An interesting point arises, however, in this connexion. As Jerusalem is situated at an altitude of about 700 m (2300 ft), the subtropical date palm was unlikely to be grown there for fruit. It is known that date palms were grown in the hill country, but their fruit was so poor that the Talmud forbade its use as an offering of first-fruits. These had to come from the lowland, such as 'Jericho the city of palm trees' (2 Chronicles 28:15), from where the cut leaves could have come for traditional use at Passover and the Feast of Tabernacles. Judges 4:5 states that Deborah 'used to sit under the palm of Deborah between Ramah and Bethel in the hill country of Ephraim'. Presumably this tree was something of a rarity in those parts. However, by New Testament times date palms would have been frequently planted in Jerusalem and they must have been readily available at the time of Jesus' entry.[2]

There is no doubt that palm leaves had already acquired a symbolic significance for they were used by Judas Maccabaeus during his processions at the restoration of the temple in 164 BC (1 Maccabees 13:51; 2 Maccabees 10:7; 14:4). The ancient Greeks and Romans used to give palm leaves to the victors in athletic games and it is significant that Jesus should have been welcomed with them, for he indeed was victorious, the victor over death (Romans 6:9, 10). Later the palm leaf was taken as a symbol of immortality and resurrection, especially for the martyr whose triumph was his death. Even today the leaves are frequently carried at the head of a Muslim funeral. The two-palm-leaf motif used on Jewish coins during Herod's reign is thought to be symbolic of the prayers of praise and thanks to God at the Festival of Tabernacles.

The Hebrew for the date palm is *tamar*, and Greek *phoenix*, from which came the scientific name. As the palm was found on the east Mediterranean coast it may have given its name to the land of Phoenicia. There is some dispute about this and how the fabulous phoenix bird is related. In the interior of Syria the city of Palmyra takes its name from the Latin *palma*. Place-names such as Hazazon-tamar (Genesis 14:7), incorporating the Hebrew name, are also found in Palestine; Elat and Elim, said by authors to be derived from 'date', are from *elah*, terenbinth. The name Tamar was actually given to Hebrew women (2 Samuel 13:1) since the date palm was considered to be elegant and graceful (Song of Solomon 7:7).

The date palm has distinct male and female trees (dioecious) and the clustered fruits are only produced when the female flowers have been pollinated. Artificial pollination of date palms has been practised for a very long time in the Mesopotamian region, yet even today in certain

Opposite: A date palm (*Phoenix dactylifera*) growing in the Kharga Oasis, Egypt. To the psalmist, the date was a symbol of elegance.

Right: Dates ripening on a palm tree.

Saharan oases no dates are produced, either because trees of only one sex have been introduced or because the inhabitants have never learnt the secret of pollination. That artificial pollination is an ancient practice may be seen from a famous Assyrian bas-relief representing the Sacred Tree, which is undoubtedly a highly modified date palm. In fact it has been suggested that the bas-relief represents a grove of female palms and a central male palm linked together by festoons such as are still seen at flowering time in those regions. A winged figure is seen to be holding a bag in one hand as a receptacle for the pollen collected from the male tree, while the other hand applies pollen to female flowers (p. 184).

Once the flowers are pollinated the fruits begin to form. They are gathered when ripe and highly esteemed by people living in the desert, where sweet items of food are scarce. Dates are eaten fresh or dried, or made into a very sweet syrup similar to honey and often called date honey. Refined sugar was unknown to biblical people and the fruit syrup made from dates must have formed a special part of their diet. Today the heavy syrup prepared from pressed dates is known as *dibs* in Arabic. As dates are rich in carbohydrates and lacking in fat and protein, Tackholm and Drar (1950) point out that it is not by chance that the Arabs nowadays tend to eat them with some form of milk, which redresses the balance. So, it is interesting that Moses should have been told that he was to deliver the people of Israel 'out of the hand of the Egyptians, and to bring them up out of that land to a good and broad land, a land flowing with *milk and honey*' (Exodus 3:8) – a land with a balanced diet! There is no doubt that bee honey is intended by certain biblical references, but date honey may be referred to in this famous phrase.

The long narrow stone (seed) of the date, with a longitudinal groove, is extremely resistent to decay. Well-preserved seeds were found in Tutankhamun's tomb and the excavations at Timna near Elat, as well as in many other sites.

Apples or apricots?

The identity of the fruit known by the Hebrews as *tappuah* is still in doubt (Proverbs 25:11; Song of Solomon 2:3, 5; 7:8; 8: 5). In most English versions of the Bible it is translated 'apple' since linguistically it corresponds closely to the Arabic *tuffah*, but the NEB calls it 'apricot' (Song of Solomon, 2:3, 5; 7:8). We may ask, however, whether apples and apricots were known in biblical Palestine.

The small crab apple (*Malus sylvestris*) is the wild ancestor of our cultivated fruit (*Malus domestica* or *M. pumila*) and it occurs throughout much of Europe and in north-west Asia, its development depending on the technique of grafting, rather than of using variable seeds. Although apples have been cultivated in Europe since ancient times, they yielded a poor type of fruit, and were unlikely to have matched the description given them by Solomon in his Song. Some well-preserved carbonized fruits were found, however, in excavations of the ninth century BC in Kadesh-Barnea (D. Zohary and Hopf, 1988).

The other candidate for *tappuah* is the apricot (*Prunus armeniaca*). Dalman (1928) argues that, because there is nothing like the Arabic name *mismis* in the Mishna or Talmud, it cannot have been known in the early Christian era. It was available to the Romans, however, who called it *armeniaca*, thus misleading many into assuming that Armenia was its place of origin, instead of this being a Latin corruption of its Assyrian name. The apricot may have come from China where its close relatives are still to be found in the wild.

Top: Apricots ready for picking; perhaps Solomon's 'apples of gold'.

Above: Ripening apples still on the tree.

Right: Flowers of a cultivated apple (*Malus domestica*).

Perhaps exceptional apricots were available to Solomon, who wrote that 'A word fitly spoken is like apples of gold in a setting of silver' (Proverbs 25:11), which is an apt description of the appearance of the apricot fruit. It is similar to a whole almond fruit, although its flesh is much thicker and more succulent, and it does not split to reveal its stone, and its seed, or nut, which is contained in the hard stone, is not as palatable. The fragrance of the *tappuah* is referred to in the Song of Solomon 7:8 and its sweetness in 2:3, 5; both characteristics attributable to the apricot. Solomon appears to have known the tree itself for he writes: 'As the *tappuah* tree among the trees of the wood, so is my beloved among young men. With great delight I sat in his shadow' (Song of Solomon 2:3).

However, problems arise in connection with this reference to the trees. Whether or not they were known in New Testament times, they were certainly unknown in Old Testament Palestine, yet Joel (1:12) links the *tappuah* with the vine, fig tree, the pomegranate and the date palm, thereby indicating its relative importance in the Holy Land. Long before Joel's time we find Tappuah being used as a place-name for localities where the fruit must have been important. We have here an unresolved problem which is similar to that concerning the identity of the *etrog*. The Hebrew words used in Leviticus 23:40 literally mean 'goodly tree' or 'tree of loveliness' and possibly refer to no particular species. Yet Hebrew writers have long held that they refers to *etrog*, citron, *Citrus medica*, which may have come from India, while most *Citrus* species – oranges and lemons – came from China. Although it has been claimed to have been grown in ancient Egypt and Cyprus, it is doubtful whether it reached western Asia before classical times.

Sycamine: the mulberry tree

In the New Testament we find a reference to the sycamine tree (Luke 17:6 KJV), in modern versions referred to as the black mulberry (*Morus nigra*). If this is correct, it must have been introduced into Palestine from Iran and cultivated for its fruit, rather than as the food plant of the silkworm (see p. 169). This is the only time the Greek *sycaminos* is used in the New Testament, but in the Septuagint it is substituted for the Hebrew word for the sycomore fig. That the trees are similar in appearance is shown by the fact that the sycomore is sometimes called the mulberry fig! The 'mulberry trees' in the KJV rendering of 2 Samuel 5:23 ff and 1 Chronicles 14:14 ff are now considered to be more likely to refer to poplar trees (aspen NEB; balsam RSV, NIV) (p. 72).

The black mulberry is a stout, deciduous tree, growing slowly and attaining a great age. Its gnarled trunk may collapse in time, but the tree is unlikely to disappear on that account, for its place is usually taken by one of the lesser trunks arising from its base. The piling of stones and turves around the base of the trunk to support the tree and to encourage the growth of new shoots is an old practice. The resulting tree would be extremely difficult to uproot, which gives point to Jesus' remark that if the apostles 'had faith as a grain of mustard seed, you could say to this sycamine tree, "Be rooted up, and be planted in the sea," and it would obey you' (Luke 17:5–6).

The stiff, heart-shaped leaves are rough, hairy and have coarsely toothed margins. Particular interest centres on the greenish catkins of the two distinct sexes. The male catkins wither, while the female flowers enlarge like raspberries yet with a very different structure. All the sepals and petals become very fleshy and they ultimately turn red, with abundant crimson juice. This rather acid fruit, botanically known as a sorosis, is usually cooked or used for preserves.

Almonds

Wild almonds (*Prunus amydalus* or *Amydalus communis*) may still be found here and there in Palestine. They usually grow as gnarled shrubs, rather than trees, since the ubiquitous goats inhabiting the

Far left: The citron (*Citrus medica*), known as *etrog* to the Jews.

Left: Ripe fruits of the black mulberry tree (*Morus nigra*), the sycamine tree of the New Testament.

rocky hills seldom allow them to grow to their full extent. The cultivated almond (*Prunus dulcis*) makes a small tree about 4 m (13 ft) high, with spreading branches and narrow, toothed leaves. Almond trees in full bloom are a splendid sight. The white petals are only flushed pink towards the base and the flowers are borne in great profusion, giving each branch a white head: 'the blossom whitens on the almond-tree' (Ecclesiastes 12:5 NEB). The pink-flowered trees (often hybrids), frequently cultivated in English gardens for their ornamental value, are not often seen in the Mediterranean region, where almond trees are grown for their nuts. The sweet almond is most delicious and has always been popular, but the primitive variety yielding bitter almonds has prussic acid in its kernel. However, oil of bitter almonds or almond essence (benzaldehyde) may be distilled from them after crushing without any of the poison being present.

The Mediterranean climate suits the almond tree well. It flourishes in the hot dry summer, since its roots penetrate into the subsoil and its fruits ripen easily in the hot sun. The velvety fruits look like small peaches, but differ by splitting open at maturity to expose the nut. One often sees unripe fruits offered for sale in Arab markets in springtime. The fruit is botanically a drupe like an apricot and olive, although it is convenient to call the hard shell a nut, as it has to be cracked to release the delicious, fragrant seed.

The almond in Hebrew is *shaqed*, which means waker or watcher and refers to the early flowering of the tree. Apparently in Jeremiah 1:11, 12 there is a play on this word:

' "Jeremiah , what do you see?" and I said, "I see a rod of almond [*shaqed*]". Then the Lord said to me, "You have seen well, for I am watching [*shoqed*] over my word to perform it".'

Long before Jeremiah's time we read that it was an almond twig which sealed the authority of Aaron when it flowered and fruited overnight in the Tabernacle (Numbers 17:1–8), an event that has no natural explanation. Moreover the great golden lampstand of the Tabernacle was ornamented with almond designs:

'*... there shall be six branches going out of its sides, three branches of the lampstand out of one side of it and three branches of the lampstand out of the other side of it; three cups made like almonds, each with capital and flower, on one branch, and three cups made like almonds, each with capital and flower, on the other branch – so for the six branches going out of the lampstand; and on the lampstand itself four cups made like almonds, with their capitals and flowers*' (Exodus 25:32–6; also 37:19–20) (see p. 185).

Most recent translations of the Bible substitute 'almond' for the 'hazel' of older versions of Genesis

Above: Flowers of the almond tree.

Right: An almond tree (*Prunus dulcis*) in full flower on the Mount of Olives.

30:37. Thus the RSV reads 'Then Jacob took fresh rods of poplar and almond [Heb. *luz*] and plane, and peeled white streaks in them, exposing the white of the rods'. At that time Jacob was at Paddan-aram near Haran in Upper Mesopotamia where almonds grew wild. It is worth pointing out, however, that hazel trees grow there, too, and their nuts were found during the excavation of Nimrud.

Although almonds as food are mentioned only once in the Bible, when they were taken to Egypt as a gift (Genesis 43:11), it is known that they were popular and eaten by all classes. Professor Helbaek thinks it is curious, therefore, that almonds are so seldom reported from excavations in the Near East. He did find a split shell at Apliki in Cyprus, and a small heap of shells in the Catal Hüyük excavations in Anatolia, but he says the latter may have been wild ones as they were so small. D. Zohary and Hopf (1988) bring together information on recent studies of the wild and cultivated almonds.

Stone-pine seeds

A very popular 'nut' in the Mediterranean region is the seed of the stone-pine (*Pinus pinea*). This lovely tree, with its spreading umbrella crown, sheds edible seeds in considerable quantities as the cones become dry. The white seeds are narrow, about 2 cm (0.75 in) long, and rich in oil and proteins, which has made them popular since classical times. Stone-pine nuts have even been found in Roman-occupied Britain, where they must have been imported for the troops. In Hosea 14:8 an edible fruit from a coniferous tree (Heb. *berosh*) is mentioned and the only likely candidate is the seed of the stone-pine.

Wild pistachio nuts

The small round nutty fruits of the wild Atlantic and Palestine terebinths (*Pistacia atlantica* and *P. palaestina*) which one sees on sale in Arab markets, are sometimes called 'pistachio' but should not be confused with the much larger true pistachio nut, *P. vera*, a native of Turkey and Central Asia. The nuts of the Palestine terebinth can be eaten whole, fresh or roasted, but those of the Atlantic terebinth, having green skin and bitter flesh, are used for dyeing and tanning, although the seed can be eaten roasted. The native terebinths were carried to Egypt by Joseph's brothers (Genesis 43:11; pistachio nuts NEB, NIV, RSV). The Hebrew word used there is *botnim*, which the Septuagint renders *terebinthos*, fitting this identification of the wild terebinth. Fruits of these trees were used for food in the Chalcolithic Age, and shells dating from the Early Bronze Age have been found during excavations at Lachish, not far from the valley named after this tree (Heb. *elah*), and other sites, including Timnah and Arad.

Walnuts

Apart from almonds, wild pistachio nuts and stone-pine seeds, there were no naturally occurring 'nuts' in Old Testament Palestine. Even the walnut (*Juglans regia*) did not grow so far west, and had to be cultivated in gardens. Nobody knows exactly when it was introduced into the Mediterranean region from its native area in Persia and northern India, but the Greeks and Romans held the walnut in high esteem, and Josephus reported its occurrence by the Sea of Galilee. Walnut trees may even have been in cultivation as early as Solomon's reign, since in the Song of Solomon 6:11 we read: 'I went down to the nut orchard'. The Hebrew word *egoz*, here rendered 'nut', could have been the walnut. The Greeks knew that this fruit came from Persia and called it *persicon* after that country. They also likened its seed to the brain within the skull and called it *caryon* after the Greek *kara*, a head. The Romans, however, regarded the walnut as Jupiter's nut, *Jovis glans*, whence comes the scientific name *Juglans*. Our English name of walnut is a corruption of the nut that came to us via Gaul!

The walnut tree grows to a height of at least 30 m (92 ft) and its stout trunk supports a well-branched rounded crown. Its wood is very useful for furniture and is well known today as a figured veneer. The large leaves are compound (pinnate) with several pairs of leaflets. Male and female flowers are borne separately on the same tree: the male catkins are 5–15 cm (2–6 ins) long and fairly thick, with numerous small greenish-yellow male flowers, while the female flowers occur later in small clusters on the new shoots. The spherical fruit is surrounded by a thin, fleshy layer which dries up as the fruit matures. Technically it is a drupe, like an olive, rather than a true nut. The unshelled nuts of shops have been cleaned of the skin, but the venation still shows as an impression on the hard inner layer, which must be cracked to release the much folded, oil-rich kernel.

Above: Shelled and unshelled walnuts (*Juglans regia*).

Carob pods

In sandy areas near the coast, and dotted about the foothills of Palestine, the carob tree (*Ceratonia siliqua*) is conspicuous for its dark, evergreen crown of pinnate leathery leaves. It is an important constituent of certain types of Mediterranean vegetation where the chalky soil is deep or where the limestone is cracked, allowing entry of its roots. The rounded crown, up to 12 m (40 ft) high, almost obscures its trunk, which never becomes large. As a leguminous tree, it is interesting that it is one of few Middle Eastern species in the pea subfamily *Caesalpinioideae*, which is mainly tropical in its distribution. The Judas tree is another species in this category. A curious feature of the carob is that it flowers in the autumn, out of step with most other Mediterranean species. Its male and female flowers are borne on separate trees in short inflorescences on the shoots of the previous year. They are bee-pollinated, although not as conspicuous as many pea-flowers since there are no petals and only the red-tinged stamens are displayed. The following spring the pods develop but do not ripen until late in the year.

Left: A carob tree (*Ceratonia siliqua*) growing in Galilee.

Right: Wadi Qilt (Kelt): olives, palm trees and other fruits are cultivated near the monastery.

Below: Young male flowers of the carob.

These whole pods with the seeds inside are used as fodder for cattle, horses and pigs. They are in fact the husks or pods (Gk. *keration*), said to be eaten by the swine in the parable of the prodigal son (Luke 15:16). Until recently only poor people and children regularly ate them for the sweet flavour. Now they have become popular, especially in Britain and the USA, as quite an expensive health food! In spite of the widespread name St John's bread for the carob or locust-bean, the 'locusts' eaten by John the Baptist were probably not the bean, but the insect (Gk. *akris*).

The Greek for the carob is *keratia*, from which was coined the scientific name *Ceratonia*, the epithet *siliqua* referring to the pods. When the Greeks found that the seeds were reasonably constant in weight they used them as a standard, which we know as the *carat* weight of 200 milligrammes, used for the fineness of gold. Originally there were 140 carats to the ounce; nowadays there are 142. The tree is also the source of the carob seed gum. Unfortunately the pods may be attacked by the carob moth (*Ectomylelois ceratoniae*) and a proportion of seeds are destroyed. However, since propagation is usually by grafting high-yielding varieties on to poorer quality trees raised from seeds, this is not a serious pest. Trees bear fruit in the fifth or sixth year after grafting.

Modern fruits

Nowadays Mediterranean countries yield a rich harvest of fruits unknown in biblical times. Perhaps foremost of these are the citrus, such as orange, lemon and grapefruit, while exotic avocado pears fetch high prices in the world's markets. The Holy Land is a fruitful land. Jesus warned his followers to

'Beware of false prophets ... You will know them by their fruits. Are grapes gathered from thorns, or figs from thistles? So, every sound tree bears good fruit, but the bad tree bears evil fruit. A sound tree cannot bear evil fruit, nor can a bad tree bear good fruit. Every tree that does not bear good fruit is cut down and thrown into the fire. Thus you will know them by their fruits' (Matthew 7:15–20).

Left: Female flowers of the carob, with some of the previous year's pods still on the tree.

[1] Talmudic references to the pomegranate are quoted by Goor (1967) and Goor & Nurock (1968).

[2] Date palms (*Phoenix dactylifera*) are seen in Jerusalem nowadays where they grow well in the more sheltered parts. However, a very similar tree, the Canary date palm (*Phoenix canariensis*) is now frequently planted in the city and especially by the coast. It is distinguished by the stouter, shorter trunk. As its name implies, it is native to the Canary Islands.

Bibliography

Avigad, N., 'The Inscribed Pomegranate from the House of the Lord', *Biblical Archaeologist* (Baltimore, 1990), 53:157–60.

Davies, W. N. L., 'The Carob Tree and its Importance in the Agricultural Economy of Cyprus', *Economic Botany* (New York, 1970), 24:460–9.

Garlick, C., 'Note on the Sacred Tree of Mesopotamia', *Proceedings of the Society for Biblical Archaeology* (Washington, 1918), 40:111–12, figs. 1, 2.

Goor, A., 'The History of the Date through the Ages in the Holy Land', *Economic Botany* (New York, 1967), 21:320–40.

Goor, A., and Nurock, M., *The Fruits of the Holy Land* (Jerusalem, Israel Universities Press, 1968): pomegranate, pp. 70–88; date, pp. 121–51; citron or etrog, pp. 202–207; walnut and almond, pp. 228–54; carob, pp. 255–67.

Harrison, S. G., 'Edible Pine Kernels', *Kew Bulletin* (London, 1952), 6:371–5.

Lemaire, A., 'Probable Head of Priestly Scepter from Solomon's Temple Surfaces in Jerusalem', *Biblical Archaeology Review* (Washington, 1984), 10(1):24–9.

Kislev, M. E., 'Reference to the Pistachio Tree in Near East Geographical Names', *Palestine Exploration Quarterly* (London, 1985), pp. 133–8.

—. 'Fruit Remains', in B. Rothenberg, *The Egyptian Mining Temples* (London, University College, 1988).

Popenoe, P., *The Date Palm*, H. Field (ed.) (Miami, Field Research Projects, 1973).

Simon, H., *The Date Palm: Bread of the Desert* (New York, Dodd, Mead and Co., 1978).

Zohary, D., and Spiegel-Roy, P., 'The beginnings of fruit growing in the Old World', *Science* (Washington, 1975), 187:319–29.

13. Vegetables of Egypt and Spicy Herbs

'We remember the fish we ate in Egypt for nothing, the cucumbers, the melons, the leeks, the onions, and the garlic.' (Numbers 11:4–5.)

Out in the parched desert of Sinai the wandering Israelites cried for the succulent vegetables of Egypt. The rich soil beside the Nile was a fine place in which to grow crops, and the Egyptians had many different vegetables. The annual flood brought silt to fertilize the river bank and the narrow plain beside it. In this chapter we discuss the various kinds of vegetables known to the ancient Egyptians and Israelites, and then look at the spicy herbs that flavoured the meals of patriarch, peasant and pilgrim.

CUCUMBERS AND MELONS

What, we may ask, were the cucumbers and melons that the people of Israel pined for? Most of us are familiar with gourds of one sort or another belonging to the marrow family, *Cucurbitaceae*. Today we see the fat American squashes, the cool Asian cucumbers and ornamental bottle gourds from Africa. The plants producing these fruits are all rather similar, being trailers or climbers with spiral tendrils, and are mainly tropical or subtropical.

Below: Water-melon (*Citrullus lanatus*) flowering shoot, with a cut-open fruit behind.

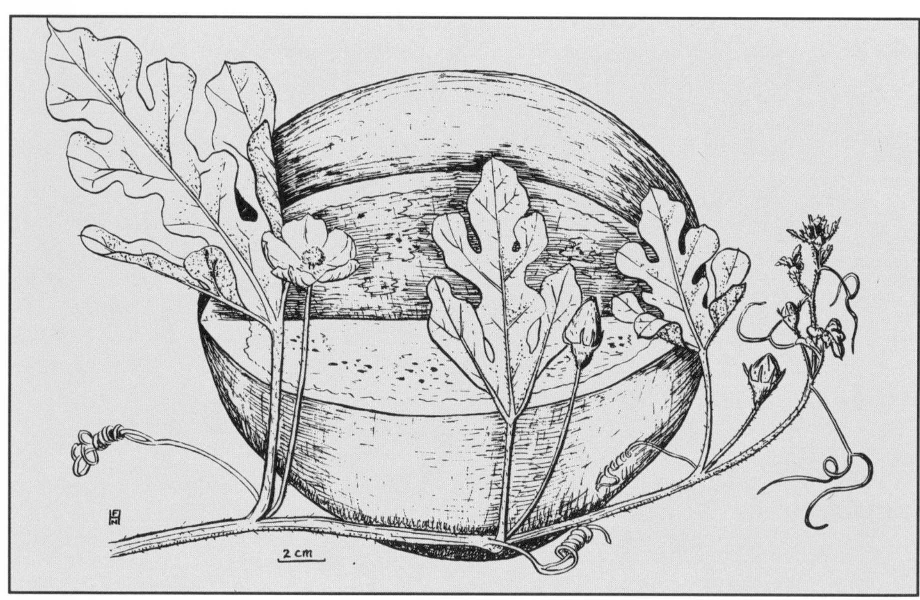

Water-melon

The water-melon (*Citrullus lanatus*, formerly *C. vulgaris*) is one of them, with large round fruits of white or pink flesh, and divided leaves. It is native to tropical Africa, being derived from the poisonous desert colocynth (*C. colocynthis*) (D. Zohary and Hopf, 1988). Water-melon was cultivated in Pharaonic Egypt, so little wonder the Israelites remembered its refreshing quality. Its large black seeds occur abundantly almost throughout the fruit. These seeds were eaten and have often been found in Egyptian tombs, showing that they were introduced very early into cultivation there. The Hebrews knew melons as *abattichim* (water-melons NEB) and it is strange that they are only mentioned in the Bible in Numbers 11:5.

Cucumber

The cucumber, however, presents a problem. The cucumber of today (*Cucumis sativa*) originated apparently in India, which means that it is very unlikely that it was in cultivation in Egypt at the time of the Hebrew captivity. However, it has a related species that used to grow in ancient Egypt, namely the musk-melon (*Cucumis melo*), and this appears to be the one referred to by the Israelites as *qissuim* (Numbers 11:5). It has long trailing stems with broad, undivided five-sided leaves and small yellow flowers, either male or female. In some varieties the fruit is rounded, but in one variety it is narrow and curved like a short snake, hence its name snake-cucumber.[1] Along its sides are grooves and markings which were copied by an Egyptian craftsman when he made the little box with a swivelling lid (p. 182). Out in the fields, growing cucumbers were protected by watchmen who sheltered from the sun under rough lodges (Isaiah 1:8).

LEEKS, ONIONS AND GARLIC

The Israelites also remembered the leeks, onions and garlic of Egypt. Well they might, for these vegetables were popular and important foods of ancient Egypt all belonging to the genus *Allium*, which has hundreds of species.

Onions

The onion (*Allium cepa*, Heb. *besalim*) is familiar to everyone. The rather large, smooth solitary bulb is made up of layers of fleshy scale leaves which yield a strong smell and cause tears to form in one's eyes. The small black onion seeds germinate rapidly after sowing and a tuft of tubular leaves develops. At ground level a bulb is steadily formed from the food manufactured by the leaves. If the bulb is allowed to remain in the ground, it will produce a tall

Left: Water-melons (*Citrullus lanatus*) on sale in an Italian market.

Left: Ancient Egyptian box in the form of a snake-cucumber (*Cucumis melo*) at the British Museum.

inflated stem supporting a round head of small purplish flowers.

Garlic

Garlic (*Allium sativum*, Heb. *sumim*), however, does not produce seeds from its flowers, and propagation is entirely vegetative. Unlike the onion, the garlic bulb is composed of a number of scales (known as 'cloves') which can be separated and planted to form new ones. Botanists suppose that the garlic is derived from *Allium longicuspis* which is wild in Central Asia. However, no ancestor is known for the garlic, except that it apparently developed as a cultivated plant in Iran and neighbouring countries (Jones and Mann, 1963).

Garlic has been found in many Egyptian tombs, where bulbs were left as offerings or associated with the mummy. When I was working on plant remains from tombs and temples at Saqqara, I received several collections of garlic. They were well preserved and had their leaves bound round with grass to keep the bunch together. Still older, well-preserved bulbs occurred in the tomb of Tutankhamun. Onions and garlic had religious significance and were depicted in paintings of offerings, as well as being mentioned in hieroglyphic literature. Herodotus and other classical writers mention the vast quantities of onion, garlic and radish consumed by the builders of the pyramids at Giza according to inscriptions on them. Some Egyptologists now believe, however, that this is a misreading and that these vegetables were offerings rather than ration-lists. Garlic was used medicinally, and also to preserve meat, which may explain its association with mummies!

Leeks

The leeks of Egypt referred to in the Bible (Heb. *hatzir*) present a slight problem, too. The Israelites were probably familiar with the salad leek (*Allium kurrat*), rather than our common leek (*A. porrum*). Both are apparently cultivated forms of the wild plant *A. ampeloprasum*, which is widespread around the Mediterranean. The salad leek has narrower leaves than the common leek. Two samples of the salad leek have been recorded from Egyptian tombs, whereas none of the other has been found. As the name implies, the salad leek is eaten raw; in Egypt the leaves may be cropped for more than a year.

All kinds of onions are soft-tissued plants and it is not surprising that they have seldom been recorded from Palestinian excavations. Some which have been found in the mounds of ancient Jericho were long and slender and said to be more like wild leeks (*A. ampeloprasum*) than onions. It is certain, however, that they were as popular there as in Egypt.

PULSES

Lentils, broad beans, peas and chickpeas were cultivated in the Fertile Crescent from very early times. They were commonly grown alongside the cereal crops, wheat and barley, and formed an important part of the peasants' diet. In 2 Samuel 17:28 and Ezekiel 4:9 beans and lentils are actually mentioned in association with grain. The Hebrew word used for beans in those verses is *pol*, stemming from the root 'to be thick', which applies well to the broad bean. Since it could also cover peas and chickpeas, I shall deal with all of them in this section. Other pulses, such as bitter vetch (*Vicia ervilia*), common vetch (*Vicia sativa*) and grass pea (*Lathyrus sativus*), are dealt with by D. Zohary and Hopf (1988).

These pulses are all members of the pea family (*Leguminosae*) and the edible seeds are rich in protein (20–25 per cent) as well as carbohydrates. This may account for the healthier condition of Daniel, if the vegetables (Heb. *zeroah* or *zeroim*) he ate were pulses, in preference to the king's rich food (Daniel 1:12). However, they are so rich in protein that peasants who eat large quantities in an unbalanced diet suffer from favism, which causes anaemia, or lathyrism, resulting in paralysis. Agriculturally, the pulses are beneficial to the ground as the bacteria in

Right: Carbonized lentil seeds (*Lens culinaris*, formerly *L. esculenta*) from an ancient Egyptian tomb.

Far right: A broad bean with long pods.

Right: Broad beans (*Vicia faba*) in flower in a large field at Faiyum, Egypt.

nodules on the root fix nitrogen from the air, which is available to successive crops:

The lentil

The lentil (*Lens culinaris*) is probably the most ancient of the cultivated pulses, as it was one of the first crops grown at the beginning of agriculture (2 Samuel 23:11); yet in the Holy Land today one can still see small patches of lentils being grown by Arab farmers. The slender annual vetch-like plants grow into one another, forming a low tangle about 23 cm (9 ins) high. The minute bluish flowers produce flat pods, containing only two lens-shaped seeds about 3–6 mm (1/8–1/4 ins) in diameter. They become reddish brown when ripe. The small seeded variety (*microsperma*) is said to be more primitive than the large seeded one (*macrosperma*), which occurs in sites dating from after the time of Solomon.

Lentil seeds dating from very early times have been found in numerous excavated sites in Egypt and the Near East. One of the earliest finds (of the seventh millennium BC) was that by Helbaek at Jarmo, in the foothills of Iraqi Kurdistan. In the Holy Land, excavations at Beth Shean in 1933 yielded substantial quantities of lentil seeds, according to Albright datable to 3000–2500 BC. As usual they were carbonized, but perfectly recognizable and found to be mixed with a bedstraw (*Galium tricornutum*), which also contaminated another large hoard at Yiftahel found in 1983 at the pre-pottery site. It is interesting to note that in Palestine this weed still regularly associates with lentil and is harvested with it.

In the Bible the first reference to lentils (Heb. *adasim*) occurs in the story of Jacob and Esau, in which red lentil stew was exchanged for Esau's birthright (Genesis 25:29–34). Lentils were among the foods brought to David and his men mustered against Absalom (2 Samuel 17:28). Mixed with cereal flour, ground lentils were baked into bread (Ezekiel 4:9).

Broad beans

The broad bean (*Vicia faba*) is also known as the field bean. In ancient times it was much smaller than our popular vegetable, which is *V. faba* var. *major*. The ancient seeds were small and bolster-shaped, compared with the large, flat broad beans we know. The small ancient bean should be called the horse bean (*V. faba* var. *equina*), and a very small variety is the tick bean (*V. faba* var. *minuta*, also known as var. *minor*) (Townsend and Guest, 1974).

The ancestry of the broad bean is still obscure. In spite of a claim by Ladizinsky (1975) that it originated in Afghanistan, D. Zohary and Hopf (1988) dismiss, for genetic reasons, the suggestion that the wild vetch *V. narbonensis* was its progenitor. Helbaek considers that the dispersal of the cultivated bean was tied up with sea traffic, since it is recorded from Bronze Age sites not far from the sea. It has been recorded in Troy, dating to 2300 BC; also in Crete, Malta and Cyprus, as well as places in Palestine, such as Beth Shean and Yiftahel near Nazareth, in early Neolithic pre-pottery time. By the Iron Age the broad bean had become much more widely distributed in Europe and the Near East (Bond, in Simmonds, 1976).

The broad bean is an annual plant with a stout square stem 60–90 cm (2–3 ft) high. The leaves are pinnate with several large dark green leaflets and no terminal tendril. Its flowers occur in short clusters in the upper axils and the whitish petals are conspicuously marked with a black spot. The long pods are white and velvety within.

Garden peas

Garden peas (*Pisum sativum*) are also often excavated in the Near East. They have been discovered in Jarmo, ancient Jericho and in Turkey, where they were unearthed in Catal Hüyük. All of these date from the sixth millennium BC. Many finds were made in much more recent sites in the region, as well as across Europe. The wild peas occurring in the Eastern Mediterranean *maquis* are usually known as *P. elatius*, while those in the open park-like areas are called *P. humile*. Botanists now consider them both to be wild *P. sativum*. Readers are probably familiar with the cultivated garden pea plant. It is an annual, climbing by means of the tendrils at the end of its pinnate leaves. Leafy appendages (stipules) are conspicuous at the base of the leaf stalks. The large flowers are usually white, or mauve like its ancestors in the Mediterranean region, and produce smooth pods that are packed with a number of rounded seeds (D. Zohary and Hopf, 1988).

Left: Cultivated garden peas (*Pisum sativum*) in Egypt, where coloured flowers are more usual than white.

Chick-peas

The seeds of chick-peas (*Cicer arietinum*) are very popular in the Middle East. They are made into a delicious and sustaining paste called *hummus*, which is mixed with olive oil and eaten with fresh pitta bread. The seeds are often roasted and even the young shoots are boiled as a vegetable. The plant is an erect annual about 20 cm (8 ins) high, with pinnate leaves bearing up to eight toothed leaflets. The very small bluish or white flowers pro-

Opposite: A market in Taiz, Yemen, selling onions and dried dates in the traditional way (1975).

Right: Chick-pea plant (*Cicer arietinum*) with a mauve flower and hairy pods.

duce a short one- or two-seeded pod. Characteristically shaped seeds have given rise to various names such as chick-pea, falcon-head and ram's-head (hence the scientific epithet *arietinum* from the Latin *aries*, ram) as it takes little imagination to see these creatures in the seed.

Chick-peas have not been found in ancient Egypt earlier than about 1400 BC. However, in the ground of ancient Jericho and Arad large numbers of seeds were excavated from a low level, datable to the Early and Middle Bronze Age, from c. 2000 BC, while claims have been made for very much older (c. 7000 BC) seeds at Jericho and near Damascus. Chick peas have also been found in Lachish, where seeds were excavated in the Bronze and Iron Age layers (*c.* 1000 BC) and in seventh-century BC Nimrud. Chick-peas are mentioned only once in the Old Testament: 'and the oxen and the asses that till the ground will eat salted *provender*, which has been winnowed with shovel and fork' (Isaiah 30:24). Here, according to M. Zohary (1982), provender (Heb. *hamitz*; fodder KJV) should be rendered as chick-pea. Botanists have concluded that this cultivated pulse originated in the northern part of the Fertile Crescent, where similar wild species occur in grassy glades among the oak trees (D. Zohary and Hopf, 1988).

GATHERED HERBS AND SPICES

When, in biblical days, cultivated crops failed during periods of drought, wild plants were sought for food to relieve the famine. In Elisha's time, for instance, one of the sons of the prophets 'went out into the field to gather herbs' (2 Kings 4:39), but he brought back the bitter colocynth. A peasant farmer, however, familiar with the lore of the countryside, would have known the edible wild plants from the inedible: Isaiah described them as 'what grows of itself' (Isaiah 37:30). This subject of wild plants and culinary herbs is so vast that we must limit ourselves to those actually mentioned in the Bible and others implied by certain references. (Some are also referred to elsewhere in this book: for fragrant plants see chapter 14.)

Bitter herbs

The 'bitter herbs' (Heb. *merorim*; Gk *pikrides*) eaten with the Passover lamb were probably gathered from wild plants, the exact species depending on the locality and its environment. The first Passover occurred in Egypt: 'They shall eat the flesh that night, roasted; with unleavened bread and bitter herbs they shall eat it' (Exodus 12:8). During the flight through Sinai, God instructed Moses and the Israelites to keep the Passover in the same way, but the bitter herbs available there would have been less palatable than those in Egypt. Later, in the Promised Land, no doubt others again were used. The herbs consumed by the Jews today are not necessarily those used in biblical times.

The Jewish Mishnah actually names lettuce (*Lactuca*), chicory (*Cichorium*), eryngo (*Eryngium*), horse-radish (*Armoracia*) and sow-thistle (*Sonchus*). These are typical salad plants with rather bitter leaves. In ancient Egypt lettuces (*Lactuca sativa*), with upright, quite bitter leaves, similar to our Cos variety, are known to have been cultivated, as records suggest that enormous quantities were consumed by the builders of the pyramids.

For chicory, the common and dwarf blue-flowered chicories, *Cichorium intybus* and *C. pumilum*, have often been suggested; also the dandelion (*Taraxacum* spp.), which is restricted to moister, hilly regions of Palestine. Several species of eryngo (*Eryngium*) are native to Palestine, the young leaves of *E. creticum* being edible, but horse-radish (*Armoracia rusticana*) is native to Europe. Sow-thistles (*Sonchus oleraceus*) occur as weeds in gardens and waste places everywhere.

In every Arab market and by the roadside in Old Jerusalem one still sees offered for sale bundles of leaves, close inspection of which reveals a wide range of species. In Jerusalem and Tiberias, for instance, I found not only cultivated mint, parsley and lavender, but also dandelion, round-leaved mallow and Jerusalem sage, some of which are bitter.

Below: A herb-seller in Jerusalem; both wild and cultivated plants are on sale.

Right: Dill (*Anethum graveolens*).

Far right: Coriander in flower (*Coriandrum sativum*).

Below: A plant of cumin (*Cuminum cyminum*).

Spicy herbs

Spicy condiments are especially favoured in warmer countries. As incense and fragrant plants perform a special function by smothering unpleasant smells, so edible spices brighten dull food or cover the taste of bad meat.

Before the pepper of our tables was known in the Near East, other seeds and leaves were used for similar purposes, such as coriander, cumin and dill. These three herbs, belonging to the parsley family (*Umbelliferae*), are cultivated for their seeds, which were, and still are, used to flavour bread and stews. Jesus condemned the Pharisees when he said to them 'you tithe mint and dill and cummin, and have neglected the weightier matters of the law, justice and mercy and faith' (Matthew 23:23).

Coriander

The coriander (*Coriandrum sativum*; Heb. *gad*) is well known in the Mediterranean region, with its aromatic leaves, used to flavour wine, and its spicy seeds. The Israelites likened the granular white appearance of manna to coriander seed, with which they were familiar in Egypt (Exodus 16:31; Numbers 11:7). The lower leaves of this annual herb, up to 60 cm (2 ft) high, are much broader than the upper ones and are sold in markets as salad. The whitish-pink flowers produce round 2-seeded fruits about 4 mm (0.2 in.) in diameter.

Cumin

Cumin, or cummin (*Cuminum cyminum*; Heb. *kammon*; Gk. *kyminon*), grows wild in western Asia and has been in cultivation since ancient times as food and medicine. In Assyria, however, it does not seem to have been so popular. An annual plant about 40 cm (1 ft 4 ins) high, it has deeply divided leaves and a flat head of white flowers.

Dill

Dill (*Anethum graveolens*) was widely used in ancient Egypt and Palestine as a spice and a medicinal herb. It is called in Greek *anethon*, which has been rendered as 'anise' in the KJV. But since anise or aniseed (*Pimpinella anisum*) is of southern European origin, it is unlikely that it was grown in Palestine, even by New Testament times. Dill is an annual about 60 cm (2 ft) high, with finely divided leaves and heads of greenish yellow flowers.

Mint

Mint (Gk. *hedyosmon*) was another spice mentioned in Matthew 23:23, as well as in Luke 11:42. The mint family (*Labiatae*) abounds in the Near East and many species are very fragrant and edible, but the word 'mint' is usually limited to certain culinary herbs in the genus *Mentha*. The plant frequently used in the Mediterranean region is the horse-mint (*M. longifolia*), though British gardeners are more familiar with the spearmint (*M. spicata*), which apparently originated in the central European mountains and would not have been available in biblical times.

The horse-mint is a perennial with creeping underground stems, its fragrant lance-shaped leaves borne on the erect stem which is four-cornered and about 60 cm (2 ft) high. Numerous small bluish flowers are carried in whorls on the long inflorescence terminating each stem. A variety of *M. longifolia*

Far left: Mint (*Mentha longifolia*).

Left: White mustard (*Sinapis alba*).

with very narrow leaves, which I noticed growing along a stream bed near Mount Sinai, is favoured by the Bedouin as a tea.

Rue

Surprisingly, wild rue is given in Luke as one of the herbs tithed by the Pharisees, since Talmudic law laid down that only cultivated herbs had to be tithed, hence the phrase 'and all other kinds of *garden* herbs' (Luke 11:42 NIV). The common rue of European gardens is *Ruta graveolens*, but the wild plant of the Palestinian hills is *R. chalepensis*, which is so similar that when I found it growing in thickets on Mount Meron I took it for the former. Close inspection of the flowers, however, shows that *R. chalepensis* has fringed petals which are not present in the other species. Perhaps both species were in use by New Testament times because of their very aromatic blue-green foliage. Like other species in the rue family (*Rutaceae*), such as the citrus fruits, oranges and lemons, the leaves are spotted with translucent glands which yield the strongly scented oil used medicinally for many ailments. Small pieces of rue leaves were also used for flavouring.

Incidentally, the Greek word *peganon* for rue has been taken up as the scientific name for a closely related genus of plants, *Peganum*. The species of this genus that is common in sandy places in Palestine is the peganum shrub (*P. harmala*; Arab *harmal*). I have also found it abundant in the semi-desert as far south as the Yemen, where the sheep leave it left strictly alone. Like rue, it was used in many Assyrian prescriptions and its alkaline ashes are still sometimes used instead of soap. Oil is extracted from its seeds which are narcotic, while in Turkey red dye is prepared from its roots.

Black cumin

In Isaiah 28:25, 27 the Hebrew word *qesah* is rendered 'fitches' in KJV, 'dill' in RSV and NEB and 'caraway' in NIV. It appears to be none of these, but the black cumin or nutmeg flower (*Nigella sativa*). The round aromatic seeds are black, hence the generic name *Nigella*, derived from the Latin word *niger*, and they have been used since ancient times both as a medicine and to flavour bread. They are easily damaged and have to be threshed, as Isaiah (28:27) well knew, by knocking with a light stick. Its flower is a dull bluish and not as decorative as the well-known garden annual love-in-the-mist, *Nigella damascena*, which is otherwise similar, with its finely cut foliage and growth to a height of 30–60 cm (1–2 ft).

Mustard

Mustard is familiar to us as a condiment, but in ancient times it seems to have been more valuable medicinally for its seed oil in mustard poultices, and for cooking oil, than for seasoning. Jesus' parable of the mustard seed seems to teach that a small work of God will develop tremendously, as a tiny seed grows to become a large, fully-grown plant (Matthew 13:31–32; Mark 4:31–2; Luke 13:19). Jesus also referred to this seed when teaching what can be achieved by even the smallest amount of faith (Matthew 17:20; Luke 17:6).

However the identity of the biblical mustard seed is a great problem, the controversy centring around the description of mustard as a tree (KJV) or large shrub (RSV) in the first parable, and the supposed small size of its seed in both. (Moldenke [1952] provides an exhaustive account of the suggestions as to its identity.)

Mustard plants (white mustard *Sinapis alba* and black mustard *Brassica nigra*) certainly occur both wild and cultivated in the Near East, and the Greek word for mustard, *sinapi*, is unambiguous. They are annuals, seldom growing higher than 1.5 m (5 ft), and the four-petalled flowers, typical of the cabbage family *Cruciferae*, are bright yellow. Although some commentators have claimed that tree-like black mustard plants have attained a height of 3–4 metres (10–13 ft) in Palestine, mustard seeds are not particularly small, and in any event Luke 13:19 seems to indicate a garden plant, not a wild one, which may indicate that this is the smallest of *cultivated* seeds. I consider the identity of the New Testament mustard remains an open question (p. 47).

Fenugreek

Although fenugreek (*Trigonella foenum-graecum*) is a legume, it has spicy seeds and can hardly be considered as a pulse in the usual sense.

Below: Garden rue (*Ruta graveolens*).

Above: Wild mallows (*Malva sylvestris*).

It is a small annual herb with long curved horn-like pods and trifoliate leaves. The whole plant is intensely fragrant of new-mown hay, owing to the presence of the chemical coumarin. In Assyria and in Egypt it was used as a fodder, to flavour meat and fish stews, and as a medicine, and in Egypt also in religious rites. Seeds have been found in Lachish in Palestine where it may have been wild or cultivated. Some authors have suggested that these were the 'leeks' yearned for by the wandering Israelites in the wilderness (Numbers 11:5).

Purslane

Purslane (*Portulaca oleracea*), a small annual plant with numerous fleshy leaves, frequent in lowland Palestine, was formerly gathered and used for medicine and eaten as salad. Job 6:6 reads 'Can that which is tasteless be eaten without salt, or is there any taste in the slime of the purslane [Heb. *challamuth*]?' in the RSV (but 'white of an egg' KJV, NIV). Various linguistic sources now support rendering the tasteless substance as the juice of a plant, according to Alan Millard (1969), whilst M. Zohary (1982) is certain it is to be identified as the slimy vegetable prepared from the leaves of the mallows *Malva sylvestris, M. nicaeensis,* and *Alcea setosa*. It is interesting that Professor Feinbrun of the Hebrew University told me that she had to collect these plants for food during the siege of Jerusalem in 1948; poor people regularly gather them.

Bay leaves

Gathered herbs and seasoning spices need not necessarily be strictly herbaceous plants. The well-known bay leaves come from the laurel or bay tree (*Laurus nobilis*), often found in the Mediterranean *maquis* type of vegetation, where it occurs as a dense, evergreen shrub or tree. The translators of the KJV rendered Hebrew *erah* in Psalms 37:35 as 'a green bay tree', while several modern versions have simply 'a green tree'. Bay leaves have been used since ancient times as an important flavouring agent, and oil extracted from the leaves was used medicinally.

Linseed

At one time the seed of the flax plant (*Linum usitatissimum*) was a very important source of oil for culinary purposes. Helbaek (1959) considers that flax was originally known in its wild state for its nourishing seed (linseed), and it came into cultivation as a food plant rather than as a source of fibres for linen textiles (see p. 166). It was only later that primitive peoples discovered that its fibres could be utilized for string and thread, which ultimately gave rise to the art of weaving. In the Near East linseed is encountered sporadically from the early eighth millennium BC onwards, and seeds from northern Iraq, not far from Nimrud, the biblical Caleh, are dated to a period between 5000 and 4500 BC, when cultivation of linseed became important. A convincing argument is also given by Helbaek for regarding the pale flax (*Linum bienne*), of the foothills region north and east of the Euphrates–Tigris plain, as the progenitor of the cultivated flax *L. usitatissimum*.

Ancient records frequently mention sesame seed as food, yet the plant we call sesame, *Sesamum indicum*, is a tropical Indian species which was not introduced into the Near East until later times, and certainly sesame seeds have not been found in excavations of ancient sites. Again, Helbaek (1966) has proposed a solution to the dilemma. He considers that sesame used to be the name for linseed, which was an important source of cooking oil, but the name was transferred to the more palatable oil from the Indian plant when that replaced the oil from the flax plant. However, on linguistic grounds Kraus (1968) and Bedigian and Harlan (1985) dispute this conclusion.

The principal food plants of biblical times have now been dealt with. In the following chapters we shall consider plants that were used for other purposes.

---

[1] Not to be confused with the tropical Asian *Trichosanthes cucumerina* (*T. anguina*), which is usually called the snake gourd.

Bibliography

Bedigian, D., and Harlan, J. R., 'Evidence for the Cultivation of Sesame in the Ancient World', *Economic Botany* (New York, 1985).

Helbaek, H., 'Notes on the Evolution and History of *Linum*', *Kuml* (Arhus, 1959), pp. 103–29.

—. 'Late Cypriot Vegetable Diet at Apliki', *Acta Instituti Atheniensis Regni Sueciae* (Lund, 1963), series in quarto 8(4):171–86.

Jones, H. A., and Mann, L. K., *Onions and their Allies* (London and New York, Interscience Publ., 1963).

Ladizinsky, G., 'On the Origin of the Broad Bean *Vicia faba L.*', *Israel Journal of Botany* (Jerusalem, 1975), 24(2–3):80–8.

Millard, A. R., 'What Has No Taste? (Job 6:6)', *Ugarit Forschungen* (1969), 1:210.

Simmonds, N. W., *Evolution of Crop Plants* (London, Longman, 1976). D. A. Bond, Field bean, pp. 179–82; D. Zohary, Lentil, pp. 163–4; Ramunujam, Chickpea, pp. 157–9; D. R. Davies, Peas, pp. 172–4; T. W. Whitaker and W. P. Bemis, Cucurbits, pp. 64–9; G. D. McCollum, Onion and allies, pp. 186–90.

Zohary, D., 'The wild progenitor and the place of origin of the cultivated lentil, *Lens culinaris*', *Economic Botany* (London, New York, 1972), 26:326–32.

—. 'The origin of cultivated cereals and pulses in the Near East', *Chromosomes Today* (New York, 1973), 4:315–20.

—. 'Comments on the origin of the cultivated broad bean, *Vicia faba L.*', *Israel Journal of Botany* (Jerusalem, 1977), 26 (1):39.

Zohary, D. and Hopf, M., 'Domestication of pulses in the Old World', *Science* (Washington, 1973), 183:887–94.

14. *Fragrant Incense*

'The pure fragrant incense, blended as by the perfumer ...' (Exodus 37:29.)

The words 'frankincense and myrrh' carry a special mystique for Christians. Christmas cards and carols remind us each year that Magi brought them, together with gold, as gifts for the infant Jesus. Yet few people know anything about the origin and uses of frankincense and myrrh, or even that they are plant products. It is difficult today to appreciate how highly incense was regarded by the civilizations of biblical times; here was a substance of the gods – one that came from distant lands, for which no price was too great.

Long before the birth of Jesus there was a queen of Egypt who sent an expedition to 'the land of Punt' to bring back living incense trees to grow beside her own temple. This extraordinary project was initiated by a remarkable woman during the fifteenth century BC, while the Israelites were still in Egyptian captivity.

Queen Hatshepsut was a women known for remarkable exploits. Indeed, she was buried in the Valley of Kings, and not among the queens! As a woman she could not go to war, but she is remembered for architectural feats, especially her obelisks at Karnak and her magnificent mortuary temple to the west of Thebes at Deir el-Bahari. Anyone who has not gazed at the temple, lying at the foot of sun-drenched cliffs, can scarcely imagine its grandeur, some 3400 years after its completion. Broad central ramps rise between three spacious terraces with colonnades stretching on either side. As I wandered along these cool dim passages I could follow the main events of this woman's life as they stand in relief along the walls. Even the colour persists, in spite of their age and the lack of any real protection.

It is here that the story is told of Queen Hatshepsut's famous expedition in 1490 BC to the land of Punt, probably present-day Somalia or possibly India, to bring back living trees for planting on these very terraces. Many expeditions to Punt had been undertaken by her predecessors for the sake of exotic tropical treasures, as Solomon later sent out 'ships of Tarshish' to Ophir (1 Kings 9:26–8; 2 Chronicles 9:21), but this was the first known attempt to bring back living trees. There is some question, however, whether the trees were myrrh or frankincense: the heaps of resin are pink like myrrh. Unfortunately it is not possible to be sure from the rather stylized reliefs, but the trees

Left: Queen Hatshepsut's mortuary temple at Thebes, where incense trees were planted on the terraces.

Above: Myrrh or frankincense trees being transported from the Land of Punt for cultivation in Egypt. Drawings after the murals in the colonnades of Hatshepsut's temple.

do seem to me to be more like leafy species of *Boswellia*, which yields frankincense, than the myrrh-producing *Commiphora*. Moreover the frankincense trees are known to grow near to the coast of Somalia (Hepper, 1967).

Carved on the walls of the temple are accurate pictures of ships that were despatched down the Nile, and perhaps along an ancient canal linking the Delta with the Gulf of Suez and the Red Sea. Even the fish on the reliefs are depicted with such accuracy that it is possible to distinguish fresh-water from marine species as the fleet passes from the Nile to the salt water of the sea. Once at Punt, the expedition persuaded the local chief of their friendly intentions and the ships were loaded with 'all goodly fragrant woods of God's Land, heaps of myrrh resin, of myrrh trees, with ebony and pure ivory, with green gold of Emu, with incense ... Never was the like of this brought for any king who has been since the beginning' (Breasted, 1905). The reliefs depict in great detail the loading of the ships, with the trees, their roots neatly bundled, being carried on poles resting on the shoulders of four or six bearers.

The return to Thebes must have taken many weeks, for it involved a voyage from the Horn of Africa. At last the triumphant fleet reached Thebes and the joyous Queen had fulfilled her ambition, to plant the trees on her temple terraces, at fantastic cost.

Frankincense (*Boswellia*)

The white resin known as frankincense, or olibanum (Heb. *lebonah*), is extracted from trunks of certain tropical *Boswellia* trees. The genus was named after John Boswell, uncle of James, the famous biographer of Dr Johnson. There are some fifteen species of *Boswellia*, but most of them are not commercially useful. When trade opened up with India during the later biblical period or afterwards, frankincense was obtained from the Indian tree, *B. serrata.* But in earlier times the principal resin-producing trees were *B. frereana* and *B. carteri*, now both included under *B. sacra*, in Somalia; *B. papyrifera* in Ethiopia; and *B. sacra* in Arabia. They are all small trees with peeling papery bark, compound leaves and little star-like pink or greenish-white flowers according to species.

There is an excellent eye-witness description of the Somali frankincense trees by a Victorian traveller named G. B. Kempthorne (1857), in which he describes these unusual species as:

'one of the most extraordinary plants I ever saw ... for the trees actually grow out of the sides of the almost polished rocks ... The trees were about 40 feet high, the stem was about two feet in circumference, rising straight up, with a bend outwards of six or seven inches. They are attached most firmly to the rocks by a thick oval mass of substances about a foot or so in diameter, something resembling a mixture of lime and mortar. Branches spring out rather scantily at the top and extend a few feet down the stem; the leaves are five inches or so long and one and a half broad, narrowing and rounding towards the point, but not serrated at the edges; the upper surface is of a rich dark shining green, while the lower is of a lighter hue; they are thin and smooth and crimped like that beautiful species of seaweed so often found on the coast of England.'

The frankincense tree grows profusely near the southern coast of the Arabian Peninsula in Hadhramaut and Dhofar, a remote, mountainous region on the edge of the Arabian Desert. They are bush-like trees, with several trunks and stout branches covered by the paper-thin outer bark that is so typical of most species. Professor Theodore Monod, who studied the Hadhramaut frankincense trees in 1978, found that their size depended on where they grew: the largest occur in the valleys, the smaller ones on the rocky slopes, and the little ones on the dry plateaux. Monod observed the extraction of the resin by immigrant Somali people who use a special knife, called a *manqeb*, to cut deeply into the rust-coloured inner bark. The oval scar was immediately covered with little pearl-like drops of resin, with the consistency of condensed milk.

Surgeon Carter, who reported on the Arabian frankincense trade as long ago as 1848, stated that the hardened resin was 'collected by men and boys employed to look after the trees by different families who possess the land in which they grow'. This practice continues today, as observed by James Mandaville (1979) in Dhofar. Frankincense collection begins there in about December, reaching a peak from March to May. Thereafter it is stored for some months in clean-swept caves in dry country before being sold at the coast.

It is surprising to realize how accurate were both Theophrastus and Pliny in their statements about

Left: Frankincense tree (*Boswellia sacra*) growing in Dhofar in southern Arabia, from where incense resin was transported on the spice route to Jerusalem. (Photo: A. Radcliffe-Smith).

the distribution of frankincense in the region they called Saba. They even described the tree which they had never seen in such a manner that a botanist could reasonably recognize it.[1]

Today incense continues to be burned in the Roman Catholic, Coptic and Orthodox churches as part of their ritual, but in Arabia it is also widely used for personal and household fumigation. The frankincense is burned on small pottery burners that are still made in the pattern of those recovered from ruins of the Hellenic period, being square with square legs. Incense is also credited with some magical potency, being used to drive off devils or the evil eye from livestock and people (Mandaville, 1979).

Myrrh (*Commiphora*)

The myrrh bush (*Commiphora myrrha*)[2] grows about 2 m (6 ft) high in the semi-desert country of Somalia and the Yemen, where I found it on rocky slopes. Like many desert plants, it is thorny, with the long, stout, branch thorns protruding in all directions bearing the small three-lobed leaves, small whitish flowers and beaked fruits. For most of the year the bush stands gaunt and leafless. A thin papery bark peels naturally from the stems exposing a thicker green bark which contains the fragrant myrrh. Exudation of myrrh is encouraged by cutting the stems, and, as in ancient times, the reddish tears of aromatic resin are still collected into baskets by local people for sorting before sale to incense dealers and transport to the markets of the worlds, since it is still used in modern pharmacy and perfumery.

Frankincense and myrrh compared

Although *Boswellia* and *Commiphora* are similar in many respects, such as the exudation, the peeling bark, and their growing in arid conditions, there are excellent botanical characters for separating them. Unfortunately, as both usually grow in such dry places, their leaves soon fall off and the branches remain bare for many months of the year. They are seldom in an attractive state and tend to be overlooked by travellers in those regions. The African *Boswellia* species are usually trees with a single stem, but if they have been lopped, a more shrubby growth may result. The myrrh-yielding *Commiphora*, on the other hand, are thorny branched shrubs, often with several sizeable stems as well.

The fruits of *Boswellia* are dry (capsules), while those of *Commiphora* are juicy (drupes). There are five petals and sepals with ten stamens in *Boswellia* flowers, compared with four and eight respectively in *Commiphora*. The

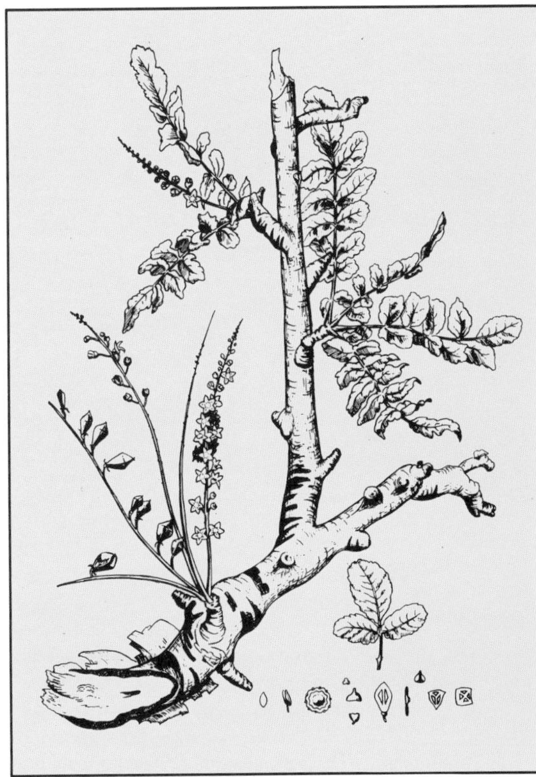

Below: A leafy branch of the Arabian frankincense tree. (After Carter, 1848.)

Above: A fiercely-armed myrrrh bush (*Commiphora myrrha*) in the foothills of northern Yemen.

myrrh resin is reddish in colour, while frankincense is whitish. In fact the Arabic names for the various frankincense resins refer to the milk-like appearance as *luban*, meaning milk.

Frankincense was burnt as an expensive, powerful incense for ancient Egyptian religious rites, as it was by the Israelites. Myrrh, on the other hand, was not burnt, but was used as a perfume, cosmetic and medicine. While both were considered to have medicinal value, myrrh was by far the more important, having many healing properties ascribed to it both internally and externally. Frankincense is still widely used in Arabia to fumigate houses, and for personal cleansing in a hot climate with limited availability of water.

ANCIENT TRADE ROUTES FOR EASTERN SPICES

There are two important general points to bear in mind when discussing the identification of spices and ancient trade routes. First we should beware of assuming that the *name* of a spice[3] has been applied through the centuries to the same plant species and its product. This is in fact seldom the case, the only permanency being the popular name of the spice, irrespective of its origin, which may vary from species to species through the ages.

The second point concerns the length of time with which we are dealing. Several thousand years are covered in the Bible. Conditions changed markedly during that time: on land the camel and the horse came to be used extensively as beasts of burden; at sea the later centuries saw the introduction of large ships well navigated by Phoenicians and Greeks.

Most writers on biblical plants have assumed that the aloes, cassia and cinnamon mentioned in the Old Testament (Exodus 30:23, 24; Psalms 45:8; Proverbs 7:17; Ezekiel 27:19; Song of Solomon 4:14) were all of Asiatic origin. The aloes have been identified as eagle-wood or lign-aloes (*Aquilaria agollocha*) in the daphne family, *Thymelaeaceae*; cassia as *Cinnamomum cassia;* and cinnamon as *Cinnamomum verum* (formerly *C. zeylanicum*), the last two both in the laurel family, *Lauraceae*. Since these are native to Assam, China and Ceylon respectively, a highly organized spice trade is presupposed if these identifications are correct. Furthermore, the cassia of Psalm 45:8 (Heb. *qesiot*) is regarded by Moldenke (1952) and others to be a product not of *Cinnamomum cassia*, but of the Himalayan plant *Saussurea costus*, formerly *S. lappa*, in the daisy family (*Compositae*), the roots of which have been used in India since very ancient times as a universal antidote for sickness. It is doubtful, however, whether this was known in the ancient Near East.

As far as I know, no eagle-wood, cinnamon, or cassia (in the modern sense) have ever been traced in Egyptian tombs. If they really were present in the kingdom of Israel it seems strange that they did not find their way to the richer land of Egypt, too. Lucas and Harris (1962), in their exhaustive treatment of ancient Egyptian materials, do not even mention eagle-wood, and they are very doubtful of cassia and cinnamon. They point out that these names have probably 'been applied to different substances at different periods ... the cassia of the ancients sometimes having been the modern cinnamon' (p. 308). Although cassia and cinnamon in the modern sense were well known to the Greeks and Romans, Lucas and Harris conclude that the two identifications of these substances in mummies of Pharaonic times cannot be considered as either satisfactory or final. Yet Moldenke (1952) blandly stated that 'there is no doubt about the cinnamon of the Bible' (p. 76). He goes on to say that the cinnamon of Exodus 30:23 (Heb. *qinnamon*), as well as the later references in Proverbs etc., was obtained from the tropical Asiatic *Cinnamomum zeylanicum*, now *C. verum*. If we examine the context of Exodus 30, however, we find Moses on Mount Horeb, in the depths of

Right: Rocky bridle paths in northern Yemen recall the ancient spice routes along which precious incense and spices were transported to the centres of civilization around the Mediterranean Sea.

Left: Leafy shoots of the cinnamon tree (*Cinnamomum verum*) in Sri Lanka.

Sinai, where it must have been difficult to obtain the more local spices, let alone exotic Indian ones.

Of the Far Eastern cassia, *Cinnamomum cassia*, Burkill (1935) writes:

'It had long been cultivated in Java, and from plants grown there Blume described it [in the nineteenth century]. Nees suggested that the classical name 'cassia' should be given to it. It is a pity that Blume adopted Nees' name, for by no argument can the Chinese tree be demonstrated to yield the cassia which reached Egypt at the time of the Exodus of the Israelites, and then and afterwards furnished the article called cassia, used in the ritual of their worship, and used, too, in the ritual of other worship around the Mediterranean' (1:549).

I think we should look to southern Arabia and especially to north-east Africa for fragrant woods, barks and spices. The natural route was northwards along the western side of Arabia parallel to the Red Sea. Job (6:19) mentions: 'The caravans of Tema' and 'the travellers of Sheba'. The oasis of Tema mentioned in that verse lies in the Arabian desert some 400 km (250 miles) north-north-west of modern-day Medina, and it probably indicates a trans-Arabian route from Mesopotamia which could be traversed only by camels. Isaiah 21:13 (KJV) mentions the 'travelling companies' of Dedanites, who were the commercial people of Dedan in the region of central western Arabia, which lies on the route from Sheba.

Ancient paintings of the patriarchal age show caravans of loaded donkeys, which were replaced by camels earlier than is generally allowed for by most authors. Evidence for the domestication of the camel even in patriarchal times is drawn from many extra-biblical sources by Kitchen (1966). But there is no doubt that the widespread use of the camel as a beast of burden revolutionized land transport across deserts. By the time of Solomon the Queen of Sheba 'came to Jerusalem with a very great retinue, with camels bearing spices, and very much gold' (1 Kings 10:2), visiting the city of Sela *en route*. Sela means 'rock' in Hebrew, as does Petra in Greek, the latter the name by which the city is known today (see p. 58).

We know that Solomon established a fleet based at Ezion-Geber near Elat on the Red Sea, from which he sent ships to Ophir, the exact location of which is doubtful, and has been placed in India, Arabia and Africa (see 1 Kings 9:26–8). We also read in 2 Chronicles 9:21 of ships bringing to Solomon such tropical items as ivory and apes, just as Queen Hatshepsut sent her expeditions from Egypt, already described.

But when was regular trade established with India? There is evidence from Indian lapis lazuli that ancient Egypt had some relationship with India during the Middle Kingdom, before 2000 BC, but this does not necessarily mean that a regular trade link was established. Moreover this link was apparently broken soon afterwards. It seems to me reasonable to assume that on very rare occasions certain exotic items of far eastern origin were brought in by these special expeditions, and for this reason I am including notes on some of them. These may even be the plant products mentioned by Solomon in his Song, but it is highly unlikely that they were included in the regular rites of the tabernacle or temple; for those products we must look to plants native in more accessible lands with a ready source of supply. By New Testament times, however, the situation had changed radically and exotic substances were more readily obtainable.

Cinnamon and cassia

The cinnamon tree (*Cinnamomum verum*, formerly *C. zeylanicum*) grows to a height of 6–10 m (18–33 ft) and bears shiny, leathery evergreen leaves with three characteristic nerves radiating from the base of the blade. It belongs to the laurel family, of which there are numerous species in the south-east Asian tropical rain forests, with insignificant flowers. The cinnamon of commerce is the inner bark, which is stripped off young trees as half-cylinders and tied in bundles for transport. The bark of 'cassia', the closely related *Cinnamomum cassia*, is collected in a similar manner. It is even more doubtful whether this spice reached the Mediterranean region earlier than late Old Testament (Heb. *qidda*) times, since the tree grows even further to the east than cinnamon.

Lign-aloes

The aloes of the Old Testament (Numbers 24:6; Proverbs 7:17, Heb. *ahalim*; Psalm 45:8; Song of Solomon 4:14, Heb. *ahalot*) are, like cinnamon and cassia, usually considered to be the product of a tropical Asian tree. For the same reasons as apply to them, I am not certain that the particular substance we now know as lign-aloes or eaglewood was, as suggested by many writers on biblical plants, available at that time. I am, however, including an account of it in default of any other suggestion. The aloes of the New Testament is positively identifiable as the bitter aloes, which is dealt with in the next chapter.

The lign-aloes tree (*Aquilaria agallocha*) occurs wild in Assam and northern Burma.[4] It is an evergreen tree with a moderately straight trunk which is often fluted.

Right: Marjoram (*Origanum syriacum*), the hyssop of Old Testament rites, growing among rocks in Palestine.

Old trees can be 20 m (65 ft) high, and some say up to 39 m (120 ft). The valuable resinous wood is hard and brown, and is known as *agar* in the incense trade in India, or as eagle-wood, lign-aloes or aloe-wood in English.[5] It is sold as chips or small blocks, and has been prized since ancient times as an incense and for making beads and ornaments. Although the wood itself has a characteristic odour, the full fragrance is obtained by burning it as incense, as the Parsees of India have done for generations. However, it has recently been found that the normal wood of this tree is soft and light, lacking resin or fragrance, and of no particular merit. In fact, the resinous eagle-wood is a pathological product of the tree formed as a result of a fungal disease: the organism concerned belongs to a group known as *Fungi imperfecti*. It is in fact possible to infect other trees artificially by driving pegs of resinous eagle-wood into them. Unfortunately the trees are felled indiscriminately by collectors, who have exploited the trade to such an extent that the species is now becoming rare.

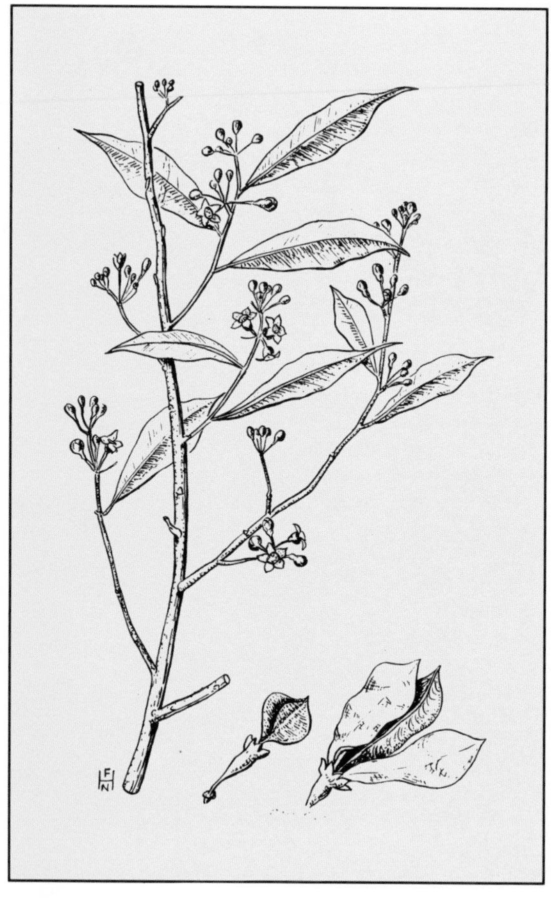

Below: A branch of the lign-aloes or eagle-wood tree (*Aquilaria agollocha*) from Assam.

PLANTS AND OLD TESTAMENT RITES

Cedar-wood, hyssop and scarlet stuff

The first rite to be instituted by the Israelites was Passover, while they were still in Egypt: 'Take a bunch of hyssop and dip it in the blood which is in the basin, and touch the lintel and the two doorposts' (Exodus 12:22). Hyssop dipped in blood with cedar wood and scarlet wool was also to be used for the rite of cleansing the leper (Leviticus 14:1–32), the disease-ridden house (Leviticus 14:33–53) and for the removal of sin according to the Law (Numbers 19:6; Hebrews 9:19).

The plant intended by the Hebrew word *ezob*, translated into Greek as *hyssopos*, and into English as hyssop, was probably the marjoram *Origanum syriacum* or *Majorana syriaca* (see p. 26). The fragrant stems of the marjoram and the cedar were dipped in the blood as a kind of brush. The cedar referred to here is the Phoenician juniper (*Juniperus phoenicea*) (described on p. 64), whose green twigs with their numerous scale leaves were used rather than the wood itself. Perhaps the purpose of the scarlet wool was to bind up the bunch. Certainly the scarlet dye was derived from the scale insect infesting the evergreen oak (p. 170).

Holy anointing oil

Moses was instructed to make up holy anointing oil as follows:

'Take the finest spices: of liquid myrrh five hundred shekels, and of sweet-smelling cinnamon half as much, that is two hundred and fifty, and of aromatic cane two hundred and fifty, and of cassia five hundred, according to the shekel of the sanctuary, and of olive oil a hin; and you shall make of these a sacred anointing oil blended as by the perfumer;[6] *a holy anointing oil it shall be'* (Exodus 30: 23–25).

This oil was for sacred, and on no account for private, use. The quantities specified were considerable, with 'sweet smelling cinnamon' and 'aromatic cane' equivalent to two hundred and fifty shekels weight (not value) of silver, as well as five hundred shekels each of 'liquid myrrh' and 'cassia', 'according to the shekel of the sanctuary'. This temple shekel was a standard weight equivalent to about

10 gm or 0.351 oz which, during the period covered by Exodus, was half the weight of the ordinary shekel. In present-day terms 250 shekels weight would equal 2.5 kg (5 lbs 7 oz). These spices were mixed in a hin of olive oil, which was equivalent to 3.66 litres or 6.5 pints.

What were the spices in this anointing oil? Myrrh is certain, but the actual identity of the substances 'cinnamon' and 'cassia' is still open to speculation, as discussed previously (p. 139), while 'sweet cane' is dealt with in this chapter (p. 144).

Sacred incense

After giving the composition of the holy anointing oil, the Lord instructed Moses how to prepare incense for ritual use: 'Take sweet spices, stacte, and onycha, and galbanum, sweet spices with frankincense (of each shall there be an equal part), and make an incense blended as by the perfumer, seasoned with salt, pure and holy' (Exodus 30: 34–35). We shall consider each of these in turn.

Stacte

The use of the word 'stacte' for one of the spices in the sacred incense follows the Septuagint rendering of a Hebrew word *nataph*, meaning drops. Several well-known incense plants yield gummy exudation in the form of drops when they are cut, and it is not easy to decide which one is intended here. It may have been the well-known opobalsamum (*Commiphora gileadensis*), the resin of which was obtained from a shrub growing wild in southern Arabia, and which seems

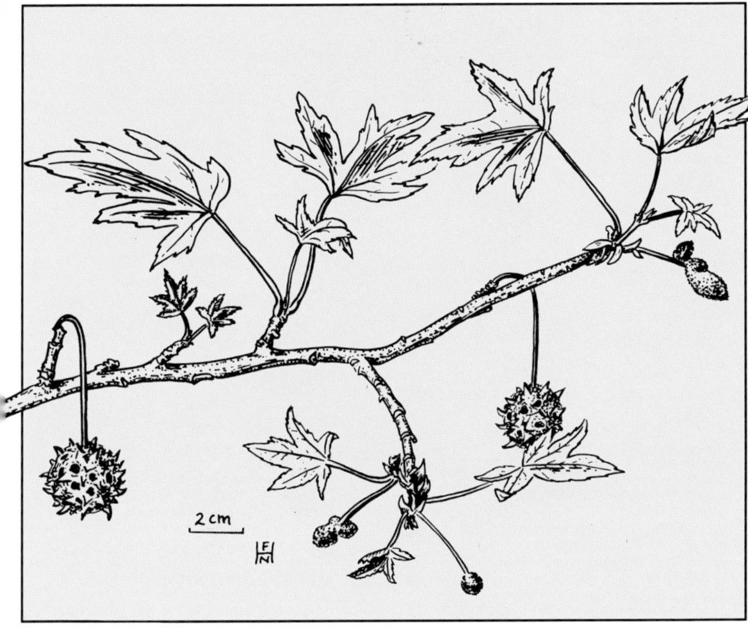

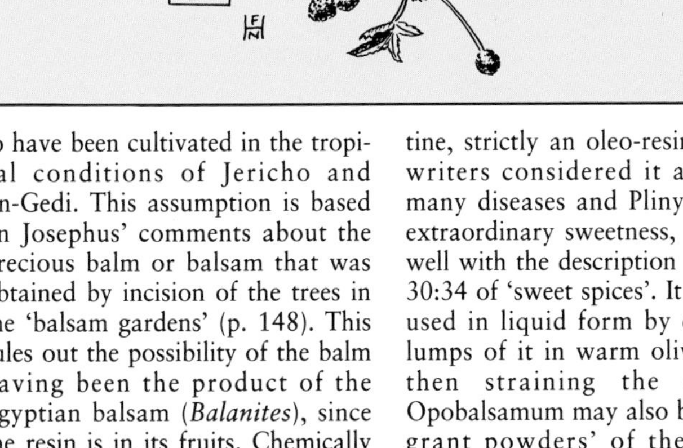

Above left: Branch of the *Liquidambar orientalis.*

Above: This tree, *Liquidambar orientalis*, yields a resin which may have been the ancient stacte.

to have been cultivated in the tropical conditions of Jericho and En-Gedi. This assumption is based on Josephus' comments about the precious balm or balsam that was obtained by incision of the trees in the 'balsam gardens' (p. 148). This rules out the possibility of the balm having been the product of the Egyptian balsam (*Balanites*), since the resin is in its fruits. Chemically opobalsumum is a kind of turpentine, strictly an oleo-resin. Ancient writers considered it a cure for many diseases and Pliny noted its extraordinary sweetness, which fits well with the description in Exodus 30:34 of 'sweet spices'. It was often used in liquid form by dissolving lumps of it in warm olive oil and then straining the solution. Opobalsamum may also be the 'fragrant powders' of the Song of Solomon 3:6 (Heb. *avkat rockel*).

The plant yielding this balm is a much-branched non-spiny bush about 2 m (6 ft) high or more. It frequently has branches chopped off by herdsmen for their flocks to graze upon, and the regrowth is even denser and more profusely branched. The leaves are small and wrinkled, each leaf having three leaflets, borne on congested short shoots. For much of the year the bush is leafless, with grey bark on

Left: A model of the priests officiating at the tabernacle, in the Bible Museum, Amsterdam.

Right: Storax bush (*Styrax officinalis*), said to yield a resinous balm.

the younger shoots and browner bark peeling off in flakes on the larger branches. It is pleasantly and strongly aromatic when cut, and exudes the resin which is collected for sale. Flowers develop and wither quickly, and being very small they are seldom seen. They give way to the small berry-like fruits with a soft exterior, which becomes dry and slits open to reveal their single seed, which has a fleshy resinous covering (aril) around its base. This shrub is rather common in the dry mountainous districts of north-eastern Africa and south-western Arabia where, in 1975, I found it growing among the rocks in sparse thickets in northern Yemen.

Two other trees yielding gummy exudation have also been suggested as possible sources of the stacte in the sacred incense. These are the storax (*Styrax officinalis*) and *Liquidambar orientalis*, trees whose products are said to have been regular articles of trade in the Fertile Crescent since remote times. Dioscorides and Pliny undoubtedly considered *Styrax officinalis* to be the tree which yielded resin from incisions in the branches. Storax is a bush or small tree common among oaks in the hills of the Mediterranean region. The paired white pendulous flowers are waxy and rich in nectar. The white stems and undersurfaces of the leaves give the plant a distinctive and elegant appearance. As recently as 1755 there is an account of French monks collecting the resin, yet nowadays this tree produces none! This is a puzzle which has not as yet been satisfactorily solved.

Some authors consider stacte to have been obtained only from *Liquidambar orientalis*, which is the source of storax resin. It has been identified in ancient Egyptian perfumes and from material taken from mummies. This liquidambar tree occurs in Cyprus, Rhodes and in western Turkey, where it grows near streams. It is a medium-sized tree with numerous twiggy branches and a somewhat weeping habit. The stacte is obtained by beating the bark in spring, which caused the resin to accumulate until it is collected in the autumn. After extracting with boiling water, the viscid greyish liquid turns yellowish-brown when purified. It contains cinnamic acid, having an odour like benzoin (Lucas, 1962).

Onycha

Nobody can be certain at present as to what substance was intended by 'onycha', in Exodus 30:34. English versions of the Bible again follow the Septuagint (Gk. *onyx*) rather than the Hebrew word *sehelet*, but I doubt whether onyx, part of a shellfish from the Mediterranean coast, was really intended. It was much more likely, at the time of the exodus, to have been a fragrant plant the identity of which is still not positively known.

Galbanum

The third spice in the sacred incense was *galbanum* (Heb. *helbena*), a well-known green resin obtained from a giant fennel (*Ferula galbaniflua*), a member of the parsley family. It grows in the high mountains of northern Iran at an altitude of about 2700 m (8900 ft). The handsome heads of yellowish flowers are borne on a stem 2 m (6 ft) or more high. The basal leaves of this plant are much divided, like parsley, but they are covered with small hairs which impart a grey appearance to them. As with all the fennels, its stem leaves have an inflated sheath-like base.

The juicy galbanum resin exudes from the large carrot-like root, as well as from the cut-off stem, especially near the base. Once the juice has dried the resinous gum may be collected and it contains 50–60 per cent resin, 5–20 per cent volatile oil, and 20 per cent gum (Howes, 1949). It is a brownish colour, with a green tinge. In ancient times it was used for toothache and for various internal ailments, but its effectiveness is doubtful, in spite of its use in Mesopotamia since the third millennium BC. There are references in Assyrian literature to galbanum being used as a fumigant, which recalls the inclusion of it in the sacred incense of the tabernacle. Although no trace of this resin has been recorded from Pharaonic Egypt, there is no reason why it should not have been included in the merchandise brought from the north. One may recall, for instance, that some 400 years before the exodus: 'Ishmaelites coming from Gilead [and from further north?], with their camels bearing gum' (Genesis 37:25) were on their way to Egypt (see gum tragacanth, p. 148).

Other Iranian and Afghanistan species of *Ferula* (*F. assa-foetida, F. foetida, F. narthex*) yield a similar resin known as *assa foetida*, which has an appalling smell when burnt! The related species, *Ferula communis*, often found in Galilee and other parts of the Mediterranean region, has more finely divided leaves and does not yield galbanum. In Roman times a very important spice was yielded by a similar plant inhabiting parts of North Africa. It was known as *silphion*, but its precise identity is not known, as it appears to have been exterminated by over-collection and by devastation of the wild plants, owing to intensive cultivation of the land at a time when North Africa enjoyed greater rainfall than at present. Silphion is represented on coins of Carthage, which used to pay tribute to Rome in the product, and most authorities agree that it was a species of *Ferula*, probably *F. tingitana*.

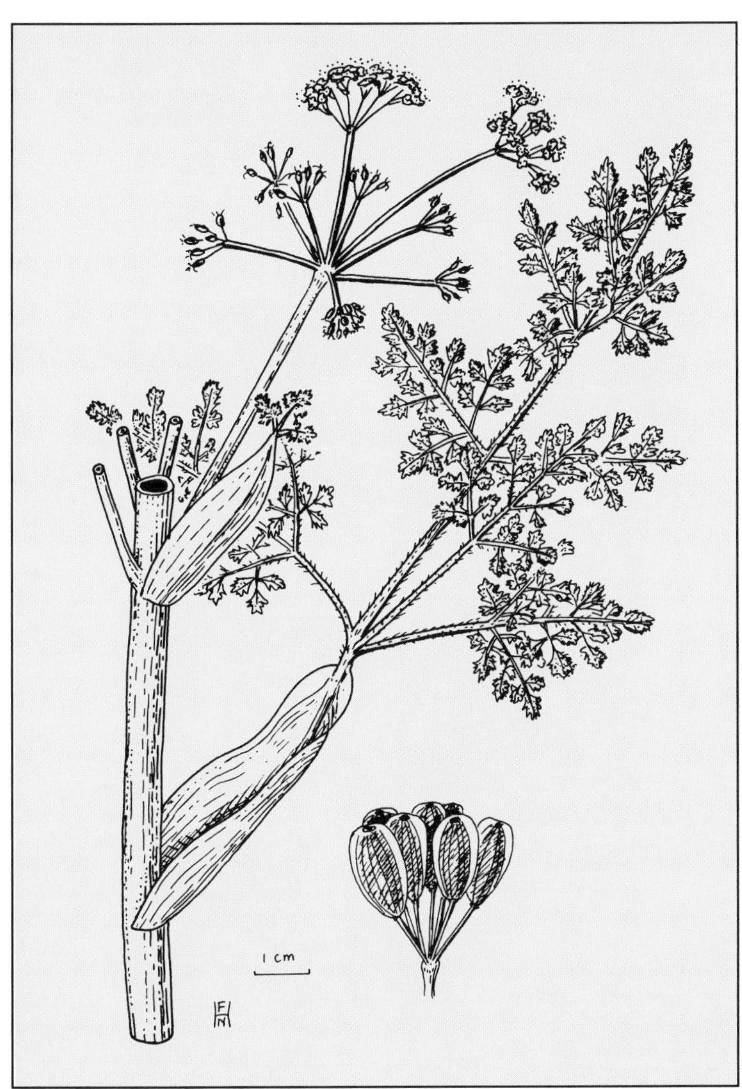

Left: The giant fennel (*Ferula galbaniflua*) yielded the resin galbanum which was used in the sacred incense.

Exotic perfumes and spices

Solomon was fond of perfumes and spices, judging from his frequent reference to them in his Song. For instance, he writes of his love as 'an orchard of pomegranates with all choicest fruits, henna with nard, nard and saffron, calamus and cinnamon, with all trees of frankincense, myrrh and aloes, with all chief spices' (Song of Solomon 4:13–14). Until comparatively recent times, strong scents were necessary to counteract the other smells that frequently pervaded the dwellings and which were not always very hygienic by our standards! We can now look at the histories of the spices mentioned in the verse quoted above.

Henna

The first of these is henna (Heb. *kopher*; camphire KJV), which is hardly an exotic, since elsewhere in the Song of Solomon we read: 'My beloved is to me a cluster of henna blossoms in the vineyards of En-gedi' (1:14; see also 4:13). In Solomon's time it apparently grew wild in the oases by the Dead Sea, along with other tropical African plants, for henna, or Egyptian privet, (*Lawsonia inermis*) is widespread in the hot, drier parts of lowland Africa. It is a much-branched shrub about 2 m (6 ft) high, bearing opposite leaves and inflorescences with numerous small white-petalled flowers. These are extremely fragrant, and the plant is often cultivated for the sake of the flowers. More important, however, are the leaves which yield a red stain[7] used to this day for colouring the skin and hair, for example in the Yemen, where I saw old men with reddened beards, which indicated that they had made the pilgrimage to Mecca. In ancient Egypt the soles and palms of mummies were dyed, as well as the finger-nails.

Nard

The nard, or spikenard, of the Song of Solomon 4:13 was obtained from the camel grass (*Cymbopogon schoenanthus*). This is an important fodder grass with aromatic leaves, inhabiting the Arabian and North African deserts. It continued to be used throughout classical times, being known by the Hebrew word *nerd* and the Greek *nardos pistike*, and by the Assyrians as *lardu*.

As with so many names of plant products, nard was also applied to an entirely different species, referred to in the New Testament as 'precious' or 'pure' nard, used by Mary to anoint Jesus (Mark 14:3; John 12:3). Small wonder it was so costly, since the perfume comes from a plant growing on open mountainsides at an altitude of 4000 m (13,000 ft) in the Himalayas. The Hindus call it *jatamansi*, a name taken up in the scientific one, *Nardostachys jatamansi*. The recently described *N. gracilis*, which has the same Hindu name, may also be used for the perfume. Nard belongs to the Valerian family, which contains other fragrant and drug plants, such as valerian itself. The nard plant is a herbaceous perennial, with a small tuft of narrow three-nerved leaves at the tip of each short stem, which is itself covered with the brown fibrous bases of withered leaves. These stems, together with the tap root, are collected for the perfume. Even herbarium specimens at Kew are pervaded with a curious fragrance which I do not find particularly sweet; but no doubt the concentrated perfume was choice enough to make the trade worthwhile in ancient times.

Saffron

This substance is better known to the average person than many of the other exotic spices mentioned in the Song of Solomon, but how many know that it is obtained from the flowers of a crocus? Only the elongated crimson styles are collected, and it has been estimated that as many as 4320 of them are required to make a single ounce of saffron. In consequence, it has always been a very expensive substance, so there has been a

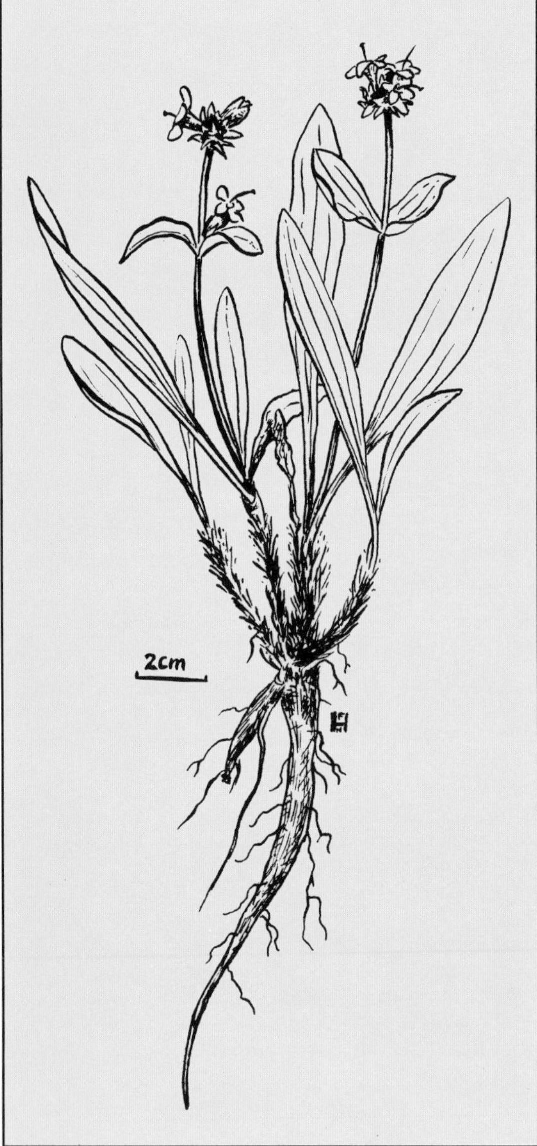

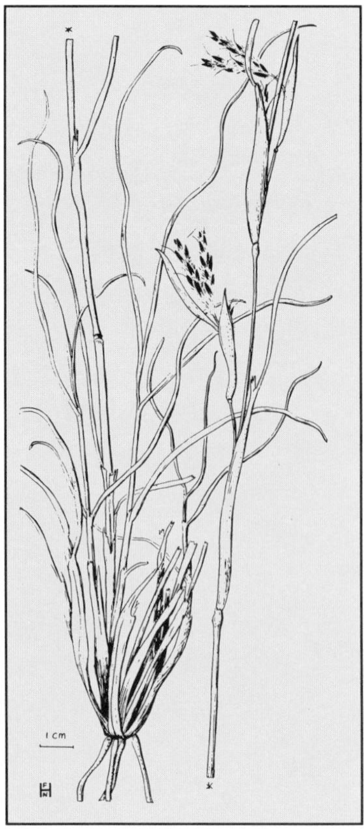

Above: Himalayan valerian (*Nardostachys jatamansi*) produced the nard perfume used to anoint Jesus.

Above right: The camel grass (*Cymbopogon schoenanthus*) yielded the nard of the Old Testament.

Far right: Saffron is obtained from the crimson styles of *Crocus sativus*.

Right: The calamus was the rhizome of the sweet flag (*Acorus calamus*).

temptation to adulterate it with cheaper substitutes such as the safflower (see p. 172). The decorative flowers of the saffron crocus (*Crocus sativus*) appear in October and are a pale reddish-lilac, freely veined with a deeper shade. The narrow leaves precede the flowers and eventually die back to the small rounded corm. In biblical times saffron was regarded as a perfume; only later, through eastern influence, was it incorporated with food as a colouring matter,[8] and also as a panacea.

In classical times the crocus was cultivated in Asia Minor, and it was later grown even more extensively in Europe, including England, especially around Saffron Walden. Since saffron crocus flowers are sterile, this plant must be increased by division of the corms. It is not found in the wild state, and appears to have been derived from *C. cartwrightianus* of Greece. The name 'saffron' is an anglicized form of the Arabic word *asfar*, meaning yellow. As a point of interest, crocus itself has come to us from the Greek *krokos*, which in turn is derived from the Hebrew *karkom*; while the original Sanskrit name for the drug *kurkuma* applies to a tropical plant called turmeric (*Curcuma longa*, also known as *C. domestica*) in the ginger family. This is another case of names being switched from one plant to another.

Calamus

This is the *aromatic* or *sweet cane* of some versions, denoted by the Hebrew *qaneh*. Apart from the reference in Song of Solomon 4:14, it is mentioned in Exodus 30:23; Jeremiah 6:20; Isaiah 43:24; Ezekiel 27:19. Most authors have taken it to refer to a grass of some kind. Sugar cane (*Saccharum officinarum*) can be ruled out since it seems to have originated in the Pacific area and there is little evidence that it had spread even as far west as India by Old Testament times. There are several tropical Indian aromatic grasses, however, which could very well be considered suitable. They occur in the genus *Cymbopogon*, and nowadays yield the lemon (*C. flexuosus*), and citronella (*C. nardus*) oils and ginger grass (*C. martinii*).

Other authors have suggested the sweet flag (*Acorus calamus*), which I would favour for the biblical plant. It has a very ancient history and the Egyptologist, Joret, believed it was used in Pharaonic times. Burkill (1935) actually says that the Greeks confused the sweet flag with the grass *Cymbopogon*, because they imported the dried rhizomes, and did not know the plant itself since it was not native to the Mediterranean region. The natural range of the sweet flag is in the

warm temperate region of Persia and northern India, although it has now been introduced elsewhere and one cannot be sure of its original distribution.

The sweet flag is a marsh plant belonging to the arum family, but it is most unusual since the green flower-head (spadix) lacks a sheathing spathe. The leafy stalk is about 45 cm (18 ins) high. The stout rhizome and iris-like leaves yield a pleasant aroma when bruised, due to the presence of a volatile oil. Apart from its use as a perfume, sweet flag has been used as a general medicine for a multitude of ailments.

No doubt there were other precious and exotic spices imported for the royal households and for use as incense in the temple at Jerusalem. In the next chapter I shall deal with fragrant ointments, since I feel they should be considered separately as personal medications and cosmetics.

----

[1] The opinions of classical authors, as well as later observations, are extensively considered by Nigel Groom in his *Frankincense and Myrrh*. He also deals with the ancient trade routes developed in and around southern Arabia.

[2] Heb. *mor*. Although *C. myrrha* is described here since it was the species from which the myrrh of the ancients was probably obtained, as well as from its variety *molmol*, several other species in the genus *Commiphora* also yield myrrh; these grow in the Horn of Africa, e.g. *C. abyssinica* var. *simplicifolia* with small undivided leaves, and *C. schimperi*. Non-spiny species of *Commiphora* yield other resins, for example opobalsamum, or balm-of-Gilead, which is obtained from *C. gileadensis* (see p. 148). Many authors refer the bdellium of Genesis 2:12 and Numbers 11:7 to *Commiphora*, especially *C. africana*. There is no reason to assume that bdellium is of vegetable origin, however, and the contexts tend to suggest an inorganic substance. In any case, *C. africana* is one of the least resinous species of the genus.

[3] Or other plant substance. See also the discussion of the use of the word 'ebony' on p. 160.

[4] At least one other species of *Aquilaria* is probably a source of the eagle-wood of commerce. It is very similar to *A. agallocha* and is known as *A. khasiana* from the Khasi Hills region of Assam. The Malaccan eagle-wood (*A. malaccensis*) with a distribution extending from Tenasserim, Burma, to Malacca and the Malayan Archipelago, also yields an aromatic wood, but of inferior quality. Ding Hou (1964) has united *A. agallocha* with *A. malaccensis* under the latter name. In view of the fact that the Malayan tree has long been known to yield an inferior quality of eagle-wood, I am reluctant to accept this taxonomic conclusion until evidence more convincing than he gives is available.

[5] Dr I. Marr, of the London School of Oriental and African Studies, informs me that the English name 'eagle-wood' is derived from the generic name *Aquilaria*, but this comes from the Portuguese *aquila*, itself a corruption of the Sanskrit *agaru* and ancient Tamil *akil*!

[6] The Hebrew *roqeah*, meaning perfumer or apothecary. Crown (1969) suggests the word applies to any person who used herbs, spices and drugs as the basic raw material of his or her craft. Although these prescriptions are the only ones in the Bible, they apparently indicate that the art of the perfumer was highly developed by the ancient Israelites.

[7] Chemically known as lawsone $C_{10}H_6O_3$, formerly called hennotannic acid.

[8] The yellow colour is chemically known as crocin, a glucoside with the formula $C_{44}H_{70}O_{28}$.

Bibliography

Bor, N. L., *The Grasses of Burma, Ceylon, India and Pakistan* (London, Pergamon Press, 1960).

Bowles, E. A., *A Handbook of Crocus and Colchicum for Gardeners*, 2nd ed (London, Bodley Head, 1952).

Breasted, J. H., *A History of Egypt* (London, Hodder and Stoughton, 1905).

Burkill, I. H., *Dictionary of Economic Products of Malay Peninsula* (London, Crown Agents, 1935).

Carter, H. J., 'A Description of the Frankincense Tree of Arabia'. *Journal Royal Asiatic Society* (Bombay Branch, 1848), 2:380–90, plates 23.

Crone, P., *Meccan Trade and the Rise of Islam* (Princeton University Press, 1984).

Crown, A. D., 'The Knowledge of Drugs in Ancient Israel', *Australian Journal of Forensic Science* (June 1969).

Deerr, N., *The History of Sugar* (London, Longman, 1949), vol. 1.

Ding Hou, 'Notes on some Asiatic Species of *Aquilaria*', *Blumea* (Leiden, 1964), 12:285–6.

Groom, N. St. J., *Frankincense and Myrrh* (London, Longman, 1981).

—. *The Perfume Handbook* (London, Chapman Hall, 1991).

Hepper, F. N., 'Arabian and African Frankincense Trees', *Journal of Egyptian Archaeology* (London, 1967), pp. 66–72.

Howes, F. N., *Vegetable Gums and Resins* (Waltham, Chronica Botanica, 1949).

—. 'Age Old Resins of the Mediterranean Region', *Economic Botany* (New York, 1950), 1:307–16.

Kempthorne, G. B., 'A Narrative of a Visit to the Ruins of Tahrie', *Transactions of the Bombay Geographical Society* (March 1856–March 1857), pp. 125–40.

Kitchen, K. A., *Orient and the Old Testament* (London, IVP, 1966).

Mandaville, J. P., 'Frankincense in Dhofar', in *Interim Report: Oman Flora and Fauna Survey, Dhofar* (Oman, Ministry of Information, 1979), pp. 52–4.

Monod, Th., *'Les arbres à encens dans le Hadramaout', Bulletin Museum National Histoire Naturelle* (Paris, 1979), 4th series, Section B, 3:131–69.

Müller, W., 'Notes on the Use of Frankincense in Southern Arabia', *Proceedings of the Seminar for Arabian Studies* (London Institute of Archaeology, 1976), 6:124-36.

Nielsen, K., *Incense in Ancient Israel* (Leiden, E. J. Brill, 1986).

Rees, A. R., 'Saffron – an Expensive Plant Product', *The Plantsman* (London, 1986), 9(4):210–17.

Thulin, M., and Warfa, A. M., 'The Frankincense Trees of Northern Somalia and Southern Arabia', *Kew Bulletin* (London, 1987), 42:487–500.

Van Beek, G. W., 'Frankincense and Myrrh', *Biblical Archaeologist* (Baltimore, 1960), 23(3):70.

15. Leaves for Healing

'All kinds of trees ... and their leaves for healing.'
(Ezekiel 47:12.)

For many centuries, in a continual fight against human illness, different societies have sought cures through medicines and magic. Most early medicines came from plants, and many botanical gardens started as medicinal, or physic, gardens. The herbalists of Egyptian, Assyrian and Hebrew cultures were well versed in the use of native and cultivated plants, and, from their investigations, different species were recognized. However, the bewildering variety of plant life frustrated the large number of attempts at sound classification.

It was not until the eighteenth century, when Carl Linnaeus regularized nomenclature, that plant systematics could be established on a scientific basis, as mentioned in Chapter 1. Linnaeus in Sweden, and his illustrious English predecessor, John Ray, raised botany from being the handmaid of medicine to a subject in its own right. For thousands of years plants were studied only as potential food or medicine, and for centuries studies had been limited because learned men referred back to classical authors instead of observing nature itself. For this reason apothecaries constantly referred to Dioscorides' *De Materia Medica,* which described the plants then thought to possess medicinal properties, and which, for some 1600 years, was repeatedly copied and uncritically accepted. The author was a Greek physician who served with the Roman army in the first century AD. However, Dioscorides owed much to his Greek compatriot Theophrastus, who lived three centuries earlier and was the first to write about plants, regardless of their usefulness.

Plants with medicinal properties, supposed or real, were better known to people in the past than they are to people today, who seek their remedies in synthetic drugs. A vast amount of pharmaceutical information has been culled from excavated inscriptions and handed down in Hebrew writings (Crown, 1969), but I cannot attempt to cover this, however fascinating it may be. In Palestine, as well as in neighbouring districts, folk medicine is still practised. Some of this information about the uses of wild plants, together with plant lore, has been collected by G. M. Crowfoot and L. Baldensperger in their book *From Cedar to Hyssop*, while a great deal more will be found in G. Dalman's monumental work in German, *Arbeit und Sitte in Palästina* and N. Krispil's *A Bag of Plants: the useful plants of Israel*, in Hebrew.

Many of the medicinal plants referred to in the Scriptures have been mentioned in the last chapter, since there appears to be a distinct connexion between fragrance and supposed therapeutic value, and between hygiene and certain cosmetics.

Below: A lentisk bush (*Pistacia lentiscus*) growing as a small tree on the island of Chios, where it is tapped for mastic resin. (Photo: B. Snogerup.)

OINTMENTS AND BALMS

Oil, and especially olive oil, was regularly used cosmetically for bodily anointing (head, Psalm 23:5; face, Psalm 104:15; foot, Deuteronomy 33:24), except during times of mourning (2 Samuel 14:2). Naomi told Ruth to: 'Wash therefore and anoint yourself, and put on your best clothes' (Ruth 3:3). The preacher exhorts: 'let not oil be lacking on your head' (Ecclesiastes 9:8). Wealthy persons, such as Solomon's lover (Song of Solomon 1:3) used perfumed oil, and Amos refers to 'finest oils' (6:6). We are told, in Proverbs, that 'Oil and perfume make the heart glad' (27:9), but that 'he who loves wine and oil [i.e. that which is perfumed and costly] will not be rich' (21:17). In Ecclesiastes, the preacher wisely observes that 'A good name is better than precious ointment' (7:1). Ointments and perfumes were kept by the well-to-do in little boxes such as those referred to by Isaiah (3:20), and many of them have been found in excavations. An ivory ointment flask dating from the fourteenth/thirteenth century BC was excavated at Lachish. We know

Left: Ladanum resin was obtained from the Turkish rock-rose *Cistus laurifolius*.

that in the fifth century BC it was customary for the wives of Persian kings to beautify themselves for 'six months with oil of myrrh and six months with spices and ointments for women' (Esther 2:12).

On the strictly medical side, oil was used to soothe and soften wounds (Isaiah 1:6); the Samaritan on the Jericho road poured oil and wine on to the injured man's bandaged wounds (Luke 10:34). However, few specific remedies are actually mentioned in the Bible, in spite of prevalent illness among the people. Jeremiah speaks vaguely of medicine (Jeremiah 30:13) and the many remedies used in Egypt (Jeremiah 46:11; Heb. *rephuah*), and occasionally a remedy is given, such as the cake of figs which acted as a soothing poultice on King Hezekiah's boil (2 Kings 20:7; Isaiah 38:21). Balm was used for pain (Jeremiah 51:8), but balm (Heb. *sori* or *tsoriy*) as a general term referred to healing ointment, which was probably made of any available oils or resins.

In the Mediterranean region in the heat of summer, every bushy hillside is wonderfully fragrant with natural resins. The scent lingers in my memory during cold northern winters, and conjures up visions of sun and blue sky, azure sea and white sails. In the *maquis*, many of the plants, such as myrtle, and members of the mint family, possess fragrant oils in their leaves, while others have glandular hairs or resin in their stems. The wooded hills of Gilead abound in such plants, yet Jeremiah poses the rhetorical question 'Is there no balm in Gilead? Is there no physician there?' (Jeremiah 8:22).

Mastic resin

The hills of Gilead and others in the region are often covered by the lentisk bush (*Pistacia lentiscus*) which yields, at least in the isle of Chios, a transparent yellowish resin, mastic, from its incised stems. (It is possible that a mastic was also obtained from the seeds of the Atlantic terebinth [*P. atlantica*], once abundant in Gilead.) The resin was imported into Egypt, where it was used medicinally as an astringent and as a kind of chewing-gum for teeth, as well as being used to varnish coffins and murals; it is still used for varnishing paintings.

This trade from the moister zones of the Fertile Crescent to drier regions of Edom and Egypt is very ancient. We read in Genesis 37:25 of Ishmaelite traders going to Egypt with 'gum, *balm* and myrrh'. The Hebrew word *sori* or *tsoriy*, here rendered as balm, M. Zohary (1982) suggested is synonymous with *nataph*, the stacte yielded by the storax tree *Liquidambar orientalis* (p. 142).

Ladanum resin

Often growing with the lentisk are rock-roses (*Cistus*), the sparkling white or beautifully crinkled pink petals of which fall by midday. These are the shrubs from which ladanum resin was obtained.[1] A surprising and amusing method of collecting the resin was that of combing the goats' beards and coats after they had browsed among the shrubs, and rubbed against the sticky foliage which exuded droplets of resin. Dioscorides tells of an alternative method, which was to beat the bushes with leather thongs and collect the resin adhering to them.

Rock-roses do not grow in the dry Egyptian climate, and it is possible that trade caravans such as those of the Ishmaelites, who passed through Gilead and Palestine on their way to Egypt, carried ladanum. Genesis 37:25 refers to traders taking 'gum, balm and *myrrh*' (Heb. *lot*). True myrrh (Heb. *mor*), however, is a tropical product which would not have been taken southwards, and it is probable that ladanum is intended, this being a true resin, not a gum, which appears as a dark brown or black mass. Ladanum was used as a perfume, but had various other medical properties. As already mentioned,

Opposite: The silhouette of an opobalsamum tree (*Commiphora gileadensis*) growing on rocky slopes in northern Yemen.

Right: The milk-vetch *Astragalus bethlehemicus*, which produces gum tragacanth, grows like spiny pin-cushions on the slopes of Mount Sinai.

the balm (Heb. *sori* or *tsoriy*) of this verse was probably mastic.

Gum tragacanth

The gum (Heb. *nekoth*; spicery KJV) referred to in Genesis 37:25 was gum tragacanth (as NEB), which is obtained as an exudate from the roots of certain leguminous plants in the genus *Astragalus*, especially *A. gummifer* and *A. bethlehemicus*.

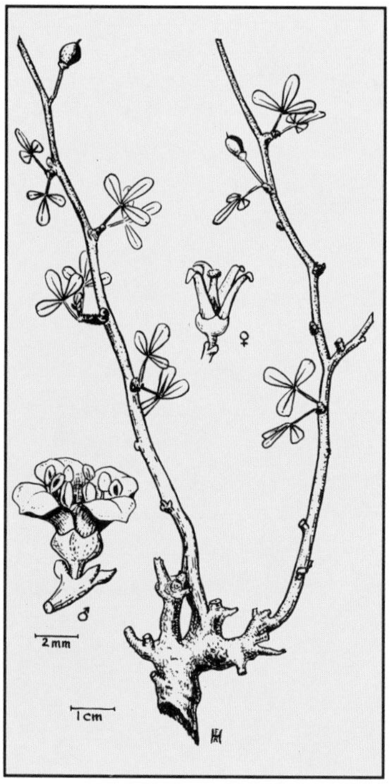

Right: Leafy shoots of the Egyptian balsam (*Balanites aegyptiaca*) with flowers and fruits which yield balanos oil.

There are over one thousand species in this genus, which are commonly known as milk-vetches, but the sixteen yielding the gum are to be found in a distinct group of small shrubby species inhabiting the dry mountains of Sinai and northwards to Turkey, Iran and neighbouring countries. The spiny cushions are scattered on the arid slopes between 1200–2100 m (4000–7000 ft), and others yielding inferior gum grow at an even higher altitude. The shrublets are protected from browsing animals by the axis of the compound (pinnate) leaves becoming spiny. When the leaflets fall, the sharp-pointed stalk remains indefinitely, resembling a pin-cushion with the points sticking outwards.

The gum itself is made and stored by the plants in the central core of their roots. This core of gum, which may be 2–10 mm in diameter according to the species, is contained under pressure in the cylinder of wood. If the root is cut off, the gum will exude from the centre at a rate of about 2.5 cm (1 in) in half an hour. The gum apparently provides nourishment and moisture for the plant during the hot dry summer, and is another example of a plant adapting to the desert environment.

Although gum tragacanth has been used since ancient times, current demand for it is greater than ever. It is used in foods where a gelatinous consistency is required, in toilet creams, and extensively in the textile industry for sizing yarns. Unfortunately the plants on the hillsides are frequently cut for fuel, in spite of recent legislation prohibiting their destruction.

The gum trade relies entirely on wild plants, which are tapped by local people. In order to expose the root of the astragalus shrublet, they dig the earth away with a small pick. One or two longitudinal cuts are then made towards the top of the root, and the gum is obtained. Gum collectors need to walk considerable distances, as the plants are scattered over the hillside, and several species may occur, each with its own characteristic gum, which should not be mixed with another. Tapping begins in June and continues for several months, until the rains start, although it is said that the best quality gum is produced during the first ten days after tapping (Gentry, 1957).

Opobalsamum

Trees that produce resins and oils from which balm was prepared occur in the oases near the Dead Sea, such as En-Gedi and those near Jericho, where the hot climate permits the growth of tropical plants. Equipment for processing balm has been excavated at En-Gedi, and a Herodian vessel containing a residue of opobalsamum was found at Qumran. There is a long-standing tradition that opobalsamum, or balm of Judea (*Commiphora gileadensis*) grew there, certainly until the time of Josephus. Whether the plant was native or introduced is still open to question, but it is most likely to have been brought from Arabia (1 Kings 10:10).

The opobalsamum is a shrub or small tree with numerous slender branches, bearing small compound leaves of three leaflets which are present for a short time after rain (see further description on p. 141). The gummy resin used as balm is obtained by making incisions in the bark, in the same way as the exudation of frankincense and myrrh was collected (see also p. 136). Opobalsamum is also called the balsam-of-Mecca, which is often considered to be the balm of Gilead, although this is likely to be one of the temperate species mentioned above.

Above: Horse-radish tree (*Moringa peregrina*) at En-Gedi.

Right: Flowers, a fruit and a seed of the horse-radish tree (*Moringa peregrina*).

Balanos oil

Another balm made in ancient times was from medicinal balanos oil, obtained from the Jerusalem-, Egyptian-, or false-balsam tree (*Balanites aegyptiaca*). This very thorny tree is abundant in the drier parts of tropical Africa, and still occurs in the oases near the Dead Sea. It is usually about 3 m (10 ft) in height, and has quite a stout trunk. Most of its slender, weeping branches have sharp thorns in the axils of the leaves, each of which bears two grey-green leathery leaflets. The small greenish flowers also occur in the leaf axils, and the young fruits are like large acorns, hence the botanical name from the Greek *balanos*, an acorn. The plum-like mature fruit develops a very hard kernel which, when crushed, yields the medicinal balanos oil.

Ben oil

In ancient Egypt ben oil was extracted from several species of the horse-radish tree, including the Palestinian *Moringa peregrina* (*M. aptera*), and was used for cosmetics and cooking. The tree itself has a dense crown of numerous whip-like branchlets bearing slender leaf stalks and scattered small leaflets. The pink flowers appear in decorative panicles in spring. Later, narrow 30 cm-long (1 ft) pods develop, each containing oily three-cornered seeds, about the size of a hazel nut. Egyptian texts frequently referred to ben oil, and to the tree itself, but these references have often erroneously been taken to indicate olive oil and the olive tree (Lucas, 1962).

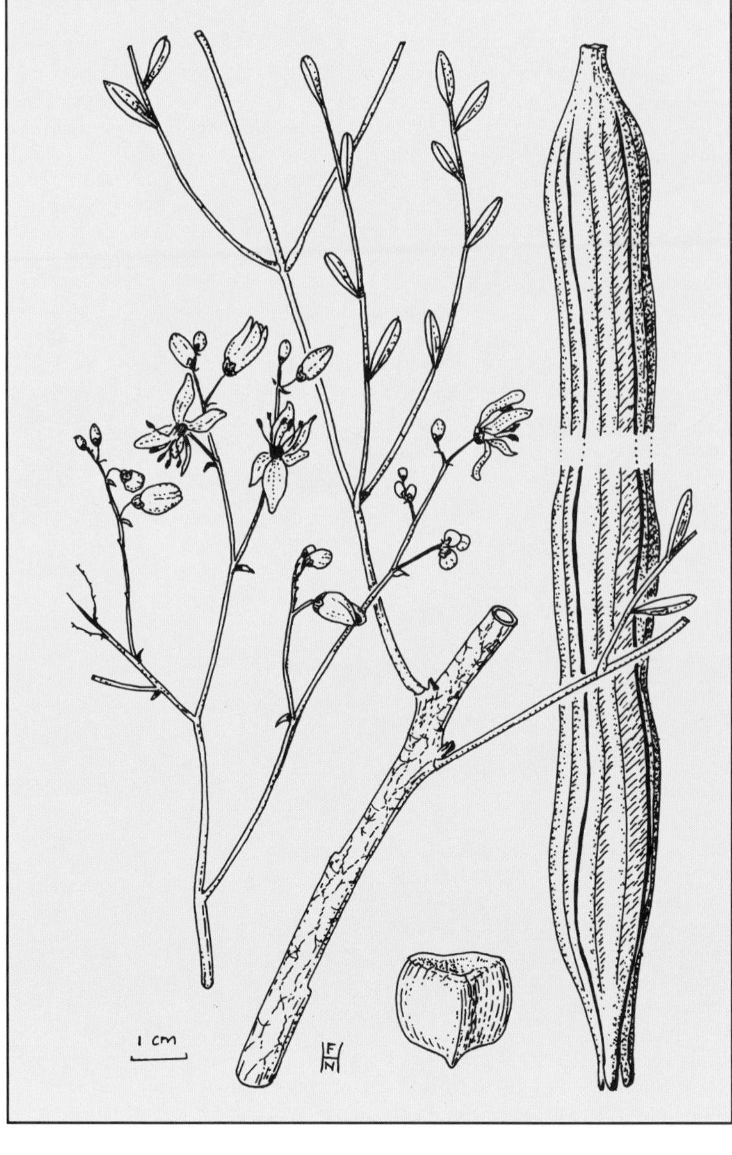

Eye salve

Eye diseases must have been common in ancient times, as blindness (from trachoma virus) is frequently mentioned in the Bible. Little could be done about most of them, and there was no treatment for cataracts, which can now be operated on. Only ointment could ease the trouble. Eye salve was produced at the Asian city of Laodicea, visited by the apostle Paul (Colossians 4:16; Revelation 3:18), a rich metropolis famous for its medicines.

Antiseptic wine

Wine was used medicinally both as a stimulant and as an antiseptic. Paul adjures Timothy: 'No longer

Far left: The mandrake (*Mandragora officinarum*) in flower. Its fruits are like little yellow tomatoes.

Left: Hemlock (*Conium maculatum*) was used to poison Socrates.

drink only water, but use a little wine for the sake of your stomach and your frequent ailments' (1 Timothy 5:23). Often mixed with resins, such as myrrh, it was drunk as a medicine or pain-killer, as we shall see in a later section. When wine was poured into wounds it acted as a useful bacteria-killing antiseptic, a practice referred to in the parable of the good Samaritan (Luke 10:34).

Magic mandrakes

Magic and superstitious beliefs have been inexorably linked with medicine and religion since ancient times. Professor R. K. Harrison (1966) points out that, in contrast with medicine in Egypt and Mesopotamia,

'the especial value of the Hebrew contribution to the development of scientific medicine was the complete repudiation of the dominance which magic was thought to exercise in the whole realm of pathology ... it is therefore unfortunate that the Jews of the Apocryphal period abandoned their inheritance and began to adopt the ancient Babylonian practice of using spells, amulets and charms in the prevention and treatment of disease' (p. 14).

One plant which has gained a reputation in many countries for having magical properties is the mandrake, which is also mentioned in the Old Testament. The English name is derived from the classical *mandragora*, of uncertain origin. Scientifically the plant is called *Mandragora officinarum*, the epithet referring to the fact that, like many other species in the nightshade family, it has long featured as a pharmaceutical drug. It grows wild in Mediterranean countries, where it can be found in rough ground at the edge of cultivation and among ruins. The forked tap root frequently becomes contorted, taking on the appearance of the human form, thus giving rise to many a superstition. It is crowned by a tuft of glossy dark green leaves with deeply set veins. In winter and early spring, pale mauve flowers are borne in the centre of the tuft, and they are followed by round, tomato-like fruits which spread out on the ground and turn yellow on ripening. The plant has a characteristic fragrance, which, I recall, scented the air on the Aegean island of Delos.

Since the flowers have a disagreeable smell, it was presumably the scent of the fruits to which Solomon referred:

'Come, my beloved, let us go forth into the fields, and lodge in the villages; let us go out early to the vineyards, and see whether the vines have budded, whether the grape blossom have opened and the pomegranates are in bloom ... The mandrakes give forth fragrance, and over our doors are all choice fruits' (Song of Solomon 7:11–13).

The fruits of the mandrake were regarded as an aphrodisiac, the use of which in fertility rites is very ancient and has persisted until recent times. Genesis 30 tells how the childless Rachel was anxious to obtain the mandrakes found in a field by Leah's son Reuben to induce fertility.[2] Although there seems to be no scientific grounds for this belief, the fruits do tend to have a narcotic effect when eaten in quantity, and a clue to the origin of this belief may be found in the shape of the fruit, which is called by the Arabs 'devil's testicles'. Here we are only concerned with the biblical references, but the interested reader is referred to the comprehensive account by Thompson (1934).

'DEATH IN THE POT'[3]

The most famous poison of the ancient world is hemlock (*Conium maculatum*), which was used to kill the Greek philosopher Socrates. It is a parsley-like plant with spotted stems about 1 m (3 ft) or more high and has numerous small white flowers. Although it occurs widely in Europe and the Near East, including Palestine, it is thought not to be referred to in the original biblical manuscripts, in spite of the KJV twice naming 'hemlock' (see p. 48).[4]

Few poisons are mentioned in the Bible. As R. K. Harrison (1966) points out, this is probably due to the fact that in Hebrew medicine, herbal therapeutics occupied a prominent position, while narcotics received little attention – although the difference between them is frequently only a matter of their strength, as many medicines are narcotic in high concentration. But the presence of poison is sometimes implied, such as the flour that caused illness when contaminated by darnel grass grains (see p. 88).

While some plants are poisonous in every part, others have the poison restricted to certain portions, such as the roots or fruits. It is not clear what plant the writer to the Hebrews had in mind when he wrote a warning about the 'root of

Opposite: Bitter aloes (*Aloe vera*) cultivated in the Arabah.

Right: Flowers and fruits of the opium poppy (*Papaver somniferum*).

bitterness' (Hebrews 12:15 KJV, RSV). This warning is extended in the NEB: 'look to it that there is no [immoral person] among you ... no bitter, noxious weed growing up to poison the whole'.

Poison was unexpectedly found in the stew pot during a famine, after one of Elisha's men had collected wild gourds (Heb. *paqquoth*) in the desert by the Dead Sea (2 Kings 4:39). Unfortunately he had gathered the small melon-like fruits of the colocynth (*Citrullus colocynthis*), a vine that trails on the sand (see p. 57). Elisha's purification of the stew by throwing in meal seems to have no natural explanation. (When Carl Linnaeus named a different gourd *Cucumis prophetarum* to commemorate the incident, he chose the wrong plant!) Its bitter pulp contains a purge which is sufficiently violent to be fatal, though the seeds are said to be harmless. The colocynth may also be the plant referred to as the 'vine of Sodom' in Deuteronomy 32:32, not 'gall' or 'poison' (Heb. *rosh*; Deuteronomy 29:18; Psalm 69:21; Jeremiah 8:14; 9:15; 23:15; Amos 6:12). The Roman Emperor Claudius is said to have been poisoned with colocynth by his wife, Agrippina in AD 54.

Gall

In Matthew's Gospel we read of Christ on the cross being offered[5] vinegar or wine (i.e. something bitter, Gk. *chole*) 'mingled with gall; but when he tasted it, he would not drink it' (Matthew 27:34), while Mark (15:22) says it contained myrrh. In New Testament days it was customary for a band of compassionate women to be in attendance at executions, seeking to alleviate the sufferings of the condemned. They brought whatever might act as an anodyne to deaden pain, such as gall and myrrh (*Commiphora myrrha*, see p. 137).

Wormwood

Often associated with gall, which in the Scriptures denotes sorrow, is wormwood (Heb. *laanah*; Gk. *apsinthos*; Proverbs 5:4; Amos 5:7, 6:12; Revelation 8:11). Wormwood is well known from ancient prescriptions as a tonic, obtained from various species of *Artemisia*. In desert regions *Artemisia herba-alba* and *A. judaica* grow abundantly, and the Arabs still drink an infusion prepared from their leaves. Some

species of wormwood can be narcotic when taken in strong doses, but others, though bitter, were favoured medicinally and the Assyrians used them for all kinds of illnesses (Thompson, 1949).

Opium

It is possible that another component of the anodyne drink offered to Jesus was an extract from the opium poppy (*Papaver somniferum*). This was widely used in ancient times in biblical lands and there are many references to its occurrence, though not in the Bible. The eastern Mediterranean seems to have been a centre for the cultivation of the poppy, from which the sap was extracted by cutting its fruit. Morphine and codeine are the well-known pain-killing drugs occurring in the opium sap, which was usually administered in drinks.

As long ago as the sixteenth/fifteenth century BC, Egypt traded in opium with Cyprus, where juglets in the shape of poppy capsules were manufactured. One of these juglets was found there in a Phoenician temple of the Bronze Age. It appears to have been associated with an amulet that was intended to protect women during childbirth, and it is probable that opium was administered to reduce pain during labour. Opium also appears in the Assyrian lists of herbs and medicines, and by the first century AD the Greek writer Dioscorides gives a good description of it.

The opium poppy is an annual plant growing quickly to about 1 m (3 ft) in height. Its grey-green leaves feel waxy to the touch, and its large flowers are white or mauve-tinged, often with large dark blotches at the base of the four petals. The large pepper-pot fruits become dry capsules which scatter their seeds through pores round the top.

Hemp

Another possible component of the drink offered to Jesus could have been hemp, the cannabis resin from *Cannabis sativa*. In ancient Egypt a drink was made from hemp, with opium-like effects, while in Assyria it was often used as a narcotic. About AD 160 the Greek physician Galen commented on the narcotic effect of hemp used in cakes. Again we have no direct biblical reference to its use.

BITTER ALOES AND OTHER PURGES

When Jesus died on the cross, Joseph of Arimathea took his body and laid it in a tomb, while Nicodemus brought 'a mixture of myrrh and aloes about a hundred pounds [45 kilos] weight' (John 19:39). Nowadays aloes are better known than myrrh, which we have dealt with in the last chapter. The bitter aloe (*Aloe vera*) is a stout, tufted plant with thick, sword-like leaves having sharp teeth along their edges. The slender flowering stalk is about 60 cm (2 ft) high, bearing numerous tubular, orange-yellow flowers.

Although plants of bitter aloe now grow in many parts of the world, it originated in south-west Arabia, where I have seen it growing wild in the semi-desert of the Yemen (Hepper, 1988). It was carried by Phoenician and Greek traders to their ports of call, and later the Portuguese took it further afield. As a succulent plant, it could withstand long periods of drought aboard sailing ships or packed up on a camel's back, and still grow on planting.

Since it is now widespread in the world, this plant has been given several scientific names. It should be known as *Aloe vera*, but it is often called *A. barbadensis* after the Island of Barbados, where was introduced in 1690. There are hundreds of species in tropical Africa, though few are economically important. The only other one known in ancient times was the plant from Socotra called *A. perryi* (or *A. soc-*

cotrina), which authors often confuse with *A. vera.*

The yellow leaf juice is the source of the drug aloes, or aloin. In order to extract the juice, the succulent leaves are cut off and placed in a receptacle for some hours. When all the juice has drained from the leaves it is evaporated until a solid mass of crude bitter aloes is obtained. It was in this form that it entered the ancient trade routes, to be sold and re-sold for use as a purge and as a spice for embalming. Nowadays we should distinguish between this juice and the colourless gel obtained from the outer layers of the aloe leaf, as it is the gel that is now popular in skin ointments, shampoos and medicines (Grindlay and Reynolds, 1986).

The purgative action of many other plants was well known in biblical times. It has been suggested, however, that the reference to 'hyssop' in Psalms 51:7 – 'purge me with hyssop and I shall be clean' – alludes to the symbolic act of cleansing in the Levitical rite, rather than to an actual medical attribute of the marjoram with which the 'hyssop' is usually identified (Moldenke, 1952).

Right: Castor-oil plants (*Ricinus communis*).

Castor oil

Even castor oil was as familiar to the Egyptian physician as it was to our grandparents. Castor-oil plants (*Ricinus communis*) grow abundantly in the warmer parts of the Middle East, in waste places and rubbish heaps. I have seen them lining the banks of the Nile at Luxor, where they grow 3 m (10 ft) high, their large erect bushes a decorative purple-green due to the colour of the new leaves and stems. Mature palmate leaves can be as much as 60 cm (2 ft) across. The green flowers with red stigmas develop into spiny fruits, enclosing three elegantly mottled, poisonous seeds bearing an aril at one end.

Many commentators on the Bible believe that the plant which shaded Jonah (4:6, 7; Heb. *qiqayon*; gourd KJV and NEB) was the castor-oil, because it grows so quickly. We do not know when this species was first introduced into western Asia from Africa, but the castor-oil features prominently in ancient Assyrian medicine, and must therefore have been well established at Nineveh in the time of Jonah in the eighth century BC.

Embalming the dead

Some years ago, on a cold and foggy afternoon I had the unusual experience of being locked in the mummy room of a London museum! The attendant who released me was as surprised to find me there as I was glad to be out, since I did not relish remaining there all night. Not only were there ancient Egyptian human mummies, but mummified cats, and grotesque shrunken heads from Ecuador.

The practice of embalming the dead is very old and widespread. We read in Genesis that 'Joseph commanded his servants the physicians to embalm his father. So the physicians embalmed Israel; forty days were required for it, for so many days are required for embalming' (Genesis 50:2, 3). Later 'Joseph died, being a hundred and ten years old; and they embalmed him, and he was put in a coffin in Egypt' (Genesis 50:26). As the Hebrews were enjoying Egyptian hospitality it is hardly surprising that this Egyptian practice was adopted. The full period of embalming was seventy days, but Jacob received only forty – perhaps, not being an Egyptian, he was not given the full treatment. Yet the verse continues: 'the Egyptians wept for him seventy days'. Margaret Murray (1949) commented that 'the extra thirty days would be required for the bandaging and wrapping of the mummy, as each bandage was put on with appropriate prayers and ceremonies'. She also points out that 'the Israelitish mourning for the dead was thirty days when they first came out of Egypt, for so they mourned for Aaron and Moses'.

Egyptian mummies have been discovered in tombs dating from the first dynasty, before 3000 BC, and bodies preserved in the dry sand date from an even earlier period. In hot Egyptian conditions bodies had to be dealt with immediately after death, and those parts (the viscera) removed which were subject to rapid decay. The whole principle of embalming was to provide the soul (the *ba*) with a continuing resting place in the after-life; hence not only must the body (the *ka*) be preserved, but it must be supplied with food and provided with its daily objects. For the rich, protection was afforded by the pyramids and subterranean tombs in which the mummy was housed, and provisions in the form of material objects or representations on the walls. In many ways the whole embalming and burial process may be considered as a magical ritual.

During the New Kingdom – the period in which the Israelites were in Egypt – the technique was to separate the viscera into four canopic jars, each with its characteristic and symbolic lid, representing the head of a baboon, jackal, falcon and man, where they were preserved in myrrh, aniseed[6] and onions after being perfumed. Desiccation of the rest of the body was achieved with the natural soda called natron, which contains sodium carbonate and sodium bicarbonate. Prolonged preservation of the body depended upon the efficiency of the desiccation. Subsequent processes involved stuffing the body cavities with tow, papyrus, sawdust or sand, anointing with fragrant oils, sometimes dyeing the finger nails, palms and soles of the feet with henna, and finally painting the body with resin. Once the body had been restored to its original shape, it was carefully bound with linen bandages – there were in all sixteen layers around Tutankhamun – and then soaked in resin.

Resin was used in great quantities both in and around the mummy, and in the tomb as an incense. It originated from the pines and junipers ('cedars') in the mountains of the eastern Mediterranean and from the terebinth (mastic) at a lower altitude. Curiously enough, spices have not definitely been found in Egyptian mummies, although Herodotus stated that 'myrrh, cassia and every sort of spicery except frankincense' were used (Baumann, 1960).

If embalming was attempted by poor people, it entailed simply soaking the body in soda, or burying it in dry sand, or washing it with cheap radish oil. For the pharaohs and rich noblemen, however, infinite pains were taken by the artistic embalmers to perfect their mummies. They were often garnished with juniper berries or with wreaths of flowers. These have sometimes survived intact and in a quite recognizable state, such as those garlanding Tutankhamun's body, which was placed in the inner of three golden sarcophagi, a stone coffin and a succession of four gilt wooden boxes called shrines (Hepper, 1990). Coffins were often made of the wood of the sycomore fig, but one from the time of Zozer (*c.* 2800 BC) was of 6-ply wood using cypress, juniper, pine and Christ thorn or sidder (*Ziziphus spina-christi*).

Joseph's body was treated in this way, as befitted an Egyptian by adoption. Although the period of Joseph's rule coincided with the period of the Hyksos (the so-called Shepherd Kings) between the Middle and New Kingdoms, many of the typically Egyptian customs were continued. Later, the Hebrews developed different methods of burial which did not include embalming, although we note that when Asa, the king of Judah, died, he was buried in a rock-cut tomb and 'They laid him on a bier which had been filled with various kinds of spices prepared by the perfumer's art' (2 Chronicles 16:14).

---

[1] It is often said that the large white-flowered *Cistus ladanifer* is the biblical ladanum-yielding shrub, but this species is limited to Spain and the opposite coast of North Africa. The closely related *C. laurifolius* is very resinous and could have been a source of the biblical ladanum, since it occurs in Turkey. Pink-flowered *C. creticus*, often referred to by its synonyms *C. villosus* and *C. incanus*, is said to become progressively more covered with glandular hairs as the summer goes on. The white-flowered *C. salviifolius*, with which it commonly grows, is non-resinous.

[2] The incident between Rachel and Leah is said to have taken place to the 'east', where Jacob lived with Laban, and it is doubtful whether *Mandragora* grew as far east, since it is a Mediterranean species. But there is good reason to disbelieve Allegro's supposition in *The Sacred Mushroom and the Cross* (1970) that they found the fly-agaric *Amanita muscaria*, as this inhabits woods, and would not have been gathered in fields. Neither is there evidence of its occurrence in the region. Eminent scholars totally reject Allegro's far-fetched theory that Christianity is derived from mushroom-based fertility cults (see J. C. King, *A Christian's View of the Mushroom Myth*, 1970).

[3] 2 Kings 4:40.

[4] The plant in Amos 6:12 (Heb. *laanah*; hemlock KJV; wormwood RSV; poison NEB; bitterness NIV) is probably wormwood, *Artemisia* species (see p. 152).

[5] When Jesus was on the cross he was passed a sponge of vinegar (see p. 102).

[6] Ghalioungni (1963) mentioned aniseed (*Pimpinella anisum*), which is a European species. However, Lucas (1962) does not include it in his list of plants used in ancient Egypt.

Bibliography

Baumann, B. B., 'The Botanical Aspects of Ancient Egyptian Embalming and Burial', *Economic Botany* (New York, 1960), 14:84–104.

Crown, A. D., 'The Knowledge of Drugs in Ancient Israel', *Australian Journal of Forensic Science* (June 1969).

Dayagi-Mendels, M., *Perfumes and Cosmetics in the Ancient World* (Jerusalem, Israel Museum, 1989).

Gentry, H. S., 'Gum Tragacanth in Iran', *Economic Botany* (New York, 1957), 11:40–63.

Germer, R., *Untersuchung über Artzneimittelpflanzen im Alten Ägypten* (Dissertation, Hamburg University, 1979)).

Ghalioungui, P., *Magic and Medical Science in Ancient Egypt* (London, Hodder and Stoughton, 1963).

Grindlay, D., and Reynolds, T., 'The *Aloe vera* phenomenon', *Journal of Ethnopharmacology* (Lausanne, 1986), 16:117–51.

Groom, N. St. J., *The Perfume Handbook* (London, Chapman and Hall, 1991).

Harrison, R. K., *Healing Herbs of the Bible* (Leiden, Brill, 1966).

Hepper, F. N., 'The Identity and Origin of Classical Bitter Aloes *(Aloe)*', *Palestine Exploration Quarterly* (London, 1988), pp. 146–8.

Howes, F. N., *Vegetable Gums and Resins* (Waltham, Chronica Botanica, 1949).

Krispil, N., *A Bag of Plants: the Useful Plants of Israel* (Jerusalem, Yara Publishing House, 1987), 3 vols.

Stearn, W. T., 'Code and Anciciae Julianae', *Graphis* (Zurich, 1954), 10:522–9.

Thompson, C. J. S., *The Mystic Mandrake* (London, Rider, 1934).

16. *Timber for the Carpenter*

'Is not this the carpenter's son?'
(Matthew 13:55.)

Noah worked with gopher wood, Moses used acacia and Solomon made his temple of cedar; in the New Testament we know that the cross was made of timber and we read of scented and expensive woods being imported into Rome. In this chapter we deal with woodworking and wooden articles, as distinct from the trees themselves which have already been described (chapter 2).

Woodworking tools

We can see at a glance that the fine furniture in Tutankhamun's tomb, for example, was made by craftsmen of the highest calibre – and he was one of the pharaohs of Egypt while the Israelites were labouring in captivity over 3100 years ago. How was such fine work accomplished? Which tools were used and what was the timber?

Woodworking requires special tools. The earliest metal ones were made of copper, which is rather soft for the purpose, even after hardening by repeated hammering. Bronze was used in early Old Testament times, since iron did not come into general use until after the exodus, and tools made of it were not common until much later. First the timber had to be obtained by felling trees, which must have been terribly hard work with primitive axes – a task relegated to slaves, who were the 'hewers of wood' (Joshua 9:21, 23). Sometimes the axe-head flew off and struck a neighbouring axeman – an eventuality which the Law covered (Deuteronomy 19:5). When 'the sons of the prophets' went to the River Jordan to cut trees for timber, a borrowed iron axe-head fell off and was retrieved by Elisha himself on casting a stick into the water (2 Kings 6:1–7). The trees cut on that expedition to the Jordan were probably tamarisk, willow or poplar, as all of these are typical of the river valley and have been identified from wood fragments excavated at Jericho by Dr Kathleen Kenyon (1953).

Once felled, the trees were cut up with copper pull-saws having erect or backward-pointing teeth, whereas teeth on modern saws point forwards and are pushed. Egyptian murals show standing carpenters sawing baulks of timber lashed to a support, and the top of the saw pointing upwards to get the best cut when the saw was drawn downwards. In early times copper chisels were used for making joints, and bow-drills with a copper bit were used for boring holes. Preparation of the timber was achieved by laboriously chipping the surface with a chisel or an adze, which had a copper blade bound to a wooden handle. The timber object was finally smoothed by rubbing with a stone, as the plane was not invented until Roman times.

Many tools of different shapes and sizes have actually been discovered in Egyptian tombs, as well as delightful models of carpenters' shops. From these we know a great deal about the tools and methods of working (Petrie, 1917; Goodman, 1964). There is no reason to believe that Israelite implements were markedly different from those of the Egyptians, with whom the Israelites were in frequent contact. Scriptural references to the carpenter's craft are numerous and an interesting word-picture is drawn by Isaiah when he writes of the carpenter who measures the wood, marks it out with rule and compass, fashions it with chisels[1] – in this case only to make an idol (Isaiah 44:13–17). Similarly Jeremiah tells how 'A tree from the forest is cut down, and worked with an axe by the hands of a craftsman. Men deck it with silver and gold; they fasten it with hammer and nails' (Jeremiah 10:3). A workman's wooden mallet was used by Jael the Kenite to hammer the tent peg into Sisera's temple (Judges 5:26).

Hewing wood, like drawing water, was a humble occupation (Deuteronomy 29:11), and although the carpenter's (and especially the cabinet maker's) craft was a skilled trade, it cannot have been held in high esteem by the people of Jesus' own country who, being astonished at his wisdom, asked 'Is not this the carpenter, the son of Mary and brother of James?' (Mark 6:3). Incidentally, it is interesting to note that Jesus drew his illustrations from agriculture rather than carpentry during his ministry, perhaps because this was an occupation more familiar to his hearers.

The tabernacle

Moses was told to make a Tent of Meeting, commonly known as the tabernacle, where the Israelites could meet with God during their desert wanderings. It had to be made of acacia wood (KJV retained *shittim*, the Hebrew word), which is actually the commonest timber tree growing in Sinai (see p. 63).[2] As we cannot deal here with the plan of the tabernacle the reader is referred to Exodus 25–7, and to Bible commentaries, for a description. We should remember, however, that it was a portable structure, consisting essentially of a series of wooden poles draped with linen, and with a wooden ark or box and other furniture inside. It is now considered that the 'boards' (KJV) along the sides of the tabernacle were in fact slender uprights joined by cross-rails, forming frames to support the curtains. They were all made of acacia wood, but overlaid with gold and fitting into silver-lined sockets. The RSV has adopted this rendering, and the constructional details in Exodus 26 are now readily comprehensible. (See also *The Illustrated Bible Dictionary*, 3:1506.)

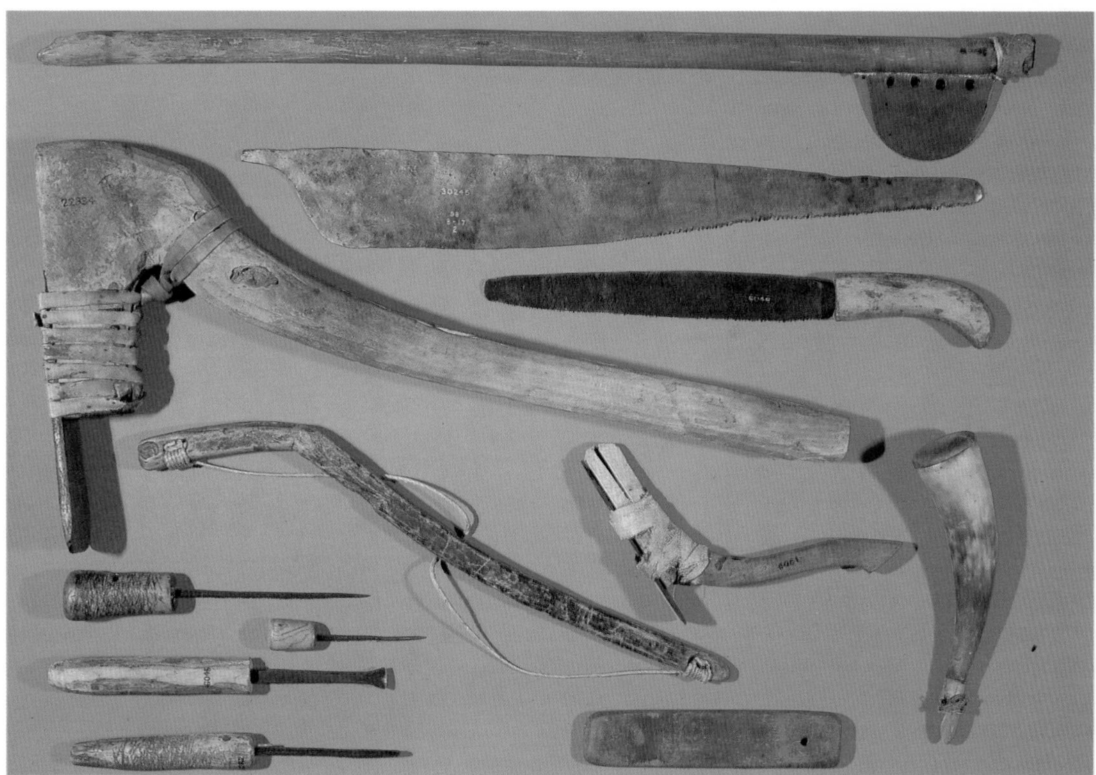

Left: Woodworking tools from ancient Egypt. (Photo: British Museum.)

Within the tabernacle there was the area known as the holy place, which was separated from the holy of holies by a veil of linen hung 'upon four pillars of acacia overlaid with gold, with hooks of gold, upon four bases of silver' (Exodus 26:32). A second screen for the door was made by Moses' craftsmen and then hung on five pillars made of acacia (Exodus 36:38).

The holy chest or ark, with two carrying poles, was made of acacia wood by the craftsman Bezalel, complete with a gold top (mercy-seat) and overlaid with gold throughout. It was 121 cm (4 ft) long and 69 cm (2 ft 3 ins) wide and deep. Other items of furniture made of acacia were the table and the altar. The former was known as the Table of the Presence of Shewbread, as it was used for the display of these twelve loaves, as well as for dishes, spoons and flagons. It was 92 cm (3 ft) long, 46 cm (1 ft 6 ins) wide and 69 cm (2 ft 3 ins) high. This table was carried on two acacia wood poles overlaid with gold. The altar was much larger being 230 cm (7 ft 6 ins) square and 138 cm (4 ft 6 ins) high, also with carrying poles. The whole was overlaid with bronze, and although it is described as hollow it must have presented a formidable object to be carried across the desert. Finally there were pillars forming the outer court. Although not expressly indicated, they too were probably made of acacia wood.

Solomon's house and temple

Three hundred years after the Tabernacle was made King David set his heart on building God a 'house of cedar' (2 Samuel 7). But it was ordained that Solomon, his son and heir, should build it and not David himself.

However, both David and Solomon had their own houses made of cedar obtained from Lebanon. Logs were floated as rafts to Joppa and carried to Jerusalem (2 Chronicles 2:16), as described in Chapter 2. Hiram of Tyre sent the carpenters and masons, as well as the timber, to build David's house (2 Samuel 5:11; 1 Chronicles 14:1). Solomon's own house was so magnificent and complex that it was thirteen years in building (1 Kings 7:1). Solomon boasted that 'the beams of our house are cedar, our

Below: Ancient Egyptian woodworkers rubbing, glueing, sawing and adzing.

rafters are of pine' (Song of Solomon 1:17). The House of the Forest of Lebanon, thought to be a public building, was 46 m (150 ft) long, with forty-five cedar pillars in three rows of fifteen, which must indeed have given the impression of a forest. Most of these buildings appear to have been finished with cedar panelling, both on the walls and on the ceiling, and the Holy of Holies had a cedar-wood floor.

Cedar beams were used together with the masonry in the following manner: 'The great court had three courses of hewn stone round about, and a course of cedar beams; so had the inner court of the house of the Lord and the vestibule of the house' (1 Kings 7:12 and 6:36). It is again referred to in the rebuilding of the temple in Ezra's time (Ezra 3:8). The use of timber in construction work is attested by excavations at Hazor in northern Israel. There may have been a structural reason for this type of construction, and Harding (1959) has suggested that the wooden beams used in the Roman temple at Petra were an anti-earthquake device. In the course of time, however, the timber rotted away and the gaps resulting were a contributory factor in the collapse of the buildings.

In 1 Kings 6 there is a description of Solomon's temple itself. The walls of this magnificent structure were made of limestone blocks, which were chiselled square by the men of Gebal (i.e. Phoenicians of Byblos), who also prepared the timber beams. Inside, it was panelled throughout with ornamentally carved cedar, while the folding doors and floor were of wood from a coniferous tree (1 Kings 6:34; Heb. *berosh*; fir KJV; cypress RSV; pine NEB, GNB and NIV).

Olive wood was used for certain parts of Solomon's temple, such as the nave doorposts and the doors to the inner sanctuary. These doors, like the panelled walls of the temple, were ornamented with carved figures of cherubim, palm trees and open flowers, all overlaid with gold. Within the inner sanctuary rested two cherubim carved in olive wood. Each was ten cubits (4.45 m = 14 ft 7 ins) high and had the same span from wing tip to wing tip. It is unlikely that the body of the cherubim would have been carved from a single piece of olive wood, and in fact it is probable that both the body and the wings were composed of numerous small pieces of wood somehow joined together and then carved to the required shape. The heavy wood of the slow-growing olive becomes contorted and, due to difficulty in obtaining a large enough piece of perfect wood, it is usual to find only small objects made from it. Olive is strong, durable, and when seasoned, it takes a fine polish and is beautifully veined and spotted; it is subject neither to cracking nor to attack by insects.

Almug and algum trees

Before leaving the subject of the temple, we should mention the mysterious almug tree of 1 Kings 10. We read that

'the fleet of Hiram ... brought from Ophir a very great amount of almug wood and precious stones. And the king made of the almug wood supports for the house of the Lord, and for the king's house, lyres also and harps for the singers; no such almug wood has come or been seen to this day' (1 Kings 10:11–12 and parallel account in 2 Chronicles 9:10–11).

Yet in 2 Chronicles 2:8, when Solomon was ordering timber from Hiram, he said 'Send me also cedar, cypress and algum timber from Lebanon'.

It is evidently that two timbers are indicated here: almug imported from Ophir and algum felled in Lebanon. Moldenke, following Celsius, William Smith and others, has identified the almug with the Indian red sandalwood tree (*Pterocarpus santalinus*) and algum with the Grecian juniper (*Juniperus excelsa*).[3] The juniper was described earlier (p. 27), together with other trees native to Lebanon. Red sandalwood occurs in India and Ceylon, and is a large tree. It is a member of the pea family (*Leguminosae*), with heavy, hard wood which polishes well.

After the Babylonian invasion and capture of Jerusalem by Nebuchadnezzar in 587 BC, the temple and city walls were ruined. However, some seventy years later, Nehemiah and his colleagues returned from captivity with the vision and enthusiasm to restore the temple and rebuild the walls, using timber originating from countries near and far (Ezra 3:7; 5:8; Nehemiah 2:8).

Other houses

Although the walls of ordinary houses in biblical Palestine were built of stone or mud, the roofs were constructed of twigs and reeds laid across beams, hence the ability of the four men to let down the paralytic through the roof to Jesus' feet (Mark 2:4, not 'tiles' as Luke 5:19). Traditional Arab peasant houses are made with domed stone roofs because, as Professor Albright points out, timber is now scarce in the region. A roof made of reeds on wooden beams (sycomore, Isaiah 9:10) affords protection from the sun and is sufficient for a dry climate such as that of Egypt, but Palestinian conditions require some waterproofing in the form of a layer of mud or plaster. Unfortunately such roofs need to be rolled after each shower, and cracks develop when they dry out. Lime-plastered roofs, together with lime-plastered rainwater cisterns, enabled the Israelites to settle wherever there was rain, instead of being restricted to sites near springs or streams. During the excavations at Masada the changing room (*apodyterium*) of the great public bathhouse, which must have been constructed early in the first century AD, was found to have had a plastered ceiling. The plaster fragments bear on one side the impression of the reeds of which the roof was constructed, and on the other side floral motifs with a pattern of squares (Yadin, 1966).

Timber was also used for the gates and gate-posts, for house door frames and for the door itself, which was pivoted. The 'hinges' referred to in Proverbs (26:14) would in fact have been a pivot. Doors in Old Testament times were fastened by a wooden bolt or lock, which was opened by a wooden key (Judges 3:25; Heb. *mapteah*).

The key was a flat piece of wood furnished with pins corresponding to holes in a shallow bolt. The bolt was inside, shot into a socket in the doorpost and fastened by pins which fell into the holes in the bolt from an upright piece of wood (the lock) attached to the inside of the door. To unlock the door one put one's hand in by a hole in the door (Song of Solomon 5:4 KJV), and raised the pins in the bolt by means of the corresponding pins in the key (F. F. Bruce, quoted in *The Illustrated Bible Dictionary*).

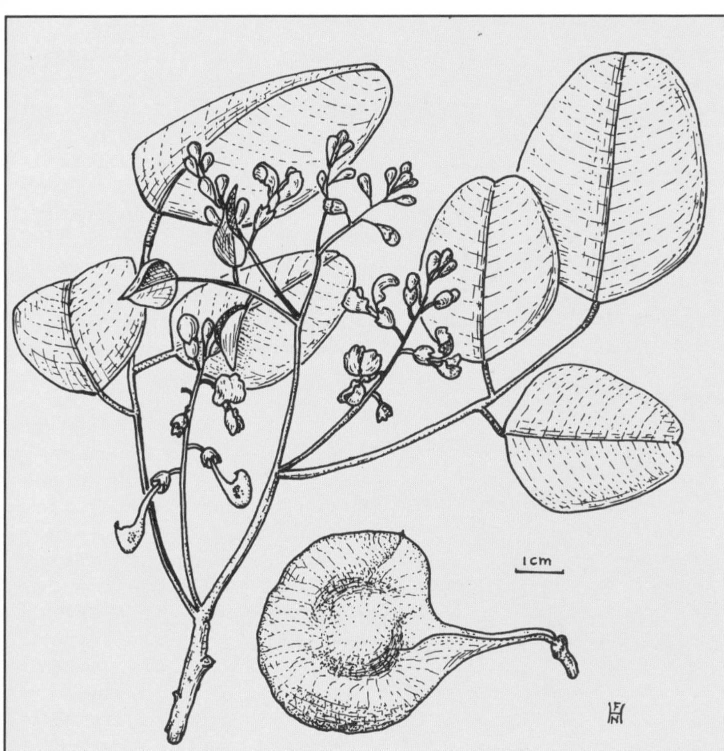

Left: The Indian red sandalwood tree (*Pterocarpus santalinus*), said to be the almug imported by Solomon.

Windows were usually placed to illuminate upstairs rooms and the opening was covered with a lattice of wooden slats or reeds, not glass (see 2 Kings 1:2; Proverbs 7:6). The interior walls of richer houses were panelled in wood, but this could be taken as a sign of extravagance (Haggai 1:4).

FURNITURE

Superb examples of ancient furniture are still in existence: some of them are so well preserved it seems incredible that they were made so long ago. For instance, the famous treasures from Tutankhamun's tomb remind one of the highly embellished furniture made in England during the eighteenth century. However, I find just as fascinating the wood joints in the simple stools and tables of those times. Even when wooden parts are badly rotted, it is often possible to see how the joints were made, and certain pieces of furniture, such as those from ancient Jericho, have been successfully reproduced according to the old designs.

A great contrast is apparent between the furniture of royalty and that of the ordinary person of biblical times. Indeed, the peasant farmer may have been too poor to have possessed anything that would really justify the name of furniture. Elisha was well provided with 'a bed, a table, a chair [stool] and a lamp' by the wealthy woman of Shunem (2 Kings 4:10), but the ordinary person could not have afforded so much. It is obviously impossible for us to deal with ancient furniture at large (see Baker, 1966) and we must limit ourselves here more or less to the main biblical references.

Thrones

As thrones have always symbolized dignity and authority, it is accepted that they should be worthy symbols. In the Bible the symbolism is especially significant since the earthly occupant of Israel's throne was regarded as God's representative. Large and ornate thrones of gold and precious woods are typical of ancient sovereigns, and many are represented on stone reliefs, engravings and tomb paintings. From an ivory panel found at Megiddo, dating from the twelfth century BC, we are able to gain an impression of the kind of throne flanked by winged beasts used by Solomon. Although it was made of ivory and gold (1 Kings 10:18) its basic construction was surely of wood. Tutankhamun's golden throne and elaborately inlaid ceremonial chair have both been preserved in all their brilliance. As I looked at the footstools in the Egyptian Museum it occurred to me that they illustrate a phrase in one of David's psalms: 'The Lord says to my lord: "Sit at my right hand, till I make your enemies your footstool" ' (Psalm 110:1). Inlaid on the surface of Tutankhamun's footstools are representations of several bound figures of non-Egyptian physiognomy. Clearly they were symbolic of the king's enemies, upon whom he put his feet while sitting on his throne. Perhaps King David's own throne had a similar footstool of which he was thinking when he wrote this psalm.

Stone reliefs at Nimrud and Nineveh show the thrones of the kings of Assyria. Both Tiglath-pileser III (745–727 BC), who attacked Israel during the reign of Pekah (2 Kings 15:29), and Sennacherib (705–681 BC) whose army was decimated in the reign of Hezekiah (2 Kings 19), are represented sitting on their thrones, which have upright backs with simple carved arms. We also know what the throne of Darius I of Persia looked like, as there are many reliefs of it on his palace walls at Persepolis dating from *c.* 520 BC, the time of Zerubbabel (Ezra 4:5). It was a heavy chair with an upright back, rounded legs and no arms, probably made of wood rather than of bronze (Baker, 1966).

Stools, tables, and beds

Chairs are hardly mentioned in the Bible, and we must conclude that the frequently mentioned stools were the common piece of furniture for sitting on. By New Testament times sitting at table had given place to reclining on couches at meals (see John 13:23).

Stools are frequently depicted on reliefs, and actual fragments of them and other furniture were excavated in Jericho by Dr Kathleen Kenyon. These stools date from the Canaanite period, *c.* 1600 BC, and their design was very similar to those of the present day, with mortised joints holding the top-sides, and stretchers. Fragments of benches and tables, as well as of a bed, were also found at Jericho. As wood rapidly decomposes, it is surprising that these samples have survived. They have been examined microscopically at Kew Gardens laboratory and found to be of

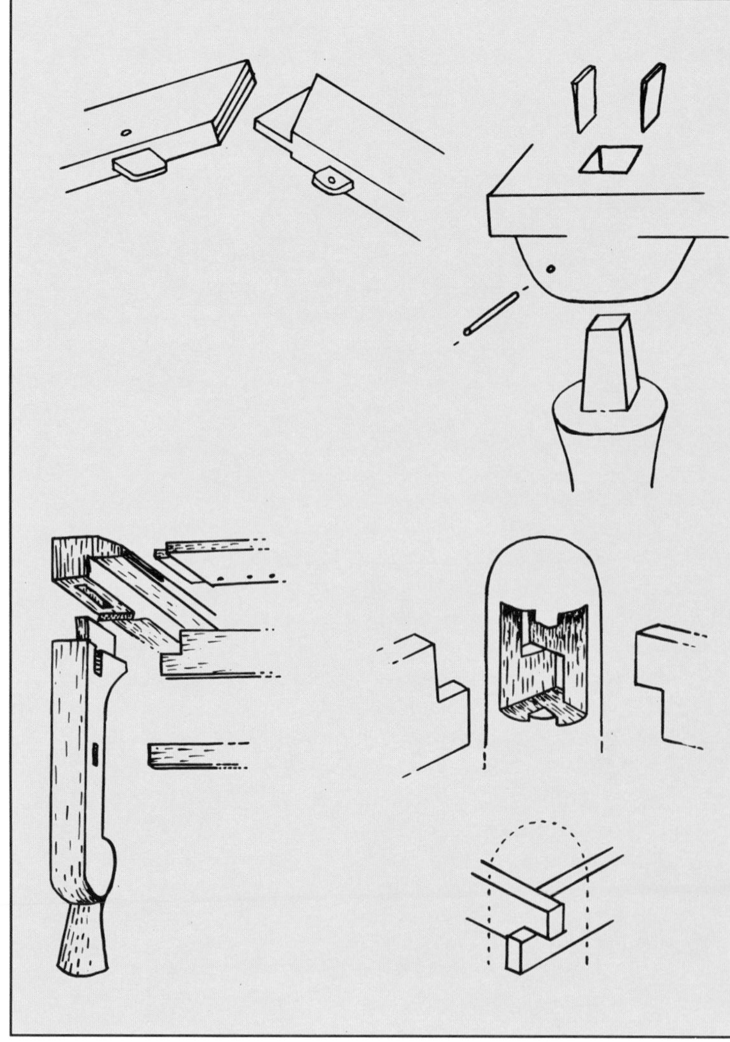

Right: Construction details of furniture from Canaanite Jericho, *c.* 1600 BC. (after Kenyon, *Jericho fig.* 229).

tamarisk, willow and a wood resembling cherry.

One of the narrow tables from Jericho was quite modern in appearance, with three legs of a simple, inward-directed scroll design and complicated mortise-and-tenon jointing. Others had a circular depression cut into the top for some unknown purpose. The benches, too, must have been pleasant in appearance, as is shown by the drawing of a reconstructed bench with a woven top. The bed was of a curious construction, with short legs and a rush top. Albright (1949) writes that the Hebrews of both Old Testament and New Testament times slept in beds, the height depending upon their wealth.

In Amos (6:4) we find the warning: 'Woe to those who lie upon beds of ivory' following a reference 'to those who feel secure on the mountain of Samaria' (6:1). We now know that in the great palace Ahab built at Samaria he had furniture overlaid with pieces of carved ivory. Many of these pieces were found by the Crowfoot expedition in the 1930s and are now displayed in the Rockefeller and British Museums. As well as explaining Amos' reference to ivory beds, it also sheds light on the 'ivory palaces' mentioned in Psalm 45:8. Small pieces of ivory of a few square centimetres must have encrusted furniture and panelling to give a very ornate effect. (Some of the details of this ornamentation relating to botanical motifs are dealt with in chapter 20.)

Ebony

Ivory was a very important and costly article of trade from early times. We read of the Tyrian trade in 'ivory tusks and ebony' (Ezekiel 27:15), while the Phoenician ivory-carving is known to have been first class. The ebony (Heb. *hobnim*) of ancient times was not the tree so called today, which is a species of *Diospyros* from tropical Asia. Our word *ebony* is taken from the ancient Egyptian hieroglyph *hbny,* which would be pronounced more or less as we say it. Microscopic examination of the dark wood found in Egyptian tombs has proved to be the leguminous tree *Dalbergia melanoxylon*,[4] which grows in the drier country along the southern edge of the Sahara. It would therefore have been much more easily available than the *Diospyros* trees, which were imported into the Near East at a much later date. This, as in the case of cinnamon, is another example of a name being transferred from one product to another (Hepper, 1977).

Thyine wood

A fine timber favoured by the Romans for inlay work on table tops was thyine wood (Gk. *thuinos*), referred to in Revelation 18:12 as being imported into 'Babylon'. It comes from a coniferous tree confusingly known as citron or citrus (but not true *Citrus*), *Tetraclinis articulata* (formerly *Callitris articulata*), which occurs wild in Malta, Algeria and Morocco. The slender resinous twigs are covered with green scale-leaves like a cypress, and the small cones split open into four parts to release the seeds. The fragrant wood is brown or yellowish and finely grained. The well-known varnish called sanderac is obtained from resin that exudes from the tree trunk.

Chests and utensils

In biblical times an important piece of furniture combining the function of a wardrobe and chest-of-drawers was the wooden chest (Heb. *aron*). Chests were also used for the collection of the temple taxes (2 Kings 12:9; 2 Chronicles 24:8). Paul states: 'In a great house there are not only vessels of gold and silver but also of wood and earthenware, and some for noble use, some for ignoble' (2 Timothy 2:20). Wooden trays and plates have actually been found in the same early deposits at Jericho referred to above (Kenyon, 1952–3). Other utensils, such as spoons and the shallow kneading troughs used in bread-making, were also made of wood (Exodus 12:34). The Law said that any wooden ves-

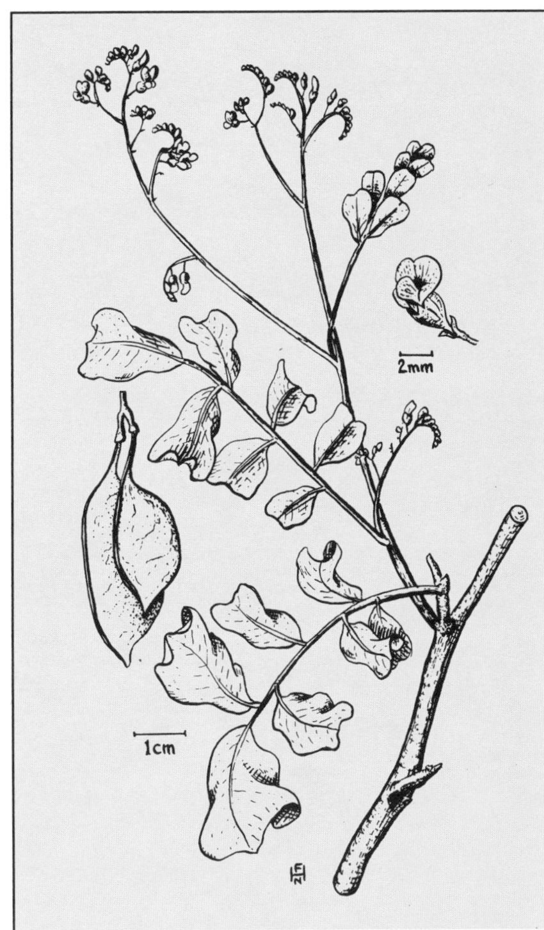

sel touched by a man with a discharge must be washed, while an earthen vessel had to be broken (Leviticus 15:12).

Coffins

Great attention was paid to proper burial in the family tomb. Exceptional treatment was given to Joseph's embalmed body which was placed in a coffin in Egypt (Genesis 50:26), where sycomore wood was frequently used for their manufacture. A coffin found in the Jericho hills and dating from the Hasmonean period (first century BC – first century AD) has a gabled roof and was constructed of sycomore, cypress and Christ-thorn timber (Hachlili, 1979).

Above left: The ebony of Old Testament times was obtained from this African tree, *Dalbergia melanoxylon*, in the pea family, here seen growing in Senegal.

Above: A leafy shoot of this African ebony, with flowers and pod.

Left: Thyine wood for fine cabinet work in Rome came from the coniferous tree *Tetraclinis articulata*, growing in North Africa.

MUSICAL INSTRUMENTS

When the people of Babylon heard the sound of music they had to fall down and worship the golden image that King Nebuchadnezzar had set up (Daniel 3). Among the instruments mentioned in this passage and elsewhere in the Scriptures

Above: A painting of musicians in ancient Egypt, photographed on the walls of Nakht's tomb at Thebes, *c.* 1400 BC.

are several made of wood, besides those of metal and of reed (see p. 70) which need not concern us here. A good deal of difficulty has been encountered by translators in rendering the names of the ancient instruments into comparable English words.[5] The wooden stringed instruments were either played with a plectrum or plucked with the fingers. The strings were made from sheep's intestines. A superb example of a lyre was found in the royal tombs at Ur dating from about 2500 BC – about two thousand years before the time of Nebuchadnezzar and more than 500 years before Abraham left the city! The wood itself had disappeared, but it was possible to restore the instrument extrapolating from the shapes of the ornately inlaid lapis-lazuli, red limestone and shell, and with a golden bull's head at one end.

We may easily imagine the magnificence of the instruments of almug wood in Solomon's temple (1 Kings 10:12), while the lyres used by David's people to celebrate the return of the ark were apparently made of Aleppo pine (2 Samuel 6:5). It was lyres that the Jewish exiles hung on the 'willows' of Babylon (Psalm 137:2).

DOWN TO THE SEA IN SHIPS

Noah's ark

Many kinds of wood have been used for boats and several are mentioned in the Bible, but their identity is not always certain. The gopher wood of which Noah constructed the ark is a case in point (Genesis 6:14). Its identity depends to a large extent on Noah's location at the time, and this the narrative does not tell. It is unlikely that a barge type of ship would have drifted far from its place of construction and one may assume that it was built in the area of the Ararat mountains where it grounded.

In this case the frequently suggested identity of 'gopher', which remains untranslated in most English versions, with cypress (*Cupressus sempervirens*), as in the NEB and NIV, would be a possibility. On the other hand it could have been any of the more readily obtainable coniferous trees, such as pine. These, too, would fit in with a suggestion that a resinous tree was intended, owing to the similarity of *gopher* and *kopher*, the Hebrew word for bitumen. However, fragments of timber brought back from Mount Ararat by Fernand Navarra's expeditions in 1952 and 1969 were examined by French plant anatomists, who declared them to be of oak (Bailey, 1978).[6]

The case for these fragments being part of the actual ark remains a matter of doubt, since they were dated by the carbon technique to the seventh or eighth century AD! Whatever wood was used, the ark was a sizeable craft. Noah's instructions were to make

'an ark of gopher wood; make rooms in the ark, and cover it inside and out with pitch [bitumen]. This is how you are to make it: the length of the ark three hundred cubits [134 m, 439 ft], its breadth fifty cubits [22 m, 72 ft], and its height thirty cubits [13 m, 43 ft]. Make a roof [or window] for the ark, and finish it to a cubit above; and set the door of the ark in its side, make it with lower, second, and third decks' (Genesis 6:14–16).

Egyptian ships

In ancient Egypt shipbuilding in wood had reached a high state of development as long ago as the Old Kingdom period. One inscription from Snefru dated c. 2700 BC tells of ships 51 m (167 ft) long made of 'meruwood' from Lebanon. Cheops' 43.4 m (142 ft) ship has actually been excavated at the foot of his Great Pyramid. The 1224 pieces, including cedar planks up to 24 m (74 ft) long, have been reassembled as the huge complete ship in its own museum building beside the Pyramid. Delightful models of ships complete with rigging have been preserved in other tombs. Reliefs and paintings usually depict the boats used for long distance voyages, such as expeditions to the land of Punt (probably present-day Somalia), to bring back incense, spices and precious woods. (See chapter 14 for an account of Queen Hatshepsut's expedition to Punt.) The ships used on the Punt expedition were 23 m (70 ft) long, 6 m (19–20 ft) wide and 1.5 m (4–5 ft) deep (Barnett, 1958). We know that contracts were made from time to time with the king of Lebanon to supply cedar for the Egyptian fleet, but Herodotus tells us that the trading vessels on the Nile were built entirely of acacia wood. These boats carried the heavier loads and were equipped with a sail and oars. Other boats, however, were made of papyrus (see p. 69).

Solomon's fleet

In the tenth century BC, 'King Solomon built a fleet of ships at Ezion-geber' (1 Kings 9:26, 28) on the Red Sea coast, and enlisted the help of Hiram king of Tyre to crew it. Obviously these 'ships of Tarshish', as the Bible calls them (1 Kings 10:22), were sea-going vessels capable of very long journeys to places such as Ophir which may have been as far away as India. The wood of these ships, as well as those built by Jehoshaphat (1 Kings 22:48), must have been sturdy and available in sufficient quantity for such large vessels. The surroundings of the Gulf of Aqaba are extremely arid and the only timber likely to be available would have been from acacia trees and Phoenician juniper from Sinai. On the other hand, there is evidence that the mountains bordering the eastern side of the Red Sea were afforested, for even today African pencil cedars (*Juniperus procera*) of some size are still to be found there (Hepper and Wood, 1979). If this Arabian timber was used, it must have been accessible for the kings to obtain and transport to the shipyard at Ezion-geber.

A Tyrian ship

Another biblical reference to the kinds of timber used for ships occurs in Ezekiel, where the prophet pictures the city of Tyre as one of its own vessels:

'O Tyre ...
They made all your planks
of fir trees from Senir;
they took a cedar from Lebanon
to make a mast for you.
Of oaks of Bashan they made your oars;
they made your deck of pines
from the coasts of Cyprus,
inlaid with ivory.
Of fine embroided linen from Egypt
was your sail,
serving as your ensign;
blue and purple from the coasts of Elishah
was your awning
... skilled men were in you,
caulking your seams'
(Ezekiel 27:3–9).

Perhaps it is rash to analyse these references too closely, as Ezekiel can have been no naval architect, yet he shows a remarkable knowledge of the material necessary for ships. The 'fir trees of Senir' (Heb. *berosh*) would have been a coniferous tree, probably cypress, which was famous on that part of the Mount Hermon range known as Senir. Strictly 'fir' should be applied to species of *Abies*,[7] which in this context would be the Cilician fir (*Abies cilicica*), which still grows in the north of Lebanon. It is interesting to note that the Cilician fir is said to have been the tree imported into Egypt to form the high masts erected in front of the temple pylons (Offord, 1918). Ezekiel refers to cedars being used as masts for the ships of Tyre, but the stout trunks of cedars seem to be much less suitable than the tall slender trunks of the Cilician fir, which would fit the context very well.

The oars of Ezekiel's ship were strong if they were made from the timber of the Tabor oak, which is still present on the hills of Bashan east of the Jordan. It seems a long way to transport it, since a more accessible supply would have been available to the shipbuilders of Tyre. The ship's decks were planked with pine from the coasts of Cyprus.[8] Reference to coasts calls to mind the stone-pine (*Pinus pinea*), which often grows near the sea. Theophrastus actually stated that Cypriot shipbuilders used coastal pine which, he said, seemed to be better quality than the mountain pine – presumably Calabrian pine (*P. brutia*).

Ezekiel completed his word picture of the fine Tyrian ship, with its gaily coloured, embroidered linen sails from Egypt, by reference to the careful caulking of the timbers to ensure water-tightness. This plugging was achieved by filling the seams with tow, bitumen and wax, before the hull was covered overall with bitumen. Fully seasoned timbers were never used for ships as they would have been too stiff to take up the curvature of the ship; they were, however, given time to settle once they were fitted before being caulked (Torr, 1895). Trading vessels such as these were called 'Byblos ships', Byblos being the principal port from which timber was exported to Egypt. As mentioned above, we frequently have puzzling references in the Bible to 'ships of Tarshish' (e.g. Psalm 48:7; Isaiah 2:16). The identity of this place ranges from Tartessus in Spain to the Levant. Barnett (1958) believed it was Tarsus, later famous as the home of the apostle Paul, a town known for its manufacture of ships' oars; hence the name came to be applied to ocean-going ships bearing numerous oars.

Some of these vessels were quite large with several decks, since Jonah was able to go 'down into the inner part' of a ship sailing from Joppa to Tarshish to lie down and sleep (Jonah 1:5).

Roman ships

The Romans, however, were not seafarers. During the first Punic War with Carthage, in the third century BC, they copied a captured Carthaginian ship (a quinquereme). They set up a crash programme to build their own fleet with the help of Greek naval architects. In the ensuing naval battles many ships were sunk by ramming, and two of the Punic vessels have recently been studied by Honor Frost on the seabed off Sicily. Much of the analysis of the timber and other plant content has been done in the laboratories of Kew Gardens,

Below: Model wooden ship with linen sail from an Egyptian tomb. (Photo: British Museum.)

London (Hepper in Frost, 1981).

Briefly, it was found that the ships were constructed from a surprising number of different kinds of timber. Pine was used for the planking, with tenons and dowels of oak, and ribs of oak and maple. There was a ram of pine (which was probably tipped with iron) protruding in front below water level. Between the ribs, bundles of twigs and leaves ('dunnage') had been placed, in order to prevent the ballast stones wearing the planking as they moved around in the swell. Sand overlying this dunnage had preserved the waterlogged plants, which were found to be composed of myrtle, phillyrea, bracken and others. While sifting through the sludge in which these remains occurred, I was intrigued to find olive stones, pistachio and hazelnut shells and to wonder who dropped them there. Perhaps hungry members of the crew ate nuts to fortify themselves for the ensuing battle in which their ship was sunk.

In New Testament times the wooden sea-going merchantmen, such as that in which Paul sailed and was wrecked, were sizeable vessels with several decks, able to carry a cargo of wheat and some 300 people (Acts 27:37). James (3:4), marvelled how so small a rudder could steer these great ships.

Fishing boats

The small fishing boats used on the fresh-water Sea of Galilee by the disciples (Matthew 14:22; John 21:3) could have been made of any of the timbers, such as oak and pine, readily available in the surrounding country. Remarkably, a first century AD boat of the kind Jesus could have used was exposed on the shore of the Sea of Galilee during a drought in 1986. It has been dated to the first century AD from a cooking pot, an oil lamp and fifteen other pieces found inside it, lying there since it sank nearly 2000 years ago. The boat is 7.5 m (27 ft) long and 2 m (6 ft) wide. The waterlogged timbers have been removed and treated with a synthetic wax (polyethylene glycol) to preserve their form for further scientific and archaeological study. Examination of its construction shows that the cedar planking was held together by mortise and tenon jointings which swelled on contact with water, forming a tight seal against seepage into the boat – a method used for centuries up to the Byzantine period. Many of the timbers were thought to have been re-used from older boats – there were small samples of Christ-thorn, pine, hawthorn and Judas-tree wood, according to Dr Ella Werker of the Hebrew University (Wachsmann, 1988).

WOOD AND WARFARE

Perhaps it will cause surprise that plants should be associated with warfare. Yet the lands of the Bible are so intimately connected with wars and weapons, and the Scriptures so full of accounts of battles, that it is inconceivable that this book should say nothing about warfare. Indeed we find certain botanical aspects of war in the Mosaic Law, under which it was prohibited in wartime to fell trees that provided food (Deuteronomy 20:19–20). At the time of the divided kingdom, however, when Moab was defeated by Jehoshaphat, 'on every good piece of land every man threw a stone, until it was covered; they stopped every spring of water, and felled all the good trees' (2 Kings 3:25–26).

Later we read of Jeremiah's prophecy of the fall of Jerusalem: 'for thus says the Lord of hosts: "Hew down her trees; cast up a siege mount against Jerusalem" ' (Jeremiah 6:6). From earliest times fire had been used during sieges; for example, Abimelech and his men cut down bundles of brushwood and set fire to them around the Tower of Shechem (Judges 9:46–49). This would have been very effective as many of the bushes in the *maquis* are highly inflammable, while towers and fortresses were often partly constructed of timber.

Weapons

Weapons of war are frequently mentioned in the Bible, and many actual examples have been excavated from ancient sites, but their wooden handles are seldom preserved. The haft of bronze or iron battle-axes fitted into a hole or was simply lashed on, whereas the blades of swords and daggers were inserted into wooden handles. Metal heads were fixed on the wooden handle of the spear (Heb. *hanit*), lance (Heb. *romah*), and javelin (Heb. *kidon*). Bows (Heb. *qeset*; 1 Samuel 2:4) were usually made of seasoned wood, and no doubt species with particular resilience were used. However, yew trees (*Taxus baccata*), which were traditionally used for bows in England, have a very restricted distribution in the Near East and are unlikely to have been available to the people of the Bible. Reeds were used as arrows (Heb. *hes*; Psalm 144:6), which were tipped with stone or metal, or simply sharpened (Jeremiah 51:11). Personal protection was afforded by shields made of wood or wickerwork overlaid with leather, such as the one found at Masada by Yadin in 1963.

Finally, prisoners such as Jeremiah were put in wooden stocks which held their feet (Jeremiah 20:2). Tree branches were used to hang victims (Joshua 10:26) or a gallows, such as the 22 m (72 ft) high one on which Haman met his death (Esther 5:14; 7:10). In New Testament times the death sentence was often carried out by hanging the victim from a tree, whilst the Romans especially favoured crucifixion. The cross-bar (Latin *patibulum*) had to be carried by the victim, as Jesus did until relieved by Simon of Cyrene (John 19:17; Matthew 27:32). The bar was fixed to an upright, which was only slightly taller than the victim crucified. Normally reserved for the worst type of criminal, crucifixion would have had a heavier meaning to those onlookers familiar with the Law, which stated that 'a hanged man is accursed by God' (Deuteronomy 21:23).

----

[1] As NIV, not a plane (KJV, RSV, NEB) which was not invented until Roman times.

[2] Some commentators see symbolism in the very kind of wood used and the Septuagint calls acacia the Wood of Life (Offord, 1919).

[3] Greenfield and Mayrhofer (1967), however, conclude on philological grounds that, in spite of the biblical text, algum (Heb. *algummim*) and almug (Heb. *almuggim*) are one and the same. They identify it with a Lebanese tree which they do not attempt to name.

[4] The African blackwood *Dalbergia melanoxylon* is not as black as species of *Diospyros*, especially *D. ebenum* from Ceylon. Nevertheless it is very heavy, dark reddish and so hard it would have been difficult to cut with the ancient copper saws. The *Dalbergia* trees I saw in Senegal were about 5 m (16 ft) high, with numerous

branchlets, pinnate leaves and white flowers producing flat pods containing 2 or 3 seeds.

[5] The Heb. *kinnor* (e.g. Psalm 137:2), rendered harp in KJV, was a small lyre (as RSV), and the Hebrew *nebel* is a larger harp-like psaltery. A similar type, referred to by the Aramaic word *sabbeka*, was one of Nebuchadnezzar's Babylonian instruments. A ten-stringed instrument (Psalms 33:2; 92:3; 144:9; Heb. *asor*; lyre RSV) may have been a kind of zither (Seller, 1941).

[6] The cellular structure of thin sections of plant tissues can be examined under the microscope and each species has its own characteristics which are recognizable by trained plant anatomists. Provided that ancient plant fragments are not decomposed, it is frequently possible to recognize by microscopical examination the genus and sometimes the species to which they belong. Ancient woods often survive as charcoal, which is examined by incident light. To be able to recognize the tissues the charcoal fragment needs to be fractured, in order to reveal a radial longitudinal and tangential longitudinal surface, as well as a cross-section. No chemicals or staining techniques can be applied since charcoal is an inert substance. Occasionally ancient woods survive entire, owing to delayed decomposition in the absence of air in very wet situations. These types of material can be sectioned and examined by transmitted light like fresh tissues, but they have often been subject to pressures which have distorted the structure and make identification more difficult. Sometimes chemicals can be used to restore the section to its original form. In any case positive identification is only possible if there is a set of standard reference material available, prepared from known species likely to be encountered in the investigation.

[7] For this reason the popular usage of Scots fir for Scots pine (*Pinus sylvestris*) is misleading.

[8] KJV rendering of this phrase is now considered to be erroneous: 'the company of the Ashurites have made thy benches of ivory, brought out of the isles of Chittim'.

Bibliography

Bailey, L. R., *Where is Noah's Ark?* (Nashville, Abingdon Press, 1978).

Baker, H. S., *Furniture in the Ancient World* (London, *The Connoisseur*, 1966).

Barnett, R. D., 'Early Shipping in the Near East', *Antiquity* (London, 1958), 22:220–30.

Goodman, W. L., *A History of Woodworking Tools* (London, G. Bell and Sons, 1964).

Greenfield, J. C., and Mayrhofer, M., 'The Algumin/Almuggin problem re-examined', *Vestus Testamentum* (1967), 16:83–9.

Hachlili, R., 'Ancient Burial Customs Preserved in Jericho Hills', *Biblical Archaeology Review* (Washington, 1979), 5(4): 28–35.

Harding, G. L., *The Antiquities of Jordan* (London, Lutterworth Press, 1959).

Hepper, F. N., 'On the Transference of Ancient Plant Names', *Palestine Exploration Quarterly* (London, 1977), 109(2):129–30.

—. 'Note on the Botanical Components of the two Punic Ships', in H. Frost, *'Lilybaeum' Notizie degli scavi di antichita* (Rome, 1981): supplement to vol. 30, 1976.

Hepper, F. N., and Wood, J. R. L., 'Were there Forests in theYemen?', *Proceedings of the Seminar for Arabian Studies* (London Institute of Archaeology, 1979), 9:65–71.

Herman, Z., *People, Seas and Ships* (London, Phoenix House, 1966: transl. by L. Ortzen).

Liphschitz, N., and Biger, G., 'Cedars of Lebanon *(Cedrus libani)* in Israel during Antiquity', *Israel Exploration Journal* (Jerusalem, 1991), 41:165–75.

Meiggs, R., *Timber in the Ancient World* (Oxford University Press, 1980).

Offord, J., 'The Egyptian Name for Lebanon', *Palestine Exploration Quarterly* (London, 1918), pp. 183–4.

—. 'The Mountains of Jahveh', *Palestine Exploration Quarterly* (London, 1919), p. 42.

Seller, O. R., 'Musical Instruments of Israel', *Biblical Archaeologist* (Baltimore, 1941), 4(3):33–47.

Torr, C., *Ancient Ships* (Cambridge University Press, 1895).

Wachsmann, S., 'The Galilee Boat', *Biblical Archaeology Review* (Washington, 1988), 14(5):18–33.

Yadin, Y., *Masada* (London, Weidenfeld and Nicolson, 1966).

17. Flax, Linen and Dyes

'Oholiab ... a craftsman and designer and embroiderer in blue and purple and scarlet stuff and fine twined linen.'
(Exodus 38:23.)

Although Adam and Eve 'sewed fig leaves together and made themselves aprons' (Genesis 3:7), these can hardly be called clothes as we know them today. Yet in parts of the tropics bunches of leaves are still used in this way. Animal skins have been used since 'the Lord God made for Adam and for his wife garments of skins, and clothed them' (Genesis 3:21), and leather is still popular for clothing. Wool from sheep, and animal hair, form warm clothing, and were used for the sackcloth of biblical times and for tents, but we cannot stop to discuss these fibres of animal origin. Let us look at fibres from plants used for spinning and weaving, which have a long history, too.

FLAX FOR LINEN

Flax (Heb. *pista* or *pisteh*) is probably the oldest known textile plant and is still used for making linen material. Linen is frequently mentioned in both the Old Testament and New Testament, although it was expensive and used, as we shall see, for special purposes.[1] As long ago as the fourth millennium BC flax is known to have been used in Egypt, and flax fibres have often been found in Near Eastern sites of that period.

The flax plant (*Linum usitatissimum*) is an annual, completing its life cycle within three or four summer months. In Egypt, however, to avoid the scorching heat, it is sown in late October and harvested the following April or May. Flax grows very rapidly, attaining, according to some measurements, a rate of 36 mm (1·5 in) in 24 hours at some stages of its growth (Carter, 1920). When full grown it is up to a metre (3 ft) high, with narrow alternate leaves along the stem, and a number of branches in the upper part on which are borne the beautiful, delicate blue flowers. Two flat, glossy seeds develop in each of the five compartments of the fruit, and from these linseed oil is extracted. At one time flax was a very important crop for this purpose (see p. 134).

When flax is cultivated for its fibres, the plants are grown very close together to encourage tall stems and few lateral branches. Wider spacing is better when linseed is required, since the numerous lateral branches bear flowers and hence seed more profusely. Some varieties yield more oil than others, which are better for fibres.

Right: Flax (*Linum usitatissimum*) in flower.

Flax for fine linen is pulled up by the roots when the stems are yellowish at the base and before the seeds are ripe. The fibre for fine thread is said to be yielded from very young plants, while tough fibres for ropes are obtained from thoroughly ripe stems. The harvested stems are bunched together with the roots and dried before stacking, or sent off to be retted when still green. Special rock-cut retting tanks of Roman age have been discovered at Tel Shosh in Jezreel. The retting process involves soaking the stems in stagnant water to separate the phloem (or bast) fibres which occur on the exterior of the woody, cylindrical core of the stem.[2] This is achieved, in fact, by bacterial action[3] which breaks down the thinner cells in the stem. After a week or more, depending on the temperature of the water, the flax is removed at just the right moment to ensure easy separation of the fibres, but at the same time avoiding the discoloration that may take place rapidly if they are left too long. The flax stems are dried off after retting and in ancient Palestine, where linen production was a home industry, the rooftops provided a suitable place for spreading the stems. Hence Joshua's spies, in Jericho, were hidden under 'the stalks of flax which [Rahab] had laid in order on the roof' (Joshua 2:6). It is interesting to note in this verse that the flax was 'in order', presumably indicating that it was not tossed like hay but the stems were kept parallel. It is important not to mix the roots with the tops, so as to facilitate the subsequent processes in the preparation of the fibres.

After retting, the fibres have to be separated from the thin outer layer and woody core by gentle beating or rolling, a process called scutching. The fibres are then combed out (hackling) before they are ready for spinning. The object is to keep the fibres as long as possible for the best thread, whereas the broken fibres, known as tow, are used for coarser linen material and lampwicks. Isaiah twice mentions this: 'the strong shall become tow, and his work a spark' (Isaiah 1:31), and 'Behold, my servant ... he will not ... quench a smouldering wick' (Matthew 12:18–21).

The cultivation of flax was apparently never very important in Palestine, although Beth Shean is said to have been famous for its fine linen, which presumably was made from local flax. It must also have been a well-known crop at Gezer, since it was given a special place in the agricultural calendar by mentioning the 'month of pulling flax' (Thomas, 1958; see also p. 77).[4]

The great source of flax was Egypt, so it was disastrous that the flax crop, as well as the standing barley, were ruined by hail during one of the plagues (Exodus 9:23–25, 31). Later, Isaiah prophesied that when the Nile dried up 'the workers in combed flax will be in despair' (Isaiah 19:9), as the fields needed to be irrigated to produce any flax. Linen was exported to Palestine, where a harlot decorated her bed 'with coverings, coloured spreads of Egyptian linen' (Proverbs 7:16). It was also used for sails of the ships of Tyre (Ezekiel 27:7). There were many different kinds of linen of various qualities and grades from flax plants cultivated in ancient Egypt.

Nowadays flax is grown not so much for its linen as for the linseed oil which is used extensively in the manufacture of paints and linoleum – the latter being named after it (*linum + oleum*). Formerly the flax stalks remaining after harvesting the seed were considered to be useless, since they were unsuitable for linen, so were burnt. But today they are used for the manufacture of the India paper on which Bibles are often printed, as well as for lightweight airmail writing paper.

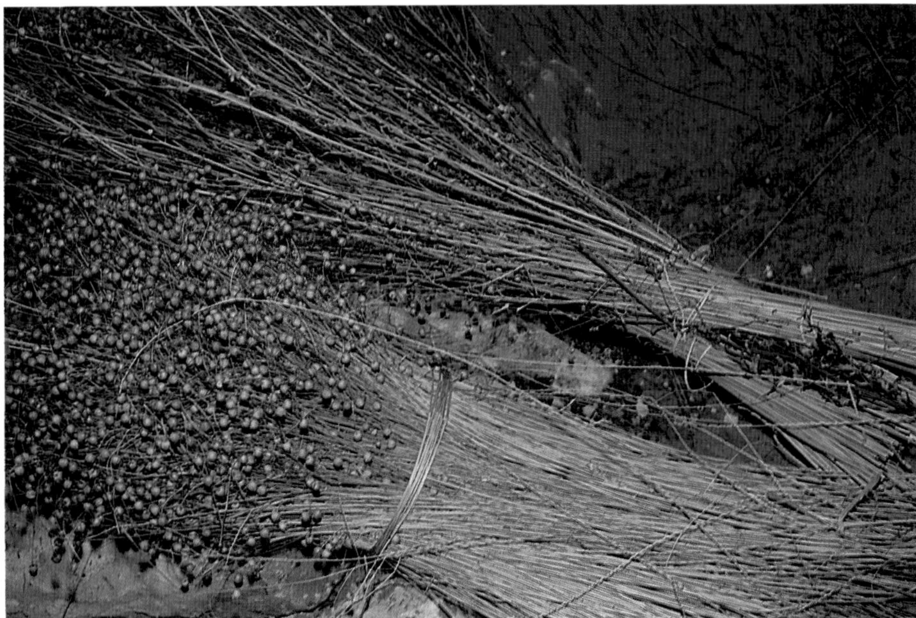

Above: Stems of flax plants pulled up and bundled in preparation for the retting process.

We cannot here take up the matter of spinning and weaving, since it would go beyond the scope of this book. Any reader who wishes to be informed on the subject should consult Crowfoot's fascinating and authoritative account in Singer, Holmyard and Hall (1958).

Linen furnishings of the tabernacle

Explicit divine instructions were given for the furnishing of the tabernacle, including the provision of curtains. The ten curtains were to be made of 'fine twisted linen [Heb. *sheshi, shesh*] and blue and purple and scarlet stuff' (Exodus 26:1), and another curtain screening the door of the tent was similarly made (Exodus 26:36). Between the inner sanctuary and the most holy place hung the linen veil: 'in skilled work shall it be made, with cherubim' (Exodus 26:31). When Herod's Jerusalem temple was built it is possible that the great veil which was torn from top to bottom on the first Good Friday was also of linen (Matthew 27:51).

Linen garments for the priests

Aaron and his sons had to wear certain clothes for personal adornment and utility. Aaron, as high priest, had a special ephod around his waist 'of gold, of blue and purple and scarlet stuff and of fine twined linen, skilfully worked' elaborately ornamented with gold and precious stones (Exodus 28:6). The robe of Aaron's ephod was to be:

'all of blue. It shall have in it an opening for the head, with a woven binding around the opening, like the opening in a garment, that it may not be torn. On its skirts you shall make pomegranates of blue and purple and scarlet stuff' (Exodus 28:31–33).

This contrasts with the simple linen ephod worn by the ordinary priests, such as those of Nob, which was apparently just a loincloth. Similar garments would have been worn by Samuel and David on certain occasions (1 Samuel 2:18; 2 Samuel 6:14). The instructions for further garments continued later in the chapter (Exodus 28:39–43).

Right: Cotton bolls still on the plant before harvesting.

Linen for the rich

Linen was an expensive textile which was worn usually by the rich and by those of high rank or for special occasions. For instance, Joseph changed his clothing (Genesis 41:14) when called from the Egyptian prison; then, having successfully interpreted the dream, he was given by Pharaoh his signet ring and a gold chain and was arrayed 'in garments of fine linen' (Genesis 41:42). Similarly, about one thousand years later Mordecai received a signet ring from the Persian King Ahasuerus and 'royal robes of blue and white, with a great golden crown and a mantle of fine linen and purple' (Esther 8:15). A bride was given linen clothes (Ezekiel 16:10, 13) and the 'good wife' of Proverbs 31:10 *ff*. 'seeks wool and flax, and works with willing hands ... she makes herself coverings; her clothing is fine linen and purple ... she makes linen garments and sells them'. In the parable of the unnamed rich man and the poor man, Lazarus, the former 'was clothed in purple and fine linen' (Luke 16:19). Yet a linen cloth was worn by the young man who followed Jesus to Gethsemane, who when he was seized 'left the linen cloth and ran away naked' (Mark 14:51).

Linen for the dead

Linen is well known from ancient Egyptian tombs as mummy cloths for wrapping the dead, so it is not surprising to find that another Lazarus had 'his hands and feet bound with bandages, and his face wrapped with a cloth', as he emerged from his tomb on being raised from death (John 11:44). Before his crucifixion, Jesus wore a seamless garment (John 19:23), while after it his body was bound 'in linen cloths with the spices, as is the burial custom of the Jews' (John 19:40). It was these linen cloths that were left lying in the tomb on the morning of Christ's resurrection (John 20:5).[5]

Symbolism of linen

Fine white linen holds a certain significance in the symbolism of the priestly garments of the Old Testament, although it was worn principally for coolness in the tabernacle and temple:

'When they enter the gates of the inner court, they shall wear linen garments; they shall have nothing of wool on them, while they minister at the gates of the inner court, and within. They shall have linen turbans upon their heads, and linen breeches upon their loins; they shall not gird themselves within anything that causes sweat' (Ezekiel 44:17–18).

Yet there was something particular about these garments for the passage continues: *'And when they go out into the outer court to the people, they shall put off the garments in which they have been ministering, and lay them in holy chambers; and they shall put on other garments, lest they communicate holiness to the people with their garments'* (Ezekiel 44:19).

Elsewhere Aaron's and other priests' clothes are spoken of as 'the holy linen coat' and 'the holy linen garments' (Leviticus 16:4, 32).

The symbolic purity of linen is implied in Revelation. The church at Laodicea was instructed to buy from the Lord gold, as well as 'white garments' (Revelation 3:18). The twenty-four elders were 'clad in white garments' (Revelation 4:4), and the 'souls of those who had been slain for the word of God and for the witness they had borne ... were each given a white robe' (Revelation 6:9–11). More specifically at the marriage of the Lamb, his bride, the church, 'has made herself ready; it was granted her to be clothed with fine linen, bright and pure – for the fine linen is the righteous deeds of the saints' (Revelation 19:8).

Linen and the Dead Sea scrolls

The famous Dead Sea scrolls were wrapped in linen covers before being hidden some 2000 years ago. Owing to the dry desert air the material was found to be in quite good condition at the time of the excavation in 1947. The largest cover was 57 by 60 cm (about 2 ft sq.), and the quality of the original linen was judged good, but not very fine. For various reasons there seems to be no doubt that the linen originated from Palestinian flax, rather than from imported stuff. Some of the linen found at Qumran was tested by the 'radio-carbon test' to find its age.[6] On this evidence, as well as other finds, Harding (1952) considered the scrolls were probably deposited in the cave in about AD 70, rather later than was at first thought. We may compare this with the more precise dating from burnt fragments of date-palm wood used in rafters at Qumran (Zeuner, 1960). These were dated to AD 66, a remarkable confirmation of the year, now thought to be AD 68, established by direct archaeological evidence (Bruce, 1966).

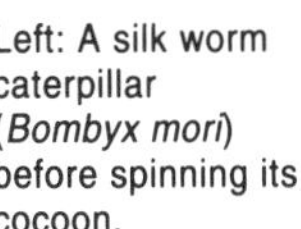

Left: A silk worm caterpillar (*Bombyx mori*) before spinning its cocoon.

COTTON

Today cotton cloth is so commonly used that it is hard to realize that it is not a very ancient material in the Near East, although it is mentioned in Esther (1:6). In fact it is doubtful whether it was known in Palestine in Old Testament times. There is still considerable mystery about both the origin of the cotton plant and when it developed its characteristic cottonwool fruits.[7]

There are several species of cotton in the genus *Gossypium* belonging to the mallow or hollyhock family, *Malvaceae*. Stem fibres are characteristic of the family as a whole, for example *Hibiscus*, which has very fibrous stems which are widely used for string in many parts of the world. However, cotton fibres are obtained from the white lint around the seed of cultivated cotton plants. This lint, or staple, is extremely dense on each of the large oily seeds. The capsular fruit containing the seeds bursts on ripening to become the typical white ball, called cotton boll. For textile purposes the cotton fibres are well suited to spinning since they are twisted two to three hundred times per inch. The Levant cotton plant (*G. herbaceum*) favours humus-rich soil with plenty of moisture and grows as a shrub to a height of 1.3–2 m (4–6 ft). It has palmate leaves arising alternately on the stems. The large flowers scattered over the upper parts of the bush are yellow with a reddish centre. On either side of the calyx is a pair of large, deeply toothed bracts, which are characteristic of all the cotton species.

It is certain that the use of cotton as a textile originated in India. From India cotton ultimately spread to the eastern part of the Fertile Crescent. It was known in Assyria at the time of Sennacherib, who besieged Jerusalem during Hezekiah's reign in 701 BC (2 Chronicles 32), for 'trees that bear wool' are mentioned on a cylinder seal. Herodotus, in the fifth century BC, described the excellent wool that grew on Indian trees, while later Hebrew writers referred to cotton as 'wool vine' (Dalman, 1937). The use of cotton for royal curtains in the Persian capital at Susa during the fifth century BC was therefore quite possible. King Ahasuerus (Xerxes) gave a banquet in his palace and 'There were white cotton curtains and blue hangings caught up with cords of fine linen and purple to silver rings and marble pillars' (Esther 1:6).

The reference to cotton in this verse is lost in KJV etc., since the phrase is rendered 'where were white *green* [Heb. *karpas*] and blue hangings'. Scholars are now generally agreed that cotton is correctly used in most modern versions, so it is surprising that the NIV refers to 'linen'. However, there is no agreement as to the meaning of the Hebrew *chowr* in Isaiah 19:9 variously translated 'networks' KJV; 'white cotton' RSV; 'linen' GNB; 'fine linen' NIV. Clearly the cotton curtains were very rare and precious. Even Egypt did not boast cotton until Roman times, judging by the available evidence.

SILK

Silk is obtained from the chrysalis cocoon of the large Chinese silk moth called *Bombyx mori*. The caterpillar of this moth is the silkworm, which in its natural state feeds on the leaves of the white-fruited mulberry tree (*Morus alba*). When silkworms were introduced into the west by Byzantine monks in AD 552, they managed to live on another species of mulberry with deep crimson fruits, the so-called black mulberry (*Morus nigra*). This tree grew wild in Iran and had long been cultivated in the eastern Mediterranean area for the sake of its fruits alone (see p. 120). After the establishment of silkworms and the spread of the silk industry, the black mulberry was more widely cultivated simply as the food plant of the caterpillars. Although the white mulberry is said to be superior to the black mulberry for silk production, the former apparently was not brought from China and established in the west until about the sixteenth century.

There is, however, another silkmoth indigenous to the eastern Mediterranean whose cocoons were used for silk. The presence of this moth (*Pachypasa otus*), which feeds on cypress and oak trees, had been overlooked until it was brought to notice by Professor Zeuner (1963). This satisfactorily accounts for the early silk industries of Cos and Sidon, formerly attributed to the import of raw cocoons from China. It also accounts for the transparency of certain silk garments referred to by classical authors – a property not shared by Chinese silk.

Dalman (1937) did not know at what date the *Bombyx* silkworm arrived in Syria and the earliest definite record he could find was the twelfth century AD! Yet during the first century silk was well established as a fabric in Rome, although the only certain reference to it in the Bible occurs in Revelation (18:12) where it is listed among the imports of 'Babylon', presumably here a pseudonym for Rome. The mention of silk (Heb. *mesi*) in Ezekiel 16:10, 13 is considered doubtful on philological grounds, but if it really refers to the silk from the *Pachypasa* moth, then the former difficulty of Chinese trading at such an early date would be overcome.

PLANTS FOR THE FULLER

The removal of the natural grease from woollen cloth had to take place before the material could be dyed. The washing processes

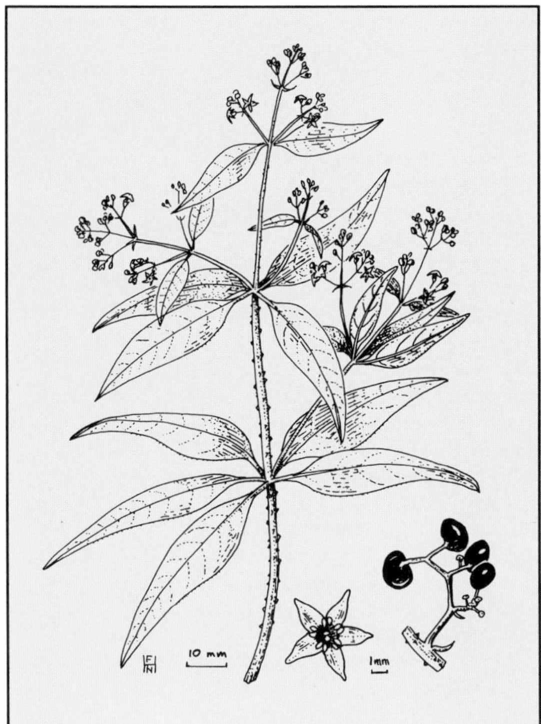

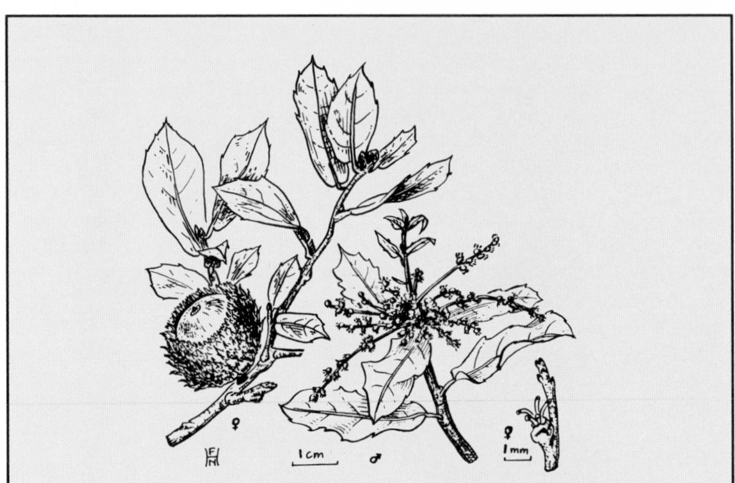

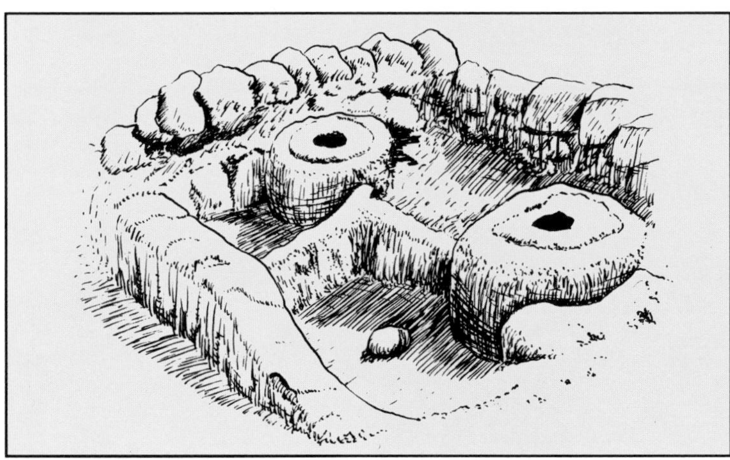

Above: Madder plant (*Rubia tinctoria*); the roots are used as a red dye.

Above right: An African species of *Indigofera*, with pink flowers and similar to *I. tinctoria*, from which indigo dye is obtained.

Centre right: The kermes oak (*Quercus coccifera* or *Q. calliprinos*) on which the kermes insects live. Scarlet dye was prepared from these insects.

Bottom right: Dye vats of the 7th century BC at Tell Beit Mirsim (after W. F. Albright, 1949, plate 22).

included the use of alkaline ashes, which were readily available from household fires since wood was used as fuel (see p. 40). Also used was a kind of soap prepared from various species of saltworts in the orache family (*Chenopodiaceae*), which grow abundantly in the salty areas around the Dead Sea (see p. 55). After washing with this fuller's soap (Malachi 3:2), the cloth was bleached by the sun while laid out in a fuller's field (2 Kings 18:17). At the transfiguration, Jesus' garments 'became glistening, intensely white, as no fuller on earth could bleach them' (Mark 9:3).

PLANTS FOR DYEING

Until recently most of the dyes used for material were plant products, notable exceptions being scarlet and purple dyes. The former was produced from the pulverized female kermes or karmil insect, *Kermes ilicis*, which is similar to the familiar scale insects occurring on fruit.[8] It infests the evergreen Mediterranean Kermes oak, *Quercus coccifera*, of which the Palestinian Kermes oak, *Q. calliprinos*, is probably only a form. The Israeli entomologist, Professor Moshe Sternlicht (1980), considers these insects used in biblical times should be called *K. biblicus* and *K. spatulatus*. Scarlet has, therefore, some association with plants, while purple and crimson, which are frequently mentioned in the Bible, were obtained solely from the shellfish (bivalve) *Murex* and *Purpura*.[9]

These dyes were used in the curtains of the tabernacle which were of 'fine twined linen and blue and purple and scarlet stuff' (Exodus 26:1; 36:8). Professor D. J. Wiseman points out that blue and purple, as well as crimson, were variants of the same dye.

Blue

True blue was obtained from fermented leaves of indigo plants (*Indigofera* species) and of the famous woad (*Isatis tinctoria*), but not until shortly before New

Left: Another red dye is produced by the alkanet plant (*Alkanna lehmannii*).

Left: Safflower (*Carthamus tinctorius*), which yields yellow and red dyes.

Testament times. Indigo plants are herbs belonging to the pea family with slender, but tough, stems and many leaflets. The numerous small pink flowers, borne in slender unbranched inflorescences, develop into narrow curved pods. The four principal indigo-yielding species are *Indigofera articulata*, *I. coerulea*, *I. tinctoria* and *I. arrecta*, all belonging to the same section of the genus (Sect. *Tinctoriae*). There is good evidence for considering them all as tropical African in origin. This includes *I. tinctoria,* which has been regarded as coming from India and only later introduced into Africa.

Probably just as important was *I. arrecta* which was one of the chief indigo-producing species in Africa. The plant referred to in Near Eastern archaeological literature (e.g. Lucas, 1962) as '*I. argentea*' is either *I. coerulea* or *I. articulata,* which prefer lower altitudes than *I. arrecta*; true *I. argentea* is a desert species in a different section of the genus. However, at least some of these would have been available to ancient civilizations. Most of them have been cultivated for the sake of their dye, and it is probable that the *Indigofera* plants still found in the tropical conditions of the Dead Sea area are relics of plants introduced in antiquity and cultivated until recent times.

Red

The Hebrews commonly used red wine to dye cloth, but I wonder how satisfactory it was for this purpose. More effective red dye is known to have been extracted by the Phoenicians and ancient Egyptians, and therefore probably by the Israelites, from madder, safflower and alkanet.

Madder is obtained from the roots of the perennial herbs *Rubia tinctoria* and *R. peregrina*, which have whorls of leaves on their trailing stems and bear small green flowers. These members of the bedstraw family are widespread in the Mediterranean type of vegetation, and *R. peregrina* spreads across Western Europe to Great Britain.

The red dye alkanet is extracted from the roots of *Alkanna lehmannii* (formerly *A. tinctoria*), and possibly from other species in the borage family. Alkanet is a herb of sandy places with rather prickly, hairy leaves. The cultivated safflower (*Carthamus tinctorius*) is

Right: Sumach tree (*Rhus coriaria*) yields tannins for tanning leather.

remarkable in that it yields two colours, yellow and red, from its florets. It is an annual thistle, with thick heads of florets which appear as yellowish-orange.

Unfortunately the yellow colour is washed out of cloth, but the red dye is permanent unless it comes into contact with alkali. It was used to dye mummy wrappings, and material discovered in a Dead Sea cave and dated AD 135 was shown to be dyed yellow with safflower, as well as kermes scarlet and indigo blue.

Yellow

The only yellow dye actually mentioned in the Bible is saffron, and then apparently in connexion with its scent (Song of Solomon 1:14; 4:13, 14). Saffron (*Crocus sativus*) was such an expensive substance that safflower or pomegranate rind were often used instead. In Assyria the Indian turmeric (*Curcuma domestica*) is said to have been used as a yellow dye.

Palestinian dyes

Several wild Palestinian plants were used for the sake of their dye (Dalman, 1937; M. Zohary, 1962), but the art has now been displaced by synthetic substances. In biblical times, however, there were local industries concerned with dye extraction and the dyeing of cloth. For instance at Tell Beit Mirsim, a possible site of ancient Debir to the north of Beersheba, a series of dye vats was found. In the dyeing process the cloth was first treated with a mordant, often alum, to fix the dye, and then dipped or steeped in the coloured solution.

PLANTS FOR TANNING

The apostle Peter 'stayed in Joppa for many days with one Simon, a tanner' (Acts 9:43). Tanning as a trade is as old as tanned leather, which in Egypt goes back to at least the fourth millennium BC, and there is no doubt that leather was extensively used throughout biblical times. Leather as an animal product is well known, but perhaps less familiar are the processes of tanning and the plant products used.

Before the tanning could take place, the hides were washed with lime to clean them and to remove the hairs. The prepared skins were then suspended in a tanning solution containing a fairly high concentration of tannin extracted from suitable plants. Most trees and shrubs contain these naturally occurring organic compounds, but some species are particularly rich in them.

In Palestine a ready source of tannins was the oak, especially the Tabor oak. Tannins occur in the bark as well as in the acorn cups, which were ground and boiled in water to produce a brown liquid, called *daba* by the Bedouin, in which hides were soaked. Pine bark, the leaves of the sumach tree (*Rhus coriaria*) and pomegranate rind were also important sources. But in Egypt, where trees are scarce, tannins were obtained principally from the Nile acacia (*A. nilotica*). Fortunately the pods of this spiny tree growing beside the water are rich in tannins (about 30 per cent) and they are still used today. The tanned hides assume the characteristics of leather on stretching and drying, the treatment varying according to the purpose for which it is required.

---

[1] An interesting and amusing story is given by Dalman in his encyclopedia on the trades of Palestine, quoted in the *Palestine Exploration Quarterly* (1938, p. 262). The Queen of Sheba asked King Solomon this riddle: 'the young panther leapt up, gave a bitter cry and his head was as the head of a reed. He became a praise to the noble, shame to the poor, praise to the dead, shame to the living, the joy of birds and a grief to fishes'. Solomon replied: 'flax, for it shoots up rustling in the wind, makes fine clothes for nobles, rags for the poor and winding sheets for the dead, is shame as the hangman's rope, feeds birds with its seeds, and makes nets for fishes.'

[2] The fibres used for linen are, as already mentioned, obtained from the phloem. The individual cells are mostly 20–40 mm (0.75–1.5 ins) long, but they may reach nearly 120 mm (4.7 ins) in length. They are polygonal in transverse section, with very thick walls which leave a very small central cavity. In British conditions an acre of flax yields two tonnes or more of flax straw from which about 200 kg (4 cwt) of fibre may be extracted. The combed fibres are spun into thread for the weaving of linen cloth which, in biblical times, was bleached, probably by exposing it to sunlight.

[3] The bacterium involved (*Clostridium butyricum*) is present in the mud of the ponds used for retting. It breaks down the pectin which holds the fibre cells together. As the flax plant ages, the pectic substances in the middle lamella between the cells are replaced by hard lignin. This nicely explains the relationship of fineness of thread to the age of the plant mentioned since the lignin would not be attacked by the bacteria and the fibres will remain together, thus producing a much coarser thread suitable for ropes.

[4] Since flax is harvested by pulling up, and not by hoeing up, the rendering of the fourth line of the Gezer calendar quoted above is preferable to Albright's translation (in Prichard, 1950) which reads 'this month is hoeing up of flax'.

[5] Joseph of Arimathea 'took the body, and wrapped it in a clean linen shroud' (Matthew 27:59). Interesting scientific and historical investigations of a linen cloth, known as the shroud of Turin, have taken place in an attempt to prove the claim that it is the one used to wrap Jesus' body (Wilson, 1978; Bortin, 1980), but carbon-dating has now shown that the linen was a fourteenth-century fake (Wild, 1984).

[6] The radio-carbon test estimates the amount of radioactive isotopes of carbon 14 remaining in a plant product and, as the annual breakdown of the isotope is known, it is possible to judge the age of the sample. All plant tissues are composed of a large proportion of carbon, some of which is radioactive and which breaks down at a steady rate.

[7] In recent years a great deal of research has been carried out into the origins of cotton. We know that *Gossypium arboreum* and *G. herbaceum* are recognizable in spite of the enormous amount of variation within them, and they may have originated in tropical Africa. Sir John Hutchinson and his collaborators traced the spread of the cottons around the world and considered that ancient records all point to the Sind (Pakistan) as the original centre of cotton cultivation. Levant cotton may have been derived from the Sind kind as it spread westwards in Greek times. These Old World cottons had shorter lint fibres than the New World species (*G. hirsutum* and *G. barbadense*) which are the usual plantation crops of today.

[8] The pigment obtained from this insect is kermesic acid. In water it is yellow-red but it turns violet-red when acid is added.

[9] Dor, at the foot of Mount Carmel, was one of the centres for producing the dye known as Tyrian purple from Tyre, the great Phoenician city. It was also called imperial purple 'for it was so expensive it was confined to kings and nobles ... It was only with the development of synthetic chemical dyes that the Tyrian purple could be matched' (Comay, 1963). I might add that the first of these synthetic dyes was the aniline dye discovered in 1854 by my ancestor, Professor Sir William H. Perkin of Leeds, who gave his name to the 'Perkin reaction'.

Bibliography

Bortin, V., 'Science and the Shroud of Turin', *Biblical Archaeologist* (Baltimore, 1980), 43(2):109–17.

Bruce, F. F., *Second Thoughts on the Dead Sea Scrolls* (Exeter, Paternoster Press, 1966).

Carter, H. R., *Flax and its Products* (London, Bale and Danielsson, 1920).

Comay, J., *Introducing Israel* (London, Methuen, 1963).

Crowfoot, G. M., 'Linen Textiles from the Cave of Ain Feshkha', *Palestine Exploration Quarterly* (London, 1951), pp. 5–31.

—. in C. Singer, E. J. Holmyard, and A. R. Hall, *History of Technology* (Oxford University Press, 1958), 1:429–45.

Harding, G. L., 'Khirbet Qumran and Wadi Muraba'at', *Palestine Exploration Quarterly* (London, 1952), p. 105.

Hutchinson, J. B., Silow, R. A., and Stephens, S. G., *The Evolution of Gossypium* (Oxford University Press, 1947).

Metcalfe, C. R., and Chalk, I., *Anatomy of the Dicotyledons,* vol. 2 (Oxford University Press, 1950).

Siegelmann, A., 'Flax growing and Processing in Roman Palestine', *Israel Land and Nature* (Jerusalem, 1984), 9(4):144–7.

Sternlicht, M., 'The Dye of the Coccid', *Israel Land and Nature* (Jerusalem, 1980), 6(1):17–21.

Thomas, D. W., *Documents from Old Testament Times* (London, Nelson, 1958).

Wild, R. A., *Biblical Archaeology Review* (Washington, 1984), 10(2):30–46.

Wilson, I., *The Turin Shroud* (London, Gollancz, 1978).

Zeuner, F. E., 'Notes on Qumran', *Palestine Exploration Quarterly* (London, 1960), p. 27.

—. *A History of Domestic Animals* (London, Hutchinson, 1963).

Ziderman, I. I, 'Sea Shells and Ancient Purple Dyeing', *Biblical Archaeologist* (Baltimore, 1990), 53(2):98–101.

18. Baskets, Mats and Cords

'And making a whip of cords he drove them all ... out of the temple.'
(John 2:15.)

BASKETS

Baskets are still familiar general household items and, since the material from which they are made is in an almost raw state, their plant origin is easily recognizable. Such receptacles for carrying fruit, bread and other objects, as well as for their storage, are essential in even the most primitive community. Plaiting for baskets is so ancient that it preceded the weaving of cloth, which entails a much more complicated preparation of fibres.

A good deal is known about the baskets of ancient Egypt, as they were frequently placed in tombs. It is, in fact, an Egyptian basket that is first mentioned in the Bible, when Pharaoh's baker, imprisoned with Joseph, dreamed of three baskets containing cakes (or white bread) and baked food (Genesis 40:16–17). These bread baskets were flat trays (Heb. *sal*) and similar ones would have been used by the Israelite priests for their unleavened wheaten bread, cakes and wafers for the wave offering (Exodus 29:2–3, 23; Leviticus 8:2, 26, 31).

A larger basket, often used for storage in the home, is referred to in Deuteronomy: 'When you come into the land ... you shall take of some of the first of all the fruit of the ground ... and you shall put it in a basket' (Heb. *tene*; Deuteronomy 26:1–2). Both Jeremiah and Amos had visions of fruit baskets (Jeremiah 24:2; Amos 8:1), but different Hebrew words are used for basket in each case. The true fruit basket (Heb. *dud*), seen in Jeremiah's vision to be full of figs, was a small round one used for carrying fruit, yet it was large enough to hold a human head after the slaughter of Ahab's seventy sons (2 Kings 10:7). The other kind was a basket for trapping birds, or perhaps holding trapped birds, as mentioned by Jeremiah: 'For wicked men are found among my people; they lurk like fowlers lying in wait. They set a trap; they catch men. Like a basket full of birds, their houses are full of treachery' (Jeremiah 5:26–7).

It is perhaps surprising to find that the plaited or woven wickerwork basket with which we are familiar was seldom made by the ancient Egyptians. In its place they had coiled baskets, which G. M. Crowfoot (1958) described:

'Coiled work requires two elements, the coil or core, and the wrapping or sewing-strip. The core,

Right: An ancient Egyptian basket of coiled work. (Flinders Petrie Collection, University College, London.)

Far left: Cotton grass or lalang (*Imperata cylindrica*) was also sometimes used for baskets.

Left: Halfa grass (*Desmostachys bipinnata*), the principal grass for basket-making.

usually consisting of a bundle of grass, rushes or fibres, is coiled spirally, the different layers being fastened together by a sewing strip.'

Date-palm leaflets and fibres, as well as the split midrib for stiffer work, were the chief material used for basket-making, with halfa grass (*Desmostachya bipinnata*) and cotton grass or lalang (*Imperata cylindrica*) sometimes used, and ornamented by dyeing the stems. Papyrus and reeds were also occasionally used for making baskets, although more frequently for constructing little framed boxes.

All these materials decompose rapidly in damp conditions and generally have not survived, but sometimes the plants used for making coiled baskets and matting can be identified from their impressions left on the bottom of freshly-moulded clay vessels. Such have been found on pots unearthed at Jericho and other Palestinian sites. The impressions were so clear that the reed-mace (*Typha domingensis*), sharp rush (*Juncus acutus*) and two species of true bulrush (*Scirpus lacustris, S. litoralis*) have been identified (Crowfoot, 1958). There is little doubt that the basket in which the infant Moses was hidden was made of papyrus, and conifer pitch (rather than inorganic bitumen), was used to waterproof it (Exodus 2:3). Both substances effectively preserve the fibres. Forbes (1955) tells of the discovery of an entire ancient Babylonian basket made of plaited plant leaves, which survived in damp foundations because it had been dipped in melted bitumen. There is also a Babylonian legend in which a baby was hidden in a basket, waterproofed with bitumen.

In the New Testament we find that the twelve baskets used by the disciples to collect the fragments of food remaining after the feeding of the five thousand were really hampers (Gk. *kophinos*; Matthew 14:20; 16:9; Mark 6:43; 8:19; Luke 9:17; John 6:13). After the four thousand had been fed, the fragments were collected in seven even larger hampers (Gk. *spyris*). It was in the latter kind of basket that Paul was lowered from the walls of Damascus in order to make his escape from the city (Acts 9:25). Paul later refers to this event himself (2 Corinthians 11:33), and uses yet another word for the basket (Gk. *sargane*), literally a plaited container. Perhaps this indicates more accurately the Syrian type of basketry used in its construction, contrasting with the coiled basketry formerly popular in Egypt. No doubt willow twigs (osiers) were used in Syrian basketry during New Testament times, as they are at the present day.

MATS

The plaiting methods used for matting are in many respects similar to ancient basketry. It is known that mats were extensively used in biblical times. For instance, when Jericho was excavated in 1952 by Kathleen Kenyon, some tombs of Early Bronze Age, well before Joshua captured the city, yielded many interesting pieces of furniture,

Right: The leaves of the reed-mace or cat-tail (*Typha latifolia*) were often used for mat-making.

Far right: An ancient Egyptian besom—handleless brush—such as would have been used in biblical times. (Flinders Petrie Collection, University College, London.)

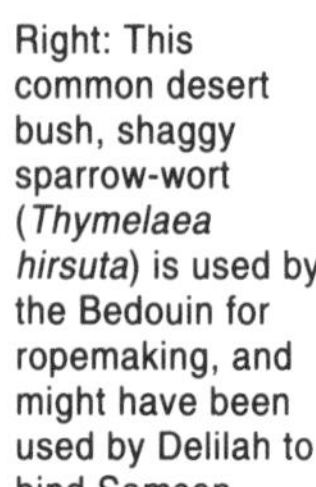

Right: This common desert bush, shaggy sparrow-wort (*Thymelaea hirsuta*) is used by the Bedouin for ropemaking, and might have been used by Delilah to bind Samson.

as well as rush mats. It is surmised that as only one actual bed was found – and this in the principal grave – people normally slept on rush mats similar to those on which the bodies were lying. Much later, in New Testament times, the bed which the paralytic man was told by Jesus to take up and carry home (Matthew 9:6) was no doubt a similar rush pallet.

The material from which mats were made varied according to the availability of suitable species. Waterside plants, such as the reed (*Phragmites australis*), rushes (*Juncus* species), reed-mace (*Typha domingensis, T. latifolia*), and papyrus (*Cyperus papyrus*), were perhaps the most frequently chosen, but halfa grass (*Desmostachys bipinnata*), date-palm fibres and flax have also been identified in Egyptian mats.

The various kinds of ancient mat-making were studied by G. M. Crowfoot (1958), summarized by Lucas (1962), who listed the following methods, as well as the coiled work for baskets already mentioned: *twined work*, in which single rushes or bundles of fibres are laid side by side and interlaced by two threads; *wrapped work*, akin to weaving, in which a single wrapping strand passed round bundles of fibres; *matting work*, also akin to weaving, in which one series of fibres forms the warp and another the weft; *plaited work*, in which plaits are made separately and sewn into the required shape.

Brushes

Ancient Egyptian brushes, and probably also those used by the Israelites, were not of the type we know with wooden handles. They were simply bundles of fibres tied together at the top to form a handle, as commonly used in Mediterranean countries today. Such a broom or besom was referred to by Isaiah (14:23) and was probably also the type that Jesus had in mind when he told the parable of the woman who swept the house to find a lost coin (Luke 15:8–9). Almost any suitable fibrous plant material, such as grass, reeds and date-palm fibres, was utilized. It is interesting to note that the finer brushes made of date-palm fibres were used, according to ancient Egyptian texts, for cleaning the horns and hoofs of the holy bulls, those revered animals that undoubtedly gave the Israelites the idea of the golden calf.

Date-palm fibres occur at the base of the young leaves and originate from the partial disintegration of the sheaths that at first enclose the developing leaves. Such fibres were also normally used in paint brushes of various sizes for the tomb paintings, while other paint brushes were made from woody pieces of palm midrib, beaten out at one end to expose the fibres. When I examined a brush of this kind excavated in 1973 at Saqqara and now at Kew, I noticed that the fibres had remained unwashed and had dried twisted: it would be intriguing to know who last used it and what latest work was so hastily relinquished. In spite of the primitive and clumsy appearance of the brushes, the wonderful execution of the tomb paintings is sufficient witness to their effectiveness.

CORDAGE[1]

'Arrogant men have hidden a trap for me', wrote David, 'and with cords they have spread a net' (Psalm 140:5). Cords and string for nets were made of twisted or intertwined plant fibres or animal hair, and sometimes of strips of hide, the thickness of the rope or string depending on the size and number of the component strands. Once again we must turn to ancient Egypt for examples of cordage preserved in tombs. When one considers the Egyptians' gigantic engineering feats such as the building of the pyramids, it soon becomes clear that strong ropes in the nature of hawsers must have been necessary to secure and haul the stone blocks into position. The famous pyramids of Giza date from the fourth dynasty, *c.* 2600 BC, and the Step

Left: Cords and ropes, such as these made of papyrus rind, are often referred to in the Bible.

Pyramid at Saqqara was built two hundred years earlier. It has been estimated that the larger blocks in the Great Pyramid, which gangs of labourers had to haul on rollers up steep ramps of sand, weigh fifteen tonnes/tons (Edwards, 1947). What tensile strength the ropes required!

A rope about 5.2 m (18 ft) long was actually found inside the Step Pyramid. Other ropes of varying thickness, which I examined from temple remains of a later period excavated at Saqqara, were all composed entirely of the green papyrus rind. When Solomon's men built the temple in c. 960 BC they must have used great ropes to haul the cedars of Lebanon to the coast and the stones from the quarry. These ropes, too, may have been made of papyrus, although ropes of date-palm fibre are much more frequent, at least in Egypt, even to the present day.

We have no means of knowing of what material ropes mentioned in the Bible were made. However, Israeli botanists believe that the ropes used by Delilah to bind Samson (Judges 16:7; green withes KJV; bowstrings RSV; thongs NIV) were of the green stems of shaggy sparrow-wort (*Thymelaea hirsuta*). This desert shrub about 2 m (6 ft) high is common in the sandy coastal plain around Gaza where the incident occurred. Its fresh stems traditionally have been used for ropes and they are very tough (Danin, 1975). When Jesus went into the temple and found God's house 'a den of thieves', he made a whip before driving them out. This probably entailed unpicking the component strands of a rope. Here the Greek *schoinion* means literally a papyrus rope (John 2:15).

Fine thread and string were made from flax, and the string in turn was used to make nets. As already noted (p. 167), Beth Shean, just south of the Sea of Galilee, was famous for its flax, which probably supplied the material for James, John and Zebedee as they sat in their boat 'mending their nets' (Matthew 4:21).

---

[1] The following Hebrew words were used in the Old Testament for cordage: *hebel* (Joshua 2:15; 1 Kings 20:31; Isaiah 33:23); *bot* (Job 39:10; Judges 15:13, 14; Psalm 118:27; Isaiah 5:18); *yeter* (Judges 16:7; Job 30:11; Psalm 11:2); *metar* (Exodus 35:18); *hut* (Ecclesiastes 4:12). In the New Testament Greek, *schoinion* (John 2:15; Acts 27:32) was used.

Bibliography

Baker, H. S., *Furniture in the Ancient World* (London, *The Connoisseur*, 1966).

Crowfoot, G. M., in C. Singer, E. J. Holmyard, and A. R. Hall, *History of Technology* (Oxford University Press, 1958), 1:418–24.

Danin, A., 'Living Plants as Archaeological Artifacts', *Biblical Archaeology Review* (Washington, 1975), 1(4):24–5.

Edwards, I. E. S., *The Pyramids of Egypt* (Harmondsworth, Penguin Books, 1947).

Forbes, R. J., 'Bitumen and Petroleum in Antiquity', *Studies in Ancient Technology* (Leiden, Brill, 1955), 1:89.

19. Papyrus, Pen and Ink

'A written scroll ... and it had writing on the front and on the back.'
(Ezekiel 2:9–10.)

PAPYRUS

Papyrus writing material is one of the most important inventions of the ancient world. It is of special interest to us since papyrus was used for many of the biblical manuscripts. In fact our word Bible is derived from the Greek *byblos,* which was their name for the white pith in the stalk of the papyrus sedge. It was this pith that was used for the manufacture of the paper. In course of time the Greek word *biblion* was applied to all scrolls or books, and subsequently to the Bible itself.

However, the etymology is even more involved, since the Greeks called the whole plant *papyros*, after a similar ancient Egyptian hieroglyph; hence our use of the word 'papyrus' for both the plant and its product. Moreover, the English word 'paper' is directly derived from papyrus. But the Greeks themselves called a sheet of the writing material *chartes*, which the Romans latinized as *charta*. This starts another train of derivatives such as chart, charter, carton and cartoon!

We have already seen how the papyrus sedge (*Cyperus papyrus*) grows in great stands in the swamps of Huleh (chapter 6). Many of its uses are described elsewhere in this book (boats, p. 69; baskets, p. 175; ropes, p. 176), but its use for writing material outweighs all these. Light sheets of papyrus had great advantages over other writing surfaces, such as heavy stone slabs, irregular pieces of pottery (ostraca) and clay tablets used for cuneiform writing by the Babylonians. Papyrus sheets could be used separately, or pasted together into scrolls for longer works.

The manufacture of papyrus is extremely old, since samples are known from the time of the first dynasty of ancient Egypt, about 3000 BC. The dry Egyptian climate preserved papyrus better than that of Palestine, where the oldest surviving papyrus manuscript dates only from the eighth century BC; it is inscribed in ancient Aramaic. Some papyrus wrappings and a few manuscripts about 2000 years old were found in a dry cave in the Judean Desert, among the other Dead Sea scrolls, which were mainly made of copper.

The Egyptians had a monopoly of the manufacture of papyrus, until it was finally superseded by parchment in Roman times. Parchment is made from animal skins, and its invention as a writing material is said to have occurred when Ptolemy stopped the shipment of papyrus to his Attalid rival, who was based at Pergamum. This city, in present-day Turkey, boasted a library as fine as the celebrated library in Alexandria.

Deprived of papyrus imports, the Attalid king turned to skins which were heavier and less suitable for scrolls. Hence they were bound along one edge as a paged book, called a codex. This form of book increased in popularity, and in due course facilitated reference between the Old and New Testaments. The Pergamum library was eventually transferred to the city of Alexandria, where unfortunately the combined libraries were burnt by the Muslims during the seventh century.

Right: A modern copy on a papyrus sheet of an illustration of papyrus-gathering in the swamps of ancient Egypt. The man on the right is stripping the green rind to expose the white pith used for the sheets. (Tomb of Ni-ankh-khum and Knum-hotep, Saqqara, Egypt, *c.* 2400 BC.)

Making papyrus

Since the commercial production of papyrus has ceased for about 1700 years, we turn to classical writers for accounts of its manufacture. Pliny gave a description which has often been quoted and intensely analysed, with widely ranging interpretations. Many people have recorded their attempts to make samples of the paper from the papyrus plant (Bruce, 1790; Lucas, 1962; Lewis, 1974; Ragab, 1980). There are today many flourishing papyrus workshops in Cairo, and others at Syracuse in Sicily, producing commercial quantities of papyrus for the tourist industry and for export.

In 1966 I decided to try to make it myself and, after an initial success, I have demonstrated papyrus manufacture many times.[1] I used plants from the hot houses at Kew Gardens, where they grow well in saturated soil at the margin of the tropical water-lily pool. I also used wild plants during a visit to Lake Chad in 1969. Readers may be interested to know the techniques of the process, as well as the results of an unexpected piece of research that arose as a result of my first attempt.

Papyrus stalks[2] are about 3 m (10 ft) high, topped by a huge mop-like head of chaffy flowers. Just below the head, the stalk is sharply triangular, with a thickness of about 1.5 cm (0.5 in), containing broken pith. Lower down it becomes thicker, reaching 5–7.5 cm (2–3 ins) at the base, and with rounded corners. Cut off a 30 cm (1 ft) length near the bottom and slice away the hard, shiny green outer cortex or rind, exposing the pure white spongy inner pith. Much longer portions may be used, but they take longer to prepare. Cut lengthwise slices of pith as thin as practicable. If they are too thin, holes tend to appear; and I found a suitable thickness was about 2 mm (0.08 in).[3] This is thinner than some people recommend, but it means a shorter process.

After laying the strips side by side on a smooth board covered with muslin cloth, with the same number on top and at right angles to the first layer, cover the papyrus with cloth. It is now ready for pressing or hammering. But even a gentle tapping with a round ended metal-worker's mallet tends to move the pieces apart, and care must be taken to maintain the edges in a contiguous position, so pressing is necessary. It is important that the pieces are as close together as possible, with their edges touching for their whole length, but not actually overlapping. If the strips are first rinsed, then rolled with a bottle or rolling-pin before placing on the board, whiter paper results. In Syracuse, the strips are actually bleached with oxalic acid, whilst Dr Hassan Ragab of Cairo always soaks the whole stems before slicing them. At both Syracuse and Cairo, where commercial quantities are made, the hand-presses are fitted with alternate layers of papyrus and absorbent sheets.

Pliny stated that the strips were 'moistened with water from the Nile; the muddy liquid serving as the bonding force' (translation by Lewis, 1974). There is no evidence, however, that muddy Nile water has the peculiar properties imputed to it by Pliny, and one may question whether any additional substance is necessary, since the strips adhere by themselves. I used tap-water and nothing at all, with equal success. I therefore asked my Kew colleague, Tom Reynolds, to make a biochemical analysis of the sap in the papyrus stalk. His analysis revealed the presence of certain complicated, but well-known, vegetable gums which are liberated

Above: Stages in the preparation of a sheet of papyrus (from left to right).

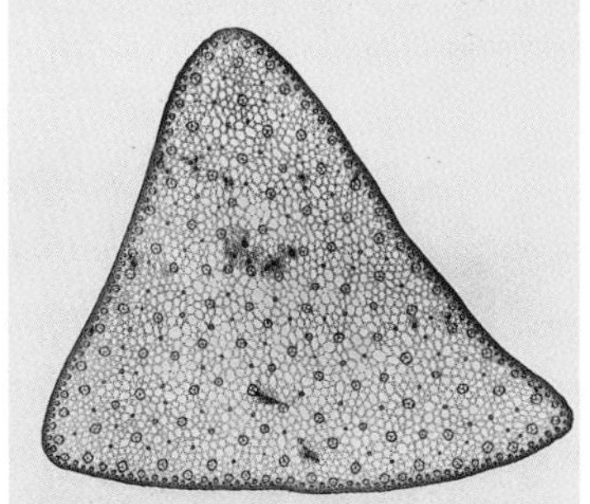

Left: The triangular stalk of the papyrus plant (*Cyperus papyrus*), showing the thick rind and inner pith with vascular bundles.

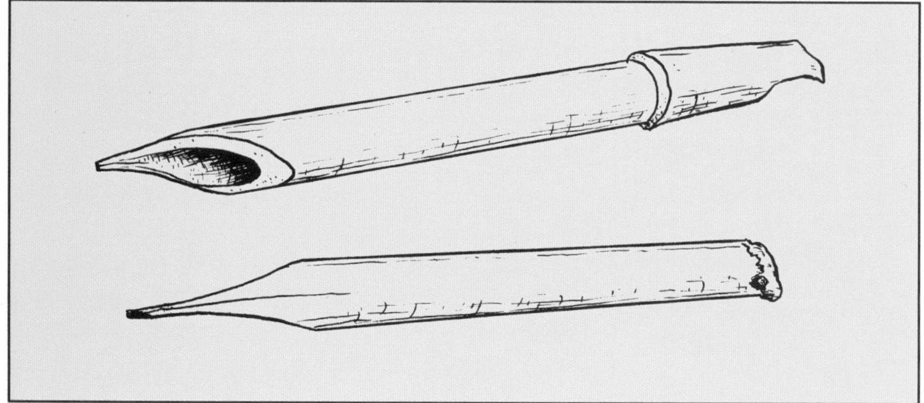

Above: Two pens cut from reeds such as were used in Roman (New Testament) times.

when the cells are crushed during paper manufacture, and these are clearly very suitable for gluing the strips together (Hepper and Reynolds, 1967). However, another suggestion has been made by Dr Ragab (1980), that the strips adhere by the physical interlocking of the cells. After thoroughly drying the sheets Pliny recommended burnishing with a piece of ivory or shell, but I found this raised the fibres and even caused the ink to smudge.

Papyrus scrolls

Writing would have been made on the surface with the fibres running horizontally, the *recto*. The other side, the *verso*, has vertical fibres which, due to contraction of the thin-walled pith between them, are prominent and impart a roughness to the paper; hence that side was not normally used. However, in Revelation 5:1, we read of writing 'within and on the back', and in Ezekiel 2:10 we also find the scroll was written 'on the front and on the back'. A scroll was composed of many individual sheets of papyrus glued together. The longest scroll known is the 'Great Harris Papyrus' of Rameses III, which is 42 m (140 ft) in length. The scrolls and rolls often mentioned in the Bible (Ezra 6:2) could have been made of papyrus, although parchment or even linen were also used. Jeremiah had to write on a scroll (Jeremiah 36:2), and Jesus read from a scroll of the prophet Isaiah in a synagogue on the Sabbath day (Luke 4:16–20 NIV – an actual scroll of Jesus' time found at Qumran is now exhibited in the Israel Museum). It has been estimated that the Gospel of Luke would have occupied a roll 8 m (about 26 ft) long (Thompson, 1965). The 'books' which the apostle Paul asked Timothy to bring (2 Timothy 4:13) would also have been papyrus rolls. John even doubted whether the world would hold all the 'books' that could be written about Jesus (John 21:25).

Right: The author making papyrus sheets from fresh papyrus sedge gathered in Lake Chad, West Africa; 1969.

Papyri have often been recovered from ancient sites, especially in Egypt, where they were frequently wrapped around or stuffed inside mummies. Some were re-used, with the first writing more or less erased, and the second writing appearing on top; such papyri are called *palimpsests*. Much information on the life and times of the writers has been obtained from these papyri. The earlier ones deal with Egyptian government affairs, some being mundane accounts, others letters pleading for help from cities facing attack. A great deal of light has been shed by later papyri on almost every aspect of New Testament times, especially linguistics. It is fascinating to examine such sheets, kept between glass in the Papyrus Room of the British Museum, the world's largest collection of papyri, and to compare the variations in the material. Indeed Roman emperors recognized various qualities of papyrus, often by naming the best ones after themselves.

OTHER WRITING MATERIALS

Papyrus was not the only writing material available to the scribes of biblical times. Leaves of various trees were also used for writing on: 'for all purposes they write on olive leaves' states the Mishnah, and 'they wrote with an ink of coagulated blood and coagulated milk on olive leaves, on carob leaves and anything else that was durable' (Goor, 1966). When Zechariah, the father of John the Baptist, asked for a tablet on which to write his son's name (Luke 1:63), he probably received a wooden writing board with a covering of beeswax. This type of writing surface, with two or three hinged leaves, was very common in New Testament times, and it is known to have been used in Assyria from about the time of Isaiah onwards. In fact, the tablets referred to by Isaiah (30:8) and Habakkuk (2:2) may also have been boards of wood or ivory of this type, on which the wax in a shallow recess could be melted for re-inscription with a pointed stylus.

Linen provided another writing material and, although it is not mentioned in the Bible, it is interesting to note that some of the Dead Sea scrolls were made of it. Scroll number 4 Q Sam^a in the Palestine

Museum is made of linen with a backing of papyrus. This is an unusual feature and probably accounts for the relatively good state of preservation of the scroll. It dates from about 50–25 BC, and is part of a manuscript that included 1 and 2 Samuel.

PEN AND INK

In spite of the age of papyrus sheets and their brownish appearance, the writing remains very clear. This is because the ink normally used was permanent, made of the element carbon, in the form of lamp-black scraped from the bottom of pots and mixed with gum and water. Similarly the other principal ancient ink pigments – iron oxide and other iron compounds – do not fade like the dyes used for inks today. Ancient ink (Heb. *deyo*) was made as required by rubbing a moist pen on to a small prepared block of the lamp-black. Spendid ivory and gold writing palettes were found in Tutankhamun's tomb, together with a pen-case in the form of a column with a date-palm capital (Hepper, 1990).

Scribes, at least in Egypt, originally used pens cut not from reeds but from rushes, such as the sea rush (*Juncus maritimus*) and Arabian rush (*J. arabicus*). These were very slender and rather long, with the writing point formed by an oblique cut at one end. The fibres were 'split by chewing so as to produce a fine brush. With the flat side the thicker lines were made and, with the fine edge, the thinner lines' (Lucas, 1964). Perhaps the writers of the Old Testament used rush pens (Heb. *et*), too, since the split-reed pen was used only from the third century BC by the Greeks and Romans. Reed stems, *Phragmites*, like our familiar bamboo canes, were sharpened at one end to form a pen with a split point.

By New Testament times the split-reed pen was in general use and one can imagine the imprisoned apostle using one for his conclusion: 'I, Paul, write this greeting with my own hand. This is the mark in every letter of mine; it is the way I write' (2 Thessalonians 3:17). Thus handwriting, even with a reed pen, was just as characteristic of the writer as it is today. John wrote that he would prefer to see the 'elect lady': 'though I have much to write to you, I would rather not use paper [Gk. *chartes*] and ink [Gk. *melan*]' (2 John 1: 12). The same thought occurs in his next letter, written to Gaius, that he 'would rather not write with pen [Gk. *kalamos*, i.e. reed]' (3 John 13). Paul even wrote to the church at Corinth saying that 'you show you are a letter from Christ delivered by us, written not with ink but with the Spirit of the living God, not on tablets of stone but on tablets of human hearts' (2 Corinthians 3:3).

----

[1] For example in the film 'Alphabet: the story of calligraphy' (Parker Pen International, 1980) and Thames TV in November 1980.

[2] Most authors refer to the flowering stalks as stems, but the *stem* of papyrus is a reduced stout rhizome rooting in the mud from which these *stalks* arise. They support the flower-head, or inflorescence, and they are therefore known botanically as the culm or peduncle. In any case the word stalk is preferable to stem in this context.

[3] Wiesner measured some slices from an ancient Egyptian papyrus and found that the dry thickness was only 80μ (.08 mm).

Bibliography

Bruce, James, *Travels to the Source of the Nile* (Edinburgh, Murray, 1790), vol. 5.

Goor, A., 'The Place of the Olive in the Holy Land and its History through the Ages', *Economic Botany* (New York, 1966) 20:226.

Hepper, F. N., and Reynolds, T., 'Papyrus and the Adhesive Properties of its Cell Sap in Relation to Paper Making', *Journal of Egyptian Archaeology* (London, 1967), 53:157–7.

Lewis, J., *Papyrus in Classical Antiquity* (Oxford University Press, 1974).

Pliny, *Natural History*, transl. H. Rackham – W. H. S. Jones, 1938–56 (Cambridge, Harvard University Press).

Ragab, H., *Le Papyrus* (Cairo, dissertation, 1980).

Ryan, D. P. 'Papyrus', *Biblical Archaeologist* (Baltimore, 1988), 53(3):132–40.

20. Art, Architecture and Symbolism

'He covered the two doors of olivewood with carvings of cherubim, palm trees and open flowers.'
(1 Kings 6:32.)

EGYPTIAN INFLUENCES

Most people appreciate the beauty of flowers, as well as the patterns of leaves and fruits, and botanical motifs have been an inspiration for ornamention since time immemorial. In ancient civilizations plants were frequently symbolic, as well as ornamental. For example the lotus water-lily and papyrus plant represented Upper and Lower Egypt, just as the rose and thistle represent England and Scotland today.

The magnificent temples and tombs of ancient Egypt were covered with drawings, carvings and hieroglyphics which were often taken from the form of plants and animals. Plants were depicted either singly or as part of a scene, such as those showing Pharaoh hunting in the Nile marshes (p. 66). In the tombs of the nobles the wall paintings were not for decoration, but to represent the owner's fields, in which his servants were depicted cutting corn or picking grapes to benefit him in the life hereafter. Even objects for daily use were modelled in the form of plants. For example, a little box with a swivel lid looks like a small snake-cucumber (p. 126), and an alabaster lampstand in Tutankamun's tomb is in the form of water-lilies.

As Palestine lies so close to Egypt it is not surprising that its art was subject to continuous Egyptian influence. Albright has pointed out that most artistic productions, at least in the Canaanite period, were crude imitations of Egyptian originals. Later, Syro-Phoenician art became the dominant influence.

When the Israelites left Egypt they established the tabernacle with its rites, and we have already seen how the wooden furniture for it was constructed. The golden seven-branched lampstand, the menorah, carefully detailed in Exodus 25 (see p. 185), has been likened to the Palestine and Judean sages (*Salvia palaestina*, *S. judaica*) with some justification (Hareuveni, 1980), but this is not accepted by all Jewish botanists.

Unlike the Egyptians and the Phoenicians, however, the Hebrews did not permit the representation of animals or humans in their art forms, although this was not always strictly observed. From the ivories found at Samaria we can obtain considerable insight into the type of ornamentation used in a royal Israelite palace at the time of Ahab (ninth century BC). When this palace was excavated in 1931–2 by the Crowfoots they found numerous ivory plaques, evidently carved to decorate panels or the framework of cabinets, couches, tables or stools which have long-since disintegrated (see chapter 16). In addition to gods, cherubs, the lion, the bull and other animals, botanical motifs were also prominent. A drooping, somewhat stylized, palm tree was evidently popular for several centuries in other cultures. The water-lily, the famous lotus of Egypt, was used either as the background to a principal theme, or by itself in a chain of flowers and buds. The petals are clearly depicted, and the stalks are formed of two lines in relief, on which traces of gold leaf were found.

Right: The symbolic union of Upper and Lower Egypt, represented by the tying of the lotus water-lily and papyrus respectively.

The Crowfoots made interesting observations on the subjects used in relation to the Bible:

'the style and subjects of the ivories suggest an immediate comparison with the decorations of the temple of Solomon. Figures borrowed from the Egyptian pantheon naturally would be ignored by biblical writers, but most of our other subjects are mentioned not once but several times in the chapters devoted to Solomon's work (1 Kings 6–10). *The 'lions, oxen and cherubim', the 'cherubim, lions and palm trees', the 'lions on the steps of the great throne of ivory', the 'oxen beneath the laver', the 'nets of checker work', the 'wreaths of chain work', the 'lily work on the chapiters', to all these we can find parallels, the pomegranates only are wanting at present. And such a verse as that about the doors of the temple – 'he carved thereon cherubim and palm trees and open flowers, and he overlaid them with gold fitted upon the graven work'* (1 Kings 6:35) *– describes not only the subjects but the treatment we have studied on the ivories. 'Ivory work overlaid with sapphire' (Song of Solomon 6:14) no longer seems an extravagant picture of the body of the beloved, and the spirit of [these] ivories is the same spirit which is reflected in the forty-fifth Psalm'* (Crowfoot, 1933).

PLANTS AND ARCHITECTURE

It is strange to realize that the form of the massive stone pillars in many Egyptian temples was derived from bundles of the weak papyrus plant. In the absence of readily available

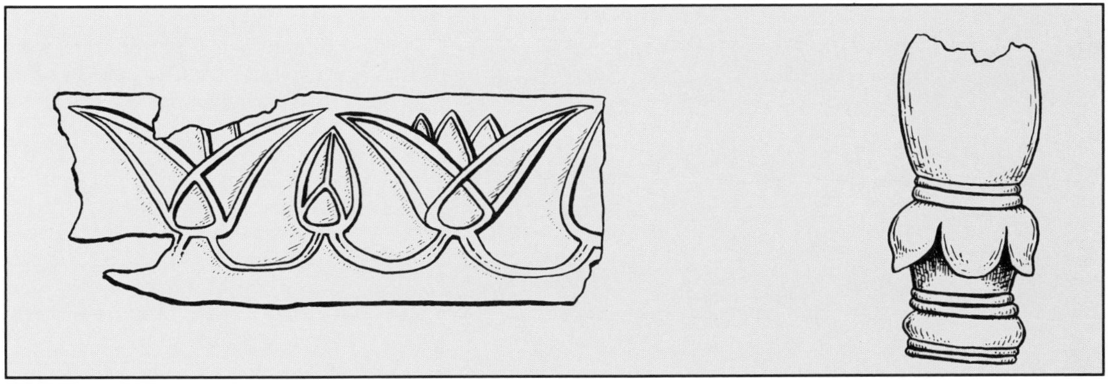

Left and below: Ivory carvings from Samaria in the form of palm trees and lotus water-lilies (After *Palestine Exploration Quarterly* 1932, plate 2.) Lotus and pommel from Arslan-Tash that may be similar to the two pillars in front of Solomon's temple. (After *Palestine Exploration Quarterly* 1959, plate 3.)

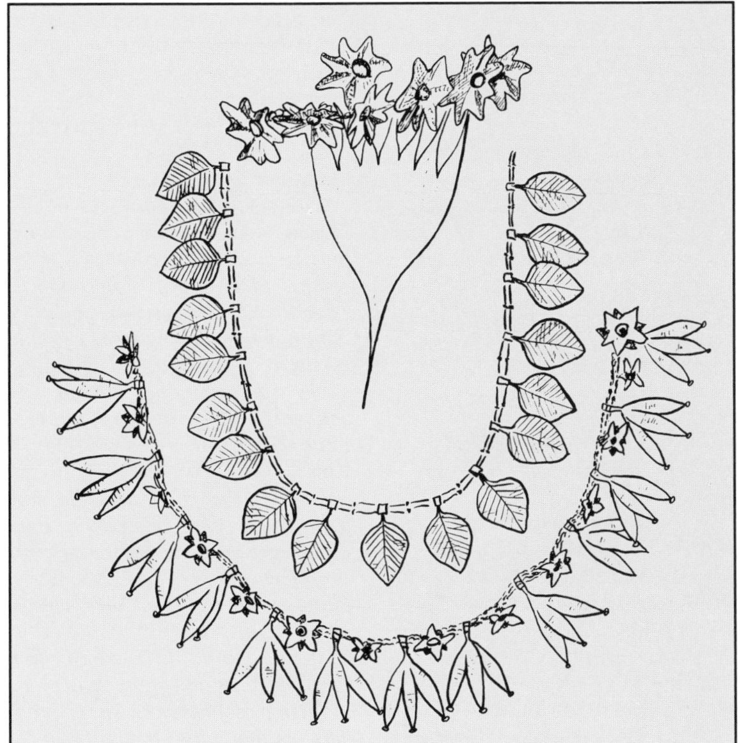

Far left: Golden jewellery from ancient Ur, with leaves and flowers. (After H. Frankfort *The Art and Architecture of the Ancient Orient*, 1958, Harmondsworth, Pelican.)

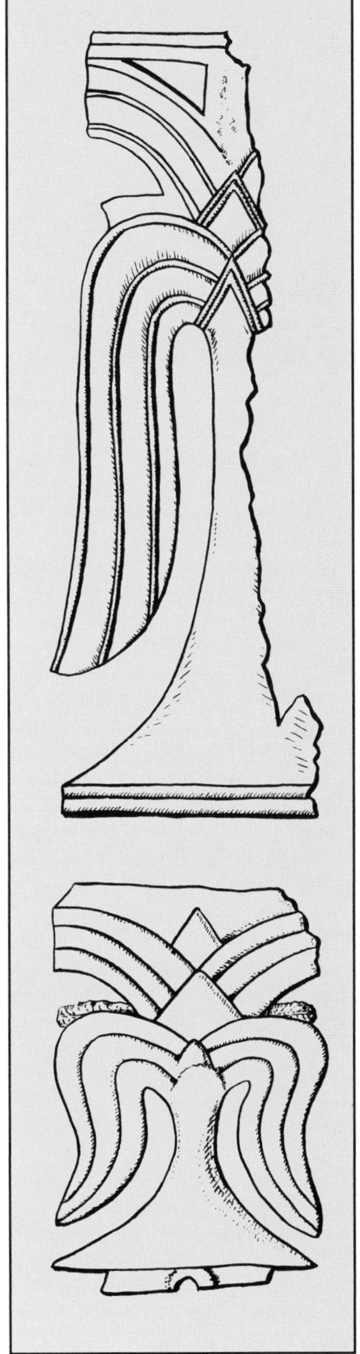

timber, the Egyptians had to use whatever they could find to support the roofs of their houses and primitive temples in remote pre-dynastic times. Apparently they collected the tall papyrus stalks from the Nile-side marshes, tying several together to form support for a flimsy roof. Dr Margaret Murray has shown how this familiar theme was adopted by the first architects and stonemasons of the ancient Egyptian temples. One frequently discovers stone columns fluted as if each were composed of eight (or rarely, six) papyrus stems, with horizontal bands at the top. Typically they are swollen below the middle, as if they are bulging under the weight of the roof.

The Hebrews in Egypt must have been very familiar with this type of 'clustered column'; moreover, during their captivity they would have seen a marked change in the traditional form. With the establishment of what we now know as the New Kingdom and the eighteenth dynasty with 'a new king over Egypt, who did not know Joseph' (Exodus 1:8), the fluted columns eventually gave way to a smooth surface covered with incised hieroglyphic inscriptions and figures, although the bands still appeared at the top and the bulging outline remained unchanged. In the Old Kingdom during Zozer's reign (2800 BC) the form of single triangular papyrus stalk was occasionally used, with the inflorescence serving as the capital (Rowe, 1962). Later the untidy form of the clustered papyrus heads was often

Opposite: The seven-branched lampstand or menorah, here seen outside the Knesset in Jerusalem, was originally based on the form of the almond flower. Some botanists see the branching like that of the sage inflorescence.

Right: Ancient Egyptian stone temple columns were usually modelled on plant forms such as the lotus water-lily, papyrus and palm leaves.

replaced by the more elegant enlarged lotus bud.

The precise appearance of the pillars known as Jachin and Boaz, standing in front of Solomon's temple, has been the subject of much discussion. A logical interpretation of the form of the pillars has been propounded by Yeivin (1959), who accounts for all the points mentioned in the biblical descriptions (1 Kings 7:15–22; 2 Chronicles 3:15–17). The capitals were ornamented with botanical motifs, and it is now possible to reconstruct them more precisely. The 'lily-work' (Heb. *shushan*)represented the open lotus water-lily flower with four pendant sepals corresponding to the four sides of the capital, each side being 4 cubits (1.8 m, 5 ft 6 ins) long. This flower supported a rounded projection, probably like that represented in one of the Arslan-Tash ivories. The rounded part was covered by a network of seven chainlets, each one formed from a succession of interlocked links. Around the edges of the net, which overhung the lotus petals, were suspended small replicas of pomegranates in two superimposed rows, each of one hundred fruit. Jeremiah (52:21–23) slightly amplifies the description, implying that there were four pomegranates, possibly larger than the others, at the corners, with the remaining ninety-six round about to make the exact hundred.

It has been suggested that the ornamental protrusions on the walls of the temple and on the brim of the brass sea (rendered 'knobs' in KJV, 1 Kings 6:18; 7:24), were in the shape of the colocynth fruit. The Hebrew words are similar, and indeed the RSV, NEB and NIV replace it with 'gourd', but NKJV has 'ornamental' buds. The walls and doors throughout the temple were ornamented: Solomon 'carved all the walls of the house round about with carved figures of cherubim and palm trees and open flowers' (1 Kings 6:29 and passim). Likewise the olive and cypress wood doors were carved before they were overlaid with gold.

We know less about the form of Nehemiah's restored temple, which was no doubt a pale reflection of its former glory. When Herod the Great built his temple of imposing proportions, he ornamented the front with a vine, the symbol of Israel (Psalm 80:8; Hosea 10:1).

BIBLICAL SYMBOLISM OF TREES AND PLANT LIFE

As Judaism is highly symbolic in art and object, it is hardly surprising that symbolic significance is also attached to plants. The Talmud is a storehouse of botanical information in relation to Jewish worship and practice and many examples of symbolism have been given in the preceding chapters. Others are mentioned here to underline their importance in the context of the Scriptures, mainly from a Christian viewpoint.

Plants are referred to in the Bible in remarkably diverse ways as literary images, and are used as parables, as direct symbols, as similes and as illustrations. The reader may be able to add other examples.

Trees

Trees were often used figuratively. In a dry land they were seen as symbols of luxuriance and richness, as when Isaiah visualized the desert as a green forest (Isaiah 41:19; 55:13). Thus trees were seen in the Bible as symbols of life. Many civilizations have revered certain trees as sacred, such as the date palm of Mesopotamia, represented in a famous carving as being pollinated by a beaked figure (p. 118). However, the Canaanite 'groves' (KJV) were cult images of Asherah which the Israelites were commanded to destroy (Exodus 34:13; Deuteronomy 12:3) and not to

replant (Deuteronomy 16:21).

The tree of life in the Garden of Eden reappears in the Book of Revelation, although its symbolism is open to various interpretations (Genesis 2:9; 3:24; Revelation 2:7; 22:2, 14, 19). We also read that '[wisdom] is a tree of life to those who lay hold of her' (Proverbs 3:18), 'The fruit of righteousness is a tree of life' (Proverbs 11:30); and 'A gentle tongue is a tree of life' (Proverbs 15:4). When Abimelech was made king, Jotham chided him with an allegory about the greatest of the trees (Judges 9:5 ff.).

Trees often figure too as symbols of uprightness or might, as in Jehoash's allegory of the thistle and the cedar (2 Kings 14:8 ff.; 2 Chronicles 25:17 ff.). Ezekiel also has allegories of the cedar (Ezekiel 17:3–10, 22–24). The psalmist says that 'The righteous flourish like the palm tree, and grow like a cedar in Lebanon' (Psalms 92:12), and 'The voice of the Lord ... breaks the cedars of Lebanon ... The voice of the Lord makes the oaks to whirl' (Psalm 29:5–9). God also 'destroyed the Amorite before them, whose height was like the height of the cedars, and who was as strong as the oaks' (Amos 2:9). The dream of Nebuchadnezzar featured a tree which was symbolic of his life (Daniel 4:4 ff.).

Plant-life

A favourite biblical simile is to liken the transience of life to rapidly fading wild plants. 'The grass withers, the flower fades; but the word of our God will stand for ever' says Isaiah (40:8; see also 1 Peter 1:24). The wicked 'will soon fade like the grass, and wither like the green herb' (Psalm 37:2). A tree, unlike grass, lives for a very long time (Isaiah 65:22).

Thorny and prickly plants (see chapter 3) symbolize sin (Genesis 3:18) and its consequences. Contrast between the wicked and the righteous, between evil and good, is reflected in comparisons between thistles or weeds and good fruitful plants (Hebrews 6:7–8; 2 Samuel 23:4 ff.; Matthew 13:7, 24 ff.) The same thought is used in relation to worthless chaff and (by implication) the good grain, for example in Psalm 1:4. Even the wicked at times 'take root; they grow and bring forth fruit' (Jeremiah 12:2), but 'Blessed is the man who walks not in the counsel of the wicked ... He is like a tree planted by streams of water, that yields its fruit in its season, and its leaf does not wither' (Psalm 1:1–3). The prophet Jeremiah compares the man who trusts in the Lord to a tree planted by water, whereas one 'whose heart turns away from the Lord ... is like a shrub in the desert' (Jeremiah 17:5–6).

Isaiah saw the day of the Lord as a glorious time when even 'the desert shall rejoice and blossom; like the crocus [rose KJV] it shall blossom abundantly, and rejoice with joy and singing' (Isaiah 35:1–2). 'Luxuriant trees shall also grow in the desert that men may see and know that the Lord has done it' (Isaiah 41:18–20). 'Then shall all the trees of the wood sing for joy before the Lord, for he comes, for he comes to judge the earth' (Psalm 96:12–13). When this time will be is known to God, but it was about this that Jesus said to his disciples: 'From the fig tree learn its lesson: as soon as its branch becomes tender and puts forth its leaves, you know that summer is near. So also, when you see all these things, you know that he is near, at the very gates' (Matthew 24:32–33).

To the Greeks and Romans the laurel, like the myrtle, attained particular significance as a wreath or crown. Perhaps the garlands on the sacrificial oxen brought out by the priests of Lystra, to the horror of Paul and Barnabas, were made of laurel (Acts 14:13), the fragrant leathery leaves of which are very suitable for such a purpose. The Roman Caesars themselves were usually depicted wearing such a crown. Athletic champions, too, obtained them at the games, which explains Paul's reference to an athlete's crown (2 Timothy 2:5). But Paul also contrasts the athlete's 'perishable wreath' – wilting laurel leaves – with the imperishable one aimed at by the Christian (1 Corinthians 9:25; see also 1 Peter 5:4). Paul used other botanical analogies such as that he had planted the word and Apollos had watered it, while God gave the increase (1 Corinthians 3:6).

The fruitfulness of plants is frequently used figuratively, as in the description of Joseph as a fruitful bough (Genesis 49:22), and the call to the Christian to be spiritually fruitful (John 15:8, 16). But this fruit has to be of the right kind: 'Can a fig tree, my brethren, yield olives, or a grapevine figs?' (James 3:12). 'You shall know them by their fruits,' Jesus taught his followers. 'Are grapes gathered from thorns, or figs from thistles? So every sound tree bears good fruit, but the bad tree bears evil fruit. A sound tree cannot bear evil fruit, nor can a bad tree bear good fruit' (Matthew 7:17–18).

Certainly, other authors will write and speak about the plants of the Bible and of biblical lands, each, we trust, adding to our understanding of the Scriptures. Each of us attempts to follow King Solomon who 'spoke of trees, from the cedar that is in Lebanon to the hyssop that grows out of the wall' (1 Kings 4:33). Yet we are also told to 'Consider the lilies of the field, how they grow; they toil not, neither do they spin: And yet I say unto you, That even Solomon in all his glory was not arrayed like one of these' (Matthew 6:28, 29 KJV).

Bibliography

Crowfoot, J. W., 'Recent Discoveries of the Joint Expedition to Samaria', *Palestine Exploration Quarterly* (London, 1932), pp. 132–3, pl. 2.

Crowfoot, J. W., and G. M., 'The Ivories from Samaria', *Palestine Exploration Quarterly* (London, 1933), pp. 7–26, pl. 3, fig. 1.

Myers, J. L, 'King Solomon's Temple and Other Buildings and Works of Art', *Palestine Exploration Quarterly* (London, 1948), pp. 14–41.

Rowe, A., 'The Famous Solar-City of On: Egyptian Columns', *Palestine Exploration Quarterly* (London, 1962), p.141.

Yeivin, S., 'Jachin and Boaz', *Palestine Exploration Quarterly* (London, 1959), pp. 6–22.

Glossary

annual	plant completing its life cycle in a year.
awn	bristle projecting from the back of glumes of grasses (including cereals).
axil	angle between the stem and leaf-stalk.
batha	dwarf shrub association of plants up to 50 cm. (6 in.) high.
caprifig	a male fig inflorescence (see explanation of caprification).
capsule	a dry fruit opening to liberate seeds.
chlorophyll	green colouring of leaves.
corolla	the petals as a whole, usually joined petals.
cotyledon	the first leaf of a plant usually seen on germination.
cultivar	a cultivated variety of a plant (not wild).
digitate	form of a leaf with more than 3 leaflets arising from the same point.
dioecious	separate male and female plants.
embryo	the 'germ' or living part of a seed.
endocarp	the inner layer of a fruit, such as an olive 'stone'.
epicarp	the outer skin of a fruit.
floret	small flowers such as those of a daisy head or lining a fig cavity.
garigue	a type of vegetation with shrubs, usually up to 1 m (3 ft) high and no trees.
glume	the scaly chaff surrounding a cereal grain.
halophyte	a salt-loving plant.
haustoria	attachments of parasitic plants to their hosts.
hermaphrodite	a flower with both stamens and ovary.
hulled	a cereal grain remaining covered by chaffy glumes.
inflorescence	a flowering branch or flower head.
loculus	compartment of a fruit.
maquis	evergreen thicket with occasional trees.
mesocarp	the flesh of a fruit such as the olive.
mutation	a genetic change.
node	point of attachment of a leaf to a stem.
osmosis	diffusion of water from a weak to a strong solution through a membrane.
ovary	the female portion of a flower containing ovules which may develop into seeds.
parasite	a plant deriving its food wholly or partially from another plant to which it is attached.
parthenocarpy	non-sexual development of fruits.
phloem (bast)	tissues in the stem transporting food downwards.
photosynthesis	the manufacture of food by chlorophyll in light.
pinnate	a leaf composed of 4 or more leaflets in two rows along the stalk.
plumule	the shoot arising from a seed.
pollination	the transference of pollen grains to a stigma in a flower prior to fertilization.
radicle	the root produced by a seed.
rendzina	greyish soil derived from chalk and soft limestone.
rhizome	a horizontal underground stem.
shatter	breaking up of cereal fruit heads (ears) into individual grains.
spadix	the fleshy inflorescence in *Arum, Acorus,* etc.
sorosis	a fleshy multiple fruit, e.g. mulberry.
spikelet	a partial inflorescence of a grass.
stamen	one of the male reproductive organs, yielding pollen.
stigma	receptive surface on the female part of a flower to which pollen grains adhere.
style	the structure between the stigma and the ovary.
syconium	the fruit of a fig having a cavity lined by florets.
terra rossa	red soil derived from hard limestone.
valve	a piece of capsular fruit separating naturally at maturity.
viable	seed having the ability to germinate.

Bibliography

Selected General References

To find a reference cited in the text first look in this list and then in those works listed under the relevant chapter. Uncited publications are also listed.

The Illustrated Bible Dictionary, N. Hillier (ed), (Leicester, Inter-Varsity Press, 1980), 3 vols.

Albright, W. F., *Archaeology of Palestine* (Harmondsworth, Penguin Books, 1949; reprint Gloucester, Mass., Peter Smith, 1971).

Al-Eisawi, D. M., 'Vegetation of Jordan', *Studies in History and Archaeology of Jordan* (1985), 2:45–58.

Alon, A., *The Natural History of the Land of the Bible* (London, Hamlyn, 1969; US ed. New York, Doubleday and Co. Inc., 1978).

Balfour, J. H., *The Plants of the Bible* (London, Nelson and Sons, 1866).

Crowfoot, G. M., and Baldensperger, L., *From Cedar to Hyssop* (London, Sheldon Press, 1932).

Dalman, G., *Arbeit und Sitte in Palästina* (Gutersloh, C. Bertelsmann, 1928-37; reprint 1964, Hildesheim), 7 vols.

Darby, W. J., Ghalioungui, P., and Grivetti, L., *Food: the Gift of Osiris* (London, Academic Press, 1977): vol. 2: grains, p. 457; bread, p. 502; beer, p. 529; wine, p. 551; aquatic marsh plants, p. 619; vegetables and legumes, p. 653; fruit, p. 697; spices and herbs, p. 791.

Darom, D., *Beautiful Plants of the Bible* (Herzlia, Palphot Ltd, 1991).

Davis, P. H., *Flora of Turkey* (Edinburgh, University Press, 1966–88), 10 vols.

Feinbrun, N. D., 'New Data on some cultivated Plants and Weeds of the Early Bronze Age in Palestine', *Palestine Journal of Botany*, 1:238-40.

Feinbrun, N. D., and Koppel, R., *Wild Plants in the Land of Israel* (Tel Aviv, Hakkibulz Massada, 1960).

Feinbrun-Dothan, N. D., and Danin, A., *Analytical Flora of Eretz-Israel* (Jerusalem, Cana Publishing, 1991). (Hebrew text, with many colour photographs and line drawings.)

Forbes, R. J., *Studies in Ancient Technology* (Leiden, Brill, 1921, 1955).

Hareuveni, N., *Nature in our Biblical Heritage* (Israel, Neot Kedumim, 1980).

—. *Tree and Shrub in our Biblical Heritage* (Israel, Neot Kedumim, 1984).

—. *Desert and Shepherd in our Biblical Heritage* (Israel, Neot Kedumim, 1992).

Hays, J. H., and Miller, J. M., *Israelite and Judaean History* (London, SCM Press, 1977).

Helbaek, H., 'Plant Economy in Ancient Lachish' (Appendix A), in O. Tufnell (ed.), *Lachish IV* (London, Oxford University Press, 1958).

—. 'The Plant Remains from Nimrud', in M. Mallowan, *Nimrud and its Remains* (London, Collins, 1966), 2:618.

Hepper, F. N., *Bible Plants at Kew* (London, HMSO, 1981).

—. *Planting a Bible Garden* (London, HMSO, 1987).

—. *Pharaoh's Flowers: the Botanical Treasures of Tutankhamun* (London, HMSO, 1990).

Hopf, M., 'Plant Remains and Early Farming in Jericho', in P. J. Ucko and G. W. Dimbleby (eds), *Domestication and Exploitation of Plants and Animals* (London, Duckworth, 1969), pp. 355–9.

Horowitz, A., *The Quaternary of Israel* (New York, Academic Press, 1979).

Kenyon, K. M., 'Excavations at Jericho', *Palestine Exploration Quarterly* (London, 1952), pp. 5–6, 72–3; (1953), pp. 83–8.

—. *Archaeology in the Holy Land*, 3rd ed. (London, Ernest Benn, 1970).

Löw, I., *Die Flora der Juden* (Vienna, Kohut Foundation, 1922–34; reprint Hildesheim, Georg Olms, 1967), 4 vols.

Lucas, A., *Ancient Egyptian Materials and Industries*, 4th ed. J. R. Harris (London, Edward Arnold, 1962).

Manniche, L., *An Ancient Egyptian Herbal* (London, British Museum, 1989).

Mazar, A., *Archaeology of the Land of the Bible 1000–685* BCE (New York, Doubleday, 1990).

Moldenke, H. N., and A. L., *Plants of the Bible* (New York, Ronald Press, 1952; reprint Dover Publications, 1986).

Mouterde, P., *Nouvelle Flore du Liban et de la Syrie* (Beyrouth, Edition de l'Imprimerie Catholique, 1966–83), 3 vols text, 2 vols figs.

Murray, M. A., *The Splendour that was Egypt* (London, Sidgwick and Jackson, 1949).

Nehmeh, M., *Wild Flowers of Lebanon* (Beirut, National Council for Scientific Research, 1978).

Petrie, W. M. F., *Tools and Weapons* (London, Egypt Exploration Fund, 1917).

Plitmann, U., Heyn, C., Danin, A., Shmida, A., *Pictorial Flora of Israel* (Jerusalem, Massada Ltd, 1983), Hebrew text with English preface and index.

Polunin, O., and Huxley, A., *Flowers of the Mediterranean*, 3rd ed. (London, Chatto and Windus, 1987).

Post, G. E., *Flora of Syria, Palestine and Sinai*, 2nd ed. J. E. Dinsmore (Beirut, American Press, 1932).

Pritchard, J. B., *Ancient Near Eastern Texts*, 2nd ed. (Princeton University Press, 1950).

Reicke, B., *The New Testament Era: the World of the Bible from 500 BC to AD 100* (London, A. & C. Black, translated from German, 1969).

Rosenmüller, E. F. K., *Biblische Naturgeschichte* (Leipzig, 1830).

Smith, G. A., *Historical Geography of the Holy Land* (London, Hodder and Stoughton, 1894; revised 1931).

Tackholm, V. *Student's Flora of Egypt* (Cairo, University Press ed. 2 1974).

Tackholm, V., and Drar, M., *Flora of Egypt* (Cairo, University Press, 1941-54), 4 vols.

Thompson, C., *Dictionary of Assyrian Botany* (London, The British Academy, 1949).

Thompson, J. A., *The Bible and Archaeology* (Exeter, Paternoster, 1965; Grand Rapids, Michigan, Eerdmans, 1965).

Thomson, W. M., *The Land and the Book* (London, Nelson and Sons, 1887).

Townsend, C. C., and Guest, E. (eds), *Flora of Iraq* (Baghdad, Ministry of Agriculture, 1966–85), 9 vols.

Tristram, H. B., *The Survey of Western Palestine: The Fauna and Flora of Palestine* (London, Palestine Exploration Fund, 1884).

Ucko, P. J., and Dimbleby, G. W. (eds), *Domestication and Exploitation of Plants and Animals* (London, Duckworth, 1969).

Zohary, D., and Hopf, M., *Domestication of Plants in the Old World* (Oxford, Clarendon Press, 1988): cereals, pp. 13–81; pulses, p. 83; flax, p. 114; olive, p. 131; vine, p. 142; fig, p. 142; sycomore, p. 145; other fruits, pp. 146–65; vegetables, p. 167; condiments, p. 172.

Zohary, M., in *The Interpreter's Dictionary of the Bible* (Nashville, Abingdon Press, 1962): flora, vol. 2.

—. *Plant Life of Palestine* (New York, Ronald Press, 1962).

—. *Plants of the Bible* (Cambridge University Press, 1982).

Zohary, M., and Feinbrun-Dothan, N., *Flora Palaestina* (Jerusalem, Israel Academy of Science, 1966–86), 8 vols. (English text; every species represented by a line drawing.)

General Index

*This index excludes the names of plants, which are found in the separate index on pp. 6-11 in both scientific and English forms. It does however include plant applications and products. Numbers in **bold italic** type represent the pages on which illustrations will be found.*

Index of Bible References